The European Tragedy of Troilus

EDITED BY
PIERO BOITANI

CLARENDON PRESS · OXFORD
1989

Oxford University Press, Walton Street, Oxford OX2 6DP
Oxford New York Toronto
Delhi Bombay Calcutta Madras Karachi
Petaling Jaya Singapore Hong Kong Tokyo
Nairobi Dar es Salaam Cape Town
Melbourne Auckland
and associated companies in
Berlin Ibadan

Oxford is a trade mark of Oxford University Press

Published in the United States
by Oxford University Press, New York

British Library Cataloguing in Publication Data
The European tragedy of Troilus.
1. European literatures. Special subjects. Troilus. Critical
studies
I. Boitani, Piero
809.'93351
ISBN 0-19-812970-X

Library of Congress Cataloging in Publication Data
The European tragedy of Troilus / edited by Piero Boitani.
p. cm.
1. European literature–History and criticism. 2. Troilus (Greek
mythology) in literature. 3. Chaucer, Geoffrey, d. 1400. Troilus
and Criseyde. 4. Shakespeare, William, 1564-1616. Troilus
and Cressida. 5. Trojan War in literature. 6. Tragic, The, in
literature. I. Boitani, Piero.
PN671.E9 1989   809.'93351–dc19   88-39424
ISBN 0-19-812970-X

Typeset by Joshua Associates Limited, Oxford
Printed in Great Britain by Biddles Ltd
Guildford and King's Lynn

Preface

The reasons for devoting a book to the European tragedy of Troilus are so obvious that one wonders why it has never been done before. A volume which appeared as the present one was being composed studies, through the figure of Achilles, the 'paradigms of the war hero from Homer to the Middle Ages' (K. C. King, *Achilles* (Berkeley and London, 1987)). To examine Troilus, a character whose destiny is so indissolubly linked to Achilles, means to look at the other side of the epic coin, the tragic one. Troilus is a 'hero' only inasmuch as he is a *victim*—of Achilles' wrath and lust, of Troy's fate, of Fortune, of love. Furthermore, within the context of that primeval conflict, the Trojan War, upon which mighty beings like the gods themselves and semi-divine men such as Achilles, Ulysses, and Hector cast their shadows, the episode of Troilus, and later of Troilus and Cressida, represents as it were a small but extraordinarily significant cameo of humane feelings, a story of death and love which occupies an important place in European consciousness and culture.

The fascination this 'myth' has held for almost three thousand years for the Western imagination is then less surprising than one might at first think. From archaic Greece it travels to Italy, where it haunts the minds of Etruscans and Romans alike. From Sophocles and Virgil it passes into the hands of late antique writers; it surfaces again in the Latin Middle Ages; it acquires new importance with Benoît de Sainte-Maure, Guido delle Colonne, Boccaccio, and Chaucer. Transmitted by Lydgate, Caxton, and Henryson it becomes part of Renaissance culture. Shakespeare writes a play on it. In a 'neoclassical' spirit Dryden rewrites Shakespeare's piece. Then the theme is resurrected in the twentieth century, and the last passages examined in this volume are from Christa Wolf's *Cassandra*, a novel published as recently as 1983.

To study the myth of Troilus means, therefore, to read the works of some of the major European writers as well as to deal with background material such as ancient figurative art, the body of 'minor' literature that underlies the production of great authors, and the wider theme of Troy's fall within which the episode of Troilus is inserted. The present volume offers a broadly chronological view of the development of the myth from antiquity to the Middle Ages, the Renaissance, and the centuries from the seventeenth to our own. Thus, the first essay analyses all the evidence we have in order to reconstruct the meaning of Troilus' tragedy in classical art and follows the theme well into the medieval period, focusing on those versions of the story which do not contain the figure of Cressida, as well as outlining some of the problems other contributors face in their articles. There follows an essay on the 'birth' of Cressida in Benoît's *Roman de Troie*, and one on her consecration (and condemnation) in Boccaccio's *Filostrato*. A series of articles then concentrate on Chaucer's *Troilus*, on Lydgate's and Henryson's treatment of the theme, and finally on its developments from Chaucer to Shakespeare and Dryden. The last piece in the volume examines modern versions and tries to draw some conclusions from both this new material and those issues that emerge in preceding chapters.

Within this chronological structure each author was invited to choose a particular approach, so that several aspects of the theme might be illustrated. Thus, it was clear from the beginning that the problem of the hero within the wider context of the Fall of Troy, besides being touched upon by all contributors, needed separate treatment. This is the aspect that Malcolm Andrew examines, choosing as his period the late Middle Ages, in an original chapter devoted to a comparison between Troilus and Gawain. It was likewise necessary to have an essay such as David Benson's, even though in some parts it overlaps with topics treated by Anna Torti, because only such treatment could provide a general view of the theme in English literature from the fifteenth to the seventeenth century and centre on less well-known versions of the story.

Chaucer's and Shakespeare's *Troilus* have more space in our volume than any other single works of literature. This is partly because the book is primarily directed to an audience of English speaking scholars and students, but mainly because of the special place which these works occupy in the development of the tragic story of Troilus and Cressida. Chaucer's *Troilus and Criseyde* is the greatest narrative poem in English, but also the work in which our theme is treated on the largest scale. Shakespeare's play is so problematic that it conditions all subsequent versions and even determines the apparent death of the story in the eighteenth and nineteenth centuries. In the case of Chaucer and Shakespeare a general introduction to their treatments of the myth was therefore felt to be needed. Derek Brewer's and Agostino Lombardo's essays provide the necessary information for the non-specialist reader and form the basis for subsequent discussion of the texts, highlighting specific problems. They are followed by articles which deal with particular themes, such as Barry Windeatt's on the mixture of genres and Karl Reichl's on the philosophical problem and the language of Chaucer's *Troilus*. When we come to Shakespeare we choose a comparative approach which we hope may throw light on his text as well as on those of his predecessors and successors. Thus, Jill Mann discusses the fundamental question of Cressida's 'value' in Chaucer and Shakespeare, while Sergio Rufini reads Shakespeare's *Troilus* through Dryden's version.

Finally, three specific aspects of the present volume must be pointed out. In the first place, the idea of publishing a book on this topic arose from a series of lectures on the Troilus theme held at Rome and Perugia in 1986–7. The essays presented here have been written for this book, but the editor has thought it opportune not to impose a flatly uniform view of the subject, leaving to single contributors a certain degree of freedom in dealing with their material. This partly mirrors the original purpose of the lectures, and accounts for the fact that not all the disagreements among contributors as to the interpretation of one text (and in particular of Shakespeare's controversial play and the 'ending' of Chaucer's *Troilus*) have been smoothed out. Internal dialectic is an integral part of this collection, which exploits different linguistic and cultural experiences as well as specialist expertise in different literary areas. Our authors come from Germany, the United States, Britain, and Italy. Some are pure medievalists, others are Renaissance or seventeenth-century experts. Most are scholars of English literature, but the field of some is primarily Old French or Italian. All approach the theme with the awareness that the tragedy of Troilus transcends single historical periods, national languages, and cultures to become a typically *European* tragedy. We hope that both the unity and the diversity of our book will prove stimulating to readers.

Secondly, the essays we present here examine with varying emphasis both the imaginative relevance of the myth and the literary characteristics of specific texts. In the hands of writers the philosophical and moral issues, the questions of love, faithfulness, justice, war, destiny, and death which the story of Troilus raises, inevitably become problems of literary genre and structure, of meanings suggested by phrases, words, and silences subject to critical interpretation. In this respect it will be enough to mention the complex relation between the 'ending' of the Troilus stories and the 'end' of Troilus as a character, his death—a problem at once formal and cultural, narrative (or dramatic) and moral.

Thirdly, I wish to stress that if the title of the collection centres on Troilus because he is present from the beginning to the end of our story, the role of Cressida becomes, after the first article, increasingly and ever more intriguingly fundamental. The true protagonist of Roberto Antonelli's, Jill Mann's, and Sergio Rufini's essays, to choose but three, is the fascinating character and the peculiar fate of this woman created and manipulated by men. Thus, illustrations 1 and 2 (on pp. 14 and 112) mirror the double aspect of our topic, showing the two extremes of the myth: the tragedy of Troilus' death as both antiquity and the most recent version of the story conceive it, and the pathos of Troilus' *and* Criseyde's love relationship (itself ready to turn into death) which dominates the imagination from the twelfth to the twentieth century.

P.B.
Rome

Contents

List of Contributors

Malcolm Andrew:	*Queen's University, Belfast*
Roberto Antonelli:	*University of Rome*
C. David Benson:	*University of Connecticut*
Piero Boitani:	*University of Rome*
Derek Brewer:	*University of Cambridge*
Agostino Lombardo:	*University of Rome*
Jill Mann:	*University of Cambridge*
Giulia Natali:	*University of Rome*
Karl Reichl:	*University of Bonn*
Sergio Rufini:	*University of Perugia*
Anna Torti:	*University of Verona*
Barry Windeatt:	*University of Cambridge*

The essays by Roberto Antonelli, Agostino Lombardo, Giulia Natali, Sergio Rufini, and Anna Torti have been translated into English by Evelyn Bradshaw, Eanna O'Ceallachain, Peter Mark Eaton, Felicity Lutz, and Anita Weston.

Note on the Illustrations

Fig. 1 (p. 14) Attic black-figure hydria from Vulci, *c.* 510 BC, attributed to the Leagros Group (London, British Museum B 326). The horses of Achilles' quadriga paw the ground. Achilles climbs the steps of the altar in the temple of Apollo, holding Troilus' head in his right hand to throw it against two Trojans (identified on other vases as Hector and Aeneas), while Troilus' dead body lies on the altar. Reproduced by courtesy of the British Museum.

Fig. 2 (p. 112) Fifteenth-century French MS of Louis de Beauvau's prose translation of Boccaccio's *Filostrato* (Bibliothèque Nationale, Paris, Fonds des Manuscrits Français 25528). It illustrates *Filostrato*, iv. cxiv–cxx, which corresponds to Chaucer's *Troilus and Criseyde*, iv. 1149–90. (See also *Le Roman de Troilus*, ed. L. Moland and C. D'Hericault, in *Nouvelles françoises en prose du XIVe siècle* (Paris, 1858), 228–9.) Briseida swoons for grief when she and Troilus meet for the last time before her departure from Troy. Troilus thinks she has died and draws his sword to kill himself. Reproduced by courtesy of the Bibliothèque Nationale.

Fig. 1 points to the death of Troilus as one of the most significant features of the story in antiquity as well as in later ages. A particularly cruel version of this has been deliberately chosen to underline the element of violence. It will be noticed that Fig. 2 picks up this theme of death by showing us an apparently dead Cressida and a Troilus ready to die (the picture actually makes it look as if Troilus had managed to run his breast through with his sword). The 'tragedy' could, Romeo-and-Juliet-like, end here with a scene of supreme melodramatic pathos. In Boccaccio and Chaucer it will in fact become a much more painful process through Cressida's betrayal and Troilus' meaningless death.

Note on the Texts

Chaucer's works are quoted from *The Riverside Chaucer*, 3rd edn., general editor L. D. Benson (Boston, 1987; Oxford, 1988). Unless otherwise specified, Shakespeare's plays are quoted from the volumes of the Arden Shakespeare; in that series *Troilus and Cressida* is edited by K. Palmer (London and New York, 1982). References to the classics, unless otherwise specified, are to the volumes of the Loeb library. Editions of all other texts cited are indicated in the footnotes.

1

Antiquity and Beyond: The Death of Troilus

PIERO BOITANI

At first sight Troilus may seem to be a decidedly 'minor' mythological figure, one of the many sons begotten by the prolific king of Troy, Priam, and one of the many killed in the course of that ten-year-long war between Trojans and Greeks which marks the beginning of Western legendary history. In the *Iliad* Homer liquidates him in one line when, in the very last Book of the poem, he builds the background for the master scene between Priam and Achilles. Hector has been slain and, inspired by Zeus, his father wants to ransom his body by asking the murderer himself, Achilles. Nine surviving sons, 'sad relics of his numerous line', surround the old king as he prepares to leave for the Greek camp. He reproaches them in a rage:

> Inglorious sons of an unhappy sire!
> Why did not all in Hector's cause expire?
> Wretch that I am! my bravest offspring slain,
> You, the disgrace of Priam's house, remain!
> Mestor the brave, renown'd in ranks of war,
> With Troilus, dreadful in his rushing car,
> And last great Hector, more than man divine,
> For sure he seem'd not of terrestrial line!
> All those relentless Mars untimely slew,
> And left me these, a soft and servile crew,
> Whose days the feast and wanton dance employ,
> Gluttons and flatterers, the contempt of Troy![1]

Troilus is nowhere else mentioned in the *Iliad.* Yet, this single appearance in Homer's poem is highly significant. In Priam's outburst, Troilus is as brave as Mestor and almost as great as Hector himself—which is no small praise for an apparently 'minor' hero. Furthermore, what the three men have in common is the fact that

---

[1] xxiv. 253–62, Pope's translation. The line references are to the Greek original.

they have died at the hands of the Greeks. Their deaths plunge us into the atmosphere of impending doom that characterizes the last days of Troy—the *Dämmerung* of an entire civilization.

Troilus' death is so important that several centuries later, in the other great epic of antiquity, Virgil's *Aeneid*, it occupies a central place among the Trojan scenes—veritable 'lacrimae rerum'—painted on the walls of the temple of Juno which Dido has built in Carthage. Here, we see the last act of Troilus' life through the eyes of another Trojan hero, Aeneas, and this adds to the pathos of what Virgil calls an 'empty picture'. Troilus is but a boy, yet he dares to defy Achilles. In the end, like Hector's, his body is dragged along the ground by horses. In the dust the spear traces a sort of tragically meaningless inscription:

> Parte alia fugiens amissis Troilus armis,
> infelix puer atque impar congressus Achilli,
> fertur equis curruque haeret resupinus inani,
> lora tenens tamen; huic cervixque comaeque trahuntur
> per terram et versa pulvis inscribitur hasta.

> [Elsewhere, he saw where Troilus defied
> Achilles, and unequal combat tried;
> Then, where the boy disarmed, with loosened reins,
> Was by his horses hurried o'er the plains,
> Hung by the neck and hair, and dragged around:
> The hostile spear, yet sticking in his wound,
> With tracks of blood inscribed the dusty ground.][2]

From the very beginning, Troilus is an epic figure who lives in an exclusively tragic dimension. It is his death, and his death alone, that interests classical art and that part of the medieval tradition which is directly or indirectly influenced by it. From the epic cycles collected in the *Kypria* to Homer, from Sophocles to Lycophron, from Callimachus to Apollodorus, from Cicero to Virgil, Horace, Hyginus, and Seneca, down to Quintus Smyrnaeus, Ausonius, and Servius between the third and fourth centuries AD, to the Latin versions of Dictys and Dares between the fourth and sixth, and on to Joseph of Exeter in the twelfth and Albert von Stade in the thirteenth, to the *Ovide Moralisé* and the erudite Boccaccio of the *Amorosa Visione*, the *De Casibus*, the *Genealogie*,

---

[2] Dryden's translation of *Aeneid*, i. 474–8. The line references are to the Latin original.

and the *Esposizioni* on the *Divine Comedy*,[3] the constant feature of Troilus' figure is his death at the hands of Achilles, a consequence of that 'wrath' of the Greek warrior which inspires the *Iliad* and which slowly becomes, as we shall soon see, not merely resentment at Agamemnon's vexations but pure *mēnis*—anger, 'furor bellicus'. The Boccaccio of the *Filostrato* and the Chaucer of *Troilus and Criseyde*, who prefer the new theme of Troilus' love, cannot eliminate his death from their stories, and with supreme tragic irony show the connection between it and Achilles' wrath by inverting the sequence. The stanzas devoted by both authors to the hero's death begin with *Troilus'* wrath, only to end with Achilles' slaughter of his opponent, matter of fact and 'wretched' in Boccaccio, 'despitous' in Chaucer:

> L'ira di Troiolo in tempi diversi
> a' Greci nocque molto sanza fallo,
>
> . . . . .
>
>   e dopo lungo stallo,
> avendone già morti più di mille,
> miseramente un dì l'uccise Achille.[4]

> The wrath, as I bigan yow for to seye,
> Of Troilus the Grekis boughten deere,
> For thousandes his hondes maden deye,
> As he that was withouten any peere,
> Save Ector, in his tyme, as I kan heere.
> But—weilawey, save only Goddes wille,
> Despitously hym slough the fierse Achille.[5]

[3] I list here the references which will not be used elsewhere in this essay. Callimachus, fragment 363; Cicero, *Tusculan Disputations*, I. xxxix. 93, with reference to Callimachus; Horace, *Odes*, II. ix. 13-16; Hyginus, *Fabulae*, cxiii. 3; Seneca, *Agamemnon*, 748 (Cassandra recalls Achilles' slaying of Troilus: Christa Wolf may have remembered this); Boccaccio, *Amorosa Visione*, vii. 28; xxxiv. 71; *De Casibus*, I. xiii. 15; *Genealogie*, vi. xxviii; *Esposizioni*, v, esp. litt. 121, 134. In these works Boccaccio makes no mention of the love-story between Troilus and Cressida he had himself consecrated in the *Filostrato*, but conceives Troilus as a purely epic hero. This is all the more strange in the *Esposizioni* on the *Divine Comedy*, where Troilus could have served as an excellent example of the 'lustful' listed in *Inferno*, V (cf. Chaucer, *Parliament of Fowls*, 291, and Boccaccio, *Decameron*, vi, intr. 3, where Dioneo and Lauretta sing of 'Troilo e . . . Criseida'). For classical references, see W. H. Roscher, *Lexicon der griechischen und römischen Mythologie*, and Pauly-Wissowa, *Real-Encyclopädie der klassischen Altertumswissenschaft*, s.v. 'Troilos'.

[4] *Filostrato*, VIII. xxvii.
[5] *Troilus and Criseyde*, v. 1800-6.

Except for Robert Henryson, none of the authors studied in the present volume will ever forget Troilus' death. Shakespeare, who significantly omits this episode in *Troilus and Cressida*, has Rosalind talk about it mockingly and gruesomely in *As You Like It* (iv. i. 92–3): 'Troilus had his brains dashed out with a Grecian club . . .'.

The questions which arise at this point are two. In the first place, why is Troilus' death so important—indeed, at least in antiquity, so exclusively central? And, secondly, why in medieval and modern versions does it keep changing its position and perspective? The first is a question that bears upon the imaginative relevance of the story, its meaning in the classical *imaginaire*. The second is a problem that arises in a world no longer pagan but Christian, and in a story profoundly modified by the appearance of Cressida. Both questions are ultimately connected with the—at once existential and narrative—'sense of an ending'[6] which different ages have developed. It is to these problems that the present volume is devoted. After analysing these questions here in the context of antiquity, I shall leave the other contributors to provide individual answers and then pick the problems up again in my final essay.

There can be little doubt as to what Troilus' end means for Greeks and Romans. Even as late as the thirteenth century the German poet Albert von Stade shows how close is the connection between Troilus and Troy. In explaining why his poem is entitled *Troilus* he associates the prince's name and the Trojan War:

> Troilus est Troilus Troiano principe natus
> Et liber est *Troilus* ob Troica bella vocatus.[7]

'Troilos' is the hypocoristic, i.e. the pet-name of 'Tros', Troy's eponymous hero, the mythological figure who gave his name to the city. Troilus—for some the son not of Priam but of Apollo himself[8]—represents the very origin of his town and bears her name. But this affectionate diminutive of Tros sounds strangely like that of Romulus Augustulus, a child who bore the name of Rome, her founder and her first emperor, and who was destined to become

---

[6] I use this expression, of course, in the sense consecrated by Frank Kermode, *The Sense of an Ending* (Oxford, 1967), esp. ch. 5.

[7] Albert von Stade, *Troilus*, ed. T. Merzdorf (Leipzig, 1875), Prooemium, 35–6; and for Troilus see iv. 33–48, 173–80, 289–310, 311–62.

[8] Apollodorus, *Library*, III. xii. 5; Tzetzes in *Lycophronis Alexandra*, rec. and scholia G. Kinkel (Leipzig, 1880), ad 307 ff., p. 94.

the very last ruler of her empire in the West. If we were medieval etymologists we could try to play with Troilus' name in two different ways. One could see it, on the one hand, as the sum and conflation of 'Tros' and 'Ilos', Troy's founders. One could also, on the other, speculate on a more fanciful association of 'Troiē', the city of Troy, and the verb *lyō*, which means 'to destroy', 'to annihilate'. These are of course mere games. But there is no doubt that the ancients were aware of the connection between 'Troilus' and Troy's fate. There are, says Chrysalus in Plautus's *Bacchides*,[9] 'three fateful events which would prove [Troy's] downfall': the disappearance of the Palladium from the citadel, the tearing away of the upper lintel of the Phrygian gate, and 'Troili mors'—the death of Troilus. In an Attic black-figure amphora by Lydos (*c.* 550 BC)[10] as well as on a Roman sarcophagus of AD *c.* 180,[11] Achilles' pursuit of Troilus constitutes one side of the picture. The other, as if logically following the first, is Priam's death, one of the last scenes of the 'Iliupersis', the destruction of Troy.

'Troilus' contains both the beginning and the end of Troy. In this sense he is not primarily a character but a 'function'. He is his death and the fall of Troy in that war which, being the first and most famous of all, constitutes the archetypal World War.

If the decrees of Fate are to be fulfilled, Troilus must die. His dying as a *pais* or *puer*—a young boy—contains, especially in some versions, and above all in vase painting, a strong element of pathos. Originally, however, it must have represented part of the 'function' Troilus performs in the Trojan cycle. A prophecy reported by the First Vatican Mythographer states that if Troilus reached the age of twenty Troy could not be destroyed.[12] This is of course partly tied to his name, but in a particular fashion. Troilus, who bears his city's name, cannot achieve an age that would allow him to perpetuate the species by begetting children. 'Troy' must die with him, and in this sense, as a 'function', he is complementary to Hector, whose role is, as the name of his son Astyanax witnesses,[13]

---

[9] *Bacchides*, ll. 953–5. This motif probably derives from Menander's *Dis exapaton*. See *Lexicon iconographicum mythologiae classicae* (henceforward *LIMC*), i/1 (Zurich and Munich, 1981), 73.

[10] Berlin F 1685, from Vulci, *LIMC*, Achilleus, 290.

[11] Now in the Palazzo Ducale, Mantua, *LIMC*, Achilleus, 355.

[12] *Scriptores rerum mythicarum Latini*, ed. G. H. Bode (Celle, 1834), i. 66 (First Vatican Mythographer, 210).

[13] See *Iliad*, vi. 402–3; xxii. 506–7.

that of saviour or preserver of the city. In due course Troilus will in fact become, as Chaucer's Pandarus calls him, 'the wise, worthi Ector the secounde' (ii. 158). It is interesting to note that as late as the fourth century AD Quintus Smyrnaeus seems to be aware of the all-important fact that Troilus must not procreate. In describing his death, he compares Achilles cutting down Priam's son to a gardener mowing a blade of corn or poppy. Troilus is 'beardless' and 'virgin of a bride, almost a child'—the flower is cut off ''ere it may reach | Its goal of bringing offspring to the birth'.[14]

Compared to its ultimately Homeric antecedent,[15] this simile has been profoundly modified. The new element is represented by the human agent, the gardener, who does violence to nature. In the sad, elegiac atmosphere of the passage, this is an essential aspect. Another feature, however, is also present. When a gardener harvests the field with a scythe, it is inevitable that he should mow down the blades of corn or poppy—indeed he must do so if he is to do his job properly. And this is the more specifically tragic aspect of the simile. We should read Quintus Smyrnaeus carefully:

> Then Peleus' bride [Thetis] gave unto him [Ajax] the arms
> Of godlike Troilus, the goodliest
> Of all fair sons whom Hecuba had borne
> In hallowed Troy; yet of his goodlihead
> No joy she had; the prowess and the spear
> Of fell Achilles reft his life from him.
> As when a gardener with a new-whetted scythe
> Mows down, ere it may seed, a blade of corn
> Or poppy, in a garden dewy-fresh
> And blossom-flushed, which by a water-course
> Crowdeth its blooms—mows it ere it may reach
> Its goal of bringing offspring to the birth,
> And with his scythe-sweep makes its life-work vain
> And barren of all issue, nevermore
> Now to be fostered by the dews of spring;
> So did Peleides cut down Priam's son
> The god-like beautiful, the beardless yet
> And virgin of a bride, almost a child!
> Yet the Destroyer Fate had lured him on

---

[14] Quintus Smyrnaeus, *The Fall of Troy* (*Posthomerica*), trans. A. S. Way (Loeb, 1913), iv. 430–1.

[15] *Iliad*, viii. 306–8.

To war, upon the threshold of glad youth,
When youth is bold, and the heart feels no void.[16]

The complexity of motifs in this passage constitutes the best general view one can have from late antiquity of the classical 'sense' of Troilus' end. It includes the function—the end of a human race through barrenness—and the notion of Fate; it is violent and pathetic, and at once inevitable, obligatory, and tragic. Troilus' death is a 'sign' of Troy's fall: both must happen, both are dreadful.

Later on in this book Malcolm Andrew will show how the destruction of Troy is related to the adventures of the hero—Troilus or Gawain—in two medieval English poems. I shall limit myself here to setting a medieval Latin poem side by side with Quintus Smyrnaeus. When Albert von Stade describes Troilus' death in his *Troilus* he shows Achilles beheading the Trojan boy as the latter tries to rise from the ground. 'Thus', he concludes, 'the young soldier is cut down in the bloom of life, the flower of the world shines but for a short time':

> Sic tiro juvenis rapitur florentibus annis,
> Flos mundi rutilat tempore valde brevi.[17]

With this biblical image[18] Troilus' end has become emblematic of the transience of the whole earthly world.

If 'death' is Troilus' function, it will be important to see what kind of death is reserved for him and at what point it occurs. So far, we have encountered one basic version of it: Virgil, Quintus Smyrnaeus, and Albert von Stade show us a young warrior struggling against mighty Achilles and being overwhelmed by him. Although this kind of account may underlie Homer's single hint at Troilus 'fighting from the chariot', it seems to be an exceptional variation, for which we have only one witness in early figurative art. In an Attic red-figure cup by Oltos (c. 520–510 BC)[19] Troilus—who can be identified as such only by the name inscribed on the vase—appears as a man fighting a duel against Achilles and defending himself on his knees, his sword against the enemy's spear. Yet this variation obviously enjoyed great popularity, especially, it

[16] *The Fall of Troy*, 418–35.
[17] *Troilus*, iv. 341–2. The passage begins at l. 329 with the following definition of Troilus: 'At Troilus murus patriae, protectio Trojae Et rosa militiae . . .'.
[18] Job 14: 1–2; Ps. 90: 5–6; 103: 15–16; Isa. 40: 6–8.
[19] Louvre G 18, *LIMC*, Achilleus, 369.

seems, after Virgil consecrated it in the *Aeneid.* Ausonius follows Virgil's account literally, though shortening it.[20] Dares, or at least the Latin version we have of his *De Excidio Troiae Historia,*[21] expands on it and talks about Troilus at great length. Here, he has become 'great', 'very beautiful', 'worthy', 'strong', and 'desirous of valour'. With Hector, he is 'dux Troianorum', and after his brother's death 'his prowess leads him to be recognized by the Greeks as his . . . successor'.[22] The encounter between Achilles and Troilus is part of a larger battle which lasts seven days, for six of which the Trojan hero has the better of the Greeks and even of Achilles, whom he wounds and forces to withdraw. On the seventh day Achilles instructs his Myrmidons to attack Troilus *en masse.* After a long skirmish Troilus' horse is wounded and falls to the ground with his rider. Achilles runs to the spot and finally kills the Trojan.[23]

This is, then, the ultimate ancestor of the scene in Lydgate and Caxton in which Achilles commands the Myrmidons to surround Troilus the better to butcher him—a scene that Shakespeare will transform into Achilles' instructions to his soldiers to 'empale' *Hector* with their weapons 'round about' and to strike him down unarmed. The complete upheaval of heroic and chivalric codes is proclaimed by the Greek 'warrior' at the end of that 'battle':

> On, Myrmidons, and cry you all amain
> 'Achilles hath the mighty Hector slain'.[24]

Neither the classical nor the medieval tradition is so brutally explicit about Achilles' unfairness in battle. Joseph of Exeter, for instance, portrays the duel between the two as a highly epic affair,[25] at the end of which Troilus' death is lamented as an unprecedented disaster:

> Quos casus, que fata querar, quos, Troile, divos?
> [What falls, what fates, what gods shall I, O Troilus, look for?]

[20] *Epitapha Heroum*, xviii.

[21] Daretis Phrygii, *De Excidio Troiae Historia*, ed. F. Meister (Leipzig, 1873).

[22] Ibid., xii, xviii, xxix–xxx. N. R. Havely, *Chaucer's Boccaccio* (Cambridge and Totowa, NJ, 1980), 165.

[23] *De Excidio Troiae Historia*, xxxiii.

[24] *Troilus and Cressida*, v. vii. 5; v. viii. 13–14.

[25] Joseph Iscanus, *Werke und Briefe*, ed. L. Gompf (Leiden and Cologne, 1970); *Yliados*, vi. 283–331 (quotation from l. 325).

Yet, an element of brutality is present even in a pro-Greek account such as Dictys', whose Latin version has Achilles order the public slaughter of Troilus—here a boy both beautiful and bold who has been captured by the Greeks—simply because he is angry with Priam.[26]

Virgil, Quintus Smyrnaeus, Dares, Dictys, and Joseph of Exeter place Troilus' death towards the end of the Trojan War, as Chaucer was later to do. In this manner Troilus' end is no longer a 'sign', an omen of Troy's future fall, but part of the very 'ending' of the city. Individual death and general apocalypse tend to merge.

Both this timing and the actual battle scene are, it seems, later developments of the story (Dictys' account constituting a very interesting variation on the latter element, the fight between the two heroes). The earlier versions present Troilus' death as one of the first episodes of the war; the best witness to this being the short account in the *Kypria*, an epic poem which covered the preliminaries of the war and the beginning of it down to the point where the *Iliad* starts, and which has come down to us only in summaries provided by the epitome of Proclus' *Chrestomathia*.[27] The *Epitome* of Apollodorus' *Library* follows this tradition.[28] Thus, as most recently in Christa Wolf, Troilus' death really is a sign of what will come—it is the beginning of the end.

This aspect is emphasized in all the early documents known to us, by the manner in which they present Troilus' death. Troilus is not killed in battle, but murdered by Achilles in what must have been considered a pause during the war, a moment of peace at the beginning of the conflict. In his play on the subject Sophocles seems to have made it the central point that Troilus was slaughtered while exercising his horses by the temple of Thymbraean Apollo.[29] The Byzantine Eusthatius, Archbishop of Thessalonica, confirms this 1600 years later in his commentary on the *Iliad*.[30]

[26] Dictys Cretensis, *Ephemeridos Belli Troiani Libri*, ed. W. Eisenhut (Leipzig, 1973), iv. 9.

[27] *Epicorum Graecorum Fragmenta*, ed. G. Kinkel (Leipzig, 1877), 20 (Proclus, *Chrestomathia*, i).

[28] *Epitome*, iii. 32.

[29] *Scholia Graeca in Homeri Iliadem* (Scholia Vetera), rec. H. Erbse (Berlin, 1977), v, ad xxiv. 257a.

[30] *Commentaria ad Iliadem et Odysseam*, ed. G. Stallbaum (Leipzig, 1825–30), in *Iliad*, xxiv. 251, p. 1348, l. 22.

Apollodorus keeps the location in the Thymbraeum.[31] Dio Chrysostom maintains that Troilus ventured outside the walls for exercise, and was captured and killed by Achilles.[32] From a surviving fragment of Sophocles' *Troilos*[33] we can evince that the boy was going with someone else 'towards flowing drinks from a spring'; i.e. either to fetch water or to water the horses, or to do both, with his companion.

This, indeed, is the general scheme of the episode we encounter in figurative art. The sequence can be reconstructed in the following manner (often one scene only is shown): Troilus goes with his sister Polyxena to the fountain; Achilles ambushes him; Troilus flees pursued by the Greek; Achilles kills him in the temple; there sometimes follows a fight between Greeks and Trojans over Troilus' corpse.

A young boy accompanied by a girl goes to a spring—it is an idyllic scene of innocence and peace suddenly upset by Achilles' ambush. Forgotten for a moment, the war bursts back on to the stage. Yet, however realistic, this type of war is by epic standards certainly degraded. There is no duel between warriors, but an ambush (something one would associate with Ulysses and Diomedes rather than Achilles); the boy is unarmed and, supreme sacrilege, murdered in a temple.

The story was extremely popular. There are countless examples of it from sculpture to bronze laminae of shields, from gems to mirrors, from tomb to vase painting, to stone and marble urns, to sarcophagi, covering Attic, Corinthian, Laconian, Chalcidian, Etruscan, Southern Italian, and Roman artifacts from the late seventh century BC to the late second century AD.[34] Throughout these nine centuries, the episode seems slowly to change in nature. When it surfaces again in literature, with Virgil, it has become a battle scene towards the end of the Trojan War. The imaginative conception is by now clearly different. Archaic and classical Greece deal with the naked tragic brutality of the myth. This is the

---

[31] *Epitome*, iii. 32.

[32] *Orationes*, xi (Loeb edn. by J. W. Cohoon, *Discourses*, i. 505–15).

[33] No. 621 in both A. C. Pearson (ed.), *The Fragments of Sophocles* (Cambridge, 1917), ii. 257, and *Tragicorum Graecorum Fragmenta*, iv (Sophocles), ed. S. Radt (Göttingen, 1977), 455.

[34] The most exhaustive refs. and discussions are now to be found in *LIMC*, i/1 s.v. Achilleus, pp. 72–95 and s.v. Achle, pp. 200–5, 210–11. Illustrations in *LIMC*, i/2, pp. 78–95, 146–50; and see bibliog. therein.

age of tragedy, and the fact that Sophocles wrote one on the subject is emblematic. Later versions try to restore the epic element and, as we have seen, emphasize the pathetic aspect.

Not much can be gathered about the nature of Troilus' tragedy from the surviving fragments of Sophocles' play, and most of the figurative evidence needs careful interpretation. Only broken figures, for instance, remain of the Attic 'Olive tree' pediment of c. 570–560 BC,[35] whereas the roughly contemporary paintings in the Etruscan Tomb of the Bulls at Tarquinia[36] seem to underline the sacrificial aspect of the murder. The bronze laminae from Olympia, the earliest of which is dated 625–600 BC and the latest 590–580, may be seen to form an ideal sequence of three moments. In the first Troilus mounts the steps of the altar, while Achilles points his sword at the boy's back.[37] In the second Achilles holds Troilus by his right arm. The naked lad is half kneeling on the altar, and with his left arm clings to the laurel tree sacred to Apollo.[38] In the third[39] Troilus, naked, stands on the altar, moving his legs as if trying to escape. Achilles, holding his arm with one hand, is about to thrust his sword into the boy's belly with the other. On the altar, between Troilus' legs, sits a cock.

To find the meaning of this sequence, however, we have to resort to other evidence. The great François vase—an encyclopaedia of myth elegantly constructed in black-figure style around 560 BC by the potter Ergotimos and the painter Klitias[40]—presents a scene that precedes the actual slaughter. It is framed by two buildings, the fountain on the left and Troy's walls on the right. Before the walls sits old Priam, with Antenor turning to him in alarm. Polyxena is running towards them, her jug fallen to the ground between the legs of Troilus' horse. Troilus, on horseback, is pursued by Achilles on foot. Athena incites the Greek, standing behind him, while Hermes talks to Achilles' mother, Thetis. A boy and a girl, called 'Troon' and 'Rhodia', draw water at the fountain. At the extreme left Apollo advances on to the stage. Meanwhile, on

[35] Athens, Acrop. Mus. 52, *LIMC*, Achilleus, 276.

[36] *LIMC*, Achle, 14.

[37] Olympia B 3600, *LIMC*, Achilleus, 375.

[38] Olympia B 988, 1801, 1802, 4962, *LIMC*, Achilleus, 376.

[39] Olympia B 987, 1803, 1912, *LIMC*, Achilleus, 377.

[40] Florence, Archaeol. Mus. 4209, from Chiusi, *LIMC*, Achilleus, 292; and see J. D. Beazley, *Development of Attic Black-Figure* (Berkeley, LA, and London, 1951), 26–37.

the right behind Priam a rescue party headed by Hector and Polites comes out of the city gate. On the battlements one can distinguish heaps of stones to be thrown against attackers.

Undoubtedly, this is a lively and beautifully proportioned dramatic scene, which brings us back to the atmosphere of the Homeric world, where both gods and men take part in the war. Thetis, for instance, is clearly worried, and the reason for this must be Apollo's threatening appearance. The god is obviously protecting both the fountain sacred to him and the fleeing Troilus. He will later exact vengeance on Achilles for his trespass. Troilus, however, is not seeking refuge in the temple, but riding towards Troy—a variation nowhere else to be met. We have, then, an interesting mixture of motifs. The gods are trying to direct human affairs and each of them has his or her different motivation for doing this. Yet, all the deities occupy the left-hand side of the picture, while Troilus and Polyxena hasten towards a purely human sanctuary— their city, their father and brothers. This feature would strike us as realistic, and if we had no other picture of this scene we would accept it as perfectly normal: after all, one seeks refuge where one is most likely to find it. A Greek, or indeed an Etruscan, knowing the standard version of the story, may however have reacted differently, asking himself why Klitias departed from tradition. And he may have come up with the answer that perhaps the picture was trying to point out the ultimate helplessness of both divine and human beings in the face of something that has already been decreed by Fate.

We shall find no confirmation of this hypothesis in the red-figure kalpis by the Troilos Painter, who attractively concentrates on the swift movement of Troilus' and Polyxena's flight, the former turning his face back in fear and whipping his horse, the latter dropping her jug.[41] The amphora and the hydria by the Painter of London B 76 (c. 575–550 BC)[42] are more interesting. They portray the scene of the ambush, with Troilus on horseback and Polyxena carrying a vase on the right side, while Achilles crouches behind the fountain on the left. The dramatic contrast is thus spatially underlined, but the tension is greatly increased in both cases by the presence of a black raven facing Troilus from above

[41] London BM E 175, 1899. 7–21. 4, *LIMC*, Achilleus, 341.
[42] London BM 97. 7–21. 2, *LIMC*, Achilleus, 225; and New York, Metr. Mus. 45. 11. 2, *LIMC*, Achilleus, 234.

the fountain. Traditionally Apollo's messenger, the bird seems to incarnate the prophecy concerning Troilus' death and certainly represents the god's last warning to the boy, whom some accounts consider his own son.

The famous Corinthian flask by Timonidas,[43] from the mid-sixth century, and the red-figure cup signed by Euphronios as potter and attributed to Onesimos[44] constitute in several ways two opposite treatments of the episode. In the former, in Priam's presence a bearded Troilus stands at the centre, leading his horses to the spring on foot and accompanied by Polyxena. Achilles, lying in wait, appears in a corner, his stature diminished. The scene looks supremely static, as if it were frozen one minute before the tragedy. Here, Troilus is Troy; the majesty of the town and its prospective perpetuation being embodied by the old king and his son simultaneously on the stage. Troilus, the almost immobile focus of attention, seems to incarnate the tragic hero *par excellence*—great, on the verge of falling, and unaware. The Onesimos cup presents two Troilus scenes, one on the outside and one on the inside. In the former Achilles is reaching Troilus at the altar. In the latter the last act of the drama is almost over. Achilles raises his sword against the boy, already half dead. Here, the contrast is between the extreme frailty of Troilus and the paroxysm of hate and fury in his murderer. Once more, the wrath of Achilles is overwhelming.

We move, therefore, one step further towards the tragic core of the story. Why should Achilles be so incensed with a harmless youth? Why should he, in a black-figure hydria of the Leagros group (c. 520–500 BC)[45] hold a childlike Troilus head down by one leg, as if throwing him on to the altar to smash him? Why should he impale the boy's head with his spear, or throw it to the Trojans as he does in at least two cases?[46] There are two kinds of answer to these questions. The first goes back to Troilus' 'function'; the second resorts to internal motivations, thus sketching in a figure of Troilus as character, who in some way interacts with Achilles.

The first answer is indirectly suggested by the Painter of

[43] Athens, Nat. Mus. 277, *LIMC*, Achilleus, 251.

[44] Perugia, Museo Civico 89, *LIMC*, Achilleus, 370.

[45] Munich 1700, from Vulci, *LIMC*, Achilleus, 382. Some think the scene represents Neoptolemus' slaying of Astyanax.

[46] Basel, private collection, *LIMC*, Achilleus, 359a; London BM B 326 from Vulci, *LIMC*, Achilleus, 363 (c. 510 BC). This is reproduced overleaf.

Fig. 1. Attic black-figure hydria from Vulci, *c.* 510 BC, attributed to the Leagros Group (London, British Museum B 326). Achilles has killed Troilus and throws his head against two Trojans.

London B 76 and, I think, definitely provided by an early sixth-century Corinthian crater,[47] and elsewhere by Attic and pseudo-Chalcidian ceramics. In the former, as we have seen, the raven announces the impending fate of Troilus. In the latter, Achilles holds the boy by his feet over the altar as if he were the victim of a sacrifice. The two schemes are thematically unified by the cruelty and the brutality of the episode which we have increasingly noted in the last few pages. But they also complement each other in a highly significant pattern. The ambush will produce the murder prophesied by the bird, i.e. foreseen by Apollo. Ambush and murder, themselves base acts of war, are ultimately seen as ritual. Achilles must kill Troilus if Troy is to fall. The harmless youth is sacrificed like Iphigenia. Troilus is the unconscious victim of laws that go far beyond him, of a tragic mechanism that reduces him to a ritual scapegoat. In this mechanism, the *moira* announced by the crow is mysteriously but inevitably fulfilled by the *anankē*—fate is 'explained' by necessity. Perhaps one can apply to this situation the words of Chaucer's Troilus:

> For al that comth, comth by necessitee:
> Thus to ben lorn, it is my destinee.[48]

The ultimate end of classical Troilus is, however, far more horrible to modern (and probably even to ancient) eyes than that of his medieval counterpart. If we are to believe a gloss of the Suidas,[49] Sophocles indicated that Troilus' corpse was subjected to *maskhalismos* on the part of Achilles. The Greek hero, in other words, would have cut off his enemy's extremities and hung them around his neck on a string, thus performing what Erwin Rohde called an 'apotropaic' or 'cathartic' sacrifice aimed at turning away the *mēnis* or wrath of the murdered man's *psykhē*.[50] This would undoubtedly mean that Troilus' soul survived his death—something with which we shall see Chaucer struggle later in this volume. At the same time, the sacrifice of Troilus' dead body represents the ideally

---

[47] Louvre E 638 bis, *LIMC*, Achilleus, 365.

[48] *Troilus*, iv. 958–9.

[49] s.v. *emaskhalisthē*, ed. A. Adler, *Lexicog. Gr.*, i. i–v (Leipzig, 1929–38).

[50] E. Rohde, *Psyche: Seelencult und Unsterblichkeitsglaube der Griechen* (Freiburg, 1898), 322 ff.; and see *Tragicorum Graecorum Fragmenta*, iv. 623, pp. 455–6; Sophocles, *Electra*, ed. R. C. Jebb (Cambridge, 1894), ad 444 f. and app.

logical conclusion of his ritual murder. Troilus, and Troy, are neutralized for ever. Our sense of an ending is indeed satisfied.

Let us now turn to the second answer mentioned above. When Sophocles (if not Phrynicus before him) wrote a tragic play on Troilus, and when Strattis apparently turned this into a parody, the protagonist as well as his murderer must have appeared as characters endowed with at least some inner motivation—they could not simply be 'functions' or 'signs'. An experienced playwright like Sophocles would have known how to integrate the two aspects and operate in accordance with the rules of necessity and probability which Aristotle was later to codify with regard to character as well as plot. Unfortunately, the surviving fragments of Sophocles' play allow no inference about characterization and motivation. Perhaps an erotic motif was present in Stesichorus' *Iliupersis* or in the play on Troilus which Phrynicus is supposed to have written. 'The light of love shines on the purple cheeks', says a fragment sometimes attributed to the co-founder of tragedy.[51] What is certain is that in the *Alexandra*—that bizarre and obscure poem on Cassandra's prophecies composed either by the tragedian Lycophron in the third century or by someone else with the same name between the second and first century BC[52]— we find a few lines alluding to Achilles' unrequited love for Troilus:

Ay! me, for thy fair-fostered flower [Troilus], too, I groan, O lion whelp, sweet darling of thy kindred, who didst smite with fiery charm of shafts the fierce dragon [Achilles] and seize for a little loveless while in unescapable noose him that was smitten, thyself unwounded by thy victim: thou shalt forfeit thy head and stain thy father's [Apollo] altar-tomb with thy blood.[53]

In his commentary on the passage of the *Aeneid* quoted at the beginning of this essay, Servius maintains that 'the truth of the story' is that Achilles loved Troilus and presented him with doves. Troilus wanted to keep them, was taken by Achilles, and 'in eius amplexibus periit'—perished in his embraces.[54] Virgil, adds Servius,

[51] Pearson, *Fragments of Sophocles*, p. 254.

[52] The date of the *Alexandra* is still very uncertain. See s.v. Lycophron in e.g. *Oxford Classical Dictionary*.

[53] ll. 307–13, trans. A. W. and G. R. Mair in *Callimachus, Lycophron, Aratus* (Loeb, 1977).

[54] Servius in *Aen.* i. 474.

changed this story because it was unworthy of heroic poetry. The twelfth-century Byzantine scholar Tzetzes, in his commentary on Lycophron's *Alexandra*, states that Troilus, Apollo's son and Cassandra's brother, was loved by Achilles, fled for refuge to the Thymbraeum and, as he refused to come out at Achilles' pleading, was slain by the Greek hero at the altar. Later on, Apollo was to exact his vengeance on Achilles by having him killed in the same temple.[55] Finally, a curious variation on this particular erotic motif is provided by the Clementine *Homilies* which, in complaining about the earthly loves and 'unnatural lusts' of the pagan gods, maintain that Apollo himself loved Troilus as well as Hyacinthus, Admetus, Orpheus, and others.[56]

Figurative evidence indicates that the erotic link between Achilles and Troilus may have been a very ancient and widespread tradition, above all in the West. 'Characterization' and 'motivation', in other words, may have been born together with 'functionality'. If a cock, the typical gift exchanged by lovers, is present on the bronze laminae from Olympia mentioned above, the paintings in the Tomb of the Bulls may contain more than a simple allusion to the erotic theme. The sixth-century black-figure Etruscan vase by the Micali painter[57] shows Achilles holding a dove in his right hand, ready to let it fly away. Another dove flies towards Troilus, and a third one hovers over one of his horses. Doves—the 'palumbes' of Servius' account—are sacred to Aphrodite and are 'erotic' birds. Another version of the story seems to be represented by the black-figure Etruscan neck-amphora in Reading,[58] where Achilles rides a horse while Troilus lies passively in his Phrygian costume between the legs of the animal. On the other side of the vase, Achilles runs towards the altar of Thymbraean Apollo. On his right shoulder lies Troilus, now naked, frantically moving his arms.[59] On many other vases an erotic aura seems to pervade representations of a fully armed Achilles pursuing or butchering a naked, boyish Troilus.

[55] *Lycophronis Alexandra*, rec. et scholia G. Kinkel (Leipzig, 1880), ad. 307 ff.

[56] Migne, *Patrologia Graeca*, 2. 184–5; *Clementina*, Homilia v. xv. 145.

[57] Rome, Villa Giulia 5200, *LIMC*, Achle, 13.

[58] Reading Univ. 47. vi. 1, *LIMC*, Achle, 18, late sixth cent. BC.

[59] For all this, and the interesting motif of the interchangeability between Troilus and Polyxena in some versions, see B. D'Agostino, 'Achille e Troilo: Immagini, testi e assonanze', *AION* (*Annali Istituto Orientale Napoli, Archeologia e Storia Antica*), 7 (1985), 1–8, and bibliog. therein.

Achilles' homosexual love for Troilus and the latter's rejection of it would undoubtedly provide sufficient 'inner motivation' for the murder and fit into the more general picture of the Greek warrior as 'lover' (of Polyxena, Troilus' sister and often his feminine 'double', and of Patroclus). But why choose this particular form of eros? One reason could be that this motif would agree with the atmosphere of violence that dominates the story. The aim of Achilles' violence is victory, but violence can also be an instinct, a 'lust'—in short, it can easily be coupled with love. There is enough evidence of this shaking passion, of Achilles' 'lust', in both Lycophron and Servius. *Thanatos* and *eros* are inseparable, and in our last Chapter we shall see how Christa Wolf treats this theme.

What, however, is interesting is that Troilus should be not the subject but the object of love. Of course, he almost always appears as a mere boy or, as Sophocles says, an *andropais*, a 'lad on the verge of manhood'.[60] If you want to motivate, or embellish, his story with the love theme, you either keep him a boy or make him grow up. In neither case, however, must he be allowed to procreate, or else Troy would perpetuate itself. Antiquity chooses the first solution: Troilus becomes the object of Achilles' love, rejects him, and perishes. In the different cultural climate of the twelfth century which Roberto Antonelli will illustrate in the next Chapter, Troilus has grown up. He can—indeed in that culture he must—love, and Cressida is invented. Troilus becomes the subject of love, but one inevitably destined to betrayal and death. The 'functionality' seems to survive even when characterization has changed and become dominant—myth has its hidden ways of perpetuating itself through metamorphosis.

The invention of Cressida, in any case, complicates the story to an unprecedented degree, and even the sense of Troilus' tragedy is, as Derek Brewer shows later in this volume, changed by it. The relationship between *thanatos* and *eros* acquires a different value. In antiquity, all is subordinated to the former: from Benoît de Sainte-Maure onwards the latter is first—*eros* and *thanatos*, Troilus *and* Cressida. As far as we know, in this story the ancients kept away from the theme of heterosexual romantic love. They had a Briseis and a Chryseis,[61] both present and important in the *Iliad* as

---

[60] Pearson, *Fragments of Sophocles*, p. 257.

[61] See *LIMC* i/1, s.v. Briseis and Chryseis, for full information on the figurative evidence.

well as in figurative art, the latter certainly a character in Sophocles' and Pacuvius' plays on *Chryses*, the former—in Homer, the cause itself of Achilles' wrath—protagonist of Ovid's third letter in the *Heroides*, where she desperately proclaims her love for the Greek warrior. None of the surviving literature, however, connects either with Troilus; nor, for that matter, does the *Ovide Moralisé*, much later, even though the author knows and mentions Benoît's *Roman.*[62]

Enough drama was produced in classical and late antiquity by far more illustrious couples and triangles. Helen, Menelaus, and Paris; Agamemnon, Clytemnestra, and Aegisthus; Theseus, Phaedra, and Hippolytus are quite sufficient to illustrate the themes of love, betrayal, and death. Ancient Troilus must simply die.

[62] *Ovide Moralisé*, xii. 4474-513; and see 4584ff. See also n. 3 above for Boccaccio's attitude to the myth.

2

The Birth of Criseyde—An Exemplary Triangle: 'Classical' Troilus and the Question of Love at the Anglo-Norman Court

The figure of Briseis-Cressida, the lover of Troilus, is unknown in classical and medieval literature: the efforts of scholars to discover the existence of the character in works previous to the *Roman de Troie*, written by Benoît de Sainte-Maure shortly after the middle of the twelfth century, have so far been fruitless.[1]

The figure of Troilus, the son of Priam, on the other hand, is well known; he is mourned by his father in the *Iliad*, and is also recalled by Dictys as the protagonist of a 'casum miserandum'.[2] However, the figure of Troilus as a modern character capable of surviving to the present was born together with Briseis: without Briseis Troilus would not exist. Or, to be more precise, without her *betrayal* Troilus would not be the object of discussion today, since the *Filostrato*, *Troilus and Criseyde*, *Troilus and Cressida*, and so on, would obviously not have been written. Paradoxically, those aspects of the figure of Briseis which are new and original in Romance (and consequently modern) courtly literature are essentially *negative* characteristics, drawn from the most well-known misogynous literature; had Briseis been one of the many women who were adored in vain, or who were described as (almost) perfect and

[1] On this question, and on the story of Troilus and Criseyde as a whole, K. Young, *The Origin and Development of the Story of Troilus and Criseyde* (London, 1908) is still an essential (and unchallenged) work. Generally helpful are: E. Gorra, *Testi inediti di storia troiana* (Turin, 1887); H. G. Wright, *Boccaccio in England from Chaucer to Tennyson* (London, 1957); Ch. Muscatine, *Chaucer and the French Tradition: A Study in Style and Meaning* (Berkeley and LA, 1957). Still of considerable value is L. Constans's Introd. to his edn. of vol. 6 of the *Roman de Troie*, 6 vols. (Paris, 1904–12), which I use here, and A. Joly, *Benoît de Sainte-More et le Roman de Troie, ou les Métamorphoses d'Homère et de l'épopée gréco-latine au moyen âge*, 2 vols. (Paris, 1870–1).

[2] Ibid., xxiv. 257; *Belli troiani*, iv. 9, 22.

beyond the reach of troubadours and trouvères, she would not have been distinguishable from a common stereotype (Beatrice is obviously the main example) which necessarily excludes the possibility of creating a *real* woman. Since she is a negative *exemplum*, Briseis is characterized by a strong contradiction and a trauma, and it is for this reason that she has attracted the interest of other authors.

However, the use and the interpretation of the story of Troilus and Briseis has often been turned upside down by critics. Briseis, one of the very few female characters in courtly literature who have an autonomous existence (who are not, that is, the mere projection or schematic reduction of the male imagination, and thus non-existent), has in fact been reduced to a means for identifying with the suffering of the man, Troilus. Contrary to what has often been claimed, the literature of 'courtly' love is, despite appearances, a *masculine* form: its centre is not the woman, but male narcissism. In the *Roman de Troie*, which was written by a man (a cleric, what is more), the character who appears to be both central and positive, and who attracts the narcissism of the male reader, is naturally Troilus. However, despite the fact that the intentions of the author (at times explicitly and loudly expressed) are in line with those of almost all twelfth-century literature in their hostility to the woman who has no precise institutionalized role (mother and wife), the character of Briseis is inevitably *contradictory*, and thus dynamic. Troilus had to love a woman who was free and *inconstant* (like all women, as Benoît and Guido delle Colonne would add), though not exclusively and inevitably negative: Briseis had to demonstrate in some way that she *deserved* Troilus, thus that she possessed positive qualities, and not only as regards physical appearance. The following is the author's introductory portrait of Briseis (note her joined eyebrows, already described by Dares, and their negative physiognomical significance):

> Briseïda fu avenant:
> Ne fu petite ne trop grant.
> Plus esteit bele e bloie e blanche
> Que flor de lis ne neif sor branche;
> Mais les sorcilles li joigneient,
> Que auques li mesaveneient
> Beaus ieuz aveit de grant maniere
> E mout esteit bele parliere.

> Mout fu de bon afaitement
> E de sage contenement.

[Briseida was charming and neither too short nor too tall. She was
lovelier, fairer, and whiter than a lily or the snow upon a branch; but her
eyebrows were joined, and that somewhat flawed her beauty. She had
marvellously beautiful eyes, and was very eloquent and most well-
mannered and prudent in conduct.][3]

The Troilus of the *Iliad*, of Dictys, and of Dares could only become
the Troilus of Benoît and of the *Filostrato* (that is, a man 'defeated
and downcast by love') if Briseis too was 'different'—if, that is, she
was susceptible to change; and in order to change she had to
'betray':

> Mout fu amee e mout amot,
> Mais sis corages li chanjot;
> E si ert el mout vergondose,
> Simple e aumosniere e pitose.

[She was greatly loved, and she herself loved greatly, but her heart was
not constant. Nonetheless she was very timid, modest, generous, and
compassionate.][4]

But *why* invent a story such as that of Troilus and Briseis? And
why Benoît in particular?

The *Roman de Troie* has been transmitted by about thirty manuscripts (to which we can add about fifteen fragments).[5] Thus, it
must have met with greater success than two other romances, both
anonymous, which were based on 'classical' subjects: the *Roman de
Thèbes* and the *Eneas*. As far as the concrete forms of transmission
and circulation of the books or manuscripts are concerned, the
most notable point of interest is the close connection between the
Roman de Troie, the *Roman de Thèbes*, and the *Eneas*, which are at
times significantly linked with Wace's *Brut.*

Of the five manuscripts (and the Angers fragment) described by
G. Raynaud de Lage in his edition of the *Roman de Thèbes*[6] only in

---

[3] *Roman de Troie*, ll. 5275–84. All translations from the *Roman de Troie* are
taken from N. R. Havely, *Chaucer's Boccaccio* (Cambridge, 1980), with some
modifications.

[4] Ibid., ll. 5285–8.

[5] *Roman de Troie*, vi. 1–67. Research carried out since Constans's survey has
not substantially altered the overall picture.

[6] *Le roman de Thèbes*, ed. G. Raynaud de Lage, 2 vols. (Paris, 1966–71).

one case does the work appear alone;[7] in the others it is paired with the *Eneas*,[8] with the *Roman de Troie*,[9] or with both.[10]

An analysis of the manuscripts of the *Eneas* leads to similar conclusions. Of the nine codices listed in J.-J. Salverda de Grave's edition[11] seven couple the *Eneas* with other romances based on classical subjects, or with the *Brut*: in the three examples mentioned above it is paired with the *Roman de Thèbes*, or with both the *Roman de Thèbes* and the *Roman de Troie*. In two examples it is paired with the *Roman de Troie* and *Brut*,[12] and in another two with *Brut* alone.[13] Thus, in the work of the scribes who copied and put together the three 'classical' romances and *Brut* (between the end of the twelfth century and the fourteenth century, though the tendency undoubtedly extends further back), the following connections are revealed: *Thèbes-Eneas* (1 or 2?), *Thèbes-Troie* (1), *Eneas-Brut* (2), *Thèbes-Eneas-Troie* (1), *Troie-Eneas-Brut* (2), and *Thèbes-Troie-Eneas-Brut* (1?).

Eneas is the common element in every case, with one exception. It is not difficult to perceive a progressive series of links. Beside the initial nucleus, based around the two older 'classical' romances (*Thèbes-Eneas*), there is also a historical and genealogical identification between Aeneas and Brutus, who is the descendant of Aeneas and the founder of Britain (*Eneas-Brut*); this historical identification is completed by the addition of the *Roman de Troie*. The *Roman de Troie* can also be linked to the *Roman de Thèbes*, which is recognized in its turn as part of a triad which unites all the 'classical' romances (*Thèbes-Eneas-Troie*), even without considering a direct and explicit use at a political and cultural level (and thus without *Brut*). However, the main link revealed by an analysis of the transmission of manuscripts is that between *Eneas* and *Brut* (the two works are paired in five manuscripts, with various additions): this amounts to a legitimization of the Plantagenet dynasty through a powerful myth (which goes so far as to suggest that the dynasty has Trojan, rather than Roman, origins). Thus, the

---

[7] Geneva, Bodmer, ex-Phillipps 8384.

[8] British Library Add. 34114 and Paris, Bibl. Nat., fr. 784.

[9] Paris, Bibl. Nat., fr. 375.

[10] Paris, Bibl. Nat., fr. 60, to which Constans believes we should also add the manuscript kept at Montpellier, Faculté de Medicine, 251.

[11] *Eneas: Roman du XIIᵉ siècle*, ed. J.-J. Salverda de Grave, 2 vols. (Paris, 1925–9).

[12] Paris, Bibl. Nat., fr. 1450 and Montpellier, Faculté de Medicine, 251.

[13] Paris, Bibl. Nat., fr. 12603 and fr. 1416.

'historical' (and cultural) recognition of the Plantagenet dynasty[14] seems to have been formed gradually through a unified strategy; the final element of this strategy (1155–60) was the *Roman de Troie*, which was written by Benoît, who succeeded Wace, the author of *Brut*, as official court historian. The chronological order of composition which is now most accepted (*Thèbes-Brut-Eneas-Troie*)[15] seems rather significant, though a very small number of years divides the works (the *Roman de Troie* was written between 1150 and 1160; there is strong evidence in favour of a date around 1155). The features which characterize the chronology of the four works, the relations between them, and consequently their historical, cultural, and political motivations, are more closely connected to the story of Troilus and Briseis than one might think at first sight.

In the *Roman de Thèbes* the theme of love is hardly touched upon; it centres principally around the arrival of Jocasta and her two daughters, Antigone and Ysmaine, at the camp of Polynices (see 4017–198), and Parthenopaeus' gift to his beloved of Ytier's horse (see 4579–624). Both these episodes anticipate passages in the story of Troilus and Briseis. Parthenopaeus accompanies Antigone, who has come from the opposing camp, to the encampment, falls in love with her, but does not receive a definite answer; this is exactly what happens to Diomedes when he accompanies Briseis, who has come from Troy, to the Greek camp. Antigone reproaches Parthenopaeus for his excessive haste and makes an explicit allusion, through the mention of the shepherdess, to the so-called *pastourelle*,[16] one of the

---

[14] See G. H. Gerould, 'King Arthur and Politics', *Speculum*, 2 (1927), 33–51, and esp. the discussion of the matter in R. R. Bezzola, *La société courtoise: Littérature de cour et littérature courtoise*, pp. 132 ff., (vol. I of *Les origines et la formation de la littérature courtoise en occident (500-1200)*, 3 vols. (Paris, 1944–63)).

[15] The arguments put forward by G. Angeli, *L'Eneas e i primi romanzi volgari* (Milan and Naples, 1971) do not seem to hold water. Further evidence in favour of the order *Thèbes-Brut-Eneas-Troie*, also in the light of a convincing argument for an earlier date, around 1150, for Thomas's *Tristan*, is contained in a dissertation by A. Punzi, '[Materiali] per la datazione del Tristan di Thomas', which was presented during the academic year 1986–7 at the Facoltà di Lettere e Filosofia of the University of Rome, and is shortly to be published in *Cultura neolatina*, 48 (1988).

[16] Already pointed out in R. R. Bezzola, *La société courtoise*, pp. 275–6. For an analysis of the strong ideological and polemical value of Marcabrun's *pastourelle*, see N. Pasero, 'Pastora contro cavaliere: Marcabruno contro Guglielmo IX', *Cultura neolatina*, 43 (1983), 9–25. The *pastourelle* has already been evoked as a topical exordium in the approach made by Parthenopaeus (ll. 4139–42): 'Vers lui

principal literary genres which dealt with the various aspects of love (and the debate around courtly love):

> Par Dieu, ce respont la pucele,
> ceste amour seroit trop isnele!
> Pucele sui, fille de roi,
> legierment amer ne doi,
> Ne doi amer par legerie
> dont l'em puisse dire folie;
> ainsi doit en prier berchieres
> ou ces autres fames legieres.

[By the Lord, replies the maid, this love would run too fast! I am a maid, the daughter of a king, I must not love lightly, I must not love with levity, that it might be called madness; thus should shepherdesses be addressed, or other light women.][17]

Haste, which is connected to the category of 'time', is thus explicitly related to social position and to 'folly', which the suitor Parthenopaeus might later reproach Antigone for:

> Ne vous connois n'onc ne vous vi
> ne mes ore que vous voi ci.
> Se or vos doing d'amer parole,
> bien me pouez tenir pour fole.

[I do not know you, nor have I ever seen you, not even now that I see you here. If now I give you word to love, you may well take me to be mad.][18]

Antigone is not, however, hostile towards him, as long as he is of good birth and speaks about the matter to her mother, Jocasta; the prospective change in her status, her noble origins, and the fact that she is 'fille de roi' allow her to be sure and clear about the future. She is consequently more able to commit herself than Briseis, who finds herself in a similar position, but is isolated, without the advantage of being the daughter of a king, and already engaged to Troilus:

> Pour ce ne di, celer nel quier,
> ne vos eüsse forment chier

en vet isnelement, | salua la courtoisement: | Dame, fet il, nel me celez | qui vous estes et ou vous alez' ('He went towards her quickly, | and greeted her courteously. | Lady, he said, do not hide from me | who you are and where you are going').

---

[17] *Roman de Thèbes*, ll. 4163–70.
[18] Ibid., ll. 14169–70.

s'estïez de si haut linage
que vous fussiez de mon parage
et ce fust chose destinnee
qu'a fame vous fusse donnee.
Car biaux estes sor toute gent
onc ne vis mes houme tant gent.
Parlez ent, fet ele, a ma mere,
et par le conseill de mon frere,
qui voz parens connoist et vos,
soit acordez le plet de nous.
Se il l'agreent, je l'otroi,
ja n'en seront desdit par moi.

[Therefore I do not say, nor do I hide it, that you would not be extraordinarily dear to me if you were of such high lineage as to be as noble as myself, and if it were established that I should become your wife. For you are more handsome than any other, and I have never seen a man of such noble aspect. Speak about the matter, she says, to my mother, and with the agreement of my brother, who knows you and your kin, may you be granted possession of me. If they consent, I will agree to it, I will not go against their word.][19]

In *Brut*, the wife of the Count of Cornwall, Ygerne—though in completely different circumstances—does not give a definite answer to the clear *avances* of King Uther, who has fallen in love with her from afar as a result of her reputation (like Jaufre Rudel):

Li reis en ot oï parler
E mult l'aveit oï loer;
Ainz que nul semblant en feïst,
Veire assez ainz qu'il la veïst,
L'out il cuveitee e amee,
Kar merveilles esteit loee.
Mult l'ad al mangier esguardee,
S'entente i ad tute turnee.
Se il mangout, se il beveit,
Se il parlout, se il taiseit,
Toutes eures de li pensot
E en travers la regardot.
En regardant, li surrieit,
E d'amur signe li faiseit.
Par ses privez la saluot
E ses presens li enveot,

[19] *Roman de Thèbes*, ll. 4175-88.

Mult li ad ris e mult clunied
E maint semblant fait d'amistied;
Ygerne issi se conteneit
Qu'el n'otriout ne desdiseit.

[The king had heard her spoken about, and had heard much praise of her. Before he gave her any sign of it, in fact long before he had seen her, he had desired and loved her, for she was praised enormously. He observed her much at table, his attention was turned to her alone. If he ate, if he drank, if he spoke, if he was silent, he thought of her always and observed her askance. While watching her, he smiled at her and made signs of love. Through his closest friends he greeted her and sent her gifts, he smiled and winked at her a great deal, and made many expressions of friendship. Ygerne behaved in such a way that she neither consented nor refused.][20]

There is only one other significant episode of love in the *Brut*: an episode which also involves a woman and two men, Guinevere, Mordret, and Arthur, and has tragic consequences. Thus, the *Brut* complements the episodes of love in the *Roman de Thèbes*, which were mentioned above, in constituting an important stage towards the *Roman de Troie*. For Ygerne (like Guinevere) is the vertex of a true love triangle, which is based on the simultaneous competition between two men, both of whom are present: her husband (the Count of Cornwall) and King Uther. However, Ygerne's cautious behaviour does not have exactly the same meaning as that of Antigone. Ygerne sees that she is the subject of a dispute in which she will *never* have an independent role: since she is a woman, and consequently weak, as Benoît will later point out explicitly,[21] she bides her *time*. In the end King Uther, the member of the triangle whose social position is strongest, will emerge as victor, because of the strength of his power, which consists of magic and weapons (for the male characters, too, the development of the plot of the *Roman de Troie* will be more complex).

The two main stories of love in the *Eneas* are also based around the triangle. In this work, however, the theme of love assumes greater importance than in the *Roman de Thèbes* and *Brut*, both in quantitative terms and in terms of the subtlety of psychological analysis. In the relationship between Dido and Aeneas there is not, apparently, a third person: Dido is a widow (as Briseis-Cressida will be a widow in Boccaccio), but even widowhood should not

[20] Wace, *Le roman de Brut*, ed. I. Arnold, 2 vols. (Paris, 1928-30), i. 451-2.
[21] *Roman de Troie*, ll. 13475-6.

untie the wife from the matrimonial knot and from 'faith to the ashes of Sichaeus'.[22] For Andreas Capellanus, widowhood was still a problem which merited special attention:

The woman says: ... although every other thing persuades me to love, widowhood and sadness for my excellent lost husband bar me from every pleasure in life.[23]

In the solution proposed by man, and thus by Andreas, the key, which must be found to persuade the widow to love is 'time':

In fact to mourn a husband *beyond the time* established by the law is to express contempt for legal precepts, to resist the divine will with rebellious spirit, and to think with foolhardy spirit in a way which is contrary to that which God has established. Furthermore, to mourn beyond the established time is certainly not useful to the dead husband, and may bring a great deal of harm to yourself.[24]

Thus, the relationship between Dido and Aeneas also takes the form of a triangle, though of an unusual type; the peculiar features which characterize this triangular relationship are the breaking of a bond which existed *previously* (a legal bond, in this case) and the *time* which passes between the first relationship and the second. In reality Briseis, who passes from love for Troilus to love for Diomedes, represents a more 'quintessential', more shocking version of the same problem, though at a 'lower' social level (in this case the relationship is between a *nobilior* and a *nobilis*, rather than between two *nobiliores*). Although she is a widow, Dido's breaking of the marriage bond represents the breaking of a 'law', of a social agreement, leading to 'folie' and the inevitable tragic, and *punitive*, outcome of the story. Dido's epitaph, which describes her love as 'soltain' ('legibus solutus', or 'outside the law'),[25] will sum up the meaning of the whole affair:

> Iluec gist
> Dido qui por s'amor s'ocist;

[22] Dante, *Inferno*, v. 62.

[23] Andreas Capellanus, *Trattato d'amore*, ed. S. Battaglia (Rome, 1947), 200 (the Battaglia edn. reproduced the critical text from E. Trojel, *Andreae Capellani regii Francorum De Amore libri tres* (Hauniae, 1892), with the addition of two translations into Italian). My translation.

[24] *Trattato d'amore*, 202.

[25] A. Ferrari, 'Amor soltaine', *Studi romanzi*, 38 (1981), 9-25.

> onques ne fu meillor paiene,
> s'ele n'eüst amor soltaine,
> mais ela ama trop folemant,
> savoir ne li valut noiant.

[There lies Dido, who killed herself for love; there would never have been a better heathen had her love not been so far outside the law [dis-solute], but she loved too madly, and knowledge served her no purpose.][26]

In the case of the triangular relationship involving Lavinia, Turnus, and Aeneas, however, the story is played out at a synchronic level (as had happened with Ygerne, the Count of Cornwall, and King Uther): the two male suitors are present at the same time. Aeneas wins final victory, like King Uther, through the strength of his weapons, but he has already previously won the heart of Lavinia (whereas we know nothing of Ygerne's feelings). The long description of the birth and the effects of love in the heart of Lavinia culminates in the rejection of the more famous and subversive triangle involving Tristan, Isolde, and King Mark.[27] Lavinia fears that she has favoured Aeneas too strongly and abandoned Turnus too rashly; consequently she considers sharing her love between them both:

> —Ne sai que s'est a devenir,
> se deüsse m'amor partir,
> que chascun l'aüst igalment.
> —Ce qui, ne me neüst noiant:
> l'un et l'autre deüsse atraire;
> ansi poïsse ge bien faire,
> se ges amasse andos issi;
> donc ne faillisse a un ami;
> li quels que fust morz ou vencuz,
> l'un an aüsse de mes druz.

[I know not what would happen if I should divide my love in such a way that each should have an equal part. It would not trouble me; I would have to attract them both; I could easily do so, if I loved them both: in this case I would not fail a friend; whichever of them were dead or defeated, I would have one of my lovers.][28]

[26] *Eneas*, ll. 2139–44.

[27] The above-mentioned study by A. Punzi makes a number of new points about the relation between *Eneas* and *Tristan*, including some concerning the triangle.

[28] *Eneas*, ll. 8269–78.

However, the temptation is only fleeting; Lavinia immediately rejects the 'mad' idea of sharing her love between more than one lover, not being 'leals', and *changing*, 'changier':

> bone amor vait solement
> d'un sol a autre senglement;
> des que l'an velt lo tiers atraire
> puis n'i a giens amors que faire.

[Good love only goes singly from one to another; if the need is felt to attract a third, then it is no longer a question of love.][29]

Tristan and Isolde had been defeated because of the fact that they were part of a triangle; Lavinia wishes to marry the man she loves, she does not want Aeneas to have a *parçonier* (co-owner):

> Qui fermement velt bien amer,
> son compaignon ait et son per;
> del tierz aprés ne sai ge mie;
> puis sanble ce marcheandie.
> Rire puet l'an bien a plusors,
> mais ne sont pas voires amors
> don l'an apaie dous ou trois;
> ne tient d'amor precepz ne lois
> qui plus que un an velt amer:
> ne si velt pas amor dobler.
> Par foi, ge ne ainz pas ansi,
> Eneas tien por mon ami,
> ge l'ain. Ce ne ferai ge mie
> que de m'amor face partie,
> ne li voil pas d'amor boisier,
> o lui n'i avra parçonier;

[May he who wishes to love resolutely have his partner and his equal; I do not wish to have anything to do with a third person, it would seem like a market. It may suit many people, but that which satisfies two or three is not true love; he who wishes to love more than one does not follow the precepts and the laws of love: love cannot be duplicated. Truly, for me it is not so, Aeneas is my friend, I love him. I will not do anything which would divide my love into parts, I do not wish to deceive him in love, with him there will be no co-owner.][30]

The permissibility, the various types, and the consequences of the triangle of love were matters of debate in both Anglo-Norman and

---

[29] *Eneas*, ll. 8285-8.   [30] Ibid., ll. 8289-304.

Provençal cultures.[31] The troubadours frequently raised the question whether it is permissible for a woman to have, in addition to her husband (with whom, in the opinion of Andreas, love is not even conceivable), one or even more lovers at the same time. From Cercamon onwards, the 'courtly' answer is that one lover is permissible; for Bernart de Ventadorn, almost certainly an attendant at the court of Eleanor of Aquitaine, only if forced by circumstances or by the 'folly' of love is it possible for the man to be the *parçonier* of love:

> Pois vol autre amador
> ma domn', eu no lo'lh defen;
> e lais m'en mais per paor
> que per autre chauzimen.

[Since another lover wants my woman, I do not prevent him; I agree to it more from fear than for other reasons.][32]

However, there are others, like Marcabrun (the author of the first *pastourelle* known to us, that which is cited, or at least referred to, in the *Roman de Thèbes*), who do not admit even one lover outside marriage:

> Selh'amor[s] viu de rapina
> que per un sol non defina
>   .   .   .   .
> Amors qui ves dos s'aclina,
> quer lo ters que l plec l'esquina,
> plus es puta que maustina.

[That love which does not finish at one person lives by theft ... Love which is directed towards two, and which looks for the third who breaks its back, is more whorish than a bitch.][33]

And Marcabrun is less isolated in his opinion than is usually believed, not only because of the clear links with clerical views.[34]

[31] A wide collection of material on the matter is reproduced and analysed in S. M. Cingolani, 'Estra lei n'i son trei', *Cultura neolatina*, 44 (1984), 9–47.

[32] Bernart de Ventadorn, 'Era m cosselhatz, senhor', in Bernart de Ventadorn, *Seine Lieder mit Einleitung und Glossar*, ed. C. Appel (Halle, 1915), 34.

[33] A. Dejeanne, *Poésies complètes du troubadour Marcabru* (Toulouse, 1909), 84.

[34] See Au. Roncaglia, '"Trobar clus": discussione aperta', *Cultura neolatina*, 29 (1969), 1–59, with the reply by E. Köhler, '"Trobar clus": discussione aperta: Marcabru und die beiden Schulen', *Cultura neolatina*, 30 (1970), 300–14, which was answered by Roncaglia in 'Riflessi di posizioni cistercensi nella poesia del XII secolo (Discussione sui fondamenti religiosi del "trobar naturau" di Marcabruno)',

Thomas's *Tristan* undoubtedly lies behind Lavinia's argument against divided love; so, probably, does the echo of the troubadours' debate on the permissibility of love outside marriage, and thus of love shared between two men, whatever their relationship with the woman, the vertex of the triangle: behind Lavinia, as well as Ovid, there is the Provençal *fin'amors*. However, the true development of the ideological and poetic views which are present at the court, or the courts, of Eleanor and Henry II is difficult to analyse without drawing over-simplified conclusions.[35] Marcabrun was an attendant at the court of Eleanor's bigoted father, William X of Aquitaine, and argued subtly but clearly (in a *pastourelle*) against the anti-clerical, 'court jester' views of Eleanor's grandfather (William IX, the first troubadour whose work is known to us, and probably the first troubadour of all).[36] Bernart was probably a close friend of the queen, while the *Roman de Thèbes*, the *Eneas*, and the *Brut*, which were hardly 'courtly' at all, though they were certainly Provençal (or Marcabrunian, I would say), were composed around the Anglo-Norman court of Eleanor and Henry (the young Chrétien de Troyes was also, perhaps, an attendant at the court; in *Cligès* he comes closer to the anti-*Tristan* views of the *Eneas*, whilst in *Erec et Enide* he deals with some of the questions central to the *Roman de Troie*). All except the most 'courtly' troubadours are, to some extent, critical of the triangle portrayed

in *I Cistercensi e il Lazio* (Proceedings of the study conference held at the Istituto di storia dell'arte of the University of Rome (17–21 May 1977)) (Rome, 1977), 11–20. The above-mentioned article by N. Pasero includes arguments which support Roncaglia's thesis.

[35] Still essential for an understanding of the literary role played by Eleanor of Aquitaine is the study by R. Lejeune, 'Rôle littéraire d'Aliénor d'Aquitaine et de sa famille', *Cultura neolatina*, 14 (1954), 1–57; a supplement to Lejeune, very limited and devoted to the typology of love, is to be found in M. Lazar, 'Cupid, the Lady, and the Poet: Modes of Love at Eleanor of Aquitaine's Court', in W. K. Kibler (ed.), *Eleanor of Aquitaine: Patron and Politician* (Austin and London, 1976), 35–59. The best treatment is still that of R. R. Bezzola in *La société courtoise*.

[36] It is difficult to accept the arguments put forward in E. Köhler's 'Observations historiques et sociologiques sur la poésie des troubadours', in *Cahiers de civilisation médiévale*, 7 (1964), 27–51, esp. where he denies that the Duke was the first troubadour (p. 39). On this subject see also R. Antonelli, 'Politica e volgare: Guglielmo IX, Enrico II, Federico II', in *Seminario romanzo* (Rome, 1979), 12 ff.: the discovery of the debate between Marcabrun and William IX gives further support to those who prefer to make use only of existing documents, which do not allow us to go further back than the Duke of Aquitaine.

in Thomas's *Tristan*, which is another clear example of the dramatic nature of love 'outside the law', and of its tragic fate, but also ultimately an example of love's refining force and power[37] (the procedure and development in *Tristan* are not so far from the story of Troilus and Briseis, despite appearances).

Thus, there was a whole range of people at the Anglo-Norman court: clerics, elegant Latin writers who were critical of the romance fantasies of low culture and of the invasion (obviously favoured by Eleanor) of the court by 'jesters' and courtiers from Poitou, Provençal troubadours and Anglo-Norman historians (though there were also historians from Poitou) who were critical of the dangerous precedent set by the *Tristan*, and also involved in the debate on the various aspects of love. Contemporary clerks had already noted, and frequently complained of, the characteristic feature of the court of Henry and Eleanor:[38] its complex, contradictory, and dynamic nature. The court was increasingly like a great melting-pot in which elements of an extremely wide range of traditions were analysed, discussed, and composed: the true melting-pot of the most significant developments of Old French literature. However we interpret the different viewpoints which existed in Eleanor's *entourage*, the story of Troilus and Briseis, and thus the character of Briseis, would not be conceivable outside the great and complex culture of knighthood and love of the Anglo-Norman court.

The complex and contradictory elements which lie *within* the character of Briseis and the many links which relate her to the various precedents are a just reflection of the *external* complexity and contradiction which accompanied the birth of the character. Briseis is, too, in some way an *exemplum*, in that she embodies a 'type' of the many possible varieties of the 'folie' of love.[39] In his representation of the various forms of eros, analysed in the *Roman de Troie* through three different cases, Benoît, the cleric and official court historian, seems to concentrate exclusively on 'folie': Medea

[37] The first to define his own work as an *exemplum*, underlining its demonstrative character, was Thomas himself—Sneyd fragment, ll. 831–9: see Thomas, *Les fragments du roman de Tristan*, ed. B. H. Wind (Geneva and Paris, 1960), 163.

[38] See R. R. Bezzola, *La société courtoise*, esp. pp. 88 ff (where Bezzola discusses Walter Map's *De nugis curialium*); and R. Antonelli, 'Politica e volgare', pp. 49 ff.

[39] On 'folly' and its meaning in troubadour poetry, see L. T. Topsfield, 'The "Natural Fool" in Peire d'Alvernhe, Marcabru, and Bernart de Ventadorn', in *Mélanges ... Charles Rostaing* (Liège, 1974), 149–58.

is mad to love Jason too much, leaving her father, her mother, her relations and her own people in order to be with him. Achilles is mad, though he is aware of his own folly when he falls in love with Polyxena;[40] but when the decisive moment arrives he loses this awareness, and consequently falls victim to the ambush prepared by Paris:

> Or est espris plus qu'il ne sueut.
> Amors li a le sen toleit:
> Ne set, ne veit, ne n'aparceit;
> Ne dote mort, ne l'en sovient.
> Ço fait Amors, qui rien ne crient.

[He is now more than usually overcome by love. Love has robbed him of his sense: he is not aware, he does not see, he does not perceive; he does not fear death, he does not remember it. This is the effect of Love, which fears nothing.][41]

Briseis, as we have seen, is presented as a woman of wise conduct; however, under Love's influence she recognizes the fact that she is 'Fause ... e legiere e fole' ('False ... and light and mad').[42] But Briseis in fact is the only character who does not follow the rule of 'folly'; she causes folly, but is not completely overcome by folly herself. Paradoxically, her lucid and 'secular' ability to reason, which has no equal in other female characters portrayed in medieval literature, is a result of her 'change' itself, of the fact that she expresses in their entirety the contradictions inherent in a character which was *bound* to change from 'wise' to 'mad' in the eyes of the usual courtly rules. The fact that she is perceived as 'mad' in the eyes of the prevailing moral values and social behaviour though she is perfectly wise in her own eyes is what constitutes the peculiarity of the character of Briseis (and its appeal to authors after Benoît, which was so great that the triangle of which she was the protagonist would become an *exemplum* that merited independent representation outside the framework of the story of Troy). It is not clear whether the contradictions in the character of Briseis were a reflection of Benoît himself as author; in the light of

[40] *Roman de Troie*, ll. 2217–20: 'Se fui sages, des or folei, | Quant en tal lieu me sui donez | Dont ja n'avrai mes volontez' ('If I was wise, now I am overcome by folly, | for I have assigned myself to that place, | where I will no longer have my will').

[41] Ibid., ll. 22116–20.

[42] Ibid., l. 20249.

the available evidence, the hypothesis seems unlikely—it is more probable that the element of contradiction was inherent in the *type* of character. However, the elements of contradiction which may have existed in the author's character (but how far is it possible to distinguish the author from the character he created?) are exactly those that were typical of courtly culture as a whole, of its desire to experiment and of the constraints that it was forced to acknowledge (led by Andreas Capellanus, especially in his *Reprobatio amoris*; however, the same can even be said of William IX, and certainly of Thomas).

There is, then, a series of parallels and a network of ideological allusions within the stories of Jason and Medea, Achilles and Polyxena, and Troilus and Briseis (and their predecessors). The results of love are always tragic for one of the main characters: in the case of the story based on the triangular relationship it is Troilus who meets with a tragic fate; it is probably no coincidence, even without taking the classical and medieval Latin precedents into account, that he meets Achilles in battle on several occasions, and is finally killed by him. Achilles and Troilus are the *exempla* of the knightly virtues destroyed by the power of Love (though Erec, who is married, will later prove the opposite). In the case of Troilus, the new and original aspect of the story consists in the development of the female character, which is presented as well-rounded and dynamic in order to explain more effectively the dramatic, unfortunate figure of Troilus and the 'folly' of love. For, if Benoît wished to provide a credible *exemplum* of the negative effects of the love triangle he was forced to take the character of Briseis to its logical conclusion, and to portray her as an inherently courtly *and* autonomous figure. In order to present the character of Briseis as an *exemplum* in the 'laboratory' where romances of *fin'amors* were being continually 'experimented' Benoît *was bound* to create a fully rounded character, and *was bound* to respect the development and the inner articulation of the character's feelings (unlike what was to happen in Guido delle Colonne and in other authors).

It has already been observed more than once that Briseis is presented in a positive manner. Forced into exile against her will, like 'a maid of rather low birth', she is not defended at all by Troilus, about whom it is said merely that he 'ot ire et tristece' ('was melancholy and sad'). It was only 200 years later that

Boccaccio, a courtier but also a bourgeois, would notice the incongruity of this situation, and set about filling in the gaps and the unanswered questions in the plot (as he did in many other cases): in Boccaccio, Troilus racks his brains to try to find a way to keep Briseis with him, and in the end he is only persuaded to resign himself, at least for the time being, by the woman herself. Benoît simply observes that it is a sin to separate two lovers, and that the Greeks will have to atone for it; when Briseis departs, everyone feels pity towards her:

> Les puceles e la reïne
> Ont grant pitié de la meschine,
> E mout en plore dame Heleine;
> E cele, qu n'est pas vilaine,
> Se part d'eles o plors, o criz,
> Quar mout par est sis cuers marriz:
> Rien ne la veit pitié n'en ait.

[The ladies and the queen are full of pity for the young woman, and Lady Helen weeps bitterly for her sake. And she, being by no means ungracious, departs from them with tears and lamentations, for her heart is sorely afflicted and no one seeing her could fail to feel pity for her.][43]

Troilus accompanies her. At this point the scenario changes. The sorrowful and 'wise' Briseis is denounced for what, according to Benoît, is the 'nature' of every woman. However, the author is forced to interrupt the story at length to make his own comments on the matter. The necessary internal contradiction in the character of Briseis leads to an external, formal contradiction:

Yet, although the lady is stricken with grief, she will be made happy again in time. She will soon have forgotten her sorrow, and her heart will be so altered that the Trojans will mean little to her. If she is sorrowful today, she will be made happy again by one who has never yet seen her. Soon she will have granted him her love, and soon she will be consoled by him. A woman will never be too downcast. So long as she is able to look about her, her sighs thereafter will be brief. A woman's sorrow is short-lived, for whilst one eye weeps the other smiles. Their hearts alter very quickly, and the wisest of them is foolish enough. Having loved for seven years, she will forget within three days. None of them ever knows what it is to suffer grief. Their wisdom is clearly manifest: they think that, whoever may have seen them, they can never at any time have committed any

[43] *Roman de Troie*, ll. 13913–16; 13413–19.

misdeed so hateful that they should be condemned for it. Their greatest folly is that they never believe themselves to be in the wrong; and whoever trusts and believes in them is betraying and deceiving himself.[44]

Thus, Benoît has to distance himself from the character of Briseis in order to underline—avoiding the misunderstandings that an ambiguous character can lead to—her role as a negative *exemplum* (a role which had so far in the plot not been envisaged for Briseis). However, in this way the author sets himself against the environment in which he works, and also against the woman who controls its cultural destiny, at least as far as the court itself is concerned: Eleanor of Aquitaine. In order to provide a moral 'explanation' of the figure of Briseis, Benoît is bound to condemn her for being a woman; but he is also bound to spare Eleanor, the queen of women (who, as is well known, was the frequent subject of gossip: her marriage with the pious King Louis VII had ended in divorce, and after many affairs she had married Henry II). (Almost) all women are weak and beset by folly, but one, the 'mother' of the court and the patroness of vernacular literature, is different (the hyperbolic praise and the clear analogy with the Virgin Mary are slightly suspect):[45]

> De cest, veir, criem g'estre blasmez
> De cele que tant a bontez
> Que hautece a, pris e valor,
> Honesté e sen e honor,
> Bien e mesure e saintee,
> E noble largece e beauté;
> En cui mesfait de dames maint
> Sont par le bien de li esteint;

[I fear indeed that I may be reproached for this by her who possesses such goodness and excellence, glory and merit—integrity, wisdom and honour—virtue, moderation and purity—and noble generosity and beauty. Through her virtues the misdeeds of many women are erased].[46]

Now Briseis is really *alone*: even her creator has distanced himself from her, and has made explicit her role as *exemplum*. However,

[44] *Roman de Troie*, ll. 13429–56.
[45] The identification of the 'rich lady, of rich king' with the Virgin Mary is already present in the MS in Paris, Bibl. de l'Arsenal 3340, according to L. Constans's Introd. to his edn. of vol. 6 of the *Roman de Troie* (p. 25).
[46] *Roman de Troie*, ll. 13457–64.

because of the features of the character that have been delineated
up to this point, and of the inherently courtly formal procedure of
the story, the development of the action and the psychological
observation of the characters will be *slow*. The explicit indication
of the order of events provided *en passant* by Benoît during his
strongly-worded personal intervention is contradicted *in the
work*. [47] Diomedes—though he will have to go through a great deal
before receiving a single kiss from her—acts exactly according to
the rules; Andreas Capellanus would have been able to include the
arguments Diomedes addresses to Briseis amongst the exemplary
dialogues of the *De amore*. Briseis' journey from Troy to the Greek
camp is said to take a short *time*, whilst in the narrative account it
is very long. Diomedes falls in love, and declares his love, immediately, but his speech extends to more than eighty lines. [48] Another
7,000 lines of armed battles and love skirmishes pass before Briseis
decides to choose Diomedes. Despite the internal and external
debate that has produced her, Briseis is incomprehensibly described once more as 'wise and worthy', [49] and replies as Antigone
had replied to Parthenopaeus: a decision and a change of such
rapidity would be unbecoming; she has left her friend in Troy, she
is alone, she must beware of being 'fole' and behave 'sagement' and
with discretion; Diomedes is worthy of respect, but Briseis is
unable to love: if she were forced to come to a decision nobody
would be dearer to her:

> Soz ciel n'a si riche pucele
> Ne si preisiee ne si bele,
> Por ço que rien vousist amer,
> Que pas vos deüst refuser:
> Ne jo nos refus autrement.
> Mais n'ai corage ne talent
> Que vos ne autre aim aparmains;
> Si poëz bien estre certains,
> S'a ço me voleie aproismier,
> Nul plus de vos n'avreie chier.
> Mais n'en ai pensé ne voleir,
> Ne ja Deus nel me doint aveir!

[47] See *Roman de Troie*, ll. 13445–6: 'Quant qu'ele a en set anz amé | A cele en
treiz jorz oblié' ('Having loved for seven years, | she will forget within three
days').

[48] Ibid., ll. 13532–616.

[49] Ibid., l. 13617.

[There is no lady beneath the heavens who is so noble, renowned, and beautiful that she could refuse you if she were at all inclined to love—and I am not refusing you either. But I do not intend or desire to love you or anyone else at the moment, although you may be assured that if I decided to do so I should give no one else preference over you. But I had not thought of doing that, nor wanted to—and God grant I never may!]⁵⁰

Diomedes, too, is 'wise and worthy': he acknowledges both the 'courtesy' and the implied (consequential?) willingness of Briseis ('Bien entendi as premiers moz | Qu'el n'esteit mie trop *sauvage*'):⁵¹ he will wait until she has 'merci'.

From this point until the final decision, the rhythm and the development of the story are consistent with the reciprocal acknowledgement on the part of the characters that they are not 'sauvage'. Diomedes and Briseis behave exactly like exemplary characters in the code of courtly love (counterpointed by the presence/absence of Troilus); there is, as in the case of Achilles, a consequent use of descriptions, passages, and episodes that are characteristic of courtly *fin'amors* and other romances based on classical subjects.

Troilus and Diomedes, who are only apparently less important than the more renowned pair, Achilles and Hector, pursue each other in battle throughout the entire *Roman*. Even before Briseis acts as a medium between them each of them manages to dispossess the other of his horse:⁵² the horse, and its clear role as a phallic symbol, is extremely influential in the decision of Briseis. Diomedes looks for Troilus in battle 'because of the damsel', unseats him, and immediately has the horse taken to Briseis. Briseis, however, does not appreciate the gift, and gives a lesson in courtly conduct to the new suitor: if he loves her, he must also love her people:

> 'Di mei', fait ele, 'ton seignor
> Que si me porte male amor;
> Quar, se rien se fait bien de mei
> Par le mien gré n'a mon otrei,

---

⁵⁰ *Roman de Troie*, ll. 13669–80.

⁵¹ 'From her very first words, he well understood that she was not uncourtly' (ll. 13650–1); I interpret 'sauvage' in its fullest semantic significance, that is, as *external* to the court, to that which is *civilized* (also, and here especially) by love: the meaning 'reluctant' is not excluded, but is part of a much wider meaning which is also more precise.

⁵² *Roman de Troie*, ll. 10725–79.

Ne s'aucuns est mis bienvoillanz,
Tant com vers mei iert depreianz,
Nel deit laidir ne damagier:
Ço qu'est de mei aint e ait chier.
Bien sai, s'il m'aime de neient,
Que mieuz en sera a ma gent:
A toz en deit porter manaie.'

['Tell your lord' she says, 'that I say he shows a poor sort of love for me. For if anyone seeks to please me by following my wishes, or is a friend of mine, he should, as he hopes to win my favour, neither mistreat nor harm Troilus; and thus he may gain my love and esteem. I am sure that if he loves me at all he will treat my friends better, for he should show tenderness to all of them'.][53]

She then concludes with her usual caution:

Ja nel harrai, se jo n'ai dreit,
N'ancor ne l'aim dont mieuz li seit.

[I should never be right to hate him, but neither shall I do him the favour of granting him my love.][54]

Diomedes, in turn, is unseated by Polydamas (who gives the horse to Troilus!); only when he appears to Briseis as a knight without his steed does she give back Troilus' horse, which had been given to her too *hastily* and rashly. And only then, in response to Diomedes' renewed entreaty and his humility, does Briseis give the first clear sign of acceptance, presenting Diomedes with her glove as a standard:

Des or puet saveir Troilus
Que mar s'atendra a li plus.

[From now on Troilus can know that she will no longer love him.][55]

The male characters act according to the role assigned to them by the code. When he learns of Briseis' betrayal Troilus looks for Diomedes alone on the battlefield, intent on wounding and offending him together with Briseis: Diomedes, in accepting Briseis, who has not maintained faith, accepts the role of *parçonier* of love and

[53] Ibid., ll. 14325-35. The motif is well known and from 'the courtly' William IX it will also reach Andreas Capellanus and the Italian lyric, including the Stil Nuovo.
[54] Ibid., ll. 14351-2.
[55] Ibid., ll. 15183-4.

partner of an immoral woman—a woman outside the law followed
by Lavinia, who deliberately rejected the triangle (as Fenice,
against Isolde, will reject the triangle in Chrétien's *Cligès*) and
'change':

Or sojornez o la moillier,
Avuec la fille al vieil Calcas,
Que ne vos het, ço dïent, pas.
Por soë amor vos manaidasse,
Se plus par tens m'en apensasse.
E ne por quant sa corte fei,
Sa tricherie e son beslei
E ço qu'ele a vers mei boisié
Vos a tot ço apareillié;
Sis pechiez vos a encombré
E ço qu'el m'a d'amor fausé,
Par vos li mant qu'or somes dui.
S'esté avez la ou jo fui,
Pro i avra des acoilliz,
Ainz que li sieges seit feniz;
Assez avreiz qu'escharguaitier.
S'ensi l'avez senz parçonier,
Ne s'est ancor pas arestee,
Dès que li mestiers li agree;
Quar, se tant est qu'un poi li plaise,
Li ostelain i avront aise.
Ço sera sens, s'el se porpense
Dont ele traie sa despense.

[Now go and stay with your woman, old Calchas' daughter—for she, they
say, by no means hates you. I would have spared you for love of her if I
had thought of it earlier. But, none the less, her lack of constancy, her
treachery and wrongdoing, and the way she has deceived me have
brought you to this pass. Her sins and her betrayal of my love have
alighted upon your head; now we are both here I shall send her this message through you. Although you have taken my place, there will be many
others who find a welcome there before the siege comes to an end—and
you will have to be quite vigilant. Although you as yet have no partner
[co-owner] in her favours she will not call a halt as long as the game
appeals to her. For, if she can manage to be pleased with so little, her
hosts will all benefit by it. And that will be the sensible thing to do if she
knows what is best for her.][56]

[56] *Roman de Troie*, ll. 20080–102.

As for Diomedes, having obtained the love of Briseis he no longer appears in the role of lover: he frequently appears as a valorous knight and, surprisingly, as a husband driven from Argos by his wife Egial, but not as the partner of 'Calcas' daughter'.

Briseis, too, disappears as soon as she decides to bestow her love on Diomedes, as, incidentally, happens with all the female characters in *fin'amors*. However, before making up her mind she must see Diomedes no longer as a knight, but simply as a man almost fatally wounded by Troilus, and thus humiliated once again:

> Mais n'en pot pas son cuer covrir
> Que plor e lermes e sospir
> N'issent de li a nes un fuer
> Semblant fait bien que de son cuer
> L'aime sor tote rien vivant:
> Nen aveit onc fait grant semblant,
> Jusqu'a cel jor, de lui amer,
> Mais lores ne s'en pot celer;
> Mout a grant duel e grant pesance.

[But she could not disguise the state of her heart sufficiently to prevent laments, tears, and sighs emerging from it nevertheless. She made it abundantly clear that she loved him from her heart, more than any other person alive. She had never until that day given much sign of loving him, but now she could not conceal it from him, and she suffered much grief and affliction.][57]

Thus, Briseis disappears from the story as soon as she gives up her role as a mysterious, contradictory character and dramatically takes on the role, in social and cultural terms, of negative *exemplum* ('De mei n'iert ja fait bon escrit | Ne chanteé bone chançon'— 'About me no beautiful work will be written | no good song will be sung'). However, before she disappears Benoît completes his portrayal of her as a 'true' character; in a remarkably fine monologue (which is almost Shakespearian in its dramatic and movingly human demonstration of her motives, and which, not by chance, is omitted by Shakespeare), Briseis presents an extraordinary picture of herself as a woman who, against social conventions and judgements (including those of other women), explores in almost secular manner the *reasons* behind her inner conflicts, her needs, the inevitability of her solitude, and the necessity of her 'change'.

[57] Ibid., ll. 20205–13.

Ultimately, she reclaims her status as *persona*, a result of her role as *exemplum* though more than this alone (the fact that she wishes Troilus well is part of this process: it is an important detail because it distances her first lover, implying that he was part of a simple, almost childish experience, as Troilus' conversation with his *mother* Hecuba will later confirm):[58]

And what good would it do me to repent? I shall never be able to make amends by that means. Let me then be true to this man who is a most valiant and worthy knight. I shall never be able to return to Troy nor leave him, for my heart is too firmly bound to him, and it was for his sake that I did what I did. Yet, it would not have been so if I were still within the city, for then my heart would never dream of faltering or changing. But here I have been without any true friends or advisers and hence lacking the kind of reassurance that might have eased my grief and affliction. I might have been plunged in melancholy lamentation and despair and remained so until I died without ever receiving comfort. I am sure I should have died a long time ago, had I not taken pity upon myself. Although I have acted rashly I have got the better of the problem—for,

---

[58] *Roman de Troie*, ll. 20664–82. The original text of the monologue is as follows: E que me vaut, se m'en repent? | En ço n'a mais recovrement. | Serai donc a cestui leiaus, | Qui mout est proz e bons vassaus. | Jo ne puis mais la revertir | Ne de cestui mei resortir: | Trop ai ja en lui mon cuer mis, | Por c'en ai fait ço que j'en fis. | E n'eüst pas ensi esté, | Se fusse ancore en la cité: | Ja jor mis cuers ne se pensast | Qu'il tressaillist ne qu'il chanjast. | Mais ci esteie senz conseil | E senz ami e senz feeil: | Si m'ot mestier tel atendance | Que m'ostast d'ire e de pensace. | Trop poüsse ore consirer | E plaindre e mei desconforter | E endurer jusqu'a la mort: | N'eüsse ja de la confort. | Morte fusse, piece a, ço crei, | Se n'eüsse merci de mei. | Senz ço que jo ai fait folor, | Des gieus partiz ai le meillor: | Tel hore avrai joie e leece | Que mis cuers fust en grant tristece; | Teus en porra en mal parler, | Qui me venist tart conforter. | Ne deit om mie por la gent | Estre en dolor e en torment. | Se toz li mondes est haitiez, | E mis cuers seit triz e iriez, | Iço ne m'est nule guaaigne, | Mais mout me dueut li cuers e saigne | De ço que jo sui en error; | Quar nule rien que a amor | La ou sis cuers seit point tiranz, | Trobles, dotos ne repentanz, | Ne puet estre sis gieus verais. | Sovent m'apai, sovent m'irais; | Sovent m'est bel e bien le vueil; | Sovent resont ploros mi ueil | Ensi est or, jo n'en sai plus. | Deus donge bien a Troïlus! | Quant nel puis aveir, ne il mei, | A cestui me doing e otrei. | Mout voudreie aveir cel talent | Que n'eüsse remembrement | Des uevres faites d'en ariere: | Ço me fait mal a grant maniere. | Ma consciënce me reprent, | Que a mon cuer fait grant torment. | Mais or m'estuet a ço torner | Tot mon corage e mon penser, | Vueille o ne vueille, dès or mais, | Com faitement Diomedès | Seit d'amor a mei atendanz, | Si qu'il en seit liez e joianz, | E jo de lui, puis qu'ensi est. | Or truis mon cuer hardi e prest | De faire ço que lui plaira: | Ja plus orgueil n'i trovera. | Par parole l'ai tant mené | Qu'or li ferai sa volenté | E son plaisir e son voleir. | Deus m'en doint joie e bien aveir! |

whereas my heart had been deep in grief, I can now be happy and content. Let those who failed to console me complain about this. One should never go on enduring pain and suffering simply through fear of what people will say. If the whole world is happy and my heart is full of grief and woe, that will be no help for me at all, for my heart will ache and bleed because of my distress. For, anyone who loves while his heart is at all restless, troubled, fearful, or regretful cannot be wholly involved in what he is doing. I often find myself at ease one moment and troubled the next. Often things seem indeed to go according to my wishes; and often, again, my eyes grow full of tears. Thus it is now, and I can do no more about it. May God grant Troilus happiness! Since I can no longer cherish him, nor he me, I shall yield and surrender myself to Diomedes. I should dearly love to be able to forget what has been done in the past, for the memory of it sorely afflicts my heart. But, whether I wish to or not, I must from now on devote all my energy and thought to making sure that Diomedes remains in love with me—so that he may have joy and pleasure from it and I from him, since that is how things must be. Now I feel my heart bold and eager to do what would give him pleasure, and he will meet no further resistance. I have led him on with promises so far that it is now time to grant his wish, his pleasure and his desire. God grant I may gain joy and happiness from it![59]

Despite doubts expressed in the past and recent attempts to prove the opposite, it seems that the *Roman de Troie* itself, and not one of the many prose versions that were derived from it, should be considered as the immediate antecedent of Guido delle Colonne's *Historia Destructionis Troiae*.[60] Guido's work, written in Latin, met with enormous success, greater even than that obtained by the *Roman de Troie*. In his critical edition of the work,[61] N. E. Griffin identified 136 surviving manuscripts, to which we can add the printed versions and translations into Italian as well as many other

[59] Ibid., ll. 20275–340.

[60] The southern prose version of the *Roman de Troie*, which was made known by K. Chesney's 'A neglected prose version of the Roman de Troie', *Medium Ævum*, 11 (1942), 46–67, is undoubtedly important for the circulation of the legend of Troy in Italy (see G. Carlesso, 'La versione sud del *Roman de Troie en prose* e il volgarizzamento di Binduccio dello Scelto', in *Atti dell'Istituto Veneto di Scienze, Lettere ed Arti*, 124 (1965–6), 519–60), but does not explain the fact that several details in Guido are common only to Benoît: the elements that are common only to Guido and the southern prose version of the *Roman de Troie* are very few, and can be explained in other ways.

[61] Guido delle Colonne, *Historia Destructionis Troiae*, ed. N. E. Griffin (Cambridge, Mass., 1936).

European languages.[62] Thus, the *Historia* can be seen as the cross-roads through which the *Roman de Troie* and the story of Troilus and Briseis passed into European literature (starting with Boccaccio).

Both Benoît and Guido, in different contexts, profess the truth of their own versions. However, Guido is undoubtedly more consistent than his Anglo-Norman predecessor: 150 years have indeed had an effect.[63] In general, Guido relates only that which is strictly essential:[64] his account is linear, and sticks to *facts* and events; explanatory description, bare and essential, is preferred to decorative description and digression. As a consequence the author drastically abandons the use of *amplificatio* ('eamdem rem dicere sed commutate'—'to say the same thing in a different way') and dialogues. For Guido, as we would expect from a true Sicilian, the crux of the story of Troilus and Briseis is the *betrayal*, the natural inclination of every woman to be inconstant. What interests him most in the triangular relationship between Troilus, Briseis, and Diomedes is the mechanism of *functions*, which are perceived as almost 'objective', scientific events; the explanation of these does not require any profound, extensive typological or psychological introspection. It is sufficient to narrate the sequence of events and the characters' *external* movements.

As far as the form of the work is concerned, the author makes more frequent, often emphatic, comments on the action; at the same time, he systematically and *coherently* cuts down, or eliminates, elements which are not consistent with the representation of a betrayal of a young hero by a woman who is depicted from the beginning as suspect. The fact that Briseis' eyebrows are joined, a detail which has strong negative implications, is given much

---

[62] On this subject see G. Carlesso, 'La fortuna della *Historia Destructionis Troiae* di Guido delle Colonne e un volgarizzamento finora ignoto', *Giornale storico della letteratura italiana*, 157 (1980), 230–51. The Neapolitan version has recently been published by N. De Blasi, *Libro de la destructione de Troya: Volgarizzamento napoletano trecentesco da Guido delle Colonne* (Rome, 1986).

[63] See C. Dionisotti, 'Proposta per Guido Giudice', *Rivista di cultura classica e medievale*, 7 (1965), 453–66, and esp. 457–60. Dionisotti's study is essential for the historical and cultural interpretation of Guido.

[64] For a precise and well-organized comparison between the *Roman de Troie* and Guido's *Historia*, see R. M. Lumiansky, 'The Story of Troilus and Briseida according to Benoît and Guido', *Speculum*, 29 (1954), 727–33, which I have particularly borne in mind.

greater emphasis than in Benoît, and is almost immediately followed by an accentuated description of her inconstancy, which is the final part of her portrait (unlike what happens in the *Roman de Troie*).

At the same time a significant detail is added to the description of Diomedes: 'libidinosus quidem multum' ('very libidinous'). Thus, the essence of the story as it will be presented has already been anticipated: the meeting of two characters of sensual nature, hindered neither by *time* nor by the 'refined' customs of the court: the *literary* debate, its subtle allusions, and its structural and stylistic correspondences are reduced in order to stress the elements of *fabula*. Thus Troilus, too, will be described at one point as a 'fatuus juvenis' ('fatuous youth'): he is, admittedly, unfortunate, but he is too prone to 'juvenilis credulitas' ('the gullibility of youth'). The meaning of Briseis, the problem of a woman who is inevitably characterized by conflict as a result of her complexity, is reduced to the straightforward representation of a threat which the bare narration of events and the interventions of the author must eliminate from the beginning. Thus, the speed of Briseis' change is emphasized, and the rhythm of Benoît's account is contracted by the 'objectivity' of the narrator:

Even before the day had reached the hours of evening Briseis had already changed her recent intentions and the desires of her heart ... Already her love for the noble Troilus was abating in her mind, and, having become fickle so quickly, so unexpectedly, and so immediately, she was beginning to change entirely. What, then, are we to say about the constancy of women ...[65]

The fragmentation of the character of Briseis necessitates a crudely ironic treatment of her grief when she is separated from Troilus, and the 'joyous' ('ylariter') acceptance of the gift of the horse (and Diomedes will also be immediately 'joyous', 'exhilaratus');[66] time and the female character are equally reduced until the remarkable monologue which marks the departure of Briseis from the *Roman de Troie* is completely eliminated.

Paradoxically, a society which was feudal but capable of exploring, in literature at least, the various cases and aspects of love

---

[65] Guido delle Colonne, *Historia*, p. 166.

[66] *Historia*, p. 169. Diomedes is immediately 'Ylaris' ('joyous') in Guido (p. 164), from his first meeting with Briseis.

handed down to the new mercantile society a story which was exemplary and potentially independent, but which was also too advanced to be fully appreciated: the principal character, a woman, had to be fragmented and deprived of her complexity in order to be understood by an audience who could easily identify with both of the male characters in the triangle, but not with an enigmatic figure who goes beyond her pre-established role.

3

A Lyrical Version: Boccaccio's *Filostrato*

GIULIA NATALI

Boccaccio's literary apprenticeship during the years of his youth in Naples was clearly influenced by Dante, as he himself acknowledged on more than one occasion. In the *Caccia di Diana*, now generally considered to be his first experiment in the vernacular, he adopts the metre of the *Divine Comedy*. The *Teseida*, as has often been pointed out, was intended to make up for the lack of an epic poem in Italian, deplored in the *De vulgari eloquentia*.[1] Boccaccio himself tells us this in the final stanzas of the poem where, in words that closely resemble Dante's, he proudly claims that his book is the first in this genre:

> tu ... primo ... cantare
> di Marte fai gli affanni sostenuti,
> nel volgar lazio più mai non veduti

[You are the first to sing of Mars' labours never seen before in our vulgar tongue].[2]

This is now common knowledge to Boccaccio scholars, but perhaps insufficient attention has been paid to the lines which immediately precede these and which also refer to opinions and problems discussed in the same treatise:

[1] 'Arma vero nullum latium adhuc invenio poetasse', *De vulgari eloquentia*, II. ii. 9. All quotations are from the P. V. Mengaldo edn., in Dante Alighieri, *Opere minori*, ii (Milan and Naples, 1979).

[2] *Teseida*, XII. lxxxiv. 6–8. All quotations are from the A. Limentani edn., in *Tutte le opere di Giovanni Boccaccio*, ii (Milan, 1964). The quotations from the *Filostrato*, ed. V. Branca with an interesting introd., are from the same vol. The English translations are from the R. P. apRoberts and A. Bruni Seldis edn. (New York and London, 1986) of the version of the text by V. Pernicone (Bari, 1937). The quotations from the *Filocolo* are from the E. Quaglio edn. in *Tutte le opere*, i (Milan, 1967). The quotations from *Elegia di madonna Fiammetta* are from the C. Segre edn., in Giovanni Boccaccio, *Opere* (Milan, 1963).

> Poi che le Muse nude cominciaro
> nel cospetto degli uomini ad andare,
> già fur di quelli i quai l'esercitaro
> con bello stilo in onesto parlare,
> e altri in amoroso l'operaro.

[Since the naked Muses appeared amidst mankind, many have cultivated them with beauteous style, in honest speech, and others in songs of love.][3]

Here, as Alberto Limentani has already pointed out, the poet is alluding to the other two 'most important things' which, in Dante's opinion, together with 'prowess in arms', deserve to be dealt with in the illustrious vernacular: these are the 'direction of the will' and the 'fire of love'.[4]

Now, it seems to me that, despite the misinterpretations and adaptations that Dante's ideas have undergone, Boccaccio is guided by them also in the overall design of the other two works he wrote in Naples. Indeed, the message of the *Filocolo*, although couched in a love intrigue, essentially concerns the 'direction of the will'; whereas the sole subject of the *Filostrato* is alleged to be the 'fire of love'.

The obvious, important innovation that the poem introduces is that it focuses exclusively on the love of Troilus and Briseis—renaming them Troiolo and Criseida—thus extrapolating it from the story of Troy. The episode had been woven into the account of the Trojan War in different ways first by Benoît de Sainte-Maure and later by Guido delle Colonne—the most likely sources for the *Filostrato*. Troilus and Briseis also appear in other writings deriving from the *Roman de Troie*, such as the shorter prose version known by the name of *Roman de Troie en prose* and a version in the vernacular based on this by Binduccio dello Scelto, the *Libro della Storia di Troia*, as well as in other texts in the vernacular and Latin, e.g. the *Istorietta Troiana* and the *Romanzo barberiniano*.[5] Thus, the structure of the *Filostrato* is altogether unusual in that it adopts a

---

[3] *Teseida*, xii. lxxxiv. 1–5.

[4] See *De vulgari eloquentia*, ii. ii. 7 and Limentani's Introd. to the *Teseida*, p. 231.

[5] For a systematic comparison of the similarities between these texts and the *Filostrato*, see M. Gozzi, 'Sulle fonti del *Filostrato*: Le narrazioni di argomento troiano', *Studi sul Boccaccio*, 5 (1968), 123–209. Gozzi makes it clear that he has considered 'i principali testi troiani indipendenti utili per confronti col *Filostrato*' (p. 128 n. 2).

narrative form traditionally employed to entertain the public with accounts of battles to relate a story of love.

This poem was definitely composed in Naples and is generally thought to have been written earlier than the *Filocolo*, though there are those today who date it authoritatively and, in my opinion, convincingly, after both the romance and the *Teseida*.[6] It is dedicated to Filomena, a character who later tells one of the tales in the *Decameron*, and a *senhal* deriving from the Greek word meaning 'the loved one'. This name refers to a woman whose real 'name is full of grace'[7] and therefore to a certain Giovanna and not the renowned, mythical Fiammetta-Maria d'Aquino. The title of the poem is one of the pseudonyms—also of Greek origin—for which Boccaccio showed a preference, which makes its first appearance here and is later found in the *Decameron*. Boccaccio adopts the guise of 'Filostrato' in the Proem, but he could equally well be Troiolo, who in the foreword to the work is presented as 'vanquished by love both by fervently loving Criseida and then again by her departure'. In fact, as a result of faulty etymology, 'Filostrato' is taken to mean a 'man vanquished and laid prostrate by love'.

Thus, the title itself implies that the events narrated are pseudo-autobiographical, as is made explicit a little further on in the text. The poet hints at his own misfortunes through the vicissitudes of Troiolo and Criseida, in so far as he attributes the Trojan prince's emotions to himself and lends his heroine the features of Filomena:

as many times as you find Troiolo weeping and grieving for the departure of Criseida, that many times you may clearly recognize and know my own cries, tears, sighs, and distresses; and as many times as you find the beauty, the good manners, or any other thing praiseworthy in a lady

[6] Branca and P. G. Ricci are in favour of dating the *Filostrato* around 1335, earlier than the *Filocolo*. See Branca, Introd., p. 5, and Ricci, 'Per la dedica e la datazione del *Filostrato*', *Studi sul Boccaccio*, 1 (1963), 333–47. C. Muscetta considers it later than both the romance and the *Teseida*, dating it at 1340. See Muscetta, *Giovanni Boccaccio*, in *Il Trecento* (Bari, 1972), 98 (vol. ii of *La letteratura Italiana: Storia e testi*). A. Balduino and L. Surdich use different arguments to suggest it was written in 1339, earlier than the *Filocolo* and at least a part of the *Teseida*. See Balduino, 'Reminiscenze petrarchesche nel *Filostrato* e sua datazione', in his *Boccaccio, Petrarca, e altri poeti del Trecento* (Florence, 1984), 243–7, and Surdich, 'Il *Filostrato*: Ipotesi per la datazione e per l'interpretazione', now in his *La cornice di Amore: Studi sul Boccaccio* (Pisa, 1987), 107.

[7] *Filostrato*, Proem, 16.

written of Criseida, that often you can understand them to be spoken of you.[8]

The same device is used in the *Teseida* and, though to a lesser extent, in the *Filocolo*: and in all three cases Boccaccio states that he has drawn on traditional sources for the subject-matter of his tales. For the *Filostrato* he carefully studied 'the old stories' and none seemed more suitable for expressing his secret suffering in love than that of the 'valorous young Troiolo, son of Priam, the most noble king of Troy'.[9]

The reader has now been warned: the story will focus solely on the love of the epic hero of that long war that brought about Troy's destruction. The epos will be transposed into a lyrical key, since Boccaccio has chosen Troiolo as the most suitable character to express the main purpose of the poem which is: 'in the person of someone emotionally overcome as I was and am, to relate my sufferings in song'.[10]

The first immediate consequence of this decision is that the previously existing relationship between the war component and the love component in the story is reversed. Little space is devoted to the conflict between the Greeks and the Trojans, and though it is true that the opening and closing scenes of the narrative directly refer to the war—Calchas' escape and Troiolo's death in battle—it is equally true that their function is merely to furnish a brief account of events before the poem opens and a rapid conclusion to a story whose main theme is quite different. The ten-year siege of Troy and the causes that brought it about are summarized in a single introductory stanza, entirely in the imperfect tense. This gives a first clear indication that the events are merely a backdrop and that they are repetitive:

> Erano a Troia li greci re d'intorno,
> nell'armi forti, e, giusto a lor potere,
> ciascuno ardito, fier, pro' e adorno
> si dimostrava, e colle loro schiere
> ognor la stringean più di giorno in giorno,
> concordi tutti in un pari volere,
> di vendicar l'oltraggio e la rapina,
> da Parìs fatta, d'Elena reina.

[8] *Filostrato*, Proem, 34.   [9] Ibid., 27–8.   [10] Ibid., 26.

[The Greek kings were round about Troy, strong in arms, and each one according to his power showed himself daring, proud, valiant, and meritorious, and with their troops they ever pressed the city more from day to day, all agreeing to a mutual desire, to avenge the outrage and the rape done by Paris to Queen Helen.][11]

This is clearly confirmed shortly afterwards:

> Le cose andavan sì come di guerra,
>   tra li Troiani e' Greci assai sovente.

[Things went on between the Trojans and the Greeks as they very often do in war.][12]

Only one battle is described in greater detail, and the use of the past historic tense underlines its significance, making it stand out as an exceptional event. This is the 'melée'[13] depicted in the three opening stanzas of Part IV, following which Criseida is restored to her father in exchange for Antenor. Here Boccaccio differs from his sources (I use the term only for convenience), in which Briseis was spontaneously conceded by Priam during the negotiations regarding Antenor and Thoas. His aim is also to confer greater dignity on the only battle episode destined to mark a turning point in the relationship between the two lovers.

The standpoint adopted towards the epic aspect of the story is seen very clearly in the figure of the hero. Following tradition, he is valorous—as we have already seen in the words used to introduce him in the Proem—but his heroism is destined to be employed in the service of love.[14] It increases or diminishes depending on how the amorous intrigue develops. His warrior attributes are stereotyped and conventional and the terms employed are influenced by the minstrel tradition: 'bodily strength' and 'prowess' in the words of the author; 'valiant and spirited', 'great and brave', in the words of Pandaro and Criseida respectively.[15] During his courtship these qualities are only used to win Criseida's heart. Troiolo, whose sole thought is love, works 'marvels in arms' not out of 'hatred of the Greeks . . . nor . . . to liberate Troy . . . but his desire for glory to be more pleasing caused all this; and through love, if the story speaks the truth, he became so fierce and strong in arms, that the Greeks

---

[11] *Filostrato*, I. vii.   [12] Ibid., I. xvi. 1-2.   [13] Ibid., IV. i. 8.
[14] See V. Pernicone, 'Il *Filostrato* di Giovanni Boccaccio', *Studi di Filologia Italiana*, 2 (1929), 77-128.
[15] *Filostrato*, I. xl. 3-4; II. xlii. 5; II. xlix. 1.

feared him as they did death'.[16] Here there are further stylistic devices typical of the *cantari*: the appeal to *auctoritas* (at precisely the moment of greatest infidelity!); the dittology in the clause of line 7; the final hemistich in line 8; and the common rhyme 'forte/ morte'.

These, however, are not the qualities destined to conquer Criseida's heart; and Troiolo's feats in battle, which therefore become his least concern,[17] are only referred to again after he has wholly possessed her. Before this there is only a brief reference to them which informs us that, whilst awaiting the desired event, Troiolo gave 'the night to thoughts of love and the day with his men to strenuous Mars'.[18] The young hero's courage reaches its peak when his passion has been satisfied, and through the direct intervention of Love who restores his former impetus. Boccaccio once again devotes only one stanza to this state of grace; he uses the imperfect tense which expresses habitual action and he is as anxious to regain credibility as he has proved to be earlier in the text:

> Nell'opere opportune alla lor guerra
> egli era sempre nell'armi il primiero;
> che sopra i Greci uscia fuor della terra,
> tanto animoso e sì forte e sì fiero,
> che ciascun ne dottava, se non erra
> la storia, e questo spirto tanto altiero
> più che l'usato gli prestava Amore,
> di cui egli era fedel servidore.

[In the undertakings involved in their war, he was always the first in arms, for he sallied forth from the city upon the Greeks so spirited and so strong and so fierce that everyone was afraid of him, if the story does not err. And love, of whom he was a faithful servant, lent him this spirit which was much greater than usual.][19]

A long silence falls on the feats of battle after the decision has been taken to return Criseida. Boccaccio is far more interested in showing us Troiolo's sorrow at being separated from his lover and, later, at the ever-increasing suspicion that she has forgotten and betrayed him. During this interval Boccaccio imagines a truce,

[16] *Filostrato*, i. xlv. 7; i. xlvi.
[17] Ibid., ii. iii, 4.
[18] Ibid., iii. xx. 7–8.
[19] Ibid., iii. xc.

agreed upon by the two enemy armies, that coincides with the ill-fated exchange. Towards the end of Part VII, Deiphobus, realizing what is causing his brother's anguish, reminds him of his past actions and that the term of the truce is completed.[20] This is emphasized by a rather exaggerated simile deriving from Virgil; this time Troiolo uses his renewed ardour to take his revenge on all the Greeks for the suffering they have caused him.[21] But this complete absorption of a public event such as war into the private sphere is inevitably doomed to failure:

> E 'n più battaglie poi con gli avversari
> fatte, mostrò quanto in arme valea,
> e' suoi sospiri e gli altri pianti amari
> che per loro operare avuti avea,
> oltre ogni stima li vendea lor cari,
> non però quanto l'ira sua volea;

[And in many battles then fought with his adversaries he showed how much he was worth in arms. And his sighs and the other bitter laments which he had through their actions he sold to them dearly, beyond any estimation, not, however, as much as his anger desired.][22]

In the last line there is a kind of premonition of the further negation of the character as an epic hero: the impossibility of his taking revenge on Diomede, his fortunate rival, for which he is later condemned. In Boccaccio's description, these courageous deeds on the battlefield come before the death of Hector, which is referred to in the first stanza of Part VIII. Therefore this killing, the only one mentioned in the whole mass slaughter of the sons of Priam, of which it becomes in a sense representative, has no connection with the unleashing of Troiolo's fury. His prowess in battle is described in all the texts on the Trojan War, but, apart from his encounters with Diomede, it is never directly or exclusively linked with the loss of his beloved.[23]

There are other interesting changes to be noted in the last part of

[20] *Filostrato*, VII. lxxviii. 8.

[21] See ibid., VII. lxxx; VII. lxxxi. 5-8; VII. lxxxii. 1-2.

[22] Ibid., VII. cvi. 1-6.

[23] Benoît states that Troilus avenges his brothers, while Guido adds to this motivation Troilus' desire to take his own revenge for the personal offence he has suffered. See Benoît de Sainte-Maure, *Roman de Troie*, ed. L. Constans (Paris, 1904-12), l. 20008, and Guido delle Colonne, *Historia Destructionis Troiae*, ed. N. E. Griffin (Cambridge, Mass., 1936), 194.

the *Filostrato*. Troiolo's suspicions of Diomede, which were aroused by a prophetic dream, are confirmed when he finds a brooch he gave Criseida at parting on a garment he has taken from Diomede in battle. The dream episode is Boccaccio's own invention, and in certain respects owes something to the *Vita Nuova*; it is also a topos of which Boccaccio appears to be rather fond.[24] No trace of the detail of the brooch is to be found in any other works. In the *Roman de Troie* Briseide gives Diomede her sleeve to carry into battle as her favour.[25] This motif, from the courtly-love tradition, is interpreted by Benoît and those who popularized him as the first sign of Briseide's weakening love and of her increasing inclination towards the Greek warrior. But the sleeve does not have any special significance for the protagonist, though he sees it worn by his opponent during one of their combats. In the *Istorietta Troiana*, however, things are different. Here the gift consists of a ring which had belonged to Troilus and we are told of this the moment the gift is made, which is immediately after Briseide's departure. This is also the moment in which, since the *Istorietta* is so succinct, she is said to succumb to her companion's advances. Troilus learns this from an eyewitness, a young boy he has sent to follow his lover and report back to him. Thus, even if here the object has the same sentimental value as in Boccaccio, it serves a completely different function. Boccaccio has Troiolo himself underline and complain at length of the insensitivity and untimeliness of the gesture.[26] Moreover, the fact that it comes both to the character's and to the reader's knowledge after the event—though not as a revelation but rather as a confirmation of the facts, and consequent self-awareness—makes the episode stand out and act as a catalyst of Troiolo's mortal hatred of Diomede:

> Mandimi Dio Diomedès davanti
> la prima volta ch'i' esco alla battaglia;
> questo disio tra li miei guai cotanti,
> sì ch'io provar gli faccia come taglia
> la spada mia, e lui morir con pianti
> nel campo faccia, e poi non me ne caglia

[24] See Branca, note on *Filostrato*, VII. xxiii. 4.

[25] In the *Historia* no mention is made of this.

[26] See *Filostrato* VIII. xiv. For an analysis of the episode as regards its possible source in the *Istorietta*, see Gozzi, 'Sulle Fonti', pp. 204–5.

che mi s'uccida, sol ch'io muoia, e lui
misero truovi nelli regni bui.

[May God send Diomede in front the first time that I go to battle; this I desire among my great woes so that I may make him test how my sword cuts and may make him die with lamentations in the field, and then it does not matter to me that someone may kill me, if only I may die and find him in misery in the dark kingdom.][27]

The fierce rivalry between the two, which exists right from the very beginning in the sources—perhaps a foreboding of their later rivalry in love—only emerges at this point in the *Filostrato*. Furthermore, there is no mention whatsoever of the two duels they had previously fought. In Benoît and in Guido a further three combats—the ritual number—take place over Briseide. The fact that love is the cause is especially underlined in the *Roman de Troie* where we learn that on the first occasion it is Diomede who takes the initiative in joining battle with Troilus.[28] Here the unseating, horse-stealing, wounding, and exchange of abuse is described in great detail, whereas in Boccaccio it is condensed into the last few lines. He does, however, find room to underline yet again that it is impossible for Troilus to achieve the purpose for which he threw himself into the fray:

nelle battaglie Troiol sempre entrava,
e più ch'altrui Diomedès cercava.

E spesse volte insieme s'avvisaro
con rimproveri cattivi e villani,
e di gran colpi fra lor si donaro,
talvolta urtando, e talor nelle mani
la spada avendo, vendendosi caro
insieme molto il loro amor non sani;
ma non avea la Fortuna disposto
che l'un dell'altro fornisse il proposto.

[Troiolo always entered into battle, and more than others he sought Diomede. And many times they came together face to face with vile and rude taunts, and great blows they gave each other, sometimes charging and sometimes heaving swords in hand, intemperately selling each other their love very dear. But Fortune had not disposed that the one should be dealt with as the other proposed.][29]

[27] *Filostrato*, VIII. xxi.
[28] See *Roman de Troie*, ll. 14286–7.
[29] *Filostrato*, VIII. xxv. 7–8; xxvi.

Fortune, who is evoked as a *deus ex machina* hurriedly to cut short the battle, is alleged to be responsible for the warrior's defeat (in which Diomede tangentially participates). The protagonist's fate is, on the one hand, the just penalty for his having given a purely personal interpretation to a conflict of such vast importance. On the other, this is the only ending Boccaccio could offer, this time without differing too much from tradition, because, as we have seen, he was not at all interested in creating an epic hero nor did he want to transform his character into a tragic one. The conclusion cannot really be called tragic, and the general toning down of the ending is underlined by Troiolo's death which follows immediately. It is true that he is slain after having performed incredible feats on the battlefield, but this occurs almost by chance. This is understood from the line which describes his death; its even rhythm does not stand out in the texture of the stanza,[30] and a single adverb ('miseramente') alludes to Achilles' traditional desecration of the body:

> miseramente un dì l'uccise Achille.

> [Achilles one day slew him wretchedly.][31]

This event is not even allowed the dignity of rounding off the tale, as it is immediately followed by a stanza containing the narrator's gnomic comment, which underlines that this end is above all the end of a love story:

> Cotal fine ebbe il mal concetto amore
> di Troiolo in Criseida, e cotale
> fine ebbe il miserabile dolore
> di lui al qual non fu mai altro eguale;
>
> .   .   .   .
>
> cotal fine ebbe la speranza vana
> di Troiolo in Criseida villana.

[Such an end had the ill-conceived love of Troiolo for Criseida, and such an end had his wretched sorrow, to which none other was ever equal. . . . such was the end of Troiolo's vain hope in the base Criseida.][32]

But the link so surreptitiously introduced is not sufficient to make the *Filostrato* a story of eros and death; Troiolo's is a story of

---

[30] See Branca, note on *Filostrato*, VIII. xxvii. 8. On how Troiolo's death has little of the heroic, see also G. Di Pino, 'Troiolo Criseida e la poesia dell'acqua furtiva', *Italianistica*, 8/3 (1978), 459–72; at p. 472.

[31] *Filostrato*, VIII. xxvii. 8.   [32] Ibid., VIII. xxviii. 1–4, 7–8.

love that incidentally ends in death only because it takes place within the broader canvas of the war; love is not the direct cause. The only function of this close, which is faithful to the letter though not to the spirit of the sources, is somehow to bring to an end Troiolo's 'laments and regrets'.[33] Boccaccio found a ready-made conclusion in his models; but the slaying of Troiolo may well be considered from the point of view expressed in Fiammetta's final words in the *Elegia*: 'since I could give you an accumulation of sorrow, but not of new words . . . I now choose silence'.[34]

Furthermore, the *Elegia di madonna Fiammetta* of all Boccaccio's works most closely resembles the *Filostrato* in structure. It, too, is a story of love that describes the happy moments and the pain of parting (over which hovers a suspicion of betrayal which in the end proves to be well founded). As in this work, so, too, in the *Filostrato*, the protagonist's mood is characterized as elegiac. However, in the *Elegia* the use of a purifying filter—the first person narrative—and its detachment from its antecedents (too unequivocally denounced as such) allow the ending to become one of 'feeble and plaintive uncertainty'[35]—between the wish for Panfilo's return and the coming of death—which is more suited to the elegiac atmosphere. The memory of what so disturbed the central role of love in the *Filostrato* is directly ignored in the first pages of the *Elegia*: 'you who read will not find . . . Trojan battles stained with much blood' (*Elegia di madonna Fiammetta*, Prologue). These battles have undergone striking changes, compared with how they were recounted and treated in the old stories: the relationship between eros and epos has been reversed[36] both quantitatively and qualitatively so that the former has taken over the space and importance which was previously given to the latter. And Boccaccio also reverses the traditional narrative structure. Indeed, whereas Benoît and Guido give a detailed account of even the earliest events leading up to the siege and destruction of Troy, in the *Filostrato* the brief introductory stanza quoted above (I. vii) is immediately followed by Calchas' desertion.[37] Thus, here the story of the war begins *in mediis rebus*. Till then only the story of Troilus and Briseide had

---

[33] *Filostrato*, VIII. xxv. 1.   [34] *Elegia*, VIII. xviii.

[35] See C. Delcorno, 'Note sui dantismi nell' *Elegia di madonna Fiammetta*', *Studi sul Boccaccio*, 11 (1979), 289.   [36] See Muscetta, *Boccaccio*, p. 97.

[37] Preceded in the *Roman de Troie* by around 6000 ll.; in the *Historia* by about 100 pp.

been treated in this way, being brought to the reader's knowledge as a *fait accompli*, only after the description of the Trojan decision to restore the girl to her father. In contrast, Boccaccio introduces us to the two characters before their fatal encounter actually takes place, and this is then described in great detail. He dwells at length on the protagonist falling in love and the pain he suffers until he is finally requited; he even permits us to enter the bedchamber. Generally speaking, the first three parts, except for the stanzas devoted to Calchas' escape and the Trojans' and Criseida's re-action, are the fruit of the author's imagination. This first striking innovation cannot be said to derive from the pseudo-autobiography traced in the Proem. Indeed, the relationship between Filomena and Filostrato, though in many respects similar to that between their counterparts in the poem, was purely platonic:

> non meno piacere io dagli occhi vostri traeva che Troiolo prendesse dell'amoroso frutto che di Criseida gli concedea la Fortuna.

[I drew from your eyes no less pleasure than Troiolo took from the amorous fruit which fortune granted him with Criseida.][38]

To confuse things even further, Boccaccio claims to have added what was not part of his love (or, in other words, what was lacking in previous versions) 'because the story of the noble young lover requires it'.[39] In point of fact, his real reason is rather to be found a little earlier in his apology to the woman for not having spoken only of Troiolo's suffering—which is what he most closely identifies with:

> la sua felice vita ... puosi ... perché la felicità veduta d'alcuno, molto meglio si comprende quanta e quale sia la miseria sopravvenuta.

[his happy life I set down ... because ... when someone's happiness is seen, the quantity and the quality of the misery which comes after may be much better understood.][40]

The space devoted to the elegy, which, according to medieval con-ventions, is destined to be given over to the suffering of the lovers,[41] is extended to include a contemplation of their previous happiness, and this aims at making the genre more rhetorically persuasive.

---

[38] *Filostrato*, Proem, 31.   [39] Ibid., 35.   [40] Ibid., 30.

[41] 'miserabile carmen quod continet et recitat dolores amantium', Jean de Garlande, *Poetria*, ed. G. Mari, *Romanische Forschungen*, 13 (1902), 885–960; at p. 926.

In the *Filostrato*, the author's premiss is also Troiolo's existential self-awareness, and the young Trojan warns his friend Pandaro, who tries to console him in vain for Criseida's approaching departure:

> ogni dolor trapassa quel che ria
> fortuna adduce a chi è stato felice

[what ill fortune brings to one who has been happy surpasses every sorrow].[42]

This is an adaptation of Francesca's famous maxim in the fifth Canto of the *Inferno*,[43] and this reference to Dante's authority at a central moment in the poem renders the words of the Proem axiomatic. Furthermore, they also act as a promise regarding the future development of the plot, which appears to be constructed on the basis of a kind of duplication of action and situation. Troiolo's story is designed in two juxtaposed, successive blocks which alternate hope and disappointment; the one resulting in happiness at the possession of the beloved and the other in despair at her loss.

Both originate from episodes in the Trojan War: Calchas' escape, and his oration to the Greeks begging to have his daughter restored to him. In recounting the old priest's treachery, Boccaccio omits to say that this was ordained by Apollo, thus branding Calchas as a coward. This, together with the accusation of avarice, further justifies the profound aversion Boccaccio feels towards him because he is the effective cause of the lovers' separation.

Later, Troiolo falls in love with Criseida and learns of her restoration when in the presence of the Trojan community, from whom, on both occasions, he wishes to hide his feelings. But whereas on the first, 'in order to hide his amorous wounds better, he mocked those who loved for a good while', on the second he falls in a swoon, 'pierced by profound grief'.[44] However, these different emotional reactions are followed by the same behaviour: he escapes to give vent to his feelings, 'all alone', 'without wishing for anyone's company', to his own 'locked and darkened room', when he needs to express his grief.[45] Boccaccio is here adopting a

[42] *Filostrato*, IV. lvi. 6–7.
[43] See *Inferno* v. 121–3. The comparison is Branca's, n. on *Filostrato* IV. lvi. 7.
[44] *Filostrato*, I. xxxii. 5–6; IV. xviii. 6–7.
[45] Ibid., I. xxxiii. 1; IV. xxii. 4; IV. xxvi. 2.

topos[46] from the *Vita Nuova* which Petrarch also employs and which had already become part of the courtly love tradition. This is also a point in which he differs from his sources: to the open spaces favoured in the latter Boccaccio prefers an enclosed space, which is more suited to Troiolo's soliloquies, his confidences to Pandaro, and the latter's advice (again, these elements are present in both the first and the second part of the story).

Indeed, ours is a hero of verbal effusiveness both in happy and in adverse situations. Apart from the occasions I have just mentioned this can also be seen from the two poems and two letters which he composes and which seem to mirror each other in the different sections of the work. It is the hero seen also as singer and writer that Boccaccio has created *ex novo*, and that most closely identifies him with the author: the letters remind us of the writer of the Proem and the lyrics of the composer of the whole work.[47] Troiolo's art as letter-writer and versifier reaches its highest expression after Criseida's departure. 'When he was tired of grieving, as if giving some respite to his sorrow, . . . he went about singing to himself in a low voice and refreshing his soul.'[48] Boccaccio's intention is the same: in singing his *Filostrato* he succeeds in offering to his 'hidden sorrow' 'an outlet from [his] sad breast',[49] as he promised himself when he set out to compose it. It is once more important to underline, in reference to this, the highly emblematic aspects of the writer's identification with his character. For both author and protagonist the lyrical tendency, already present in Dante, Cino, Petrarch, and the Provençal poets, to vent one's grief in song involves the process of rewriting existing material. In Boccaccio's case this is the story of the Trojan War, in Troiolo's it is the song 'La dolce vista e 'l ben guardo soave', repeated, as is known, in Part V, stanzas lxii–lxv of the *Filostrato*. The author of that canzone,

---

[46] See P. Boitani, 'Petrarch's *dilectoso male* and its European Context', in J. O. Fichte, K. H. Göller, and B. Schimmelpfennig (eds.), *Zusammenhänge, Einflüsse, Wirkungen* (Berlin and New York, 1986), 311. On the use of the topos and the importance given in the poem to closed spaces, see also Surdich, 'Il *Filostrato*: Ipotesi', p. 111.

[47] On Troiolo the poet, see S. Debenedetti, 'Troilo cantore', *Giornale Storico della Letteratura Italiana*, 66 (1915), 414–25; on Troiolo the letter-writer, see G. Chiecchi, 'Narrativa, "amor de lohn", epistolografia nelle opere minori del Boccaccio', *Studi sul Boccaccio*, 12 (1980), 176, 180, 186–8.

[48] *Filostrato*, v. lxi. 2–4, 6–7.

[49] Ibid., Proem, 25–6.

Cino da Pistoia, was mentioned in the passage from *De vulgari elo-quentia* to which I referred at the beginning, as the representative *par excellence* of love poetry written in the vernacular.[50] If we consider it in the light of Dante's pronouncement, this quotation therefore reinforces the fundamentally lyrical nature already attri-buted to the *Filostrato* in the Proem. The homage paid to the poet from Pistoia is, furthermore, perfectly in line with the importance the theme of separation takes on in this context. Within the area of Stil Novo poetry this motif may almost be said to be peculiar to Cino, who dwells at length on the nearly fatal result of not seeing the beloved (as indeed occurs in 'La dolce vista')—a theme that Petrarch, too, highlights in his *Canzoniere.*

In Troiolo's second appearance as a letter-writer he draws up an epistle requesting Criseida's return. In essentially reproposing the aims and central situation of the dedication to Filomena this is, in the part we may rhetorically describe as the *narratio*, a further variation on the theme of separation. In some cases there are precise echoes from the Proem,[51] which in turn presents certain similarities with canzone xxxvii in the *Canzoniere*, both in its language and in its description of the mood of the lover separated from his beloved. In this composition the elegiac tone is emphasized, as in the *Filostrato*, by the contrast between present sorrow and past happiness:

> et quanto era mia vita allor gioiosa
> m'insegni la presente aspra et noiosa!

[let my present life, hard and troublesome, teach me how joyful was then my living].[52]

And 'vita assai noiosa', 'a very distressful life', is Troiolo's immersed in contemplation of the 'mountains' which hide from

[50] See *De vulgari eloquentia*, II. ii. 8. The idea of having Troiolo speak lines com-posed by another poet might have come to Boccaccio from the *Roman du Chastelain de Couci* by Jakemes, where the song the protagonist composes is actu-ally by Gace Brulé. See Muscetta, *Boccaccio*, pp. 90–4. On Boccaccio's personal transposition of the story of the Trojan war, see Gozzi, 'Sulle fonti', p. 208.

[51] See *Filostrato*, VII. lx. 5–7 and Proem, 16; VII. lxii and Proem, 12; VII. lxiii–lxiv and Proem, 13; VII. lxvii and Proem, 13. On the similarity between the passages in the Proem and Troiolo's letter to Criseida, see Pernicone, 'Il *Filostrato*', p. 113.

[52] F. Petrarca, *Canzoniere* xxxvii. 47–8. All quotations are from the edn. by G. Contini (Turin, 1964). On the links between canzone xxxvii and the Proem of the *Filostrato*, and on the latter's lyrical connotation, see my 'Progetti narrativi e tradizione lirica in Boccaccio', *La Rassegna della letteratura Italiana*, 90/3 (1986), 385–90.

him 'the love-inspiring view of the beautiful eyes' and of 'the waves descending to the sea'.[53] This is a commonplace in popular poetry, and Petrarch too complains of geographical obstacles:

> Quante montagne et acque,
> quanto mar, quanti fiumi
> m'ascondon que' duo lumi.

[Those two lights hide for me so many mountains and waters, so many rivers, so much of the sea.][54]

By contrast, the model for another of Troiolo's complaints is the opening of a famous canzone in Dante's *Vita Nuova*, the product of a more cultured code:

> Li occhi dolenti per pietà del core
> hanno di lagrimar sofferta pena,
>
> .   .   .   .   .
>
> convenemi parlar traendo guai.

[My eyes that grieve because of my heart's anguish have been afflicted with weeping . . . I must lament in words.][55]

> Gli occhi dolenti, dopo il tuo partire,
> di lagrimar non ristetter giammai;
>
> .   .   .   .   .   .
>
> . . . ma sempre ho tratto guai.

[My sorrowing eyes after your departure never ceased weeping . . . but always I have uttered moans.][56]

The tears in Petrarch's 'eyes always desirous of weeping' never cease; he too is incessantly devoted 'but to lamentations'.[57] The

[53] *Filostrato*, VII. lxiv. 6; VII. lxiv. 1, 5–6; VII. lxv. 1.

[54] *Canzoniere*, xxxvii. 41–3. The fact that mountains are often an obstacle between lovers in popular poetry is pointed out by Branca, n. on *Filostrato*, VII. lxiv. 1. Also typical of popular poetry are two identical line endings: 'bel viso', *Filostrato*, VII. lxix. 7 and *Canzoniere*, xxxvii. 28; 'dolce mio bene', *Filostrato*, VII. lxxii. 8 and *Canzoniere*, xxxvii. 6, both rhyming with 'spene'.

[55] *Vita Nuova*, xxxi. 8. Quotations are from the edn. by D. De Robertis (Milan and Naples, 1980). The trans. is from K. Foster and P. Boyde (eds.), *Dante's Lyric Poetry*, i (Oxford, 1967), 83. Another possible echo from Dante may be found in the immediately preceding stanza: 'né so né posso più da lei atarmi', *Filostrato*, VII. lxix. 6, for which see 'sì ch'io non so da lei né posso atarme', 'Così nel mio parlar voglio esser aspro', 13. Quotation from the edn. by Contini (Turin, 1970). Trans. from Foster and Boyde, *Dante's Lyric Poetry*, No. 80, p. 170.

[56] *Filostrato*, VII. lx. 1–2, 4.

[57] *Canzoniere*, xxxvii. 83, 96.

topical and linguistic similarities with the more elevated poetic style of the years in which Boccaccio was composing the *Filostrato* are further evidence of its substantial debt to this higher genre.[58] The aim and inspiration of the Proem are lyrical—most of the character's story also derives from the development of an essentially lyrical situation. The frequent borrowing of images, stylemes, and whole lines from poetry, often put into the mouth of the hero, supports this view.

As this language, however, is mixed with the popular, comic, realistic idiom of the *cantari*, so the static, lyrical situation of separation is surrounded by a series of motifs that are very common in the culture of the period, and which transform it into narrative.[59]

The place appointed for Troiolo's falling in love (the description of which follows the typical phenomenology of eros) is a temple, and the object of his love a widow. It is known that these are two situations which appeal to Boccaccio's imagination. In the *Filocolo*, in imitation of an episode in the *Vita Nuova*, he uses the same setting for his encounter with Fiammetta. This interest in widows,

[58] Petrarch's *canzone* has been dated 1336–7. See E. H. Wilkins, *The Making of the Canzoniere and Other Petrarchan Studies* (Rome, 1951), 350. In Part vii of the poem there are further echoes of the same song. The most important seem to be the following: 'qual sottile ingegno, | qual piacer nuovo' (vii. xxix. 1–2), for which see 'Novo piacer che negli umani ingegni' (xxxvii. 65); 'la morte alla qual già corr'io' (vii. xxxiv. 6), for which see 'com'io corro alla morte' (xxxvii. 20). Earlier his separation from his beloved had been expressed as follows: 'quivi da lei feci dipartita' (v. lviii. 6), for which see 'l'empia dipartita | che dal dolce mio bene | feci' (xxxvii. 5–7). There seem to be further traces of the *Canzoniere* in the following: ''l mio riposo | dentro degli occhi suoi tutto portava' (v. liii. 5–6), for which see 'occhi ond' ogni mio riposo | vien' (lxxii. 35–6); 'dolce ragionare' (vii. lxxi. 3), for which see 'dolce ragionar' (lxxiii. 92); 'li tuoi atti adorni' (v. lix. 6), for which see 'gli atti per mio mal sì adorni' (lxii. 4); 'fiero disio' (vii. xxxiv. 4), for which see 'fero desio' (lxii. 3). *Canzoni* lxxii and lxxiii date from 1326–36, whereas sonnet lxii—the famous 'Padre del ciel'—dates from 1337–41 (see Wilkins, *The Making*, p. 350), the same period as sonnet cxii (to Sennuccio del Bene). The echo of this sonnet in *Filostrato*, v. liv–lv, pointed out by Wilkins (*The Making*, pp. 300–1), has been analysed in greater detail by Balduino ('Reminiscenze', pp. 231–49), who bases his thesis for a later dating of the *Filostrato* on this. What has been pointed out above appears to support this possibility, which seems even more likely since there is still another phrase that echoes sonnet cxii: 'vederti sdegnosa od altiera . . . grida fera' (i. lvi. 4, 6), for which see 'qui la vidi altera . . . or disdegnosa et fera' (cxii. v. 8).

[59] On the mixture of lyric and narrative and courtly and popular tradition, see D. Wallace, *Chaucer and the Early Writings of Boccaccio* (Woodbridge and Dover, New Hampshire, 1985), 91, 97.

which is so widespread in the literature of the period, is, as far as we are concerned, supported by the ninth question in Book Four of the *Filocolo* which the queen settles by claiming that the love of widows is to be preferred to that of maidens or wives. Many of the reasons for this put forward in the *Filocolo* are to be found as traits of Criseida's character in the *Filostrato*. Having already experienced the pleasures of love she is all the more desirous, and regrets the time she has use-lessly wasted without tasting them.[60] On more than one occasion she is seen to be aware of the advantages offered by 'furtive pleasures' which are attained by 'hidden ways' well known to her.[61]

The love of maidens is to be preferred only when the aim is mar-riage. This is an impossible solution in the *Filostrato*, given, among other things, Criseida's inferior social status, and, besides, she her-self is already quite reluctant to marry.[62] The anti-topos—all the precepts of the time prescribed falling in love only with women of a higher rank—initially acts as a brake and therefore Criseida is uncertain whether to consent to Pandaro's offers:

> questi ch'al presente t'ama
> è di troppo più alta condizione
> che tu non sei; questa amorosa brama
> gli passerà . . .

[he who now loves you is of much higher rank than you are; this amorous desire will pass from him . . .][63]

Later this will be one of the reasons that prevent a happy dénoue-ment. Troiolo considers various ways of averting the feared return of Criseida to her father, and one of these, in fact, is marriage:

> Pensato ancora avea di domandarla
> di grazia al padre mio che la mi desse,
>
> .   .   .   .   .   .
>
> né spero ancor ch'el dovesse darla,
>
> .   .   .   .   .   .
>
> perché la direbbe diseguale
> a me, al qual vuol dar donna reale.

---

[60] See *Filostrato*, ii. xxvii. 7 and *Filocolo*, iv. lii. 4; *Filostrato*, ii. lxx. 6 and *Filo-colo*, iv. lii. 8.   [61] *Filostrato*, iv. liv. 6–7.

[62] The preference for maidens when considering matrimony is discussed in *Filocolo*, iv. liv. 5. Criseida expresses her reluctance to marry in *Filostrato*, ii. lxxiii. On the obstacle that difference in rank represents, see apRoberts and Bruni Seldis, Introd. to *Filostrato*, pp. lxv–lxvi.   [63] *Filostrato*, ii. lxxvi. 1–4.

[I also thought of asking my father for her so that by his grace he might give her to me. . . . I do not hope even then that he would necessarily give her . . .because he would say she was not equal to me, to whom he wishes to give a lady of royal blood.][64]

I believe that all these factors constitute the reason for Boccaccio's departure from his sources, in which Briseide was a 'pucele', as well as a means by which he may be suggesting that he was in love with a widow at the time of composing the *Filostrato*.

Nor, on the other hand, do the succinct arguments in the *Filocolo* ever appear to be in contradiction with the betrayal of Troiolo. The heroine re-experiences widowhood in the Greek camp, as the lament before her departure foretells:

> Or vedova sarò io daddovero,
>
> .   .   .   .   .
>
> e 'l vestimento nero
> ver testimonio fia delle mie pene.

[Now I shall in truth be a widow . . . and the black attire will be a true testimony of my sufferings.][65]

The writer, in order to stigmatize her conduct in the final stanzas, that make the work an *exemplum* 'to young lovers',[66] never refers to her marital status. She is only the negative paradigm of 'fickle and desirous' youth,[67] to which he exorts the reader to prefer maturity, as it offers a greater guarantee of perfection. Though he does not respect the social dictates of the contemporary love ethic,[68] Boccaccio is quite subservient to another of its popular norms: that prescribing secrecy. Whereas the relationship between Troilus and Briseide was common knowledge, the characters in the *Filostrato* are determined to keep theirs a secret. Pandaro, who has broken the code, becomes, in his own words, the example of unhappiness in love.[69] This topical theme is reinterpreted so that its deeper meaning becomes evident: on the one hand, discretion serves to safeguard Criseida's reputation and honour; on the other—and this is even more important—by placing obstacles in

---

[64] *Filostrato*, iv. lxix. 1–2, 5, 7–8.   [65] Ibid., iv. xc. 1, 3–4.
[66] Ibid., viii. xxix, heading.   [67] Ibid., vii. xxx. 1.
[68] This position is restated in *Filostrato*, viii. 31, where young men in love are told, in no uncertain terms, to keep away from scornful and arrogant women 'd'alto lignaggio' (l. 1).
[69] See *Filostrato*, ii. xi. 1–4.

the path of love this secrecy makes the pleasures, attained so rarely, much more enjoyable. Criseida expresses this famous theory in the form of a popular saying:

> l'acqua furtiva assai più dolce cosa
> è che il vin con abbondanza avuto.

[Stolen water is a far sweeter thing than wine had in abundance.][70]

The two aspects of the topos of secrecy are also an insurmountable barrier to a happy ending. Indeed, it is impossible for Criseida to receive a regular proposal of marriage both because of her inferior rank and because of Priam's obligation to keep his word: this would be 'to accuse her and to make known the things already done'.[71] And the desire not 'to tarnish her honour and reputation with violent abduction'[72] had just dissuaded Troiolo from accepting Pandaro's suggestion that he follow Paris' example. However, Troiolo does propose this to Criseida during their final meeting, but receives a sharp refusal. After reminding him of the ill that results from 'broken faith'[73] she returns to the question of her own honour:

> la mia onestate
> e la mia castità, somme tenute,
> di quanta infamia sarien maculate,
> anzi del tutto disfatte e perdute.

[my honour and my chastity, of the highest, would be stained with infamy, would even be completely undone and lost to me].[74]

Finally, her argument reaches a climax when she warns him that their passion, if freely indulged, would soon die, since it flourishes 'because it is necessary for you to act furtively and seldom to come to this peace. . . . For if we wish our love to last, as we now do, it must always be stolen'.[75]

This night of love has a central place in the structure of the story, where it represents a counterpart to the first meeting of the two lovers. Boccaccio's technique of duplicating scenes, with which we are now familiar, is underlined by the opening and closing images. In both cases Criseida goes to meet Troiolo in the

---

[70] *Filostrato*, II. lxxiv. 1–2. On secrecy, see apRoberts and Bruni Seldis, Introd., pp. xxiv–xxviii, and Di Pino, 'Troiolo Criseida', p. 467.

[71] Ibid., IV. lxix. 3–4.   [72] Ibid., IV. lxviii. 1–2.   [73] Ibid., IV. cxlvii. 7.

[74] Ibid., IV. cli. 1–4.   [75] Ibid., IV. cliii. 2–3, 7–8.

dark with a 'lighted torch', and the cock crowing signals the coming of dawn and parting.[76] However, on these two occasions the lovers use their time very differently. The first is spent enjoying the pleasures of love-making; the second is devoted to lamentation and reasoning, while love has been pushed into the background. Their first meeting opens up a prospect of regular, though brief, moments of happiness, which is supported by the short description of their next encounter;[77] whereas their final meeting, as is only logical, remains symbolically without a follow up.

It is here, however, that the fate of the hero is sealed: being denied a happy ending he is also deprived of a tragic one. I believe this is the meaning of the scene where Criseida swoons, overcome by anguish. Boccaccio may have vaguely taken this idea from Guido.[78] In the *Historia* we read that Briseide swoons several times in the arms of her lover; but in the Latin text the fact that she falls in a faint only serves to indicate the intensity of her suffering and is not developed further. On the contrary, in the *Filostrato*, Troiolo having searched in vain for 'any sign of life'[79] believes her to be dead. After having lovingly composed her body and pronounced the traditional oath against Jove and Fortune, he decides to kill himself. But Criseida's untimely recovery prevents this dénouement, which would have been even more dramatic if she, too, had subsequently taken her own life.[80]

This episode is subtly parodied in the *Elegia di madonna Fiammetta*. During the heroine's final encounter with Panfilo she also swoons, but he departs forever without being sure whether she has fainted or is dead. Fiammetta and Troiolo are figures who are repeatedly offered and then promptly denied a tragic fate such as that of Ovid's Pyramus and Thisbe, raised to the dignity of drama by a misunderstanding similar to that which occurs in the *Filostrato*. On a subsequent occasion it is the protagonist who denies himself such an honourable destiny. His 'so bold and daring plan'[81] to use arms to prevent single-handedly the abhorred restitution is

[76] Ibid., IV. cxiv. 2; and see III. xxviii. I. See ibid., III. xlii. 1–2 and IV. clxvii. 5.

[77] See ibid., III. lxiv–lxxi.

[78] See K. Young, *The Origin and Development of the Story of Troilus and Criseyde* (London, 1908), 7–8; Pernicone, 'Il *Filostrato*', p. 95; Gozzi, 'Sulle fonti', pp. 203–4.

[79] *Filostrato*, IV. cxviii. 5.

[80] See ibid., IV. cxxvi. 2–4.

[81] Ibid., V. v. 6.

seen to be nothing more than a foolish impulse, which is immediately restrained by the fear that 'Criseida might be killed in such
an attempt'.[82] Neither does he lack an awareness of the status to
which he is condemned, this time by his own inaction, as well as by
the author throughout the story:

> non è el meglio una volta morire,
> che sempre in pianto vivere e languire?

[Is it not better to die at once than to live and languish ever in tears?][83]

He is also frustrated in his subsequent attempt to take his own
life, after a dream that reveals the existence of a fortunate rival in
Diomede, under the guise of a boar intent on eating Criseida's
heart. Pandaro, the only one who knows of the relationship
between his friend and his cousin, intervenes, causing Troiolo to
return to the dimension that better suits him—'a languishing life is
worse than death'.[84] To determine the outcome of this crisis Boccaccio uses one of the conventions out of which he constructs the
tale. Pandaro successfully prevents Troiolo from acting because he
is 'weak'[85] and this weakness is only the consequence of the malady
of love to which he has fallen prey. The 'aegritudo amoris'[86] (the illness and the anguish of love) described in Part VII, stanzas 18–20,
which results yet again in the avoidance of tragedy, duplicates an
earlier, analogous state of prostration: the hero suffers from the
same conventional symptoms[87] at the first sight of Criseida and
these are overcome thanks to Pandaro's good offices.

This motif (also codified by Andreas Capellanus, whose influence is clear throughout the *Filostrato*)[88] is found in the sources,
too, where it is, however, attributed to Diomede. Benoît especially
describes the sufferings of the Greek warrior under the assault of
Love, and his wooing which, without the aid of any go-between, is
finally successful. Briseide's conduct follows a more tortuous path:
initially hostile, she then passes to skirmishing with her lover,
cleverly keeping him at bay, until in the course of a long monologue she finally succumbs. Criseida's behaviour towards Troiolo

---

[82] *Filostrato*, v. v. 7–8.   [83] Ibid., v. iii. 7–8.
[84] Ibid., vii. xxxv. 6–7.   [85] Ibid., vii. xxxvi. 3.
[86] On Troiolo's malady of love as a topical motif, see Surdich, 'Il *Filostrato*:
Ipotesi', p. 110.
[87] See *Filostrato*, i. xlvii.
[88] See Branca, Introd., p. 8.

is equally wary. After the preliminary protestations of her honour to Pandaro, which almost parody those of Virgil's Dido, she decides to accept only a Stil Novo exchange of glances. Subsequently her decision to concede to love-making is dissembled and delayed by the elusive exchange of letters. And both decisions are preceded by decisive soliloquies. Though it is true that the love of Troiolo and Criseida as depicted in the first three parts of the poem may be said to be Boccaccio's invention, it is equally undeniable that he follows, in general terms, the account of Briseide's betrayal given in the *Roman de Troie.*

The corresponding act of treachery of her counterpart in Boccaccio undergoes a drastic *abreviatio.* It is anticipated by occasional authorial interventions (which are not however revealing, as the reader already knows the story summed up in the Proem), and it is then confined to only two stanzas.[89] They follow the conversation with Diomede, which reproduces in a different temporal collocation the same sequence as the sources. In these Diomede makes his first proposals on the way to the Greek camp, whereas Boccaccio places this first (and in his poem the only) approach after telling us that the heroine has spent four days in the enemy camp and describing how deeply she misses her city and her lover.

Her initial behaviour is the same, though to a lesser degree, as Troiolo's: they both weep, recall and gaze towards the place where their lost beloved is, and regret not having given in to the impulse to flee. Thus, in contrast, Criseida's later inconstancy and use of artful ambiguity in response to Diomede's proposals stand out even more. Though she appears here very similar to the traditional model, the difference lies in the fact that she denies she loves someone else (though Diomede has noticed this from Troiolo's reaction at her departure). This denial, in line with the convention of secrecy, also indicates, in my opinion, a first refusal of the past by Criseida and lends greater credibility to the image of Diomede departing full of hope in future 'mercy'.[90] This sudden change in the heroine's feelings after the conversation is already to be found in the *Historia.* But whereas Guido, though more briefly than Benoît, presents her to us in the act of keeping her suitor on tenterhooks, Boccaccio lowers the curtain on her as, at the end of the

[89] See *Filostrato*, VI. xxxiii–xxxiv.
[90] Ibid., VI. xxxii. 3.

scene, she passes from a 'severe torment' to a 'new hope'.[91] Because of the limited space and importance given to the account of Criseida's treachery, the *Filostrato* is not a story of betrayal like the corresponding episode in the *Roman de Troie*. This theme is under-played, as is the theme of death, in order to emphasize the new, salient features of the love plot.

The real meaning of the tale and the protagonist's true fate are contained in the night which marks the impossibility of a happy ending and at the same time the first failure in achieving a tragic dé-nouement.[92] The key lies in Criseida's promise to return within ten days, not present in earlier sources. Thus begins the deserted lover's vain and elegiac wait which, when the term expires, gradually becomes despair—though this despair is, so to speak, static. The final, fleeting appearance of the unfaithful Criseida is merely to remind us that 'she loved Diomede with all her heart, and Troilo wept. Diomede praised God, and Troiolo, on the contrary, grieved.'[93] These lines might well have put the final seal on the story, were it not for Troiolo's death, which, as we have already seen, is largely incidental. The two principal characters are destined to end their lives in radically different ways. Their fate is the same only in the paradigmatic dimension which, following contemporary narra-tive convention, shapes the story. Here the one becomes the exem-plary instance of unwariness in love; the other of the fickleness of youth. Troiolo is already aware of female inconstancy when he first appears; already experienced and disillusioned, he mocks lovers, and the author later echoes his words of popular wisdom:

> come al vento si volge la foglia,
> così in un dì ben mille volte il core
> di lor si volge, . . .
>
> né sa alcuna quel ch'ella si voglia;

[The way a leaf turns itself with the wind, so a thousand times a day their hearts change . . . nor does any woman know what she wants.]

[91] *Filostrato*, VI. xxxiv. 5–6. On the fact that Troiolo and Criseida both suffer from the same nostalgia initially, see Di Pino, 'Troiolo Criseida', p. 468; on the very little importance given to Criseida's betrayal, see Muscetta, *Boccaccio*, p. 91, and M. Marti, 'Conformismo retorico e reazioni realistiche nella responsabilità culturale del Boccaccio tra Napoli e Firenze', now in his *Dante Boccaccio Leopardi* (Naples, 1980), 152–4.

[92] *Filostrato*, IV. cxxv–clxvii.   [93] Ibid., VIII. xxv. 3–6.

Giovane donna, e mobile e vogliosa
è negli amanti molti . . .

. . . . . .

volubil sempre come foglia al vento.

[A young woman is both fickle and desirous of many lovers . . . unsteady always as a leaf in the wind.][94]

In contrast to the Proem, where Boccaccio identifies with his protagonist, here, at the end of the poem, he deliberately takes up the hero's words in order to underline his detachment from Troiolo, who, thus doubly stigmatized, is finally placed on a par with Criseida as a negative *exemplum.*

[94] Ibid., i. xxii. 2–4, 6, viii. xxx. 1–2, 8.

4

The Fall of Troy in *Sir Gawain and the Green Knight* and *Troilus and Criseyde*

MALCOLM ANDREW

Sir Gawain and the Green Knight begins with an allusion to the fall and destruction of Troy:

> Siþen þe sege and þe assaut watz sesed at Troye,
> þe borȝ brittened and brent to brondez and askez.[1]

The first line is echoed in the last long line of the final stanza, 'After þe segge and þe asaute watz sesed at Troye'.[2] What might, therefore, be described as the 'Troy frame' of *Sir Gawain and the Green Knight* has generally been regarded by commentators as having little significance beyond that of establishing a historical (or pseudo-historical) sequence and of evoking some traditional associations. The sequence is the dynastic progression which leads from the foundation of Britain to the reign of King Arthur. The associations are those of majesty, high seriousness, and the fate of nations. None of this has seemed of any great relevance to the story of Sir Gawain and the Green Knight. Thus, the frame receives scant attention from such distinguished interpreters of the poem as Larry D. Benson, J. A. Burrow, and A. C. Spearing: indeed, Burrow maintains that the Troy frame 'introduces an adventure which has no significance at all for the history of the kings of Britain'.[3] The ordering of this statement is conspicuous. It might seem more appropriate to consider the possible significance of 'the history of the kings of Britain' for the 'adventure' of Sir Gawain than vice versa.

The views of these prominent critics reflect, I think, the influence of another aspect of tradition. It has regularly been observed

[1] Quotations from *Sir Gawain and the Green Knight* and *Cleanness* are taken from *The Poems of the Pearl Manuscript*, ed. Malcolm Andrew and Ronald Waldron (London, 1978).   [2] *Sir Gawain*, l. 2525.
[3] *Ricardian Poetry: Chaucer, Gower, Langland, and the 'Gawain' Poet* (London, 1971), 96.

that allusions to Troy and the founding of Britain, broadly similar
to those in *Sir Gawain and the Green Knight*, occur in several other
alliterative poems, among them *Winner and Waster*, *St Erkenwald*,
and the alliterative *Morte Arthure*.[4] The allusions in these poems
have been deemed, by general consensus, to be of limited significance and essentially conventional in character. Thus, Dorothy
Everett praises several qualities which she discerns in the handling
of material in *Winner and Waster*, including that of relevance—
'apart from a pointless opening reference to Brutus the Trojan and
his founding of the kingdom of Britain'.[5] My intention is not to
dispute the justice of such opinions, but to suggest how easy it is to
leap by analogy from them to the conviction that the Troy frame of
Sir Gawain and the Green Knight is of similarly limited significance.
That is a view which I should wish to question. At the least, we
may observe that it is not based on the comparison of exact like
with like. The allusion in *St Erkenwald* is integral—though not
essential—to a narrative; that in the alliterative *Morte* contributes
to the process of historical placing and distancing at the end of the
poem; that in *Winner and Waster* functions as an introductory
device. Of these, the Troy frame of *Sir Gawain and the Green Knight*
has most in common with the passage from *Winner and Waster*:

> Sythen that Bretayne was biggede, and Bruyttus it aughte,
> Thurgh the takynge of Troye with tresone with-inn,
> There hathe selcouthes bene sene in seere kynges tymes,
> Bot neuer so many as nowe by the nynde dele.[6]

The parallels, both thematic and verbal, with the opening of *Sir
Gawain and the Green Knight* are plain enough. It is, however, not
possible to tell whether the author intended to reiterate this motif
at the end of *Winner and Waster*, given the incomplete state of the
manuscript in which the poem is uniquely preserved. In contrast,
the reiteration of the opening allusion to Troy at the end of *Sir
Gawain and the Green Knight*—with the resulting creation of a Troy
frame—is hardly a matter of debate.

---

[4] See e.g. Derek Pearsall, *Old English and Middle English Poetry* (Routledge History of English Poetry, i, London, Henley, and Boston, 1977), 158. The passages
in question are: *Winner and Waster*, 1–4; *St Erkenwald*, 207; *Morte Arthure*, 4342–6.

[5] *Essays on Middle English Literature*, ed. Patricia Kean (Oxford, 1955), 50.

[6] Quoted from *A Good Short Debate between Winner and Waster*, ed. Sir Israel
Gollancz (Select Early English Poems in Alliterative Verse, iii, London, 1930).

The potential contribution of this frame to the meaning of the poem is, of course, precisely such a matter. I suggest that the subtle but emphatic patterning which has been discerned elsewhere in the poem should encourage us to hesitate before concluding that the frame is merely conventional. Furthermore, if—with the great majority of scholars—we accept that the poet was also the author of *Pearl*, *Cleanness*, and *Patience*, then we may perceive the subtle shaping of narrative and the emphatic use of framing as characteristic qualities of his work. It should, therefore, seem not unreasonable to claim that the Troy frame of *Sir Gawain and the Green Knight* merits close and thoughtful attention.

This is not to imply that it has been neglected. Scholarly efforts have, however, been mainly devoted to discussion of the opening lines of *Sir Gawain and the Green Knight* in relation to the traditions which they manifestly reflect. The appearance of the first edition of the poem, that of Sir Frederic Madden, in 1839, initiates a process of explication, which is carried forward through the notes and interpretations of successive editors, commentators, and translators over the years. By the middle of the present century, a clear pattern of explication has emerged. The editors and commentators inform us that the link between the Trojans and the founding of Britain may be traced back to the early Welsh historian Nennius, and that the crucial influence in the dissemination of this idea is Geoffrey of Monmouth's twelfth-century *Historia Regum Britanniae*. While this is generally unproblematic, difficulties do arise with reference to several details—especially those to which allusion is made in lines 3–5:

> þe tulk þat þe trammes of tresoun þer wroȝt
> Watz tried for his tricherie, þe trewest on erthe.
> Hit watz Ennias þe athel and his highe kynde.

Though it is explained as early as Madden that, in the medieval version of the Troy story, Aeneas is implicated in Antenor's betrayal of the Trojans to the Greeks, the allusion continues to cause disquiet. The problem is, essentially, that of reconciling the figure described here so paradoxically as both a traitor and 'þe trewest on erthe' with Virgil's 'pius Aeneas'. Doubtless, it is this sense of difficulty which leads Sir Israel Gollancz to argue, in the notes to his edition of *Sir Gawain and the Green Knight* for the Early English Text Society, published in 1940, that the allusion is not to Aeneas but to Antenor. This case gains a considerable degree of support, and represents the majority view for perhaps a quarter of a century. By the 1960s it is, however, losing ground. The decisive contributions to this process are those of Norman Davis in the notes to his revised version of Tolkien and Gordon's edition (1967) and of Alfred David in a cogent and persuasive article on the opening of the poem (1968).[7] A few years later, J. D. Burnley points out that the syntax of a passage from *Cleanness* lends further support to the argument that 'hit watz' (line 5) refers back rather than forward—and that 'þe tulk' (line 3) is thus to be identified as Aeneas.[8]

Though I share the view that these lines refer to Aeneas, I do not believe that their problematic or paradoxical quality is something we should set out to resolve. Indeed, I take this to be a deliberate effect of the passage, and one fundamental to its meaning. The basis of my position may best be articulated by considering the first three stanzas of *Sir Gawain and the Green Knight* as a context for the story that follows. In order to create some sense of how this context may work, I shall start by looking at the third stanza, and then go back to the two preceding stanzas, to see how they may influence and qualify our reading.

The third stanza is, in fact, a natural starting point, since it functions to introduce the Arthurian society of Camelot.[9] It constitutes an essentially celebrative account. King Arthur's knights are described as 'mony luflych lorde, ledez of þe best'.[10] The poet tells us of revelry, mirth, jousting, singing, feasting, and dancing, and observes that 'al watz hap vpon heȝe'.[11] He proceeds, in a series of superlatives, to acknowledge the most famous knights, the loveliest ladies, and the fairest king, before summarizing in the statement, 'for al watz þis fayre folk in her first age'.[12] The wheel[13] provides further summary, and reinforces the impression of unqualified celebration.

---

[7] *Sir Gawain and the Green Knight*, ed. J. R. R. Tolkien and E. V. Gordon, 2nd edn. rev. Norman Davis (Oxford, 1967); Alfred David, 'Gawain and Aeneas', *English Studies*, 49 (1968), 402–9.

[8] '*Sir Gawain and the Green Knight*, lines 3–7', *Notes and Queries*, 218 (1973), 83–4. Cf. *Cleanness*, 977–84.

[9] This idea is discussed by Theodore Silverstein in a fine article: '*Sir Gawain*, Dear Brutus, and Britain's Fortunate Founding: A Study in Comedy and Convention', *Modern Philology*, 62 (1965), 189–206.

[10] *Sir Gawain*, l. 38.

[11] Ibid., ll. 40–7, 48.

[12] Ibid., ll. 51–3, 54.

[13] Ibid., ll. 56–9.

But this account, though a beginning, is not *the* beginning: it
follows an opening sequence of some thirty-six lines, arranged in
two stanzas. *Sir Gawain and the Green Knight* opens with a gradual
progression from the distant past to the Arthurian present. We
have already observed that Britain is introduced here in relation to
Troy. It is also introduced as a setting for the story which will
follow—and a setting with various and varied connotations: on the
one hand, glory, might, and dynastic pride; on the other, destruction, treachery, and treason. The wheel of the first stanza encap-
sulates this ambivalence in the splendidly resonant phrase 'blysse
and blunder'.[14] This phrase might, indeed, seem an effective motto
for the preceding survey, which has alluded, first, to the destruction of a great civilization through treachery, and then to the successful re-establishment of civilization in Rome, Tuscany,
Lombardy, and Britain.

The first stanza thus establishes a contrastive pattern, which
envisages civilization as alternating between 'bliss' and 'blunder'.
We may well discern a correspondence between this pattern and
the intriguingly (or, as some would have it, awkwardly) ambiguous
figure which we discussed earlier: that of the noble man who is also
a traitor. The second stanza brings a narrowing of focus, and a concentration on the founding of Britain—by another noble man. In
the following lines,[15] the quality of this newly-established civilization is exemplified by the conduct of bold men who love strife and
often cause harm. Though I should regard too negative a reading of
these lines as inappropriate, they may perhaps reflect an awareness
of the difficulty of reconciling the martial ideals of chivalric hardi-
hood with the peace and tranquillity which is beneficial to a settled
society. An interesting parallel occurs in *Cleanness*. There, the poet
describes the broadly similar conduct of the Giants of Genesis with
unqualified disapproval:

> þose wern men meþelez and maȝty on vrþe,
> þat for her lodlych laykez alosed þay were;
> He watz famed for fre þat feȝt loued best,
> And ay þe bigest in bale þe best watz halden.[16]

The values appropriate to a romance are, of course, distinct from
those appropriate to a religious poem, and it would be simplistic to
take the passage from *Cleanness* as a critical gloss on that from *Sir*

[14] Ibid., l. 18.   [15] Ibid., ll. 21–2.   [16] *Cleanness*, ll. 273–6.

Gawain and the Green Knight. None the less, the parallel may, I think, legitimately lend support to our sense that the praise of this brave new warrior-society is not entirely unqualified. This view may also derive support from the next few lines, which lead up to the introduction of King Arthur. The sequence is striking: from the love of strife and the causing of harm, to recognition of an un-equalled incidence of 'ferlyes', to Arthur as 'þe hendest' of 'Bretaygne kynges'—and so on to the preamble of the story itself.[17] Without labouring the point, I should wish to suggest that the logic of a progression from the enjoyment of causing harm to the noblest of British kings is apt to be at least potentially problematic.

It should, I hope, be apparent that the effect of the third stanza when read in isolation differs significantly from its effect when read in the context of the first two stanzas. While it might, in isola-tion, seem a blandly uncritical celebration of the way of life and the reputation of Arthur's court, the context of the first two stanzas functions to qualify radically this potential view. It may be helpful to specify two of the main ways in which this process of qualifica-tion works. First, if the tenor of the third stanza is 'bliss', then the logic of the opening would lead us to see this as potentially threat-ened by 'blunder'. From such a perspective, the assurance that 'al watz hap vpon heȝe'[18] will hardly inspire confidence. Second—and not unrelated—the opening image of a great civilization destroyed may imply by analogy the threat of such an end to the civilization which has, in some sense, replaced it—and is presently enjoying its own 'first age'.[19] Given the essential nature and shape of the story of Arthur, this might be interpreted specifically as an allusion to Camelot before the ideal of the Round Table was undermined by dissent. If so, it could serve to suggest the way in which the Arthur-ian story as a whole confirms to the pattern of 'bliss and blunder'.

In addition to these particular uses of context to create an effect of qualification, there is a subtle but recurring sense that the terms in which the Round Table is celebrated are not entirely or un-equivocally appropriate. The third stanza ends with an affirmation in martial terms: it would be extremely difficult to name a 'here' so 'hardy'.[20] But the foregoing account has scarcely suggested this, and has certainly not demonstrated it. The emphasis throughout the third stanza has been on revelry and celebration: indeed, the

---

[17] *Sir Gawain*, ll. 21–6.
[18] Ibid., l. 48.   [19] Ibid., l. 54.   [20] Ibid., ll. 58–9.

only allusion relevant in any way to heroic conduct is that to jousting, and even this—as a result both of its immediate context and of
the implications of phrasing (the 'gentyle kniȝtes' jousting 'ful
jolilé'[21])—sounds more like social recreation than the serious practice of martial skills.

The statements made in the third stanza are also subject to a
sustained process of retrospective qualification. Since the presence and the effect of retrospective qualification in *Sir Gawain
and the Green Knight* has been thoroughly discussed by some of
the best writers on the poem, this is a topic which may be dealt
with briefly here. It is plain enough that the third stanza makes
or implies a series of claims and value-judgements, which, in a
sequential narrative, must invite testing against subsequent events
and judgements. Thus, to take an obvious example, the claim that
the members of the Round Table are 'þe most kyd knyȝtez vnder
Krystes seluen' is directly challenged by the Green Knight some
200 lines later.[22] Although his final judgement will be that
Gawain, as the representative of Arthur's house has, in effect,
substantiated this assertion, Gawain's own evaluation is quite different; and, while modern readers usually take a view somewhat
closer to that of the Green Knight than to that of Gawain, few
would deny that the initial claim has been subjected to a searching scrutiny, which has, inevitably, resulted in some significant
qualification. Several minor instances of retrospective qualification could be mentioned, but I shall limit myself to a single
example. The statement that the 'fayre folk' of Arthur's court are
'in her first age'[23] seems at first—whatever the modifying effects
of context, as discussed above—to be predominantly one of
enthusiasm for youth, freshness, vigour, and self-confidence.
When, however, at the beginning of the fifth stanza, Arthur is
described as 'sumquat childgered',[24] we are likely (and, I think,
intended) to feel a substantial degree of uncertainty with regard
to the tone and implications of these words. About 200 lines
later, the Green Knight provides a singularly discomforting and
uncomplimentary gloss on them, and on the youthfulness of the
court, by asserting that 'hit arn aboute on þis bench bot berdlez
chylder'[25]—none of whom would be a match for him. There is a
sense in which such a judgement is already latent within the two

---

[21] Ibid., l. 42.   [22] Ibid., ll. 51, 258 ff.   [23] Ibid., l. 54.
[24] Ibid., l. 86.   [25] Ibid., l. 280.

earlier statements: all that is required to bring it out is a shift of perspective, of intention, or of implicit values.

I regard this process of retrospective qualification as closely
related to the motif of 'bliss and blunder'. Since, as we have
observed, the ordering of the first stanza of *Sir Gawain and the
Green Knight* serves to emphasize the association of this motif with
the essential pattern of the story of Troy, we may be justified in
anticipating that the Troy frame will prove a rich but ambivalent
context for the following story of Gawain. We may also anticipate
that the opening image of the poem, that of the city ruined and
burnt, will prove evocative. A parallel—striking though not exact—
occurs in *Beowulf.* There, in a procedure partially analogous to that
in *Sir Gawain and the Green Knight*, the poet approaches his main
setting through the dynastic history of the Danes, before describing the martial success of King Hrothgar. This success results in the
establishment of a society, and is symbolized by the building of a
great hall, Heorot.[26] The most striking aspect of the account is,
however, that within a few lines of celebrating the construction of
Heorot the poet predicts its destruction—by fire, as a consequence
of internecine strife.[27] While the significance of this passage and of
the image of the burning hall for a reading of *Beowulf* is a complex
matter which cannot detain us here, I should wish to stress one
aspect of the poet's narrative strategy. He predicts the destruction
of the hall—and thus, symbolically, the civilization—at the centre
of the first part of his poem, before describing the heroic endeavours of Beowulf in defence of this very hall and civilization.
Such a procedure, while not devaluing the hero's efforts, must
place them in an ironic perspective. The irony is, of course, made
possible by the retrospective viewpoint.

It seems to me that a broadly comparable effect is created by the
Troy frame in *Sir Gawain and the Green Knight.* From a retrospective viewpoint, the audience or reader—whether in the fourteenth
or the twentieth century—knows full well that the Round Table
and all it stands for is doomed to destruction through internal
strife. The key question may be simply formulated. Does the Troy
frame serve to suggest by analogy that Arthurian civilization, too,
will eventually be destroyed? While this precise question has not
often been asked, critics have regularly considered a rather more

[26] *Beowulf*, ll. 64–79.   [27] Ibid., ll. 82b–5.

general issue: whether or not the poet intended his poem as a whole to imply the future collapse of the Round Table. Opinions on this matter have been various. Some commentators argue that Gawain's quest is essentially religious, and that the poem predicts the inevitable fall of a secular society. Thus, according to Charles Moorman, the poet offers 'a microcosm, ... a semi-allegorical presentation of the whole history and meaning of the Round Table'.[28] The opposing view is propounded by several distinguished interpreters of the poem, among them Larry D. Benson. He maintains that 'there is no hint of the adultery, incest, and treachery that finally brought ruin to the Round Table, and familiar characters whose names might serve as allusions to these vices are carefully omitted'.[29] A middle way between these views may be suggested by the comments of Alfred David and Charles Muscatine.[30] It is, perhaps, not coincidental that both are among the small minority of critics to consider seriously the significance of the allusion to Troy in *Sir Gawain and the Green Knight*. David, in his article on the opening of the poem, points out that to the Middle Ages the fall of Troy 'was one of the great human catastrophes', and contends that 'in the frailty of the best of the Round Table we can see already the seeds of a catastrophe that equalled the destruction of Troy—the fall of Arthur's kingdom through treason'.[31] Less specifically, but to similar effect, Muscatine argues that the opening of *Sir Gawain and the Green Knight* is entirely appropriate, since Troy was what he terms 'that archetype of disaster'.[32] My own view coincides broadly with those of David and of Muscatine. I should, however, wish to emphasize the importance of the ironic context derived from the retrospective, historical viewpoint.

The viability of such a position will depend, at least in part, on the nature of the inherited attitude to the fall of Troy prevalent in

---

[28] 'Myth and Mediaeval Literature: *Sir Gawain and the Green Knight*', *Mediaeval Studies*, 18 (1956), 158–72 (quotation from p. 170). Cf. e.g. G. V. Smithers, 'What *Sir Gawain and the Green Knight* is About', *Medium Ævum*, 32 (1963), 171–89.

[29] *Art and Tradition in Sir Gawain and the Green Knight* (New Brunswick, NJ, 1965), 98. A similar view is taken by J. A. Burrow, *A Reading of 'Sir Gawain and the Green Knight'* (London, 1965), 8–12.

[30] Alfred David, 'Gawain and Aeneas'; Charles Muscatine, *Poetry and Crisis in the Age of Chaucer* (Notre Dame and London, 1972).

[31] 'Gawain and Aeneas', p. 408.

[32] *Poetry and Crisis*, p. 59.

the late Middle Ages: the attitude which the *Gawain*-Poet could expect his audience to share. In assessing this, the key text, without doubt, is the thirteenth-century *Historia Destructionis Troiae* of Guido delle Colonne. As C. David Benson points out in his admirable study of the history of Troy in Middle English literature,[33] Guido's account was accepted during the late Middle Ages as the authentic history of the fall of Troy. Guido is, however, significant for my case not only for his pre-eminence as historian of Troy, but also for an essential quality of his vision. That quality is a particular outlook, which Benson describes as 'deep pessimism concerning man's ability to shape or even comprehend his own destiny'.[34] Benson goes on to state that 'Guido's anguish comes from the conflict between his characters' ignorance and his own historical perspective', and to remark that 'the *Historia* does not show us the just punishment of sin, only the futility of human plans and effort'.[35] This last point notwithstanding, the potential for moralizing the story of Troy—in Guido's or in any other version—is manifest. As R. E. Kaske observes, 'one common medieval significance of Troy is as an example of pride that was humbled'.[36] Whatever their differences, all versions and applications of the Troy story in the Middle Ages share an emphatically retrospective viewpoint, which will tend to generate ironic effects concerning the impermanence of human achievement and the futility of human aspiration.

It must be acknowledged that this fundamentally pessimistic and retrospective view of Troy coexisted with another, essentially optimistic and, in some sense, forward-looking. Thus, it was possible to associate London with Troy in a positive spirit, as Gower does in the Prologue to the first version of his *Confessio Amantis*, where he speaks of

the toun of newe Troye,
Which tok of Brut his ferste joye.[37]

[33] C. David Benson, *The History of Troy in Middle English Literature: Guido delle Colonne's 'Historia Destructionis Troiae' in Medieval England* (Cambridge, 1980).   [34] Ibid., p. 23.   [35] Ibid., p. 23.
[36] *'Sir Gawain and the Green Knight'*, *Medieval and Renaissance Studies* (Proceedings of the Southeastern Institute of Medieval and Renaissance Studies, Summer, 1979), ed. George Mallary Masters (Chapel Hill and London, 1984), 24–44 (quotation from p. 30).
[37] ll. 37–8, quoted from *The Works of John Gower*, ed. G. C. Macaulay, 4 vols. (Oxford, 1899–1902), vol. 2, p. 3.

Discussing this and several other contemporary and near-contemporary examples of the association, J. A. W. Bennett maintains that 'it is not mere phrase-making to say that to an Englishman *Troy* inevitably rhymed with *joy*'.[38] He points out that the rhyme occurs about twenty times in *Troilus and Criseyde*,[39] and that the equivalent to Chaucer's 'joie' in alliterative poetry would be 'wynne' or 'blysse'—which occur in lines 15 and 18 (respectively) of *Sir Gawain and the Green Knight*. I should wish to add that in the second instance the word in question forms part of the key formula 'bliss and blunder'. While this will remind us of the existence of a pessimistic as well as an optimistic view of the Troy story, the apparent contradiction should, I think, be regarded not as awkward but as significant. It indicates that Troy could be associated in the medieval mind with either 'bliss' or 'blunder'. I shall argue that two exceptional writers had the subtlety to perceive that it might suggest both simultaneously—and thus create a context in which human history could be seen in terms of an unpredictable oscillation between these two poles of experience.

The writers I have in mind are Chaucer and the *Gawain*-Poet, the texts *Troilus and Criseyde* and *Sir Gawain and the Green Knight*. It must be admitted at once that there are substantial differences of approach between these two poems: while Chaucer foregrounds love and tells the story of Troilus, the *Gawain*-Poet focuses on the values of Christian chivalry and alludes to the story of Troy. None the less, the two poems have some significant characteristics in common. At the very least, they are virtually contemporaneous, and among a handful of truly outstanding romances in Middle English. I shall argue, furthermore, that the treatment of the Troy story in *Troilus and Criseyde* shares some striking and fundamental qualities with that in *Sir Gawain and the Green Knight*.

Chaucer relates the story of Troilus and Criseyde in such a way as to emphasize and draw out its potential for retrospective irony. The opening stanzas of the narrative inform us of things which are, indeed, 'wel wist': that Troilus will love Criseyde but be forsaken

---

[38] *Supplementary Notes on 'Sir Gawain and the Green Knight'*, 4 fascicles (Cambridge, 1972–6), fasc. 1, p. 6.

[39] My own count—based on J. S. P. Tatlock and Arthur G. Kennedy, *A Concordance to the Complete Works of Geoffrey Chaucer and to the Romaunt of the Rose* (Washington, 1927)—is 30.

by her, and that Troy will—as Calchas prophesies—'destroied be'.[40]
Thus, despite Chaucer's stated intention

> for to tellen forth in special
> As of this kynges sone of which I tolde,
> And leten other thing collateral,[41]

there is an emphatic sense that the fate of Troilus is inextricably
bound up with that of Troy. This receives emphasis not only from
the essential nature and shape of the story, but also from several
narrative devices. Among these is the handling of imagery, including that of shielding and shields. Chaucer uses this imagery to
create some significant effects: thus, Troilus is described as a 'sheld'
for the Trojans and 'a wal | Of stiel, and shield from every dis-
plesaunce' for Criseyde, while Hector, who has been praised as 'the
townes wal', is subsequently criticized by his fellow citizens for
attempting 'to shilde' Criseyde.[42] The common factor here is a
sense of futility. There is also a recurring sense of the difficulty of
judging values and predicting the course of events. Troilus will
prove an ineffectual protector of Troy, as of Criseyde; Hector, likewise powerless to defend the city, cannot withstand the demands
of the citizens that Criseyde should be exchanged for Antenor—
who will, of course, later betray them. Though it is this last
instance of retrospective irony which provides Chaucer with the
occasion to remark, through his narrator, 'o nyce world, lo, thy
discrecioun!',[43] such a reflection would be appropriate not infre-
quently during the course of *Troilus and Criseyde*.

The key factor which facilitates this use of retrospective irony is
that of differentiated levels of knowledge: the author, narrator, and
audience share information which the protagonists lack. In terms
of the story as history, the essential information is, of course, that
Troy will eventually fall to the Greeks. While the impending doom
of Troy is also of fundamental relevance to the love story, this
involves several other elements, crucial in their own right: that
Pandarus will succeed in bringing Troilus and Criseyde together;
that Troilus will love and then lose Criseyde; that she will grant
him her love, but will later be sent to the Greek camp, and will

---

[40] *Troilus and Criseyde*, i. 57; 68.
[41] Ibid., i. 260—2.
[42] Ibid., ii. 201; iii. 479—80; ii. 154; iv. 188.
[43] Ibid., iv. 206.

there forsake him for Diomede. It is reasonable to assume that Chaucer would have been fully conscious of his audience's familiarity with the essentials of the story. If this confronted him with a problem—that his account might be enfeebled by its predictability—then he turned the potential weakness into an actual strength. Chaucer's version of the story derives much of its intensity and poignancy from retrospective irony. We witness the protagonists speculating uneasily not only as to the fate of Troy, but also as to future assessments of themselves. In particular, Chaucer emphasizes the anxiety concerning Criseyde's reputation—felt not only by Criseyde herself, but also Pandarus and Troilus. This generates some telling and poignant effects—as, for instance, the progressive contrast between Criseyde's firm assertion of her faithfulness to Troilus in Book III, her plea in Book IV that Troilus should think of her reputation, and how 'foule' it would be 'shende' if she agreed to flee with him rather than go to the Greek camp, and her sad acknowledgement in Book V that she has now forfeited her reputation, and that the authors of future 'bokes' will indeed 'shende' her.[44]

Some critics have argued that the purpose of such irony is to expose the folly and ignorance of the protagonists. This strikes me as a perversely simplistic and reductive reading, which depends upon placing undue emphasis on the passage of overt Christian moralizing at the end of the poem,[45] and fails to take full account of the subtlety and complexity of Chaucer's narrative. A more intelligent and sensitive reading would recognize the sophisticated literary possibilities which Chaucer so skilfully develops, and would conclude that his purpose is less to expose the foolish ignorance of his protagonists than to create in his portrayal of their fictional situations a rich and complex sense of the sheer difficulty of knowing, of choosing, of reaching decisions, and of making judgements. Such an intention can surely be recognized in the wonderfully acute yet elusive account of Criseyde's conflicting thoughts and feelings as she falls in love with Troilus.[46] It may also be discerned more generally in several aspects of the protagonists' perception of themselves and of their situations. Thus, for instance, the recurring use of proverbial and aphoristic sayings and judgements—especially, but not

[44] Ibid., iii. 1053–4; iv. 1576–82; v. 1058–64.
[45] Ibid., v. 1835–69.
[46] Ibid., ii. 649–812.

exclusively, by Pandarus—may suggest the desire to understand, define, and predict experience. In the complex world of *Troilus and Criseyde* such efforts, while seeming entirely natural, are doomed to failure. When, to take an example almost at random, Pandarus states that 'joie is next the fyn of sorwe',[47] it will hardly escape notice that the match between aphorism and experience is unlikely to prove complete, permanent, or definitive. This tendency extends into the narrator's discourse, as when the response of Troilus to Criseyde's acceptance of his love is compared to the seasonal change of winter into summer.[48] Each statement bears within it the clear possibility of reversal. Each is, duly, reversed: the seasonal allusion by an equivalent comparison between Troilus' loss of joy at Criseyde's departure and a tree's loss of leaves in winter, Pandarus's statement by that with which Criseyde responds to a temporary set-back in her relationship with Troilus.[49] The message would seem clear enough. Proverbial and aphoristic utterances in *Troilus and Criseyde* have an immediate aptness, but their relevance is limited, and the wisdom they embody restricted in its application—and conspicuously unreliable as a guide to the probable course of future events.

I have argued that Chaucer creates the retrospective irony which is typical of this poem by exploiting the differences between the knowledge shared by himself, his narrator, and his audience, and that available to the figures who exist within the world of his fiction. I have also suggested that in *Troilus and Criseyde* the processes of knowing and of judging are presented as crucial but problematic. If there is any virtue in these views, then the considerable significance of the apparently minor role played by Calchas should come as no great surprise. The prophecy of Calchas—that Troy will fall—is pivotal in several ways. As an element of the plot, it serves to set in motion a chain of events which brings Criseyde to the Greek camp, and thus creates the situation in which she forsakes Troilus. At the heart of this sequence, the exchange of Antenor for Criseyde is richly if harshly ironic—highlighting failures of honour and of foresight in both public and private life, as the man who will betray his people is traded for the woman who will betray her lover. The prophecy is also significant by virtue of its essential nature. It represents and intensifies the sense of Troy's

---

[47] *Troilus and Criseyde*, i. 952.   [48] Ibid., iii. 351-7.
[49] Ibid., iv. 225-31; iii. 817-33.

impending doom, not only as a pervasive quality of the poem's fabric, but also, within the fictional world, as part of the protagonists' experience. In the latter connection, it is most significant for the unbearable pressure it exerts on Criseyde, 'with wommen fewe, among the Grekis stronge'.[50] The effect is, however, also witnessed from other viewpoints—both in Troilus' fearful anticipation of the potential effect on Criseyde of her father's conviction that Troy 'nys but lorn', and in Diomede's cynical manipulation of this authority, by means of which he is able, in due course, to exhort her: 'Lat Troie and Troian fro youre herte pace!'[51] One final aspect of Calchas' prophecy warrants attention. If, as I have argued, *Troilus and Criseyde* presents a sustained contrast between those outside the story, who know the future fate of Troy, and those within it, who do not, then the prophecy of Calchas takes on a special significance. It is the sole means by which the knowledge of future events—otherwise reserved to the author, narrator, and audience—may temporarily penetrate the fictional world of the narrative.

The key image of Calchas' prophecy is that of the burning city. Though this might seem entirely natural—since the sacking of a city would readily suggest burning—the treatment of the image is interesting and, I think, significant. While Boccaccio uses it once,[52] in Chaucer it is twice repeated. Calchas informs the Greeks, first:

> dredeles, thorugh yow shal in a stounde
> Ben Troie ybrend and beten down to grownde;

then that

> the tyme is faste by
> That fire and flaumbe on al the town shal sprede,
> And thus shal Troie torne to asshen dede.[53]

Finally, he reiterates that 'the town of Troie shal ben set on-fire'.[54] Given this emphatic repetition, in the space of fifty lines, it is especially conspicuous that the image occurs nowhere else in *Troilus and Criseyde*.[55] The use, in this prophetic passage, of the image of the burning city may be compared to that of the image of the burning hall in the likewise (if less portentously) prophetic passage

[50] Ibid., v. 688.   [51] Ibid., iv. 1479; v. 912.   [52] *Filostrato*, iv. 5.
[53] *Troilus and Criseyde*, iv. 76–7; 117–19.   [54] Ibid., iv. 126.
[55] The image also occurs in *The House of Fame* (163)—though Chaucer's use of it there has no particular relevance to the present argument.

from *Beowulf*, discussed earlier. It also has striking similarities with the reiterated key image in the Troy frame of *Sir Gawain and the Green Knight.*

The fact that Chaucer and the *Gawain*-Poet share this key image of destruction may encourage reconsideration of some of the other common features in their handling of the Troy story. I have argued that retrospective irony and differentiated levels of knowledge are essential characteristics of *Troilus and Criseyde*, and that Chaucer uses them to convey within the fictional world a profound sense of the elusiveness of knowledge and the uncertainty of judgement. Comparable effects may be discerned in *Sir Gawain and the Green Knight.* The first major scene of the poem focuses upon a problem of understanding and judgement: when Arthur and his court are confronted, without warning, by a huge green man on a huge green horse, their difficulties are essentially those of understanding the nature of the challenger and the challenge, and of judging what kind of response may be appropriate. Similar problems recur throughout the poem. Thus, for instance, despite the apparent security and comfort of his surroundings during the sequence in the lord's castle, Gawain is constantly aware of acute uncertainty arising from the sense that things are not quite what they seem—a sense paradoxically intensified by legalistic ritual and language. This emphasis on the problematic and elusive quality of any attempt to understand and to judge human experience may be related to the poem's characteristic pattern of retrospective qualification.

The acuteness of the difficulty arises in part from the recognition that, while change is inevitable, the precise nature and significance of any particular change is often resistant to prediction: as the poet states, 'þe forme to þe fynisment foldez ful selden'.[56] The difficulty is compounded by the tendency for ideals—whether of love, conduct, or society—to be envisaged in models which are absolute and thus prone to be static and inflexible. Having realized that he has failed to live up to the absolute standard of Christian chivalry, Gawain can do nothing but condemn himself absolutely. But, while he feels that he has failed the ideal, a more detached observer might reverse the judgement and conclude that the ideal has failed him, by proving inadequate to deal with the complexity of his

[56] *Sir Gawain*, l. 499.

experience within the poem. This is not to suggest that the ideal is seen as anything other than admirable; rather, that its absoluteness renders it extremely demanding and inflexible as a model either for inspiring or for judging conduct. Much the same could be said of love, as envisaged by Troilus. It demands total commitment, as it offers total fulfilment; conversely, it can respond to failure only with absolute rejection. Thus, the manœuvrings of Pandarus and the vacillations of Criseyde are alike both in constituting a recognition of complexity and ambivalence and in being utterly alien to Troilus—for whom the qualified and the contingent barely exist. The weakness of this ideal, too, is in dealing with the subtleties of experience in a complex fictional world.

I have argued that the aphoristic utterances in *Troilus and Criseyde* often suggest a desire or attempt to understand and control experience. The desire will be frustrated, the attempt unsuccessful, because the aphorism will prove inadequate to accommodate the complexity of the poem's fictional world. While it may provide a partial interpretation of a given experience—joy follows after sorrow, as winter gives way to summer—it will be limited in its application, and even potentially self-subverting: joy may likewise be followed by sorrow, as summer turns to winter once again. The *Gawain*-Poet makes still more striking use of the idea of seasonal change. It is, perhaps, the unforced way in which they combine the familiar with the inexorable which makes the changing seasons so rich a source of imagery concerning the inevitability of change in human experience. This potential is exploited by the *Gawain*-Poet in the magnificent passage[57] which functions as a bridge between the opening narrative sequence of the Green Knight's challenge and the following sequence of Gawain's preparation and journey in quest of the return blow. He creates a powerful impression of threat and foreboding, partly through the poignancy with which the general fact of mutability is suggested, partly through his shaping and manipulation of the narrative. Gawain's future is, indeed, unknown—at least to him. It is also partly unknown to the audience, who are obliged by the poet to share, for substantial sections of the narrative, the protagonist's ignorance of such vital facts as the identity of the lord of the castle and the significance of the temptation scenes. Such a procedure

[57] Ibid., ll. 491–535.

was available to the *Gawain*-Poet because the details of this story were not firmly established—in contrast to those of the story of Troy and Troilus with which Chaucer was working in *Troilus and Criseyde*. The degree to which the audience of *Sir Gawain and the Green Knight* share the hero's ignorance is, however, limited: here, too, levels of knowledge are differentiated. The poet and the audience have an advantage over Gawain by virtue both of their knowing that Arthur's kingdom is doomed, and of their more remote and detached perspective, in which his experiences are seen in relation to the motif of 'bliss and blunder'. This motif, as I have pointed out, is derived from the Troy frame.

I therefore conclude that the Troy frame of *Sir Gawain and the Green Knight* serves (among other things) to predict the collapse of Arthurian civilization. Previous discussion of this topic has been prone to polarization—critics tending to maintain either that the poet means to suggest the fate of the Round Table, and that his poem should therefore be read as a moral allegory, or that he avoids any such suggestion by excluding allusion to the major figures and events associated with the death of Arthur. As I have indicated, my own reading is something of a middle way between these poles. It seems to me that the Troy frame does indeed predict the downfall of King Arthur and everything for which he stands, and that this effect is reinforced by the motif of 'bliss and blunder', which is established from the outset. This does not, however, lead to a simplistically or reductively moral poem: the *Gawain*-Poet creates a fictional world in which moral issues are subtle and complex, and moral life is full of difficult choices and elusive judgements. As in *Troilus and Criseyde* (albeit to a somewhat lesser degree) the sense of the difficulty of knowing and judging in the fictional world is enhanced by differentiated levels of knowledge. While the author and his audience know that Arthur's kingdom, like Troy, will fall, this is a fact unknown to those within the fiction. The consequent effect is an intensification of retrospective irony. With hindsight, we see what was an essential part of the author's design from the outset: that Arthurian civilization, which has so much in common with that of Troy—idealism, dynastic associations, the linking of love and conflict—will follow its illustrious exemplar to destruction.

I suggest that Chaucer and the *Gawain*-Poet—two great English poets from the late fourteenth century, authors of two great and virtually contemporaneous romances—perceived in Troy the potential for a setting uniquely rich and resonant. These qualities derive not only from exotic associations with dynastic heritage and a glorious past but also from a pervasive sense of paradox and complexity. Troy combines the public and the private, love and conflict, nobility and treachery—'bliss and blunder'. As a consequence, it is a setting with the potential to generate intense responses to events and searching analysis of conduct, viewed with the retrospective irony which is facilitated by the historical perspective. Thus, for Chaucer as for the *Gawain*-Poet, Troy was not merely remote, noble, and exotic, but also a rich and subtle context for the exploration of human understanding, choice, and motivation. In *Sir Gawain and the Green Knight*, as in *Troilus and Criseyde*, this potential is triumphantly fulfilled. With all their differences, both poems constitute a profound realization of those aspects of experience suggested by the Troy story—in each case viewed with retrospective irony, qualified by deep sympathy for the human condition, and by appreciation of the sheer difficulty of knowing and of judging.

5

Comedy and Tragedy in *Troilus and Criseyde*

Troilus and Criseyde is and is not a tragedy; it is and is not a comedy.[1] How should we label or define it then? Why indeed should we wish so to do? Labels and definitions are useful in suggesting the assumptions which govern our responses to what we perceive in reading or hearing. The wrong assumptions may distort our understanding of the work of art which is the object of perception unless, like scientists, we allow what we perceive to challenge and change our assumptions as necessary. It is inevitable that we should have some assumptions before we perceive anything at all. So it is useful, if we can, to have both flexible and reasonably accurate labels or definitions to start off with. It is significant of the nature of *Troilus and Criseyde* that it is very difficult to find a suitable label for it. The reason is partly historical. Medieval literary theorists, and especially writers in the vernacular, were not much interested in 'pure' literary forms or in precise literary labels. That interest only developed with the neo-classical theorists of the Renaissance, and their theories of *genre* and decorum never suited medieval English literature, nor Shakespeare (in this respect a medieval writer) very well, as the criticism of Shakespeare by Rymer and Samuel Johnson notoriously shows.

   We must make do with what we can get, and fortunately Chaucer himself introduced the terms 'tragedy' and 'comedy' into English. We can start with them as suggestive working hypotheses without keeping them too strictly to purely modern definitions,

---

[1] Willi Erzgräber has discussed this problem with clarity in his 'Tragik und Komik in Chaucer's "Troilus and Criseyde"', now in W. Erzgräber (ed.), *Geoffrey Chaucer* (Darmstadt, 1983), 144–75. In the same volume, see the classic essays by D. W. Robertson, 'Chaucerian Tragedy', and P. G. Ruggiers, 'Notes Towards a Theory of Tragedy in Chaucer', pp. 108–43, 396–408. A. J. Minnis, *Chaucer and Pagan Antiquity* (Cambridge and Totowa, NJ, 1982), discusses the question and gives further references, pp. 27–8.

and then elaborate and modify our notions of what 'tragedy' and
'comedy' mean in relation to the poem and therefore what the
poem means to us. We can start with the label 'tragedy', attributing
to it a rather vague sense, which reading the poem will define, of a
sad story with an unhappy ending.

Chaucer himself calls *Troilus and Criseyde* 'litel myn tragedye',[2]
but the very manner of description here is self-deprecatory and
thus not entirely serious. Chaucer's very naming, within the
poem, of his poem as a tragedy, places the poet himself inside as
well as outside his own poem. In itself this act points to a major
difference from most modern literature. External information
about the poem, such as might appear on the wrapper of a
printed book, is included within the text. We are made conscious
thereby of the author presenting himself as telling us a story not
of his own invention but learnt from others and of which his own
sympathetic knowledge is only partial. Because we have a strong
sense of the story-teller presenting his story, we realize that
though he is inside the *poem* he is not inside the *story*. He is not a
participant in the action, and is not in that sense (*pace* most
modern critics)[3] a Narrator within the story. He is not like Gulliver in *Gulliver's Travels* or David in *David Copperfield* or Marcel
in *A la recherche du temps perdu.* Unlike virtually all novels, and
even unlike Chaucer's main source, Boccaccio's *Il Filostrato* (if we
can believe Boccaccio), there is clearly no autobiographical element in the telling of the story of *Troilus.* This is indeed the normal
situation and normal attitude of the traditional, oral story-teller,
telling a story of long ago—such as a Homer or some humble
minstrel repeating what he has heard or read, commenting or

    [2] *Troilus and Criseyde*, v. 1786.
    [3] Virtually every critic on *Troilus and Criseyde* now employs the concept of the
Narrator, though to very different effects and with varying degrees of sophistication. Used with care it can lead to delicate discriminations, but the concept is very
much the product of print culture and often distances the reader from the emotional impact of the story, or introduces a promiscuous irony. For some of the
subtlest formulations, see E. T. Donaldson, 'Chaucer the Pilgrim' and 'Criseyde
and her Narrator', now in his *Speaking of Chaucer* (London, 1970), 1–12, 65–83;
C. Muscatine, *Chaucer and the French Tradition* (Berkeley, 1957), 135. For specific
discussion and extended general use see e.g. M. E. McAlpine, *The Genre of 'Troilus
and Criseyde'* (Ithaca and London, 1978); E. Salter, '*Troilus and Criseyde*: Poet and
Narrator', in M. J. Carruthers and E. D. Kirk (eds.), *Acts of Interpretation*
(Norman, Oklahoma, 1982), 281–92.

guessing about the action and about the nature of the characters who appear in the story.

The traditional story-teller still in some parts of the world comes round the villages, and even in Europe has not long been extinct. Scholars still alive (such as Professor Kenneth Jackson)[4] have heard and witnessed to them. Chaucer was more than a simple oral story-teller. He was literate and subtle to an almost unique degree. But he patently chooses to adopt this traditional style of narration, creating it in the very first stanzas of *Troilus*, and it is basic to his whole conduct of the story.

This undeniable choice of a traditional oral style depends upon and evokes assumptions and expectations which are very different from those conventions of print culture which are so familiar to a modern reader that we take them for nature itself and see them where they are not, as in *Troilus*, for example. The concept of the Narrator, nowadays almost universal amongst critics, is begotten of a print culture upon an oral style, seeing the Narrator as a character inside the story rather than as a traditional story-teller and Expositor (as in the Chester plays) who is partly telling, partly explaining, at times half acting, a story whose outline he has received from elsewhere, but which takes on new life through his own participating and recreating imagination.

Chaucer begins the poem by very deliberately creating in imagination himself as poet, standing before us, emphasizing the ultimately sad conclusion of the story he is to tell by his own appearance of sadness:

> The double sorwe of Troilus to tellen,
> That was the kyng Priamus sone of Troye,
> In lovynge, how his aventures fellen
> Fro wo to wele, and after out of joie,
> My purpos is, er that I parte fro ye.
> Thesiphone, thow help me for t'endite
> Thise woful vers, that wepen as I write.
>
> To the clepe I, thow goddesse of torment,
> Thow cruwel Furie, sorwynge evere yn peyne,
> Help me, that am the sorwful instrument,
> That helpeth loveres, as I kan, to pleyne;
> For wel sit it, the sothe for to seyne,

---

[4] e.g. A. Lord, *The Singer of Tales* (Cambridge, Mass., 1960); Kenneth Jackson, *The International Popular Tale and Early Welsh Tradition* (Cardiff, 1961).

A woful wight to han a drery feere,
And to a sorwful tale, a sory chere.[5]

The poet is telling us about a well-known hero, Troilus, and expects us to know something vaguely at least about his unhappy life and his premature death. In case we are uncertain about the drift of the story he summarizes it in the very first line, and everything we read or imagine about the characters in the course of the poem is seen against this faint but sombre background, as of a menacing row of mountains to which the course of the story brings us closer and closer.

An audience listening to a story-teller's fresh version of a known story is the normal, traditional oral-social situation. Why do we attend to such a sad story as told, or in print, or on the stage or film? One thing is certain: we do not go simply to have a good laugh, or to exercise our contempt for the characters, whatever incidental moments of comedy or satire there may be in the course of narration. We go to have, at least metaphorically, a good cry. In other words, we go to hear or see enacted a sad story or a tragedy in the expectation of being moved overall in a certain way. We know that life itself is often sad and we need art to represent that as well as other facets of life, especially when the sad aspects are hard to face in ordinary life. Art gives them order and significance.

We would find it difficult to appreciate a sad story if we felt that its teller was not himself moved by, did not in some sense believe in, its pity, its pathos, even its terror. We would not be able to accept in attending to such a story that our feelings were being merely manipulated. If we became aware of some cynical or fundamentally ironic impulse in the artist we would cease to respond to the sad or tragic element. At best the story of disaster would be one to be treated with derision. If the author was in fact not openly derisive but merely trying to deceive us we would not feel that his telling of the story was worth our attention. This is not to deny that the story-teller must in the nature of his art manage the story in the most effective way. Artistry implies artistic calculation, awareness of how to create a response in the audience, rhetorical persuasion, verbal skill, and so forth. Art is not in any simple way 'sincere', any more than sincerity is in itself enough to make a work of art. But if a work of art lacks a certain quality of genuineness we

[5] *Troilus and Criseyde*, i. 1–14.

judge the work of art as bogus, hypocritical, sentimental, cynical, and so forth, and to that extent a failure. How could we admire, for example, *King Lear*, if we felt that beneath the surface of the presentation Shakespeare was really thinking to himself that Lear was just a silly old man who got what he deserved? A serious story requires the reader to experience some sense of inner conviction on the part of the author, though conviction operates according to the demands of the material and purpose. Even satire and comedy must convey this sense of inner conviction and genuine intention.

It follows that the first major point to be made about Chaucer's *Troilus*, if we recognize it as the major work of art it is, must be that it is intended to be overall a sad and moving story; that an appropriate reading or hearing will judge it to be so; and that our response tells us that Chaucer himself, the poet, found it sad and moving. Whatever else we may later have to say about the poem and the way it is told we must first say that it is basically a sad story, a tragedy; that we deeply sympathize with the hero, Troilus, and that we can easily see why he fell in love with the beautiful and charming Criseyde. Most people have been in love and very many of them have been unhappily in love: it is a process of deep human interest to us. We must therefore give our sympathy to the story as Chaucer must have done. Why otherwise would Chaucer have written the story or we bother to read it? Once Chaucer made the decision to tell it and write it, many other factors complicated the way he told it, as will be later remarked. Those factors modify our response, but the poem remains in essence what he calls a 'tragedy'.

Chaucer was the first person recorded as using the term 'tragedy' of a vernacular English work, and he uses it of *Troilus and Criseyde*:

> Go, litel bok, go, litel myn tragedye.[6]

After a slightly flippant side-reference to comedy, to which I will return, Chaucer aligns his poem at this point with the great narrative works of antiquity known to him, by Virgil, Ovid, Homer, Lucan, Statius. Not all the poems by these writers are tragedies and nor were all Chaucer's, but Chaucer knows that as a poet his place is not too far from the greatest.

Chaucer also knows and accepts the general definition of

---

[6] *Troilus and Criseyde*, v. 1786.

tragedy prevalent in the Middle Ages deriving from Antiquity and many times repeated, which he quotes from Boethius at the beginning of the *Monk's Tale*:

> Tragedie is to seyn a certeyn storie,
> As olde bookes maken us memorie,
> Of hym that stood in greet prosperitee,
> And is yfallen out of heigh degree
> Into myserie, and endeth wrecchedly.[7]

This defines what is called *De Casibus* tragedy, telling the story of how the mighty are fallen. It is narrative rather than dramatic and dominates the notions of tragedy in English from Chaucer's time to the end of the sixteenth century. It is sometimes called Gothic Tragedy.[8] It does not always end in death but it always consists of a fall into misery from happiness, and death is often treated as the ultimate calamity, the last misery. In the sequence of tragedies told in the *Canterbury Tales* by the Monk, the story of Adam may perhaps be counted as a tragedy of death, since through his fault 'came death into the world and all our woe', and Sampson, Hercules, Balthasar, Peter of Spain, Peter of Cyprus, Barnabò of Lombardy, Hugolino of Pisa, Holofernes, King Antiochus, Alexander, Julius Caesar, and Cresus all die. But Lucifer, Nebuchadnezzar, and Cenobia, in their stories, do not. Death need not be a part of medieval tragedy and is not in fact part of Troilus' own tragedy, for death does no more than conclude his woes. Troilus' tragedy conforms to the general medieval pattern; it is a reversal of fortune in its arbitrariness, yet the arbitrariness is very much the way of the world. We know that this is what life is like.

From the examples given in Chaucer's *Monk's Tale* we also note that the medieval tragic hero or heroine need not be a good or even

---

[7] *Monk's Tale*, ll. 1973-7.

[8] For a good recent discussion of these problems, see R. Haas, 'Chaucer's *Monk's Tale*: An Ingenious Criticism of Early Humanist Conceptions of Tragedy', *Humanistica Lovaniensia*, 36 (1987), 44-70. A still valuable and extensive account, though focused more on Lydgate, is W. Farnham, *The Medieval Heritage of Elizabethan Tragedy* (Berkeley, 1936). For an excellent brief summary of medieval views and the texts available see M. Doran, *Endeavors of Art: A Study of Form in Elizabethan Drama* (Madison, 1964), esp. pp. 115-28. For the notion of Gothic literary form see Muscatine, *Chaucer and the French Tradition*, pp. 167-73; D. Brewer, 'Gothic Chaucer', now in his *Tradition and Innovation in Chaucer* (London, 1982), 110-36, and, more generally, *English Gothic Literature* (London, 1984). But see also J. Norton-Smith, *Geoffrey Chaucer* (London, 1974), 160-212.

a partially good man or woman. The morality of medieval tragedy does not depend on the goodness or even the wickedness of the hero. High estate and good fortune are external qualities, to be deprived of which constitutes a tragedy, independent of the worthiness of the individual who has enjoyed them. Yet, there is a further poignancy if the protagonist is indeed a good man or woman, as Chaucer represents the two King Peters, or Cenobia. We may, if we like, reserve judgement on Troilus' goodness, though I would argue that Chaucer presents him, in order to increase the pathos, as an outstandingly good man. Nevertheless, medieval ideas of tragedy are not so internalized that we need to seek the seeds of tragedy, let alone the justification of tragedy, in the moral quality and least of all in a moral weakness or 'tragic flaw' in the hero. The notion that Troilus somehow deserves his fate because of his moral weakness is a gross simplification and deprives the story of the pathos which it is clearly intended to convey. It would also imply a view of the justice of life which it is surely impossible for any modern or medieval man to entertain. Troilus is young and natural, and in consequence is liable to rashness and self-pity, but any reading of the poem that makes him morally deserving of his ill fortune is repellent in itself, denies the pathos of the story, goes against what Chaucer tells us about him at the end of Book III, and also denies Criseyde's praise of his 'moral virtue grounded upon truth'. 'Truth' meaning loyalty, integrity, is surely Troilus' leading characteristic. In other words, you do not need to be bad to suffer a reversal of fortune in this world. Perhaps goodness suffers more. There is good precedent for such a view.

Nevertheless, the ending of the poem repudiates love of the kind that Troilus experienced and some critics have found it jarring because they have rightly responded to the beauty and goodness of Troilus' feelings.[9] The repudiation, however, must clearly follow on from the course of this typically medieval tragic narrative. Troilus ventured himself on fortune's wheel and rose with it; it is the way of the world that to give yourself to the world is to run a

---

[9] For an old-fashioned view which still finds echoes see W. C. Curry's still valuable essay, 'Destiny in *Troilus and Criseyde*', now in R. J. Schoeck and J. Taylor (eds.), *Chaucer Criticism*, ii (Notre Dame and London, 1961), 34–70, esp. 67–9. For other examples see E. T. Donaldson, 'The Ending of "Troilus"', in his *Speaking of Chaucer*, pp. 84–101; A. C. Spearing, 'Narrative Closure: The End of *Troilus and Criseyde*', in his *Readings in Medieval Poetry* (Cambridge, 1987), 107–33.

great risk, especially if you are mighty and noble, of tumbling
down to the depths. Fortune's wheel always turns. To be high
means almost certainly in the nature of things to be liable to fall. In
any event, even the lustiest and most fortunate of men must die,
often in pain and misery.

Medieval men saw tragedy as a sequential narrative paralleling
the way that we experience linear time to some extent in our own
lives. They placed the events of the story in their natural sequence.
They made such stories intelligible in relation to the risks that we
all run in life and to which those of great estate are even more liable
than those of us who creep along the ground. Seeing the pattern of
rising and falling, Chaucer, led by traditional wisdom and the
explicit remarks of Boethius, draws the obvious conclusion. He is
far less moralistic than some critics appear to wish to make him.[10]
He sees the entirely comprehensible risks and frequent result of
high estate, and that life is a great gamble. He sees that most of us
make some attempt at that gamble. Gambling is always dangerous
and, even if we win for a time, at last we may well lose everything.
A perfectly reasonable conclusion to draw from this is that it is
better not to rise into such uncertainty, better not to gamble
against such odds. Chaucer concludes that Troilus in his life, as we
in ours, would have done better to seek the certain good and the
higher truth, even if it is doubtful if they were available to him.
Since, in any event, Troilus did not seek that good and truth, he
suffered, as we will suffer. What happens after death is between us
and God, and nobody in this life can be certain of the result. The
poem describes Troilus briefly after death in a passage which must
be considered extraneous to his life story and leaves us to guess
that Troilus might have gone to Heaven, or at least to that com-
fortable limbo where good pagans go, because, though he made his
mistakes, he was a good man. That reflection, however, is external
to the actual tragedy, and the undoubted suffering, which are a
matter for this life. The story is about Troilus' life and is not even
incidentally about the fate of Criseyde. She is entirely ancillary to
him.

The drift of my argument is that Chaucer is telling a serious
story with a fundamental seriousness; that he was moved by it, as I
think any reader who is uncorrupted by literary prejudice must be
moved by it. It is a genuine medieval tragedy of fortune, a Boethian

[10] Most notably D. W. Robertson, *A Preface to Chaucer* (Princeton, 1963).

tragedy. The ending, the so-called Epilogue, is quite logical and natural since, while Troilus' moral worth is not in question, both his apotheosis and the repudiation of earthly love are legitimate conclusions to be drawn from considering his life.

Troilus is represented after his death as laughing at those who mourn for him. There is no reason to consider this laughter as ironical—a vague word too easily used, often mistakenly, to imply bitterness. What irony can there be, what sense of the double meaning intrinsic to irony, can there be in Troilus' laughter? He has escaped from the fetters of the world which he had mistakenly taken to be its joys and he celebrates with a genuine, hearty belly-laugh, as well he may, his own escape and consequently the absurdity of mourning for it. Far from denying the seriousness of the sad story the ending gives it a further perspective.

There is no reason to question the poet's own sympathetic view of his characters. Just as we cannot respond imaginatively to the poem without giving the characters some degree of credibility, and some of our sympathy, so the author himself has to give some credence and sympathy to the autonomous existence of his characters. Dickens is the classic example of the *novelist* whose imaginary characters have, as it were, taken on an independent existence of their own—most famously, contemporary readers took with the utmost seriousness the fate of his fictional character, Little Nell. We do not have to go back as far as the stories told in nineteenth-century novels to find examples of this tendency. It is well known that very many modern viewers of television 'soap operas' take the fictional characters so seriously that they send them presents for their birthdays and flowers for their funerals. While it is always dangerous to make simple analogies between modern and past modes of feeling, there are some correspondences, and in this particular respect we are surely right in referring to the universal human tendency to take the characters in fictional stories seriously. In the case of traditional stories we are on the even safer ground that such stories have a certain objective validity, even a kind of vague historical truth, simply because they are traditional, which gives them a start in the race for credibility against the ostensibly new characters of newly invented, modern, subjective fictions. Chaucer knew that he had invented much of Criseyde's story and character, but so did Dickens and Jane Austen know they had invented their characters. Yet, they had attitudes towards them, as if they were real people. So, we may assume, did Chaucer have such attitudes. The difference is that Chaucer the poet introduces his own views explicitly into his own poem while Dickens and Jane Austen, following art-forms with narrower conventions, had to restrict their comments (usually) to letters outside the work.

Another analogy may be helpful here, as in much of Chaucer's work. Although he does not introduce himself as a character within the action of *Troilus*, Chaucer's expressed presence as story-teller is universally recognized. As a traditional story-teller sometimes does, he comments on the action and his own feelings. Description of their own feelings or state of mind can analogously be found in Shakespeare's characters as they present themselves on the stage to the audience. The outstanding case is Hamlet, who does it so extensively as to be regarded normally, but not necessarily accurately, as a highly introspective character. But many other characters in Shakespeare who are not introspective also comment on and explain their own states of being. Richard III does so when he says, 'I am determined to prove a villain'.[11] Macbeth, in soliloquies, describes his own state of feeling. Neither of these can be convincingly described as introspective or self-analytical characters, unless we confuse the medium of soliloquy with the message about the nature of the character. Self-description is a dramatic convention which is already found in English in the monologues that survive from fourteenth-century plays, for example, and in the self-revelations of Chaucer's Wife of Bath and Pardoner. Such self-description seems to witness to a developing self-consciousness, but in a culture such as that of the fourteenth century, which was in many respects still relatively unself-aware, it retains a slightly artificial ring, an awkwardness or inconsistency with context which, while not a serious artistic flaw, may puzzle us moderns who are nurtured on self-consciousness and self-analysis. When presented with explicit self-description we naturally tend to look for irony or comic satire or introspection or hypocrisy. We may well be mistaken. In the case of the Wife and the Pardoner the aim is indeed satirical, but this need not be so when love, sorrow, or pity are the emotions which the character describes himself or herself as feeling. Some degree of self-awareness is attributed to

---

[11] *Richard III*, I. i. 30.

Troilus himself in expressing his sorrowful conviction that he is doomed to be lost, but there is no reason to suppose any irony put into Troilus' mouth. That Chaucer agreed with such pagan determinism is highly unlikely, but does not make Troilus' speech in itself ironical.

There is therefore little reason, other than anachronistic cynicism, to believe that when Chaucer says that he would excuse Criseyde for pity[12] he means to be ironical or satirical at his own expense. We need doubt neither the seriousness of the judgement on treachery (for he does not excuse her) nor the regret which accompanies it.

So far I have been arguing for the acceptance of *Troilus* as being what Chaucer says it is—a medieval tragedy of Fortune the contemplation of which moves and instructs, and to whose characters we respond with sympathy but also with judgement. Yet, we also notice the variations of tone and attitude intermingled with this seriousness from the very beginning of the poem. In the first two stanzas the poet refers to spoken delivery and to his own appearance, as well as to writing. He dramatizes himself in the script he has written for himself to deliver. In so doing he lightens the tone, and there must surely be an intentional touch of humour here. Many other passages later, especially concerning Pandarus, but even touching Troilus, approach such humour, or are indeed lightly comic in tone.

How different is this poem from other medieval tragedies of Fortune, although multiplicity of points of view, absence of a single dominating perspective, is a characteristic of much medieval literature, as it is of medieval painting. No poet appears to have made such free and indeed deliberate use of variation and polyphony as Chaucer did. In *Troilus* the poet constantly changes the point of view of the narration and the attitude with which he conducts the story, even apparently his own beliefs, for example, in the apparent contradiction between the praise of love at the beginning of Book III and the condemnation of love at the ending of the poem. Other variations or contradictions are well known. Sometimes the poet knows a character's inmost thoughts and at other times he is ignorant of obvious externals such as whether Criseyde had children or not. Chaucer varies his distance from the characters

---

[12] *Troilus and Criseyde*, v. 1099.

and their actions, alters the tone in which he speaks of them, though he always maintains a certain detachment even from his hero himself.

In the narration, therefore, there is no single dominant point of view, no single perspective. Usually Troilus offers the experiencing centre of consciousness. We know his inner feelings from the start and we have an intimate view of the subjectivity of his falling in love. Although I have emphasized the basic seriousness and sympathy with which this is presented, it is also narrated with touches of flippant detached humour, especially in the first book. There are no touches of humour, on the other hand, in the treatment of Troilus' misery in the fifth book.

Pandarus is hardly ever presented as a centre of consciousness. The characterization of Pandarus as a bawd is made necessary by the concept of Troilus' goodness. If Troilus is ever going to seduce Criseyde then Troilus must be distanced from the intrigue and someone else has to do the dirty work. The device of Pandarus enables Chaucer to do two remarkably incompatible things in the same poem. First, although the whole story is tragic, much of the action can then be a partially comic intrigue, carried on by Pandarus without stain on Troilus. Pandarus is a bawd, a fixer, one who responds to emergencies, one who both reacts to other people's desires and generates actions. He is an almost entirely modern character and personality, ultimately trivial in moral terms, but extremely entertaining and convincing in artistic terms. Thus, Pandarus allows Chaucer to introduce all the realism and the middle-class settings expected of medieval popular comic tales. This element represented by Pandarus is no doubt what Chaucer meant by 'comedy'. When Chaucer, at the end of *Troilus*,[13] asks that he be granted the opportunity to write some comedy, it seems likely that what he has in mind are the comic tales that he included in the *Canterbury Tales*, which we sometimes call *fabliaux*. These versions of widespread European medieval popular comic tales are cheerful, derisive narratives of the kind of delinquencies which all right-thinking minds both deplore and find amusing. Their realism of setting, their bawdiness, their ridicule, are reflected in the passages in *Troilus* where Pandarus acts. Such is one element in this tragic poem which Chaucer introduces in order both to extend and deepen the story and to relieve its gloom.

[13] *Troilus and Criseyde*, v. 1787–8.

The other element which the introduction of Pandarus allows is the passivity of Troilus. He is relieved of the need to act and of the need to face the true nature of his actions. Thus, Troilus becomes supremely the man who feels, with the utmost truth and sincerity. This, paradoxically, justifies his love which ends in tragedy, while at the same time allowing it to proceed through its dubious, partly comic, intrigue. In consequence, by the side of the comedy of intrigue we have first the joy and then inevitably the tragedy of personal feeling purified of the need for action. Troilus is of course a great warrior, but we see in him not the active but the contemplative life.

The effect of this deft mixture of, and even more deft division between, comedy and tragedy is to present a remarkably internalized version of the normally externalized medieval concept of tragedy. As already noted, medieval tragedy dealt in persons of high rank, great estate, or great importance (like Adam), who came to sad ends. It was public and external. Much later, in England, in the sixteenth century, tragedy is given a domestic middle-class setting, but this is externally expressed in crime and violent action. By contrast, Troilus, in relation to his tragedy, does nothing and loses nothing objective, neither status, nor power, nor wealth. His tragedy is one of pure and simple feeling. It is hardly even psychologically developed beyond the initial description of his falling in love. Indeed, the unchanging nature of his love, its stability, its constancy, is part of the point. Thus, we have the story of an absolutely stable, powerful, ultimately painfully frustrated passion. The secrecy of Troilus' love (apart from its being known to Pandarus), is essential to its remarkable inwardness, and its inwardness leads to self-examination. Here Chaucer uses the work of the philosopher Boethius in order to present some degree of self-awareness on the part of Troilus in the soliloquy in the temple.[14] The difficulty of this innovation for Chaucer is suggested by some degree of artificiality in both the placing and the style of the soliloquy. The text seems to have been slightly disturbed at both the beginning and the end of the soliloquy, whether or not that soliloquy was, as some have argued, an afterthought; and although Chaucer has done everything he can to assimilate the style to oral delivery (as may be seen by comparing the soliloquy with its equivalent in

----

[14] Ibid., iv. 953 ff.

Chaucer's own prose translation), there is still some awkwardness in placing it in the mouth and mind of Troilus. The sentiments are entirely suited to Troilus' situation and temperament, but their expression lacks the normal lyricism of his complaints and the realism of his dialogues with Pandarus and Criseyde. He is inevitably describing his own feelings as if he were an introspective man, but he is not.

Nevertheless, this soliloquy in the temple is a moving scene of pathos and reflection, marking an important development in the history of self-awareness in English tragedy. It should further be noted that Chaucer here, with great artistry and tact, actually postpones the moment of complete self-awareness. Troilus in the temple will not accept the implicit counter-argument which answers his own fatalistic conviction, and which had been clearly expressed in the source Chaucer was using. This counter-argument in favour of the freedom of the will, whether or not known in logical terms, would certainly have been present not only in Chaucer's mind but in that of any reader or hearer conceivable to him. Full self-awareness of potential human freedom is postponed for Troilus till beyond death. Troilus' tragedy in this life is one of inwardness and self-awareness, unlike any other medieval tragedy, and it is the more tragic because while alive his self-awareness is strictly limited.

Chaucer thus avails himself to the full of the medieval variability of narrative point of view, not only in the course of his poem but also when he comes to the summation, the rounded-off ending which all good story-tellers seek. A story told to a listening audience, even if only so told in imagination as imitated in writing, needs to be wound down, fully closed, commented on, however briefly, just as an Elizabethan tragedy on the open stage needed a slow close in order to carry the bodies off. The events the poet recounts end with Troilus' death, but this leads him to further comment in conclusion. Troilus' fate had not been, as he thought, inevitable. Freedom is within our reach. In particular Chaucer reflects that such tragedy as that of Troilus can now be avoided— this is in fact part of his tragedy—by knowledge of Christian truth, i.e., in Chaucerian terms, by better knowledge of the true self and what it should truly love.

There are, therefore, in this remarkably inward tragic story, further paradoxes relating to the curious mixture of tragedy and comedy. Death is doubly insignificant. First, it is no part of Troilus' actual tragedy, which is his betrayal by Criseyde. Secondly, far from being the expression of utmost misery, death is the conclusion of his woes and the gateway to a better and happier self-realization. The tragedy is a story which can be seen to be set within a poem which itself has a kind of happy ending. The poem can then be seen in the light of the more general medieval notion of comedy. This comedy is not the derisive bawdy comedy of the popular comic tales, which Chaucer obviously enjoyed, nor even a more subtle form of ironic humour, but simply something which accords with the basic requirement of medieval comedy, that it have a happy ending. That is more like our notion of romance than comedy, but Dante had led the way with the title of his own *Commedia*. The insecurity of medieval notions of genre, the mixture of modes and points of view, the disregard for decorum, the pleasure of variety, the paradoxes of suffering and laughter, serve Chaucer well, as they serve Shakespeare. *Troilus* is a tragedy indeed, but interwoven with and encasing the tragedy is a larger sense, call it comedy or romance, of potential human freedom and happiness, a sense indeed of ultimate value which the very existence of tragedy must itself bear witness to. Tragedy cannot exist in a nihilistic universe.

The complexity of this great poem is such that neither label, 'tragedy' nor 'comedy', nor even perhaps 'romance', nor any combination of these terms, can do more than suggest one aspect of its Gothic multiplicity. Through this, Chaucer succeeds in offering a completely new version of the traditional myth of Troilus, one in which the 'tragic' interplay of Fortune and consciousness is counterbalanced by a 'comic' leap beyond death and tragedy, towards a new awareness. It is significant that this very delicate, almost precarious, balance should become a problem in later versions of the story.

6

Classical and Medieval Elements in Chaucer's *Troilus*

BARRY WINDEATT

Go, litel bok, go, litel myn tragedye
. . . . . .
And kis the steppes, where as thow seest pace
Virgile, Ovide, Omer, Lucan, and Stace.[1]

Although such an innovative step forward in the development of the story of Troilus, Chaucer's *Troilus* seeks to cast itself as following in the footsteps of classical forebears. Yet among Chaucer's most distinctive innovations—which relates classical and medieval aspects of the poem—is his drawing together of a singular variety of genres or generic features within the same work. Before Chaucer wrote his *Troilus*, treatments of the story of Troilus may be thought of as falling into particular generic categories, whereas Chaucer's poem achieves a special mixture of different genres. Chaucer's inheritance in the Troilus story of a tradition and succession of sources, of sources in various genres, results in a special inclusiveness of genre in *Troilus and Criseyde* which is a distinctive and characteristic part of its nature, and the outcome of its classical and medieval inheritances. Chaucer's Troilus and his *Troilus* may thus be related to the larger story, the European tragedy of Troilus, by examining the effects and implications of this gathering of genres in the poem—the absorption, combination, quotation, and transcendence of genres—so as to bring out both the classical and medieval aspects of what Chaucer contributes to story and character.

But is it not anachronistic to speak of 'genre' in relation to medieval literature,[2] both in terms of its composition and the ways

---

[1] *Troilus and Criseyde*, v. 1786, 1791–2.

[2] On aspects of genre, see H. R. Jauss, *Toward an Aesthetic of Reception*, trans. T. Bahti (Brighton, 1982), ch. 3, 'Theory of Genres and Medieval Literature'; A. Minnis, *Medieval Theory of Authorship* (London, 1984); A. Fowler, *Kinds of Literature* (Oxford, 1982). Cf. D. Mehl, *Geoffrey Chaucer: An Introduction to his*

Fig. 2. Fifteenth-century French MS of Louis de Beauvau's prose translation of Boccaccio's *Filostrato* (Bibliothèque Nationale, Paris, Fonds des Manuscrits Français 25528). It illustrates *Filostrato*, IV. cxiv–cxx, and Chaucer's *Troilus*, IV. 1149–90. Briseida swoons. Troilus thinks she has died and draws his sword to kill himself. And see p. 69 above.

it would be received by its contemporary audiences and readers? Anachronistic, because of the very scarce formal discussion of matters of vernacular genre surviving from the Middle Ages? Yet there is no need to look further than Chaucer's poems to see that an age lacking in much formal discussion or definition of genre is nevertheless an age of exceptional richness in the use of genres. The *Canterbury Tales*, as a whole and in detail, evidently reveals Chaucer's sense of the possibilities of combination, variety, and contrast of genre, both in the pilgrimage tale-telling and within individual tales.[3] And Chaucer's realization of the *fabliau* as a genre in English—long after that genre's demise in its homeland, and without surviving precedent in England—is only one instance of his acuteness as to the potential in genre.

There is also the evidence of those early readers of *Troilus*—the scribes and glossators of the poem—whose notes in the margins of the extant manuscripts offer a commentary on the text which reveals contemporary alertness at several levels to that inclusiveness of genre deriving from Chaucer's combination of classical and medieval elements.[4] The way in which scribes of some manuscripts carefully notice such transitions as the beginnings of speeches, or the openings and closes of letters, songs, and other lyric units and divisions within the poem is itself a kind of formal commentary which gives recognition to some of the variety of genres in *Troilus*. And just as such scribal commentary on formal divisions has implications for contemporary responses to genre, so also do the scribal commentaries on the sources which they identified behind various passages of the poem.

Through these 'marginal' commentaries of the glossed manuscripts some early readers of the poem will always have been alerted to seeing *Troilus* in relation to sources and models, to a range of classical and medieval authorities which Chaucer has

Narrative Poetry (Cambridge, 1986): 'The poem has been associated with the classical epic, it has been described as a medieval romance, and interpreted as a predecessor of the modern novel. This variety of interpretation alone suggests that it is not strictly modelled on any particular conventional genre but attempts something new' (p. 65).

[3] Cf. Helen Cooper, *The Structure of the Canterbury Tales* (London, 1983), ch. 3, 'An Encyclopaedia of Kinds'.

[4] There is also considerable marginal annotation in some MSS which registers and explains the classical texture of Chaucer's poem: 'Mars deus belli', 'Minerva dea ingenii', 'Pluto deus inferni', 'Aurora amica sol', 'Lamedon pater Priami', etc.

drawn upon, including Virgil, Ovid, Lucan, Statius, Boethius, Dares, Cato, and Alanus de Insulis. Not all such scribal attributions of sources are correct, although a large number are.[5] Virgil is quoted as the source of a passage on fame; Statius is identified as the source of Cassandra's exposition of Theban history, and of the romance of Thebes heard read by Criseyde; Lucan is correctly identified as the source of Criseyde's maxim, but incorrectly as the origin of the invocation of the Furies.[6] A stream of marginal comments identify the origins of Chaucer's allusions to classical myth in Ovid's *Metamorphoses*, sometimes reproducing a line or two of Ovid's text.[7] There are also more speculative comments suggesting a source in Ovid's *Fasti* for Chaucer's allusion to Janus,[8] or the likely Ovidian sources of such allusions as those to Procne or Niobe ('Require in Metamorphosios'). When Pandarus echoes Lady Philosophy on the ass listening to the harp, one scribal commentator correctly refers his reader to Boethius, and some manuscripts include source passages from Joseph of Exeter and a summary of Statius's *Thebaid* adjacent to or even incorporated within the parts of Chaucer's poem based on them.[9]

Such features of the manuscripts are significant in suggesting how some of the very earliest readers of the poem at once recognized that—in varying ways and degrees—classical texts lay behind the *Troilus*. The scribal indications of sources reveal that medieval readers of the poem acknowledged the 'intertextuality' of Chaucer's poem, and with that sense of the intertextual quality of *Troilus*

---

[5] Beside these ll. of *Troilus* the following MSS make the following comments: iv. 659: 'noua infra civitatem currenc' (MS H4, quoting *Aeneid*, iv. 188); ii. 100: 'Require in libro Stach Thebaidis' (MS R); v. 1485: 'Stacius Thebaydos' (MS H4); ii. 167: 'Lucanus' (MS S2); iv. 22: 'Herine | furie infernales unde lucanus me pronuba ducit herinis' (MS H4, citing *Pharsalia*, viii. 90); iii. 721: 'Metamorphoseos x°. capitulo. hos tu care mihi' (MS H4, referring to *Met.* x. 705); iii. 723: 'perlege Methamorphoseos.ii.' (MS H4, referring to *Met.* ii. 833–75); iii. 726: 'Methamorphoseos .I. Vix precatur prece finita & cetera' (MS H4, referring to *Met.* i. 548); iii. 730: 'Methamorphoseos.ii.' (MS H4, referring to *Met.* ii. 722 ff.); iv. 791, H4 quotes *Met.* ii. 61–4; iv. 1138, H4 quotes *Met.* x. 500–1; ii. 77: 'Require in libro Fastorum Ouidii de Jano & cetera' (MS R); i. 701, 714: 'Require in Metamorphosios', 'Require in Ouidio' (MS R); i. 731, 'Baicius | de consolacione philosophie' (MS R); iii. 294: 'Cato' (MSS DgS2); iii. 1415: 'Nota Gallus vulgarus astrologus Alanus de planctu nature' (MS H4).

[6] *Troilus and Criseyde*, iv. 659; v. 1485; ii. 100; ii. 167; iv. 22–4.

[7] e.g. at iii. 721–30; iv. 791, 1138–9.

[8] Ibid., ii. 77.   [9] Ibid., i. 731; v. 799–840, 1498.

comes recognition of the various literary kinds that the poem draws upon and still embodies in itself. While to identify a source is not necessarily the same as acknowledging a role for the genre of that source in the present poem, to notice elements of the *Aeneid*, the *Thebaid*, Dares, or Boethius points to the generic inclusiveness of *Troilus* even when Chaucer's generic 'quotation' is brief.

This sense of intertextuality, and of an inclusiveness of genres, tends to a mutual, interrelating critique between genres: by being included together they ultimately react and comment upon each other. The different terminology used by Criseyde and Pandarus to describe the story of Thebes that is being read to Criseyde when Pandarus visits her suggests that the narrative known to his niece as vernacular romance has been read by Pandarus in its Latin epic form,[10] and this nicely shows an awareness of the double survival of the Theban material as both epic and romance, a mixture Chaucer's poem is itself trying to reflect. In the same scene Criseyde declares she ought to be reading saints' lives; in Book III Pandarus picks up an old romance to read.[11] In Book I he quotes one of Ovid's *Heroides* to Troilus as a piece of contemporary writing; in Book V he apparently alludes to the world of pastoral in dismissing unrealistic hopes.[12] And in the writing of letters and utterance of lyrics by the characters there is recurrent alertness to literary form and kind, as in their sense that of their experience 'Men myght a book make of it, lik a storie'.[13] Framing all, there is the compositional role of the narrating persona, with his concern for his poem in relation to *geste*, *storye*, *tragedye*, and *comedye*.

The inclusiveness of Chaucer's *Troilus* toward literary kinds is the outcome of its place in a particular sequence of texts which represent responses to the same *matière*, and of the expectations Chaucer's audience would consequently have had of a work addressing that subject-matter. It will be helpful to anticipate here in outline that distinctive conjoining of genres created in *Troilus* by Chaucer's combinative use of classical and medieval source elements, before then proceeding to examine the contributing genres.

From their knowledge of the Troilus story in Benoît de Sainte-Maure's *Roman de Troie*, with its special character as a *roman d'antiquité*, Chaucer's early readers would already have a strong

---

[10] Ibid., ii. 100; 108.   [11] Ibid., ii. 118; iii. 980.
[12] Ibid., i. 659–65; v. 1174.   [13] Ibid., v. 585.

sense of this story within the genre of romance. From Guido delle
Colonne's *Historia Destructionis Troiae*, with its imitations in
various 'Troybooks', they would also have a strong sense of how
this particular story existed as part of a history, a sense confirmed
by awareness of Troilus' martial role in the earlier 'historical' narratives of Dares and Dictys, and by various links with epic style.
From *Filostrato* Chaucer absorbs Boccaccio's invention of a beginning for the story, an ascending 'upbeat' action in the narrative of
the first three books which incorporates various generic features of
romance, before the story fulfils its traditional downwards course,
which Chaucer can associate both implicitly and explicitly with
tragedye. Medieval understanding of the genre of tragedy allows
possible associations with contemporary reading of Seneca's plays
as tragic narratives within which dialogue and monologue have an
extensive role, and from this concern with dramatic speech there
also arises a connection with the generic models offered by philosophical dialogue, as in Boethius. Related to this 'dramatic' sense of
the role of speech in the poem is the addition and extension by
Chaucer of material drawing on various lyric genres. These lyrics
express aspects of characterization in *Troilus* which are in turn
counterpointed by Chaucer's incorporation of motifs recalling the
fabliaux, or related comic tales of arranged meetings and seduction, while in the course of the whole poem there are also significant elements both of epic and of allegory.

To accumulate such an outline of the range of genres Chaucer
incorporates into his *Troilus* is not enough to exhaust his uses of
generic quotation, yet is perhaps enough to establish that some
genres inform more of the poem more sustainedly than others.
Romance—that various and inclusive genre—is the ground element
and underlying generic principle, not least by reason of the inherited form of Chaucer's main sources. That Chaucer's earliest
audiences would tend to see his version of the Troilus story in relation to those literary kinds of the story they already knew means
that generic combination and extension would be part of their perception of Chaucer's *Troilus*. Their principal knowledge of the love
story of Troilus would be from Benoît or Guido, or a memory of
both: that is, from a historically minded romance of chivalry at
Troy, or from a redaction of that work which presents its subject
as history. Here is the foundation of Chaucer's poem as romance
and history, even though his direct uses of Benoît rarely rise near

or break the surface of the *Troilus*, and Chaucer's knowledge of Guido remains elusively submerged.

It is through Chaucer's narrative debt to *Filostrato* that some of the most distinctive generic character of *Troilus* is created, both because of what is received from the generic nature of *Filostrato* itself, and because of what *Filostrato* prompts Chaucer towards. It is, after all, Boccaccio who in *Filostrato* has invented a beginning for a story which Benoît and Guido only begin to tell when it is nearly over. Only when Criseyde is about to be exchanged, as a result of events in the Trojan War, do the earlier narratives explore the relationship of Troilus and Criseyde, and not undividedly, but interwoven with other events of the siege. It is Boccaccio who makes what is one of a number of romantic episodes in the older narratives into the sole subject of his *Filostrato* and (as it were) invents 'backwards' to provide with a beginning what is a story about an ending. In so doing he creates a story—in his first three books—with many archetypal features of the ways romances develop in their earlier stages. The beginning of the action in *Filostrato* may be related to many other type-scenes in romance literature, with many stock motifs of plot, episode, and characterization. The hero's first sight of his lady in a church and the process of his falling in love; his languishing and his eventual reluctant confession to a confidant and go-between; the responses of the heroine and her first sight of the lover—all these are type-scenes of romance, and in so far as Chaucer broadly follows the structure and progression of episodes in *Filostrato* he accepts generic features of romance into his poem. Yet, in *Filostrato* Boccaccio is evidently not writing a traditional romance. As the focus is now on the personal, indeed secret, life of the hero, almost no space remains for that chivalrous outward life of the hero as a knight of prowess which is the context for Troilus' love in Benoît's *Roman*. And although the focus of *Filostrato* is on private emotional experience in a way that produces much lyrical writing, this coexists with many 'realistic' effects in the urban and domestic setting of the action.

In terms of genre, Chaucer has accepted much of the structure of *Filostrato*, with its archetypal romance episodes, while overlaying that structure with additions and modifications which consolidate in *Troilus* the ground of romance and the atmosphere of history. But that qualification of romance which *Filostrato* initiated is to be achieved in *Troilus* by a more subtle and extensive conjoining of genres. In effect, Chaucer acts to strengthen the presentation of Troilus' experience as a part of romance in each phase of the poem. In the earliest phase of his falling in love and first being in love, Chaucer colours the account from *Filostrato* with a number of added reminiscences of the Lover in the *Roman de la Rose.*[14] In the central consummation scene of the poem the solemnities of the lovers' vows and exchanges of tokens have suggested a recollection of Boccaccio's *Filocolo*,[15] and the point that Chaucer has made his poem here so resemble a type of Floris-and-Blancheflour romance is more important than whether an actual textual borrowing can be (doubtfully) established. In the fifth book of *Troilus*, where the action runs parallel to that of Benoît's *Roman*, Chaucer has incorporated into his narrative a series of incidents from the French romance which had been dropped by Boccaccio: the conversation of Diomede as he escorts Criseyde from Troy, and the heroine's later soliloquy and the narrative of her change of heart in the Greek camp, are taken into *Troilus* from Benoît, along with such quintessential romance incidents and motifs as the taking of the glove, the gift of a horse, and the token of the lady's sleeve. By acting to move his fifth book back closer to the chivalric texture of the *Roman*, Chaucer seems intent on 'restoring' to his narrative some characteristic features of the genre of romance, along with all that idiom of 'service' by knight to lady within which Chaucer casts the progress and processes of his lovers' relationship.

But although Chaucer thus builds more features of romance into his version of *Filostrato*'s narrative, his own emphasis that the reader must seek elsewhere for the history of Troilus' martial deeds ('Rede Dares') seems to follow Boccaccio's lead in focusing entirely on Troilus' experience in love not war. Yet, we need not take too literally Chaucer's recommendation to look 'In Omer, or in Dares, or in Dite'.[16] The very rehearsal of the names of these 'authorities' on the Trojan War acknowledges the keener sense in *Troilus* of how the action exists in significant relation to a sequence of historical events. Chaucer's sympathetic attempt to re-create some sense of the pagan past within which his characters are acting reflects a real interest in

---

[14] Cf. I. 241–4, 365–6, 637 ff., 743–9, 927–8, 961–2, 1053.

[15] Cf. David Wallace, *Chaucer and the Early Writings of Boccaccio* (Cambridge, 1985), chs. 3 and 4.

[16] *Troilus and Criseyde*, i. 146.

fourteenth-century England in ancient practice,[17] and suggests that Chaucer wants to associate his poem with history-writing, just as his own distinctive alertness to time and change in the *Troilus* narrative reveals in practice a historian's interest.

It is again fruitful to see how this generic extension of *Troilus* may have been prompted by the way Boccaccio's innovations in *Filostrato* challenged the earlier approach of Benoît and Guido to the structure of the story and the role of time within it. In Benoît's *Roman* (followed in this by Guido's *Historia*) the main chronological structure is provided by the successive numbering of the battles during the siege of Troy, and the significant events in the lives of Troilus and Criseyde are placed in relation to reference-points furnished by these battles. In the *Roman*, Benoît carefully prepares the context for the lovers' parting in the knightly careers of Troilus and Diomede, and thus establishes a real connection between the lovers' lives and the sequence of battles, which in his version Guido neglects. Yet, in both *Roman* and *Historia* it remains true that the story of Troilus and Criseyde is narrated within a chronology structured by a 'historical' concern with the siege of Troy. Boccaccio's innovation was that the structure of his poem reflected that span of time significant to the lovers, although Chaucer goes beyond Boccaccio in giving a sharper sense of the chronology, dating, and timing of the action in his poem, in a way that underlines the presentation of *Troilus* as history.

Boccaccio's own response to the Troilus story in selecting and shaping it as an independent unity from the *Roman* and *Historia* shows a concern for time which was in turn to have the effect of a catalyst on Chaucer's own generic modification of the narrative he took over from *Filostrato*. From Benoît and Guido Boccaccio borrowed a story which focused on the ending of a love affair, and, although Boccaccio's own contribution was to fashion a beginning, the expectation of tradition made that sad ending the characterizing part of the story, and the structure Boccaccio creates still serves that expectation. It was a romance that ended unhappily, and Boccaccio's provision of an ascending action to place before that well-known descending action, that 'fall', did not so much diminish as increase the poignant sense of loss in the lovers' emotional downfall. In refashioning that declining action, Boccaccio had also

---

[17] Cf. Beryl Smalley, *English Friars and Antiquity in the Early Fourteenth Century* (Oxford, 1960); Alastair Minnis, *Chaucer and Pagan Antiquity* (Cambridge, 1982).

invented Criseida's promise to Troiolo that she will return to Troy within a specified time. In Benoît and Guido Briseida neither makes nor is asked to make such a promise: she goes to the Greek camp, succumbs to Diomede, and so fades out of the story. It is thus Boccaccio who invents that poignant tension in the last movement of the story as Troilus waits and waits against time—first a definite, measured period, and then an open-ended passage of time.

The structure of the whole action in rise and fall Chaucer takes over broadly from *Filostrato*, for it is Boccaccio who first discerns this pattern in the story, but it is Chaucer who then crystallizes and articulates the generic potential of the structure within which the old story is now perceived. Boccaccio does not open *Filostrato* with Chaucer's anticipation of the arching structure of the *Troilus* narrative in rise and fall ('fro wo to wele and after out of joye'), and it is only Chaucer, not Boccaccio, who refers to the poem at its close as a *tragedye.* In so doing, Chaucer makes even fuller, more explicit acknowledgement of the potential which Boccaccio saw in this story about an unhappy ending, when he first decided to turn an episode in a much longer work into a separate free-standing poem, and thereby to give a different and heightened emphasis to its conclusion. Indeed, the very precociousness of the use of the terms 'tragedy' and 'comedy' in English here[18] conveys Chaucer's interest both in questions of genre in general, and in the new generic associations to which his own rewriting of the Troilus story might attain.

If tragedy was customarily defined in terms of the nature of its ending, it is not so surprising that *Troilus* should be defined as a tragedy so near its narrative close, and as if in response to that close. But since medieval understanding of tragedy is often now remembered in terms of its limits, it is important to retrieve some sense of what Chaucer meant to convey by this belated generic definition of his *Troilus*, and of how a reading of the narrative as tragedy interacts with the many generic features of romance in the poem. To see a love story as the matter of a tragedy would not be unknown, in terms of medieval understanding of classical texts. Chaucer's *House of Fame* suggests he perceived the tragedy of Dido in the *Aeneid*, and in the *Tristia* he could know Ovid's allusions to

---

[18]   *Troilus and Criseyde*, v. 1786–8.

love as the subject of tragedy.[19] Yet, medieval definitions of tragedy do often define the genre in terms of narratives very different in kind from *Troilus*, and this is true of the definitions of tragedy offered elsewhere in Chaucer's works, in the Monk's Prologue and in the *Boece*.[20] Here are the 'standard' definitions of medieval tragedy as a fall from worldly sovereignty, wealth, and well-being through the tragedy of a blindly changeable fortune. As the outlook of the worldly Monk, and as Philosophy's impersonation of Fortune's self-defence, both these definitions are ironic in their contexts, and suggest the irrelevance of 'tragedy' to those who can learn to view this world with proper detachment. Indeed, it is of course possible to imagine that the definition of *Troilus* as a *tragedye* reflects ironically on the too-worldly understanding of a narratorial persona.

But such definitions of tragedy as a fall from prosperity—however prescriptive and reductive—do nevertheless represent a contemporary working definition, and as such could be the norm in terms of which generic 'quotation' and differentiation might be made. The differences between the *Troilus* narrative and the kinds of 'tragedy' represented by Chaucer's *Monk's Tale* or Boccaccio's *De Casibus* hardly need to be spelled out. The private emotional tragedy of Troilus is not the outward political tragedy of a ruler's downfall, and there is every difference in scale, pace, and ampleness of romance narrative between *Troilus*—with its protracted sequence of ending in stages—and the abrupt but predictable turn of Fortune's wheel in the Monk's tales. The inward nature of the hero's real loss, the sense that he still has something that cannot be taken from him, the lack of simultaneity between his emotional downfall and his death: all are rather different from medieval tragedy simply defined, which also fits uneasily with the romance-like copiousness of detail in characterization in *Troilus*, characterization that promotes a sense of freedom of action in the protagonists, even if their behaviour is hard to explain satisfactorily in terms of a 'tragic flaw' of character.

But to echo selective features of a certain genre by 'generic quotation' may be achieved by economical means, and Chaucer

[19] Cf. Andrea Clough, 'Medieval Tragedy and the Genre of *Troilus and Criseyde*', *Medievalia et Humanistica*, 11 (1982), 211–27; Paul G. Ruggiers, 'Notes Towards a Theory of Tragedy in Chaucer', *Chaucer Review*, 8 (1973), 89–99.

[20] Cf. M. E. McAlpine, *The Genre of Troilus and Criseyde* (Ithaca, 1978).

incorporates at key points in *Troilus* some of the tones and motifs of conventional tragedy as if to serve as stylistic pointers to a tragedy more deeply embodied in his development of romance. It is Chaucer who begins his romance with emphasis on the destiny of a foreknown and inevitable ending, and the scene in which Troilus falls in love is elaborated by Chaucer as the fall and punishment of a proud man, the climbing on the stair, the rising of one who does not see the ensuing descent.[21] The turning-point in the lovers' lives is presented in the fourth Proem as the movement of her wheel by a changeable Dame Fortune; the characters are often dramatized in terms of their sense (however mistaken) of participating in a tragedy of Fortune; their sense of the past fate of Thebes only stresses to the reader the characters' unwitting involvement in the present tragedy of Troy. Through echoing some traditional aspects of *tragedye* Chaucer evidently wishes to articulate the philosophical implications of what started simply as a tale of disappointed love in an old romance: the intensely realized sense of human value and loss in the lovers' experience bursts the bounds of the view of worldly life implicit in the conventions of *tragedye*, but these can still be 'quoted' to measure and help define *Troilus*, as a tragedy, against them. It is a paradox that Chaucer shows his interest in genre by using (precociously in English) a generic label which—as applied elsewhere, even in Chaucer's other works—can only diminish *Troilus*. A definition of genre is offered, yet this only suggests the greater reach and inventiveness in genre of the poem of which it is used.

From the tragedies of Seneca—as these were understood and interpreted in the Middle Ages—Chaucer could also derive a powerful model of a tragic narrative.[22] For part of the impact made by *Troilus* lies in its 'dramatic' quality: the way its narrative contains 'scenes' of lively dialogue and vividly observed gesture. The manner in which classical plays were studied by medieval readers possibly had some role in providing a model for Chaucer of such scenic form in narrative, for the works of Roman playwrights were not known through performance but were read as if narratives composed in dialogue. The role thus imagined for the poet as the 'narrator' who recited the Roman play-text while actors mimed the action, is not dissimilar to the deployment of the narrator-figure by

[21] *Troilus and Criseyde*, i. 183 ff.
[22] Cf. John Norton-Smith, *Geoffrey Chaucer* (London, 1974), ch. 6.

some medieval poets, including Chaucer. If Chaucer has changed *Filostrato* by developing a narrator-figure and expressive 'scenes' of dramatic dialogue and encounter, then a central generic model was available in the plays (as read) of the Roman dramatists, interpreted as narratives in dialogue, with scene-division marking off the beginnings and endings of episodes according to the grouping and presence of characters.

It is clear from the marginal glosses in some *Troilus* manuscripts that this dialogic quality of long stretches of the poem was something scribal commentators wished to remark, for some scribes are assiduous in adding in the margin the names of those who are speaking in the text, especially where speakers are alternating in rapid exchanges of dialogue.[23] Such scribal signalling of speech units in the text can give some pages of some *Troilus* manuscripts the appearance of a play-text, and reflects a sense among contemporary readers of *Troilus* of the dramatic nature of the poem in its substantial use of dialogue. From *Filostrato* Chaucer inherits the small cast of characters, and with that a concentration on dialogue and monologue, but he makes this scene structure more dramatic through the impression of autonomy created by the sheer conversational vitality of the speeches—although Chaucer's shaping of scenes is always enfolded within a larger narratorial frame. In this way, the medieval reading of classical drama as narrative, and Chaucer's own use of scenes of very 'dramatic' dialogue within his narrative, make for intriguing resemblances between *Troilus* and medieval understanding of the genre of Seneca's tragedies.

But other models for dialogue were, indeed, available to Chaucer from other genres, and it is evident that in several parts of *Troilus* the exchanges between characters reflect the influence of that form of philosophical dialogue found in Boethius's *De Consolatione Philosophiae*. Here the use of a source brings with it a 'quotation' of the genre of that source, for at key points Chaucer inserts and develops scenes of extended, serious, and rather formal

---

[23] Thus, MS H5 identifies speakers by writing their names at relevant points in the margin, as in these dialogues: i. 568, 'Troylus'; i. 582–3, 'Pander'; i. 596–7, 'Troylus'; i. 617, 'Pandare'; i. 820, 'Troylus'; i. 829, 'Pandarus'; i. 834, 'Troylus'; i. 841, 'Pandarus'. In MS H4 speech units and dialogue are also often remarked by marginal commentary, e.g. at iv. 827, 'Verba Cressaidis P.'; iv. 875, 'Verba P. C.'; iv. 897, 'Verba C. P.'; iv. 1527, 'Responsio .C.'; v. 117, 'Verba Diomedis Cressaide'; v. 218–19, 'Verba T. in absentia C.' MS S1 also contains much signalling of speakers by marginal notes.

dialogue which has no place in Boccaccio's narrative. The dialogue between Troilus and Pandarus in the second half of Book I is an instance of this: the scene much extends the discussion between Troiolo and Pandaro from *Filostrato* and is full of quotations of Boethian phrases and arguments, just as it develops Pandarus' role towards Troilus with echoes and quotations of Philosophy's role towards the prisoner Boethius in their dialogues in the *Consolation*. In both texts there is a dialogue with somebody metaphorically deaf and sick. The scribe of the Rawlinson manuscript of *Troilus* who notes that this passage is from Boethius shows that medieval readers registered Chaucer's 'quotations' and read his poem in some relation to its sources and their genres, just as in some later dialogues between Troilus and Pandarus, or Pandarus and Criseyde, a sense of the Boethian model allows such scenes in a romance narrative to be read in relation to the Boethian genre of philosophical dialogue constructed without narrative around the participants' direct speech.

Direct speech, personal expression, brings us to the lyric nature of *Troilus*—its relation to various types of lyric genre—for this is an aspect of the generic identity of Chaucer's poem which is insufficiently recognized. It has been natural to admire *Troilus* as a narrative poem, but to admire its strongly and formally lyric nature is in no way to qualify such admiration for Chaucer's narrative achievement. Indeed, *Troilus* is often distinguished from *Filostrato* in a way that misleadingly implies that the 'autobiographical' framework used by Boccaccio (which Chaucer drops) makes the Italian poem more 'lyrical' in nature than the English. While it is true that *Troilus* is not presented as an expression of the poet's own experience in love, Chaucer does increase the formal lyric nature of his poem, both absorbing and adding to the sequence of lyric pieces already included in the Italian narrative. Moreover, Chaucer works to establish a context in which lyric set pieces become part of the accepted self-expression of his characters. All such changes to the ways lyric genres are used within the narrative are contained within an added emphasis on the formal lyric framework to the poem through its Proems.

What models would Chaucer have for a form that mixed narrative and lyric genres? In the *dits amoureux* of Machaut, which he undoubtedly knew well from his earliest days as a poet, Chaucer would know a form in which lyric genres are used so extensively as to subordinate the narrative element to the role of a supportive framework which contains and orders the elaborate lyric set pieces.[24] When given as a performance, a poem like Machaut's *Remède de Fortune* would have had some of the effect of an opera, and shows some operatic relation between narrative and lyric pieces.[25] There are many echoes in mood and theme between *Troilus* and the *Remède de Fortune*, a fourteenth-century poem which focuses on the aspirations of a lover and on how he is comforted and counselled in Boethian terms by Lady Esperance. Yet *Troilus* still has too strong a narrative impetus and shape to qualify as itself being a *dit amoureux*, and that narrative momentum which can pause over but 'contain' its lyric passages resembles, and derives essentially from, *Filostrato*. In *Filostrato* Boccaccio includes lyric passages, but these are written uniformly in the same metrical form of *ottava rima* as the rest of the poem, so that narrative and lyric are not formally distinguished. In this way Boccaccio subordinates lyric to narrative through versification in a manner quite different from the *dits amoureux*, where one of the pleasures lies in the rehearsal in the lyrics of varied and elaborate verse forms, metrically distinct from the narrative of the work. In *Troilus* Chaucer is at first glance following Boccaccio's method of a uniform versification for narrative and lyric, yet the contemporary associations of Chaucer's rhyme-royal stanza were probably still more with lyric than narrative forms, so that, where Boccaccio versifies narrative and lyric uniformly in an essentially narrative verse form, Chaucer versifies narrative and lyric uniformly in an apparently more lyric verse form. Despite the uniform versification, it is also noticeable that the lyric passages in *Troilus* are more carefully distinguished than in *Filostrato* from the surrounding narrative—by occasional rubrication and by references within the text to the beginning and ending of lyric pieces—and this suggests in Chaucer a sense of the specialness of the lyric genres embedded within the flow of the narrative. In the sense that Chaucer has made *Troilus* a more extendedly lyrical narrative, the *dits amoureux*

---

[24] Cf. James I. Wimsatt, 'The French Lyric Element in *Troilus and Criseyde*', *Yearbook of English Studies*, 15 (1985), 18–32.

[25] Cf. John Stevens, 'The "Music" of the Lyric: Machaut, Deschamps, Chaucer', in *Medieval and Pseudo-Medieval Literature*, ed. Piero Boitani and Anna Torti (Tübingen and Cambridge, 1984), 109–29. Cf. also John Stevens, *Words and Music in the Middle Ages* (Cambridge, 1986).

may indeed have served as the ultimate model of a genre that mixed narrative and lyric, just as the *Consolation* worked by alternating discussion with lyric. In the light of such models Chaucer extends the lyric element in *Filostrato*, and in so doing he has extended the 'medieval' elements in his own poem.

In the *Remède de Fortune* the role of the numerous and elaborate lyric pieces is to allow voice to the quintessential 'sentiment' of the lover, just as in *Troilus* Chaucer incorporates lyric pieces at various key emotional points in the action—which is not to say that lyric in its medieval courtly form acts simply as a symptom of individual feeling.[26] At the point where Boccaccio reports in passing that Troiolo sang a song in his bewildered state after falling in love,[27] Chaucer provides as the verbatim text of the song a translation of Petrarch's sonnet made over into the usual verse form of *Troilus*. In Book II it is Chaucer's idea to have his heroine listen to a courtly lyric sung by her niece Antigone.[28] This lyric is evidently a tissue of phrases and ideas recollected from various lyrics of Machaut, and it is striking that Chaucer makes such a direct verbal 'quotation' from the world of Machaut's lyrics here and only here in the poem, where Criseyde is moving inwardly towards accepting love. Chaucer's third book is especially studded with lyric pieces, which Chaucer is either adding or developing from a slight hint, as with the *aubades*, or lyrics complaining at the departure of night and the coming of day, which both the lovers utter after their first night of love.[29] It is essentially Chaucer's idea to include these lyrics here, which in form echo the three-stanza patterns of the courtly *ballade*, and in their highly formal, rhetorical expression of feeling bring within Chaucer's *Troilus* a relatively rare example in English of the medieval genre of the dawn-song. Through Chaucer's adding and augmenting of lyric pieces in this way in the first three books a momentum of lyric expression is set up which is continued in the later books.

In the margins of some *Troilus* manuscripts there are glosses in

[26] Cf. Stevens: 'The lyric forms were fixed because the feelings were fixed . . . The manifold references to *sentement* do not mean that courtly song had to express individual, particular experience. Indeed, if one were to call Machaut's lyrics "beautifully wrought public gestures", one would be nearer the truth', ('The "Music" of the Lyric', pp. 114–15).

[27] *Filostrato*, l. xxxvii; *Troilus*, i. 400–20.

[28] Ibid., ii. 827–75.

[29] Ibid., iii. 1421 ff.

Latin or English which offer definitions of lyric genres recognized by scribes within the narrative they are copying. Such marginal noticing of lyric genres often suggests an individual response, beyond the limits of that lay-out of rubrics and incipits in the poem which probably stems from the poet. The words *Cantus*, *Littera*, *envoy*, and *testamentum* are added in the manuscript margins at appropriate points,[30] and another lyric form noted in these marginal commentaries is *compleynt* or *lamentacio*.[31] With this the scribes draw attention to a distinctive strand in Chaucer's use of lyric genres in *Troilus*, and one which adds a distinctively medieval element.

A tendency to lament and 'complain' formally is augmented in Chaucer's poem, and even where it already exists in *Filostrato* Chaucer furnishes more careful definition, noticing the beginning and ending of such complaints, as do some scribes in their marginal commentaries ('Here maketh Troylus his compleynt upon Fortune . . .'; 'How Cressayde complaynyd'). The act of making 'complaint' in a courtly context may naturally be the impetus behind such lyric forms as songs or letters. In Chaucer's *Troilus* more frequent *compleynt* thus forms a greater part of the protagonists' characteristic behaviour, in both the ascending and the declining actions of the poem: Chaucer's Troilus complains before he gains Criseyde; he complains, as she does too, after they know they must part, and this structure of complaint is noted by the glossing scribes in their marginal commentaries and analyses of the generic

---

[30] In addition to the rubrics for songs and letters which probably derive from the poet, individual scribes also show an interest in signalling lyric units, as in the following marginal notes: i. 658: 'Littera Oenone' (MS S2); i. 659: 'Cantus Oenonee' (MS S1); ii. 875: 'Explicit Cantus' (MS H4); ii. 1065: 'Littera Troili Cressaid' (MS H4), 'Prima littera Troilus missa ad Criseid' (MS S1); ii. 1085: 'Her endes Troylus his first lettyr' (MS S1); v. 295: 'The testament of Troilus' (MS R), 'Testamentum Troili' (MS S2); v. 1421: 'Finis littere Troili' (MS H4); v. 1425: 'Risponcio Criseidis' (MS S1); v. 1855: 'Lenuoye Du Chaucer' (MS H3).

[31] 'Nota bene de Troily how he complenit . . .' MS S1 at v. 1674. Cf. the following marginal comments: i. 547: 'How Pandar fond Troilus compleynyng' (MS R); ii. 526: 'How Pandar tolde Crisseide that Troilus pleind to loue' (MS R); iii. 1422: 'How Cresseyde sorowed whan day gan for tapproche' (MS R); iii. 1424: 'Nota verba .C. in aurora' (MS H4); iv. 260: 'Here maketh Troylus his compleynt upon fortune' (MS S1); iv. 729: 'How Cresseyde comp[ley]nyd for she shuld departe oute of Troye' (MS R); iv. 743: 'lamentacio .C.' (MSS H4, Ph, S2); v. 1674: 'Nota bene de Troily how he complenit' (MS S1); v. 1681: 'complent'; 1688: 'complent'; 1695: 'complent' (MS S1).

units in the text.[32] In the latter books Criseyde's various lamentations, either augmented by Chaucer or added, are carefully presented as formal *compleynt* ('How myghte it evere yred ben or
ysonge, | The pleynte that she made in hire destresse?'), and even
Troilus' predestination soliloquy may be seen as a *compleynt* in
these terms.[33] In the fifth book Troilus' laments, on the places of
Troy, and outside the deserted house of Criseyde—an example of
paraclausithyron, itself a classical lyric genre—are considerably
elaborated by Chaucer from their Italian originals, just as Chaucer's
careful rewriting of Troilus' sorrowful letter to Criseyde, and his
invention of a last letter from Criseyde show the significance he
saw in the lover's epistle as a lyric genre.[34]

If the formal 'complaint' is part of Chaucer's incorporation of
more lyric genres into the narrative framework of his *Troilus*, this
is a reflection of the shifts in characterization and motivation from
Filostrato, where Troiolo and Criseida—more active and assertive
characters—are not so much disposed to that passive lamentation
which in Chaucer's characterization leads to a somewhat different
balance of genres within his poem. This more passive character to
the English lovers does in turn prompt further incorporation by
Chaucer of quite different, almost antithetical, generic elements.
For the way in *Filostrato* that Troiolo and Criseida proceed to meet
and go to bed together did not square with Chaucer's reinterpretation of their characters. And in inventing the action in *Troilus*
by which Pandarus as go-between brings Troilus and Criseyde to
bed together Chaucer draws on elements of plotting and characterization which resembles the genres of *fabliaux* and sundry comic
tales in which a go-between practices deceptions to accomplish the
meeting and union of lovers. The resemblances in outline and in
some details to the Latin *Pamphilus*, and perhaps to its later
versions in French, establish enough common ground for Chaucer
perhaps to intend an echo, a kind of 'generic quotation', with its
implicit comparison of the action in *Troilus* with the typical
actions in such kinds of tale.[35] In the *Pamphilus* the go-between

---

[32] At i. 547 in MS R: 'How Pandar fond Troilus compleyning'; at ii. 526: 'How
Pandar tolde Crisseide that Troilus pleind to loue'.

[33] *Troilus and Crisseyde*, iv. 742 ff.; iv. 825–47; iv. 799–800.

[34] Ibid., v. 561 ff.; v. 540 ff.; v. 1317 ff., 1590 ff.

[35] Cf. T. J. Garbáty, 'The *Pamphilus* Tradition in Ruiz and Chaucer', *Philological Quarterly*, 46 (1967), 457–70; T. J. Garbáty, '*Pamphilus, De Amore*: An Intro-

invites the girl to a meal at her house, and the youth is already waiting there, gets the girl to bed, and achieves his desire. In so many respects—of detail of texture, and of delicacy—Chaucer's *Troilus* is far removed from this, and yet at the same time it does approximate to the *Pamphilus* in some motifs in the character of the go-between, and in the archetypal pattern of the plot which bridges Books II and III. It is here that *Troilus* recalls something of the *fabliaux*, in the way that this part of the poem acquires a sharp focus on that physical setting which has such a direct bearing on the successful momentum of the action: the 'stewe' where Troilus waits, the drawn 'travers', the 'trappe-dore', the 'pryve wente', the cushion, the 'chymeneye', the curtained bed. The sudden actions, the sheer virtuosity of manipulation and contrived appearance, the darting and leaping about: all seem to bring near to the action of *Troilus*—with whatever implication—the associations of the world of the *fabliau* genre which Chaucer evidently knew so well.

Any such echo in *Troilus* of elements of *fabliau* remains a rather localized quotation of a genre in particular parts of the poem. For while genres like romance and lyric are being developed throughout the poem, other kinds of quotation of genre occur much more locally in special contexts, although the effects of such 'quotation' of genre spread beyond immediate context and contribute to the impression of the whole poem. This may be said of Chaucer's use in *Troilus* of elements of epic and of allegory.

When Chaucer at the close of *Troilus* tells his poem to follow after, and kiss the footprints of, such writers of epic poetry as Virgil, Homer, Lucan, and Statius, he echoes the very words with which Statius bids his epic *Thebaid* to follow in the footsteps of his revered model, the *Aeneid*. And when Chaucer opens his poem declaring its subject as 'The double sorwe of Troilus to tellen . . .' he is evidently picking up on the words with which, in Dante's *Purgatorio*, the poet Virgil addresses Statius, referring to how the latter has in his *Thebaid* written of the double sorrow of Queen Jocasta in the Theban wars, where her two sons killed each other.[36] The poem's opening promise to tell of Troilus 'That was the kyng Priamus sone of Troye' also has the Virgilian sweep and ambition

duction and Translation', *Chaucer Review*, 2 (1967), 108–34; G. Mieszkowski, 'Chaucer's Pandarus and Jean Brasdefer's Houdée', *Chaucer Review*, 20 (1985), 40–60.

[36] *Purgatorio*, xxii. 55 ff.

of the opening of an epic poem. Both in opening and in closing his poem Chaucer in this way recalls something of the epic dignity of Statius' poem and associates it with his *Troilus*, as well as invoking by name Calliope, Muse of epic poetry—with whatever ironic effect—at the beginning of that third book which describes the consummation of the lovers' affair. For the overall ambitiousness of scale and dignity of form with which the romance tale of Troilus is presented has some of the manner of epic writing, if not its normal focus and subject. Chaucer's generic quotation from epic in *Troilus* is at a number of levels, for the formal echoes of epic machinery betoken a thematic absorption into *Troilus* of conceptions of destiny and human character in the epic writing best known to Chaucer, like that of Statius.[37] From Statius Chaucer could recall the epic machinery of invocation, a view of the pagan gods and of the boundaries of human efforts, while—especially in the last books—there are contexts in which Chaucer associates the experience of his Troilus with that of epic heroes,[38] despite the disclaimer that he is writing of anything other than his life as a lover.

The implication of echoing and quoting so many genres in *Troilus* is that Chaucer sees so many levels of potential meaning in his story. For each genre in a sense represents a view of experience in the way that it distinctively orders it, organizes and expresses it, and to evoke a number of genres is to suggest dimensions and layers of significance. One might not readily think of *Troilus* as including elements of allegory, and yet the ambitious Proems that Chaucer has added for each book—to go no further—prepare us to see the narratives of each book that we are just about to read in terms of larger patterns than those of the immediate surface of the story. The first Proem is especially striking in this way, as lovers in the audience are urged through reflection to relate the story of Troilus to their own experience and sympathize with those in like suffering, while the narrator prays for his own success in representing the sorrows of all love's folk via this particular adventure of Troilus ('... to shewe, in som manere, | Swich peyne and wo as loves folk endure | In Troilus unsely aventure ...').[39] Again, in the second Proem the pointed explanation of meaning reminds the reader that the action is in part being represented by figurative

---

[37] On Statius, cf. Winthrop Wetherbee, *Chaucer and the Poets* (Ithaca, 1984).
[38] *Troilus and Criseyde*, v. 827–40.
[39] Ibid., i. 33–5.

means ('This see clepe I the tempestous matere | Of disespeir that Troilus was inne'). In this way the Proems acknowledge that the poem is presenting us both with a particular narrative and also with a framework of interpretation. And, in the way that the inner life of the lovers is represented, especially that of Troilus, there is some quotation and echo from the kind of texts (like the *Roman de la Rose*) which convey the inner psychological processes by means of allegory. An elusive effect of 'layers' of both character and archetype in the protagonists of Chaucer's *Troilus* will often suggest to the reader that the text is being 'shewed hym in figure'[40] in a poem so written to alert its reader to the need and the enigma of interpretation. This does not suffice, of course, to make *Troilus* an allegorical poem, any more than some of the other noted echoes and motifs of style and content turn *Troilus* into an epic, or a drama, or an opera, or a history book.

What kind of controlling purpose may then be perceived behind the exceptional richness of literary kinds, of genres, echoed and incorporated in *Troilus*? It is hardly possible to discuss *Troilus* without mentioning Boethius, and the dialogue form of the *Consolation* may itself be seen as an example of the genre of Menippean satire, questioning not so much deviations from an ideal standard but the very possibility of ideal standards on earth.[41] Granted the influence of the *Consolation* on Chaucer, it is certainly possible to see the play of genres in *Troilus* as operating through the poem in a kind of Menippean satire on the attitudes and outlooks to life of its characters. A sense of differing attitudes as crystallized in genres is achieved cumulatively as the poem progresses and is seen as a whole. As in the *Canterbury Tales*, the poem gains in richness and comprehensiveness of implication by containing those varying interpretations of experience represented by the genres, at last concluded by the striking ending or 'Epilogue', itself a remarkable juxtaposition of generic features. The Middle Ages may show scant interest in defining genres, but an age which in England produced and enjoyed *Piers Plowman* or the mystery plays was not shy of transcending genres, for a genre is in part a point of view, a structured perception, and both a style and a style of life, and a combination of genres realized both a critique of possibilities and a wisdom, as Chaucer knew.

[40] Ibid., v. 1449.
[41] Cf. F. Anne Payne, *Chaucer and Menippean Satire* (Madison, 1981).

7

Chaucer's *Troilus*: Philosophy and Language

When Eustache Deschamps calls his friend Geoffrey Chaucer a 'Socrates enlightening England with his philosophy' in one of his poems,[1] he is no doubt referring to Chaucer the 'Boethian poet'. Chaucer admired Boethius, 'l'anima santa che 'l mondo fallàce | fa manifesto' (the blessed soul that exposes the deceptive world), as Dante calls him in his *Divina Commedia*,[2] and like the Tuscan poet he had studied the *Consolation of Philosophy* in depth. In translating Boethius' most influential work Chaucer was following in the footsteps of another philosophical poet, Jean de Meun, the learned continuator of the *Roman de la Rose*, whose French translation of *De Consolatione Philosophiae* he undoubtedly knew. Boethius' concern with the relationship between free will and predestination is also Chaucer's, so much so that those interested in this question are referred to Chaucer's *Troilus* by Love in Usk's *Testament of Love*:

Myne owne trewe servaunt, the noble philosophical poete in Englissh . . . in a tretis that he made of my servant Troilus, hath this mater touched, and at the ful this question assoyled.[3]

Thomas Usk must have been one kind of reader Chaucer had in mind when he wrote his *Troilus*, a reader who, like 'moral Gower' and 'philosophical Strode', to whom he 'directed this book',[4] would appreciate his explicit and implicit 'philosophizing' of the Troilus story.[5] Ralph Strode was probably the ideal reader. He is

---

[1] See W. W. Skeat (ed.), *The Complete Works of Geoffrey Chaucer*, 6 vols. (Oxford, 1894), vol. I, pp. lvi–lvii.

[2] *Paradiso* x. 125–6; quoted from Dante Alighieri, *La Divina Commedia*, ed. and annot. C. H. Grandgent, rev. C. S. Singleton (Cambridge, Mass., 1972). As far as possible I have taken over the translations given in the notes of this edition.

[3] W. W. Skeat (ed.), *Chaucerian and Other Pieces* (Oxford, 1897), 123.

[4] *Troilus*, v. 1856 ff.

[5] On the meaning of *moral* and *philosophical* see J. H. Fisher, *John Gower:*

mostly remembered as a logician, less as an opponent of Wyclif's determinism, but he was also, according to a note discovered by John Leland in a fifteenth-century *vetus catalogus* of the fellows of Merton College Oxford, a 'nobilis poeta', hence capable of appreciating Chaucer's *Troilus* on all levels, in its 'art poetical' as well as in its 'resonyng of Goddes purveyaunce'.[6]

Strode's philosophical contributions lay in the field of logic. He was, like Pandarus, a man who could 'wel and formely arguwe'.[7] That this particular side of his scholarly activity is implied by the epithet 'philosophical' is shown by the variant readings found in two manuscripts of *Troilus*, in which Strode is called 'sophistical' instead.[8] This characterizes Strode's logic accurately in its highly formalized and sophisticated nature. Strode was, in the words of one of his commentators, 'the weightiest author of all logicians'.[9] Of his logical writings only his theories of *consequentiae* and *obligationes* have come down to us. In these late scholastic developments of Aristotelian syllogistic logic the emphasis is on laying down general rules which guarantee the validity of an inference. These rules are developed and discussed in painstaking minuteness and detail; they show, says C. Prantl in his voluminous history of Western logic, a 'hair-raising comprehensiveness'.[10]

It is highly unlikely that Chaucer had read these technical and specialized treatises; but he certainly knew Strode as a logician and he knew of the formal and complex nature of contemporary logical theory, of the *sophismata* or 'sophymes' as the Squire calls them.[11] There is a large amount of reasoning and argumentation to be found in *Troilus*, some of it fairly involved and probably a sheer delight to a fourteenth-century logician. In particular the dialogues between Pandarus and Troilus breathe the air of scholastic disputation. Already, in their first encounter, Pandarus goes through the 'contraries' like a dialectician, and the repeated occurrences of

Moral Philosopher and Friend of Chaucer (New York, 1964), 225–6. On Chaucer's connection with Strode and the 'Men of Merton' see J. A. W. Bennett, *Chaucer at Oxford and at Cambridge* (Oxford, 1974), 58 ff.

[6] *Troilus*, iv. 1046.   [7] Ibid., iv. 497.
[8] BL Harley 3949, Bodl. Lib. Rawl. poet 163.
[9] See C. Prantl, *Geschichte der Logik im Abendlande*, 4 vols. (Leipzig, 1855–70), iv. 45 n. 175.
[10] Prantl, p. 45. On the theory of consequences see also P. Boehner, *Medieval Logic: An Outline of its Development from 1240–c.1400* (Manchester, 1952), 52–75.
[11] *Squire's Tale*, l. 554. Cf. Bennett, *Chaucer*, pp. 82–3.

words like 'argument' and 'argue', 'prove', 'conclusion', and 'fyn of entent' emphasize the deliberative and argumentative element in the protagonists' actions.[12] When Chaucer apostrophizes Strode, however, he is, of course, not asking him to subsume the various arguments of his characters under the twenty-four rules of formally valid inferences (*consequentia bona formalis*). What Chaucer seems to have in mind is rather a reader who would and could appreciate the philosophical dimension of his work, including the more technical aspects of the philosophical terms employed; and both 'philosophical Strode' and 'moral Gower' qualify as such readers.

This philosophical dimension is indeed the most distinctive feature of Chaucer's version of the Troilus story. The poem is characterized by the many explicit references to Boethian thought, as well as by the frequent occurrence of terms with a complex philosophical tradition behind them.[13] Although Chaucer's use of philosophical terminology is neither systematic nor rigorous, it is by no means unintentional and accidental. It provides a continual gloss on the text, true to the Summoner's precept that 'Glosynge is a glorious thyng, certayn'.[14] The semantic ramifications of 'complex words' establish a philosophical meta-discourse, they constitute, in Nathalie Sarraute's terms, a kind of medieval *sous-conversation* to the *conversation* of the narrative.

The most striking instance of philosophizing is clearly Troilus' long speech on free will and predestination in Book IV.[15] Of all Boethian references in *Troilus* this is the longest, disproportionately so, it would seem, with over 100 lines of pure metaphysics.[16]

---

[12] *Troilus*, i. 638 ff. On 'contraries' and dialectics in Chaucer and Boethius see P. Elbow, *Oppositions in Chaucer* (Middletown, Conn., 1975), esp. pp. 49 ff., 114 ff.

[13] Most if not all studies of Chaucer's *Troilus* have stressed his indebtedness to Boethius; the basic investigation of Boethian influence on Chaucer remains B. L. Jefferson, *Chaucer and the Consolation of Philosophy of Boethius* (Princeton, NJ, 1917). For an interpretation of *Troilus* as a companion piece to the *Consolatio* see J. P. McCall, 'Five-Book Structure in Chaucer's *Troilus*', *Modern Language Quarterly*, 23 (1962), 297–308.

[14] *Summoner's Tale*, l. 1793.   [15] *Troilus*, iv. 960–1078.

[16] This passage has been repeatedly interpreted, both in relation to the meaning of *Troilus* as a whole and in relation to Chaucer's alleged determinism. Particularly influential were the studies by H. R. Patch, 'Troilus on Determinism', *Speculum*, 6 (1931), 225–43; M. W. Bloomfield, 'Distance and Predestination in *Troilus and Criseyde*', *PMLA* 72 (1957), 14–26, and W. C. Curry, *Chaucer and the Mediaeval Sciences*, 2nd edn. (New York, 1960), 241–98. They are all repr. in R. J.

Although these verses, with their convoluted syntax, do not
always make for easy reading, Troilus' argumentation is yet fairly
straightforward: if there are two alternative future events A and B
and God foresees A, then A must occur and B is, given God's perfection, an impossibility. Even if God's foreknowledge has not
caused A to happen, the future is yet determined by divine predestination, and hence there is no room for a free will. The necessity of an event, grounded in, though not caused by, God's
foreknowledge, is illustrated by an analogy. If a proposition is true
then the state of affairs it describes must be the case, otherwise it
could not be characterized as being true. This does not mean that
the man is sitting out there in reality, because my proposition
expressing this fact is true (it is rather the other way round), but he
really must be sitting there if I truly affirm this.

When set against philosophical thought in fourteenth-century
England, this passage could be read and commented upon from a
variety of points of view, ranging from Scotist voluntarism and
indeterminism to the theological determinism of Thomas Bradwardine and John Wyclif. Man has a free will, teaches John Duns
Scotus, precisely because his will alone is the cause of his willing,
but, continues Bradwardine in *De Causa Dei*, free will is ultimately
'necessitated' by God: man's acts might be free from secondary
causes, but they are necessarily dependent on the *causa prima*. [17]
This question is intimately linked to the logical problem of the
relationship between true propositions and facts. The 'cause of
soth of this | Comth of his sittyng', says Troilus.[18] It would be inter-
esting to speculate which kind of cause he means. Pandarus is more
explicit when he asks for the 'final cause' (*causa finalis*) of Troilus'
woe in Book I, as is Criseyde when she sees in Pandarus the 'cause
causyng' (*causa causans*) of her first joy in Book IV.[19] The theory of

Schoeck and J. Taylor (eds.), *Chaucer Criticism: II: Troilus and Criseyde and The
Minor Poems* (Notre Dame, Ind., 1961).

[17] For a summary see G. Shepherd, 'Religion and Philosophy in Chaucer', in
D. Brewer (ed.), *Geoffrey Chaucer* (London, 1974), 262–89, esp. pp. 272 ff. On
Duns Scotus see É. Gilson, *Jean Duns Scot* (Paris, 1952), 574 ff.; on Bradwardine see
G. Leff, *Bradwardine and the Pelagians: A Study of his 'De Causa Dei' and its
Opponents* (Cambridge, 1957), 98–109; on Wyclif see J. A. Robson, *Wyclif and the
Oxford Schools: The Relation of the 'Summa de Ente' to Scholastic Debates at Oxford in
the Later Fourteenth Century* (Cambridge, 1961), 171 ff.; A. Kenny, *Wyclif* (Oxford,
1985), 31–41.

[18] *Troilus*, iv. 1041–2.   [19] Ibid., i. 682; iv. 829.

truth behind Troilus' argumentation is in any case the familiar correspondence theory of truth, defining a true proposition, with Aristotle, as saying 'that that which is is and that which is not is not'.[20]

As is well known, the logical conclusion reached by Troilus is
refuted by Philosophy in the *Consolatio*. The argument from analogy is not valid: divine foreknowledge cannot be compared to
human knowledge. Boethius' whole theory of the relationship
between free will and predestination hinges on this difference
between divine knowledge or *intelligentia* and human knowledge
or *ratio*. It is precisely because God's knowledge transcends human
knowledge that free will is not ruled out by divine foreknowledge.[21] The metaphysical problem of determinism versus free will
is seen to be based in Boethius' thinking on the problem of knowledge; at the core of metaphysics lies epistemology.[22]

This epistemological aspect of the *Consolatio* is, I think, important for a better understanding of Troilus' long speech on predestination. The scholastic rigidity of his argumentation might be
compared to some of the doctrinal lectures in the *Paradiso*. But,
while these are part of a highly patterned poetical structure, com-
ponents of a larger philosophical and visionary exposition of
ultimate reality, the artistic propriety of Troilus' monologue has
been more than once called in question. It is certainly related to the
theme of the poem as it emerges from the plot itself: the prob-
lematical relationship between human hopes and wishes and the
workings of the world, the conflict between man's aspirations and
Fortune's wheel, the uncertainty of human love and its question-
able nature *sub specie aeternitatis*. But, for all that, three stanzas on
'the man sitting by the sea' seem curiously out of place—unless
they are taken seriously.

[20] *Metaphysics* 1101b25. C. Kirwan, trans., *Aristotle's 'Metaphysics': Books Γ, Δ, and E* (Oxford, 1971), 23. On the correspondence theory of truth see A. D. Woozley, *Theory of Knowledge: An Introduction* (London, 1949), 125–49.

[21] Boethius, *Consolatio*, v, Prose 6.

[22] For a concise exposition of Boethius' philosophy see H. Chadwick, *Boethius: The Consolation of Music, Logic, Theology, and Philosophy* (Oxford, 1981). For Boethian influence on medieval philosophy see H. R. Patch, *The Tradition of Boethius: A Study of his Importance in Medieval Culture* (New York, 1935); P. Cour-celle, *La Consolation de Philosophie dans la Tradition Littéraire: Antécédents et Posté-rité de Boèce* (Paris, 1967). On the relationship between Boethian epistemology and *Troilus* see also L. Eldredge, 'Boethian Epistemology and Chaucer's *Troilus* in the Light of Fourteenth-Century Thought', *Mediaevalia*, 2 (1976), 49–75.

Troilus' soliloquy with all its pedantic long-windedness is first and foremost 'doctryne'.[23] As such it is clearly 'intertextual' in the Structuralist sense, all the more so as Chaucer has hardly disguised his source, taking over almost *verbatim* his own translation of the *Consolatio.* The passage refers back to Boethius and invites a reading of Chaucer's text against its point of reference. In its original context, the discussion of the relationship between a true proposition and a fact is linked with a distinction into three kinds of human knowledge and a refutation of the Stoic view of the mind as a *tabula rasa.*[24] These epistemological issues are not only at the core of Boethius' argumentation, they also play an important role in the meta-discourse of Chaucer's *Troilus.*

This is already apparent in the first Book. The Boethian echoes range from the portrayal of Pandarus as a somewhat mundane version of Dame Philosophy, comforting the lover, and from invocations of Goddess Fortuna and her wheel, to more veiled and subtle allusions to the concepts of free will and foreknowledge, such as when it is said of Calchas, 'this forknowynge wise', that he knew of the destruction of Troy, 'wolde whoso nolde', or of Troilus that he thought that nothing could affect him 'ayeyns his wille'.[25] But Pandarus is also the Ami of the *Roman de la Rose*, just as Troilus is the Amant, showing like Arcite all the signs of the 'loveris maladye | Of Hereos'.[26] As in the *Filostrato*, Troilus' love at first sight is couched in the conventional language of medieval love poetry, with Amor having his 'dwellynge | Withinne the subtile stremes' of Criseyde's eyes.[27]

Despite the pervasive tone of love poetry in the first Book, there is a shift of emphasis in Chaucer's text towards reflection and analysis. This shift is, however, already foreshadowed in Boccaccio's *Filostrato*. After coming back from the temple Troiolo tries to remember what he has seen (*rammentarsi*), and begins to reason about his love for Criseida (*argomentava*).[28] Remembering and reasoning are faculties of the mind repeatedly underlined in the

[23] See C. S. Lewis, 'What Chaucer Really Did to *Il Filostrato*', *Essays and Studies by the Members of the English Association*, 17 (1932), 56–75; repr. in Schoeck and Taylor, pp. 16–33.
[24] Boethius, *Consolatio*, v, Metre 4.
[25] *Troilus*, i. 79, 77, 227–8.
[26] *Knight's Tale*, ll. 1373–4.
[27] *Troilus*, i. 304–5.
[28] *Filostrato*, i. xxxiii, i. xxxv.

poem. As in Chaucer's *Troilus*, the dialogues between Troiolo and Pandaro in particular are in an argumentative, reasoning vein, as when Pandaro attempts to give good reasons for Troiolo not to be unhappy about Criseida's departure.[29] The conclusive *dunque* of his argumentation (*gli argomenti miei*) is countered by Troiolo's equally rational retort (stanzas liii and lv begin with *dunque*), refuting Pandaro's pseudo-logic (*tu favelli divisatamente*, 'you talk rationally'), which had affirmed that loss is less painful than not having.[30] It is interesting to note in this context that *ragione*, 'reason', and *cagione*, 'cause', are frequently recurring words in the *Filostrato*, in some stanzas even standing as a rhyming pair.[31]

By the same token, the imagery associated with the heart as the 'brestes ye', elaborated in Chaucer,[32] is also present in Boccaccio. Troiolo carries Criseida's image painted in his heart (*dov' io porto dipinta | l'immagine*), a beautiful image which makes him think only of her: *l'immagine bella| di te sempre nel cor reca un pensiero.*[33] Remembering and re-seeing in the mind are particularly poignant after the lovers' separation. Although Criseida remembers (*memorando ... ricordando*),[34] it is above all Troiolo who continually thinks of his beloved and sees her again in his heart and in his mind:

> e 'l suo bel viso e le parole ornate
> nel cuore e nella mente figurava

[and her beautiful face and her eloquent words he saw painted in his heart and in his mind].[35]

Troilus too, when he comes back from the temple, re-sees what he had experienced, 'gan it newe avise':

[29] *Filostrato*, iv. xlvi ff.

[30] Ibid., iv. xlix; lxiv; lvi.

[31] e.g. vi. xv; vii. l; ix. i.

[32] i. 453. For a study of the imagery connected with the heart in *Troilus* see S. L. Clark and J. N. Wasserman, 'The Heart in *Troilus and Criseyde*: The Eye of the Breast, the Mirror of the Mind, the Jewel in its Setting', *Chaucer Review*, 18 (1984), 316–27.

[33] *Filostrato*, ii. lviii; ii. xcix, cf. iii. lxvii.

[34] Ibid., vi. ii.

[35] *Figurare* has both the meaning of 'making a figure' and 'seeing (as a figure), picturing'; Mario Marti glosses *figurava* here by *immagina corposamente*; cf. Giovanni Boccaccio, *Opere Minori in Volgare. ii. Filostrato, Teseida, Chiose al Teseida*, ed. M. Marti (Milan, 1970), 177. (Quotations from the *Filostrato* are, however, from Branca's edn.). Cf. also Chaucer's *refigure* in v. 473.

Thus gan he make a mirour of his mynde,
In which he saugh al holly hire figure[36]

The 'mirour of the mynde' is also found in Chaucer's translation of
the *Roman de la Rose*,[37] where it enables the lover in the absence of
the beloved to have Swete-Thought (Dous Pensers) for his companion. This expression, with all its conventional ring, is, however,
found neither in the *Filostrato* nor in the French *Roman de la Rose*; it
comes from the *Consolatio*, the 'epistemological' Metre 4 of Book V.
Equally Boethian is Pandarus' comparison of Troilus to an ass who is
incapable of hearing music as anything but noise.[38] Pandarus sums
his criticism up with the words: 'Now knowe I that ther reson in the
failleth'.[39]

'Reson' is the key term in the philosophical gloss implicit in the
text. If Troilus lacks reason in his love for Criseyde then, according
to Boethius, he has only exercised the subordinated faculties of cognition, sense perception (common to all living beings), and imagination (common to all living beings endowed with the power of
movement). Boethius makes these distinctions in that part of his
Consolatio to which Chaucer's text repeatedly points. It is found in
a passage which begins with the words: 'The reason for this error
is . . .',[40] by error meaning the mistake Troilus makes in the fourth
Book when he wrongly deduces a deterministic view of man's
actions from God's foreknowledge. The Boethian distinction into
sensus, *imaginatio*, and *ratio* is based on Aristotelian hylomorphism.
By the lowest type of cognition we perceive material objects—i.e.
matter put into definite shapes by form—with our external senses.
Through the power of *imaginatio* we see the shapes of objects only,
stripped of their *materia. Ratio*, finally, permits us to see the form of
things, not the form that characterizes an individual object (the particular red of this particular flower), but the general form that
transcends individual forms (i.e. the universal red as such).[41]

---

[36] *Troilus*, i. 364; i. 365–6.   [37] *Romaunt of the Rose*, l. 2806.
[38] *Troilus*, i. 730 ff.   [39] Ibid., i. 764.   [40] *Consolatio*, v, Prose 4.
[41] See also Chaucer's trans. of this passage. R. A. Peck, 'Chaucer and the
Nominalist Question', *Speculum*, 53 (1978), 745–60, interprets Chaucer's poetry
in the framework of Occam's thought on the basis of this distinction (pp. 747–9).
The similarities between Chaucer and Occam are, however, mostly, if not solely,
due to Chaucer's acquaintance with Boethius; see Peck's nn. 7, 15, and 37. For a
detailed account of *wit*, *ymaginacioun*, and *resoun* in Chaucer see also J. D.
Burnley, *Chaucer's Language and the Philosophers' Tradition* (Cambridge, 1979),

Chaucer translates *sensus* by *wit*. This word occurs about forty times in *Troilus*, but never in the Boethian sense of the five (outer) wits. As C. S. Lewis has shown, the broad range of meanings of wit reflects a complex semantic development.[42] The most common meanings in *Troilus* are the ones already present in Old English *witt*: (1) 'mind, reason', as when Troilus threatens to go 'out of his wit', and (2) 'understanding, intelligence', as when Criseyde is, before her tête-à-tête with Troilus, at her 'wittes ende'.[43] Chaucer does, however, emphasize the sensual origin of Troilus' love of Criseyde when he elaborates Boccaccio's text along the lines of an 'impression'-theory of vision:

> And of hire look in him ther gan to quyken
> So gret desir and such affeccioun,
> That in his hertes botme gan to stiken
> Of hir his fixe and depe impressioun.[44]

This looks like the theory Boethius attributes to the Stoics,[45] who maintained that external objects leave their impression (*imprimi*; 'weren enpreintid' in Chaucer's translation) on the mind, similar to the letters imprinted on a wax tablet or written 'in parchemyn'. But, Boethius continues, impression is not all. The mind is not just passive like a mirror, it is also active in that it orders and interprets the impressions it receives.

Chaucer is, I think, aware of this Platonistic trait in Boethius' thinking. The 'fixe and depe impressioun' is only possible because of 'so gret desir and such affeccioun' aroused by Criseyde's look, and when Troilus later recalls Criseyde by exercising his power of *imaginatio* he does not *have* a mind like a mirror, but he *makes* a mirror of his mind. Nevertheless, Chaucer's emphasis is not on the *vis activa* of the mind, connected to *ratio* in Boethian thinking, but on the imaginative power of the mind, which sees individual forms only. What Troilus sees in the mirror of his mind is indeed a *forma*

103 ff. On *imaginatio* see also R. Quirk, 'Vis Imaginativa', *Journal of English and Germanic Philology*, 53 (1954), 81–3.

[42] See C. S. Lewis, *Studies in Words* (Cambridge, 1960), 86 ff. This is one of the rare cases where Chaucer does not use a loan-word for the translation of philosophical terms; compare Olga Fischer, 'A Comparative Study of Philosophical Terms in the Alfredian and Chaucerian Boethius', *Neophilologus*, 63 (1979), 622–39.

[43] *Troilus*, iv. 230; v. 1262; iii. 931.

[44] Ibid., i. 295–8.

[45] *Consolatio*, v, Metre 4.

individualis—Criseyde, or rather, 'al holly hire figure'.[46] *Imagi-natio* is here intimately related to remembering, the recalling of sense impressions and past experience. This aspect of *imaginatio* is also stressed in the fifth Book when after Criseyde's departure Troilus, like Troiolo, 'refigures' her shape and remembers the sound of her voice, and Criseyde, like Criseida, 'portrays' Troilus' worthiness and 'records' his words.[47] An image in the mind can, however, also be created by words alone, as when in Chaucer's *Man of Law's Tale* the description of Custance is enough for the Sultan 'To han hir figure in his remembrance'.[48]

Imagination plays an important role in Troilus' relationship to Criseyde. The key term here is *fantasye*. *Ymaginacioun*, the word Chaucer uses in his Boethius translation, does not occur in *Troilus*, but the verb *imaginen* is found eight times. It corre-sponds to Italian *immaginare*, a verb describing the workings of Troiolo's mind, as when he thinks (*Immaginando*), that it is well worth suffering and sighing for Criseida (cf. the corresponding passage in Chaucer i. 372, *Imaginynge*) or when he imagines drawing sweet water from her eyes to cool his desire; Criseida 'makes images' in her mind as well; for instance, when she thinks of Troiolo after Pandaro has sung his praises (*Troiol immagi-nando*).[49] The noun *immaginazione* is only once used, in reference to Cassandra's prophetic gift, which is criticized by Troiolo, while Calchas' foreknowledge is once pejoratively termed *fan-tasia*, a word also employed by Pandaro to disprove the validity of Troiolo's dream.[50]

The Aristotelian concept of *phantasia* lies at the basis of the Boethian concept of *imaginatio*, so that Chaucer's use of the word *fantasye* is quite in line with Boethian thinking. According to Aristotle's *De Anima*, *phantasia* is a movement originating in perception (Boethius' *sensus*), and the *phantasmata* it creates can be both true and false.[51] These *phantasmata* or images are not only intimately connected to sense perception, but also to the *vis activa* of the mind. This is made clear in the detailed discussion of Book V, Metre 4 in the Boethius commentary by Nicholas Trivet. It is highly probable that Chaucer used this commentary for his translation of the *Consolatio*, and it seems therefore apposite to

[46] *Troilus*, i. 366.
[47] Ibid., v. 473; v. 579–80; v. 716 ff.
[48] *Man of Law's Tale*, l. 187.
[49] *Filostrato*, i. xxxv; i. xli; ii. lxviii.
[50] Ibid., vii. lxxxix, iv. xxxviii, vii. xl.
[51] *De Anima*, 429ᵃ1.

summarize Trivet's (and his sources') views on the relationship between perception, image, and Platonic idea.[52]

With reference to Aristotle's *De Anima*, and within an Aristotelian framework, Trivet attempts to justify the Platonic bias of Boethius' thought. Knowledge (*intellectio*) consists in abstraction, more precisely in abstracting the universal from the particular, in 'seeing' the intelligible form (*species intelligibilis*). This is done by the active intellect (*intellectus activus*). In order to perform its intellectual operations, it needs to be aroused by perceived images, so that Trivet can say: 'There is no knowledge without turning to *phantasmata*' (*non fit intellectio nisi per conversionem ad fantasmata*).[53] This is also Aquinas' position and phrase in the *Summa Theologiae*.[54] Unlike Aquinas, and Aristotle, Trivet posits, with Boethius, innate ideas in the receptive intellect (*intellectus possibilis*), which for Aristotle was a *tabula rasa*. He can thus maintain with Boethius that the perceived images are in the process of cognition 'applied' to the innate Platonic ideas.

In no other work by Chaucer is *fantasye* found as often as in *Troilus*. The word never translates a specific term in the *Filostrato*; in fact, in over half of its thirteen occurrences there is no corresponding passage in Boccaccio's text. *Fantasye* characterizes first and foremost Troilus, but it is also used in connection with other characters. Hector entertains *fantasies* in the sense of unrealistic,

---

[52] On Chaucer's probable knowledge of Trivet's commentary see K. O. Petersen, 'Chaucer and Trivet', *PMLA* 18 (1903), 173–93; A. Minnis, 'Aspects of the Medieval French and English Traditions of the *De Consolatione Philosophiae*', in M. Gibson (ed.), *Boethius: His Life, Thought, and Influence* (Oxford, 1981), 312–61; 342. On Trivet see F. Ehrle, SJ, 'Nikolaus Trivet, sein Leben, seine Quolibet und Quaestiones ordinaciae', in *Abhandlungen zur Geschichte der Philosophie des Mittelalters: Festgabe Clemens Baeumker zum 70. Geburtstag* (Münster, 1923), 1–63. One of the problems discussed by Trivet is 'Utrum intellectus abstrahit suum obiectum ab obiecto sensuum particularium immediate vel mediante fantasmate' (Whether the intellect abstracts its object from the object of the individual senses directly or via *phantasmata*); Ehrle, p. 57.

[53] MS Paris, Bibl. Nat. lat. 18 424, f. 157rb; this MS contains Boethius' text, Jean de Meun's French translation and Trivet's commentary, thus representing the kind of MS Chaucer might have used for his translation.

[54] Thomas Aquinas, *Summa Theologiae* 1 q.85 a.1. For a discussion see A. Kenny, 'Intellect and Imagination in Aquinas', in A. Kenny (ed.), *Aquinas: A Collection of Critical Essays* (London, 1969), 273–96; cf. M. L. Colish, *The Mirror of Language: A Study in the Medieval Theory of Knowledge*, rev. edn. (Lincoln, Nebr., 1983), 170 ff.

impractical ideas, when he wants to keep Criseyde in Troy; and
Criseyde, 'the ferfulleste wight | That myghte be', has fears in her
fantasye that more might be required of her than she is—as yet—
willing to give.[55] Pandarus does, however, succeed in overcoming
her fears; he has, as he tells Troilus, 'in my nece yput this fantasie, |
To doon thi lust and holly to ben thyn'.[56] *Fantasye* is here glossed
as 'desire', just as Troilus in Shakespeare's play calls his love to
Cressida *fancy* and affirms: 'Never did young man fancy | With so
eternal and so fix'd a soul'.[57] It is important to realize that this
fancy is based on imagination, not that of a healthy person, however, but rather the imaginings of those suffering from the lovers'
malady. 'And al it is Malencolie, | Which groweth of the fantasie |
Of love', confesses the lover in Gower's *Confessio Amantis.*[58] This
'humour malencolik', we are told in the *Knight's Tale*, has its seat in
the 'celle fantastik' of the brain.[59]

This is indeed Troilus' disease, not just at the beginning of the
narrative, when he wastes away in canonical fashion as diagnosed
by Ibn Ḥazm in the eleventh century in his *Dove's Necklace*:

Another sign of love is the predilection for solitude and preference for
being alone. Also, an excessive thinning of the body without any fever, or
any illness that would prevent a change for the better.[60]

Troilus is after all the young lover, though perhaps not as young
and innocently impressionable as in the classical tradition—or in
the second act of Jean Giraudoux's *La guerre de Troie n'aura pas lieu.*
It is in particular in the fifth Book that references to Troilus' *fantasye* denote these imaginings of the suffering lover, complaining

[55] *Troilus*, iv. 193; ii. 450–1; ii. 482. On Criseyde's states of mind see D. R.
Howard, 'Experience, Language, and Consciousness: *Troilus and Criseyde*, ii, 596–
931', in J. Mandel and B. A. Rosenberg (eds.), *Medieval Literature and Folklore
Studies: Essays in Honor of Francis Lee Utley* (New Brunswick, NJ, 1970), 173–92.

[56] *Troilus*, iii. 275–6.

[57] *Troilus and Cressida*, iv. iv. 24; v. ii. 164–5. On Middle English *fantasye* see
MED, s.v. *fantasie*, sense 5; *fancy* in Shakespeare's *Troilus and Cressida*, iv. iv. 24, is
glossed in the Arden edn. by K. Palmer as 'love; sometimes with the implication
fancy + fantasy (love + the imaginative power it engenders)' (p. 236).

[58] iii. 125–7. Quoted from G. C. Macaulay (ed.), *The English Works of John
Gower*, 2 vols., EETS ES 81, 82 (London, 1900–1).

[59] *Knight's Tale*, l. 1376. See J. L. Lowes, 'The Loveres Maladye of Hereos',
Modern Philology, 11 (1913–14), 491–546.

[60] Quoted from A. R. Nykl, *Hispano-Arabic Poetry and its Relations with the Old
Provençal Troubadours* (Baltimore, 1946), 82.

so pitiably 'That wonder was to here his fantasie'.[61] Although Pandarus urges Troilus to drive out his 'swevenes ek and al swich fantasie', and persuades him to seek distraction at Sarpedon's court, the lover's state of mind only gets worse, to the point of whimsicality, when it 'was his fantasie' to forbid all music in his presence[62]—apparently, unlike Monsieur Jaques in *As You Like It*, unable to 'suck melancholy out of a song'. While in his 'first sorrow' the symptoms of *amor hereos* had a basis in reality—Troilus' loss of appetite 'shewed in his hewe'[63]—he now grows pale and is beginning to wither away in his imagination only:

> And of hymself ymagened he ofte
> To ben defet, and pale, and waxen lesse
> Than he was wont[64]

Phantasmata and *imaginatio* are here clearly pathological, hardly steps to knowledge in the scholastic sense:

> And al this nas but his malencolie,
> That he hadde of hymself swich fantasie.[65]

The truth value of other *phantasmata* created by Troilus' imagination earlier in the narrative might be equally false, but his *fantasye* is there of a different nature. In the third and fourth Books it is linked to Troilus' jealousy and lack of faith in his beloved, at first feigned, then real. After their first love-night Criseyde warns Troilus that he must not indulge in any false imaginings concerning her, in whose heart he is now deeply engraved:

> Lat in youre brayn non other fantasie
> So crepe, that it cause me to dye![66]

Earlier on she had already told him that even justified jealousy 'and som swich fantasie' should be repressed.[67] And later she replies to Troilus' affirmation that Calchas will never return—he says: 'To trusten on nys but a fantasie'—that he must not mistrust her: 'Drif out the fantasies yow withinne, | And trusteth me . . .'.[68]

It is ironic that in these cases Troilus entertains for once no fantasies in the sense of false imaginings: his premonitions are quite realistic and they turn out to be only too true. So, there is in a way

---

[61] *Troilus*, v. 261.   [62] Ibid., v. 358, v. 329; v. 461.
[63] Ibid., i. 487.   [64] Ibid., v. 617–19.   [65] Ibid., v. 622–3.
[66] Ibid., iii. 1504–5.   [67] Ibid., iii. 1032.   [68] Ibid., iv. 1470, iv. 1615.

no need for Criseyde to appeal to his reason—'And forthi sle with resoun al this hete!'—reason which paralysed him at the council meeting, when he should have pleaded for Criseyde's stay in Troy, and which opposed his desire to ravish his beloved.[69] And it is equally ironic that Cassandra should not be believed, as always when she speaks the truth. She only provokes Troilus' anger and disbelief:

> Thow wenest ben a gret devyneresse!
> Now sestow nat this fool of fantasie
> Peyneth hire on ladys for to lye?[70]

Despite the conventional character of the lovers' sickness, and despite the non-technical use of the term *fantasye*, in *Troilus*, the emphasis on *imaginatio* as opposed to *ratio* is none the less clearly marked. It is not the *imaginatio* of the philosophers, neither in the Boethian sense of the cognition of individual forms without matter nor in the sense of the scholastic theory of abstraction. But the opposition of appearance and reality, imperfect knowledge by *imaginatio*. and perfect knowledge by *ratio*, does refer back to the ascending scale of knowledge as sketched in the *Consolatio* and elaborated in Trivet's commentary. It is only after his death that Troilus is able to climb the top rung of this ladder, when he looks down on earth from the eighth sphere and finally sees 'with ful avysement'.[71]

This last *gradus ad parnassum* follows logically from the philosophical gloss on the story and is carefully prepared for in the course of the narrative. Troilus' vision 'with ful avysement' harks back to the beginning of his love for Criseyde, when he was 'Ful unavysed of his woo comynge', and, while he was incapable then of recognizing sound as melody, he can now hear the harmony of the spheres: 'herkenyng armonye | With sownes ful of hevenyssh melodie'.[72]

---

[69] *Troilus*, iv. 1583; iv. 164; iv. 572–4. In the *Filostrato*, Troiolo, 'il timido donzello' (the timid youth), is also torn between *amore* and *ragione*; iv. xvi. For this tension between reason and desire see S. Wenzel, 'Chaucer's Troilus of Book iv', *PMLA* 79 (1964), 542–7.

[70] *Troilus*, v. 1522–4.

[71] Ibid., v. 1811. Troilus' progress from 'sensual ignorance to intellectual insight' is stressed in particular by J. M. Steadman, *Disembodied Laughter: 'Troilus' and the Apotheosis Tradition: A Reexamination of Narrative and Thematic Contexts* (Berkeley, 1972), 66 f., 75 f., 139 f.

[72] *Troilus*, i. 378; i. 731–5; v. 1812–13.

The epistemological implications of the Boethian example of the ass and the harp[73] are quite manifest:

> Or artow lik an asse to the harpe,
> That hereth sown whan men the strynges plye,
> But in his mynde of that no melodie
> May sinken hym to gladen, for that he
> So dul ys of his bestialite?[74]

Chaucer seems to be indebted to Trivet here, who says that

similar to asses are men who, when they hear meaningful utterances, use their ears only in order to listen, but not their mind in order to understand the meaning.[75]

Troilus' argumentation in his long monologue in the fourth Book is wrong in its Boethian context. Free will and divine foreknowledge are compatible, as Dante's forefather puts it in Canto XVII of the *Paradiso*:

> La contingenza, che fuor del quaderno
> de la vostra materia non si stende,
> tutta è dipinta nel cospetto etterno;
>
> necessità però quindi non prende
> se non come dal viso in che si specchia
> nave che per torrente giù discende.

[Contingency, which does not extend beyond the volume of your matter, is depicted in its entirety in the eternal vision; but it does not derive inevitability therefrom, any more than a boat going downstream from the eye in which it is mirrored.][76]

Man realizes his freedom to the fullest when he seeks after the *summum bonum*, but he is in danger of losing this freedom when, instead of looking up 'into the sovereyn day (that is to seyn, into cleernesse of sovereyn good)', he looks down, like Orpheus, 'into the put of helle'.[77]

---

[73] *Consolatio*, i, Prose 4.   [74] *Troilus*, i. 731–5.

[75] '... unde asinis similes sunt homines qui audientes sermones rationabiles tantum prebent aures ad audiendum non animum ad percipiendum intellectum'. MS Bibl. Nat. 18 424, f. 14ᵛᵃ. This passage is also printed in Minnis, 'Aspects', p. 342. I am grateful to Mrs Silk for supplying me with her husband's MS collation of Trivet's commentary.

[76] *Paradiso*, Canto xvii. 37–42.

[77] *Consolatio*, iii, Prose 12; iii, Metre 12.

True knowledge is the realization of this goal:

But the soules of men moten nedes be more fre whan thei loken hem in the speculacioun or lokynge of the devyne thought; and lasse fre whan thei slyden into the bodyes; and yit lasse fre whan thei ben gadrid togidre and comprehended in erthli membres. But the laste servage is whan that thei ben yeven to vices and han ifalle fro the possessioun of hir propre resoun. For aftir that thei han cast awey hir eyghen fro the lyght of the sovereyn sothfastnesse to lowe thingis and derke, anon thei derken by the cloude of ignoraunce.[78]

And this is, of course, what Troilus is seeing now: that man should not follow his 'blynde lust', but cast his 'herte on heven', on the measure of all things, 'the pleyn felicite | That is in heven above'.[79]

'Pleyn felicite' is the 'contrarie' of 'fals felicite'. Ironically, it was Criseyde herself who had warned against 'fals felicite', in a speech that counterbalances Troilus' monologue on free will and determinism, both in its argumentative style and its indebtedness to Boethian thought.[80] Those who, like Troilus, strive after the 'joie of worldly thyng' are not only mistaken, Criseyde affirms, they are also barred from true knowledge, they are 'of ignoraunce ay in derkenesse'.

In the tradition of the Troilus story the closest parallel to this interplay between narrative and gloss, story and commentary in Chaucer's Troilus is found in Shakespeare's play.[81] The emphasis has shifted from the philosophical theme of free will versus determinism to other, no less philosophical, topics. Order as expounded by Ulysses in a long speech on Degree[82] can be compared to the role love plays in Boethian thought,[83] and Time—'Injurious Time' in Troilus' words, 'that old common arbitrator, Time' in Hector's—is linked to the theme of transience and mutability, in short Fortune's wheel, or 'fortune's tooth':

For beauty, wit,
High birth, vigour of bone, desert in service,

[78] Consolatio, v, Prose 2.   [79] Troilus, v. 1818–19, cf. 1823–5.
[80] Ibid., iii. 813 ff.
[81] For a comparison between Chaucer and Shakespeare see M. C. Bradbrook, 'What Shakespeare Did to Chaucer's Troilus and Criseyde', Shakespeare Quarterly, 9 (1958), 311–19; D. Mehl, Shakespeare's Tragedies: An Introduction (Cambridge, 1986), 220 ff.
[82] Troilus and Cressida, i. iii. 75 ff.
[83] See E. M. W. Tillyard, The Elizabethan World Picture (London, 1943; Harmondsworth, 1963), 18 ff.

> Love, friendship, charity, are subjects all
> To envious and calumniating Time.[84]

The clearest echo of Troilus' monologue on free will in Chaucer is probably Hector's speech in Act II, when he rejects both Troilus' and Paris' reasons for keeping Helen, since they do not 'make up a free determination | 'Twixt right and wrong'.[85] Hector refers to Aristotle, and it can be argued that Aristotle's *Nicomachean Ethics* has exerted a noticeable influence on Shakespeare's play.[86]

More subtly, the epistemological issues of Chaucer's *Troilus* are also present in *Troilus and Cressida*, transformed and stressed differently. Achilles contributes to the epistemological theme when he explains, in a scholastic vein, that beauty cannot view itself but must be seen just as the eye cannot see itself but needs to be reflected:

> For speculation turns not to itself
> Till it hath travell'd and is mirror'd there
> Where it may see itself.[87]

The contrast between reason and madness, truth and imagination is embodied in various characters of the play. Ajax is represented as a 'purblind Argus, all eyes and no sight', a fool that 'knows not himself', and Achilles is shown to be immobilized by his self-deception, 'Imagin'd worth'.[88]

As in Chaucer's poem, Troilus suffers from the lovers' malady: 'I tell thee I am mad | In Cressid's love'.[89] Hector quite appropriately asks him:

> Or is your blood
> So madly hot, that no discourse of reason,
> Nor fear of bad success in a bad cause,
> Can qualify the same?[90]

In the deliberation scene of Act II, Troilus qualifies everything he finds dishonourable as unreasonable and expounds his own 'voluntarist' position: choice is made on the basis of will, 'enkindled' by

---

[84] *Troilus and Cressida*, IV. iv. 41; IV. v. 224; IV. v. 292; III. iii. 171–4.
[85] Ibid., II. ii. 171–2.
[86] See app. iii in the Arden edn. (pp. 311–20).
[87] *Troilus and Cressida*, III. iii. 109–11.
[88] Ibid., I. ii. 30–1; II. i. 68; II. iii. 173.   [89] Ibid., I. i. 51–2.
[90] Ibid., II. ii. 116–19.

the senses, not by judgement.[91] His senses are enchanted by 'Th'imaginary relish' before meeting Cressida, but later, when witnessing Cressida's tryst with Diomedes, he has to suppress his sense perceptions:

> I will not be myself, nor have cognition
> Of what I feel: I am all patience.[92]

Indeed, Troilus cannot—and will not—believe what his senses tell him; in order not to lose his reason he must deny Cressida's presence ('my negation hath no taste of madness'[93]), or at least *his* Cressida's presence:

> If beauty have a soul, this is not she;
> If souls guide vows, if vows be sanctimonies,
> If sanctimony be the gods' delight,
> If there be rule in unity itself,
> This is not she. O madness of discourse,
> That cause sets up with and against itself![94]

Truth has become 'wither'd'[95] both as the human value of fidelity and as the philosophical goal of true knowledge. If Troilus' truth becomes proverbial, so does Cressida's falseness.

Returning to Chaucer: we found that there was a progression from blindness to sight (and from seeing what there is not, as in v. 1158, to seeing what there is), from deafness to hearing, from *fantasye* to *resoun*. If such a progression is recognized, the praise of divine love and reprobation of 'feynede love' at the end of the poem will not come as a surprise.[96] Much in the love-relationship between Troilus and Criseyde is indeed feigned, both in the sense of 'contrived' and of 'fictitious'. But love is also celebrated in the poem. Troilus' love of Criseyde is not just 'lust',[97] *pace* Troilus in heaven and D. W. Robertson.[98] It is also an ennobling love:

---

[91] Ibid., II. ii. 62 ff.
[92] Ibid., III. ii. 17; v. ii. 63-4.
[93] Ibid., v. ii. 126.   [94] Ibid., v. ii. 136-42.
[95] Ibid., v. ii. 46.
[96] *Troilus*, v. 1848.
[97] Ibid., v. 1831.
[98] See D. W. Robertson, *A Preface to Chaucer: Studies in Medieval Perspectives* (Princeton, NJ, 1962), 472 ff. Diametrically opposed to Robertson's interpretation is Tatlock's view that the 'feeling in the Epilog is in no way foreshadowed at the beginning or elsewhere ...': J. S. P. Tatlock, 'The Epilog of Chaucer's *Troilus*', *Modern Philology*, 18 (1921), 625-59, 636.

And this encrees of hardynesse and myght
Com hym of love, his ladies thank to wynne,
That altered his spirit so withinne.[99]

In the Proem to the third Book there are echoes from Guido
Guinizelli's famous *canzone* 'Al cor gentil rempaira sempre amore',
which cannot be overlooked ('Plesance of love, O goodly debon-
aire, | In gentil hertes ay redy to repaire!').[100] And when Troilus and
Criseyde are finally united in love, the narrator comments that
'Felicite'—whether 'pleyn' or 'fals'—

which that thise clerkes wise
Comenden so, ne may nought here suffise;
This joie may nought writen be with inke;
This passeth al that herte may bythynke.[101]

This Proem is based on a passage in Boccaccio's *Filostrato* which
in turn, like Chaucer's *Canticus Troili* later in the third Book, goes
back to the *Consolatio*, Boethius' neo-Platonistically inspired
hymn on love as the binding force of the universe.[102] Boethian
thinking permeates, then, not only the rejection of earthly love in
the Epilogue, but also its praise in the preceding narrative. The tension remains, but the relationship between contrasting conceptions is more subtle than can be captured by simple dichotomies
such as that between divine and earthly love; nor can it be reduced
to the opposition between the true point of view of the Christian
narrator and the false points of view of the pagan *dramatis personae*.[103] The philosophical gloss cuts through this distinction and is

[99] *Troilus*, iii. 1776-8.   [100] Ibid., iii. 4-5.   [101] Ibid., iii. 1691-4.

[102] *Consolatio*, ii, Metre 8. For an interpretation of these passages as cele-
brations of human love see W. Wetherbee, *Chaucer and the Poets: An Essay on
'Troilus and Criseyde'* (Ithaca, NY, 1984), 46-52. Cf. also D. Mehl, *Geoffrey
Chaucer: An Introduction to his Narrative Poetry* (Cambridge, 1986), 80 ff. For a
Boethian interpretation see I. L. Gordon, *The Double Sorrow of Troilus: A Study of
Ambiguities in 'Troilus and Criseyde'* (Oxford, 1970), 30-40.

[103] This is basically the position of Bloomfield, 'Distance and Predestination',
modified by D. R. Howard, 'The Philosophies in Chaucer's *Troilus*', in L. D.
Benson and S. Wenzel (eds.), *The Wisdom of Poetry: Essays in Honor of Morton W.
Bloomfield* (Kalamazoo, Mich., 1982), 151-75. Gordon, *Double Sorrow*, sees the
position of the Epilogue as 'implicit in the ironies of the narrative' (p. 55). On the
relationship between the narrator's point of view and the narrative see also
D. Mehl, 'Chaucer's Narrator: *Troilus and Criseyde* and the *Canterbury Tales*', in
P. Boitani and J. Mann (eds.), *The Cambridge Chaucer Companion* (Cambridge,
1986), 213-26, esp. 215-20.

embodied in the language, in the speech of the protagonists as well as in the authorial comments of the narrating voice.

This language is rich in semantically complex terms, with varying philosophical implications in the history of ideas. As readers we are invited to 'use our discretion',[104] to explore these implications, follow the intertextual pointers the text gives, let ourselves be provoked into thought by the philosophical meta-discourse inherent in the poem. If we take the bait which the 'hier in philosophie | To Aristotle'—as Hoccleve calls Chaucer[105]—has thrown out, we can, I think, discern the epistemology underlying Boethius' solution of the problem of predestination and free will, and we can see its reflection in the poem. But Chaucer's *Troilus* is for all that no allegory on Wit, Ymaginacioun, and Resoun; however philosophical our reading, it remains what it was in Chaucer's main source: an intensely moving story of human love.

[104] *Troilus*, iii. 1331 ff.
[105] In his *Regiment of Princes*; quoted from C. F. E. Spurgeon, *Five Hundred Years of Chaucer Criticism and Allusion, 1357-1900*, 3 vols. (Cambridge, 1925), i. 22.

8

True Troilus and False Cresseid: The Descent from Tragedy

C. DAVID BENSON

The supreme expression of the tragedy of Troilus and Criseyde is Chaucer's poem of that name, and three other major British poets subsequently treat the theme: Henryson, Shakespeare, and Dryden. The eminence of these names obscures a wider, less ambitious, and more casual use of the story in the late Middle Ages and Renaissance.[1] In the first three centuries after its composition, *Troilus and Criseyde* was by far Chaucer's most popular and most frequently cited work (with Henryson's *Testament of Cresseid* generally considered to be Chaucer's own conclusion after 1532), but few of those who use the poem show any understanding of its thematic and artistic complexity. *Troilus* seems to have intimidated later writers: many acknowledge its greatness while being unable or unwilling to respond to its challenges. Most references to Troilus and Criseyde in the fifteenth, sixteenth, and early seventeenth centuries are brief and undeveloped, ignoring both the high passion and the tragedy of the lovers.

Two of the earliest responses to *Troilus and Criseyde* are found in the scribal glosses of the surviving manuscripts and in the three English translations of Guido delle Colonne's history of the Trojan War. Neither reveals any serious attempt to address the major themes of Chaucer's poem. In contrast to the important Latin commentary in almost every manuscript of John Gower's *Confessio Amantis*, which undoubtedly derives from the poet himself, the marginal glosses to *Troilus* are spotty (some important manuscripts have virtually none), clearly the product of individual scribes, and superficial. In Latin and English, the *Troilus* glosses

---

[1] My subject is a much more modest tradition than that discussed in ch. vii of Alice S. Miskimin's *The Renaissance Chaucer* (New Haven, 1975).

briefly explain words, note wise sayings, identify sources and mythological figures, and, in the later manuscripts especially, label speakers and summarize the story on the most objective narrative level.[2] The only genuinely interpretive comments among these impersonal glosses are two brief statements by one of the four Rawlinson scribes: when Criseyde coyly declares just before the consummation that Troilus should be beaten for his jealousy the scribe writes in the margin, 'ye with a Fether', and when the lovers finally embrace he describes their union with a vivid euphemism: 'How bace [base] phisik come in honde betwene Creysseyde & Troylys'.[3] It is unfortunate that this scribe wrote only a few hundred lines of the Rawlinson manuscript, for we would have liked to hear more of his response to Chaucer's poem. Yet even he reveals no understanding of the tragedy of Troilus; instead he expresses what will become a common attitude toward the lovers—the cynical moralizing of Shakespeare's Thersites.

Troilus and Criseyde seems to have created a taste for the story of Troy. Within a generation of Chaucer's death three independent verse translations of Guido delle Colonne's authoritative Historia Destructionis Troiae were produced in English, perhaps in direct response to Chaucer's advice to turn to the historians for information about the war itself.[4] But if Troilus inspired later writers, its redefinition of the story was treated cautiously. Although at least two of the translators reveal their knowledge of Chaucer's version of the story, both hesitate to retell it. All three choose to remain faithful to Guido's account, which presents Troilus primarily as a military figure.

The anonymous author of the undervalued, alliterative Destruction of Troy, usually dated at the end of the fourteenth century, borrows a few details from Chaucer's Troilus (such as Diomede taking Criseyde's horse's reins, and Troilus looking from the Trojan walls), without showing any particular engagement with

---

    [2] e.g. 'Neptunus deus maris' at ii. 443 in Harley 2392; 'Troylus schewing his first mynd to Pandar', at i. 597 in Arch. Selden B. 24, or 'How Troilus dremed of Cresseyd & told it unto Pandar & seyde hys lady hym had betrayed', at v. 1234 in Rawl. Poet. 163. All quotations and titles in my notes and text are original except that I have followed modern practice in capitalization and in the use of u and v and i and j. I have also transcribed þ and ȝ as th and gh respectively.
    [3] Troilus, iii. 1169; iii. 1191.
    [4] Troilus, i. 141–7. For an account of Guido and his Middle English translators, see my History of Troy in Middle English Literature (Cambridge, 1980).

the love story.[5] Although respecting the sincerity of the Trojan knight's passion ('For he lovit hir full lelly, no lesse then hym selvyn, | With all the faithe and affection of hys fyn hert'), the poet claims to grow tired of the grief of Troilus and Criseyde (whom he, following Guido, calls 'Breisaid') as they part ('No lengur of thies lovers list me to carpe'), and, in an echo of Chaucer's advice, declares that the reader who wants to know more about them should 'Turne hym to Troilus, & talke there ynoghe!'[6] The reference to Chaucer's poem is unmistakable (he could hardly mean Boccaccio's *Filostrato*, the only other possible candidate), but so is the reluctance to follow the lead of his great predecessor in exploring the implications of the love story. The alliterative poet gives us Guido's historical facts about Calchas' daughter and her two lovers, but sends us to Chaucer for anything more.

We cannot be sure that the author of the *Laud Troy Book* (*c.* 1400) had read *Troilus*, because the name 'Cresseide' that is twice used in the manuscript appears to have been added by a later hand.[7] Whatever his knowledge of Chaucer, the metrical poet shows even less interest in the love story than his alliterative counterpart. Although usually remarkably faithful to Guido's historical narration, the poet drastically reshapes the Troilus and Criseyde episode. He does not mention their relationship until Criseyde is already in the Greek camp (Guido's first account is when they learn they must part) and reduces all their love and sorrow to little more than a single phrase: '[Cresseide] that sumtyme was Troyle lemman'.[8]

The third translator of the complete history of Troy, John Lydgate—in his *Troy Book* (1412-20)—will be the subject of Anna Torti's essay. Lydgate knows Chaucer well and expresses the gravest reservations about retelling *Troilus and Criseyde*: 'Sith my maister Chaucer her-a-forn | In this mater hath so wel hym born'.[9] Easy as it is to scorn his many grovelling tributes to the older poet,

[5] *The 'Gest Hystoriale' of the Destruction of Troy*, ed. G. A. Panton and D. Donaldson, EETS, os 39, 56 (1869, 1874; rpt. London, 1968), ll. 8078, 8178-9.

[6] *Destruction of Troy*, ll. 8030-1; 8051; 8054.

[7] *The Laud Troy Book*, ed. J. Ernst Wülfing, EETS os 121, 122 (London, 1902-3). See R. M. Lumiansky, 'The Story of Troilus and Briseida in the *Laud Troy-Book*', *Modern Language Quarterly*, 18 (1957), 238-46.

[8] *Laud Troy Book*, ll. 9064, 13546.

[9] John Lydgate, *Troy Book*, ed. Henry Bergen, EETS es 97, 103, 106, 126 (London, 1906-20), iii. 4197-8.

Lydgate is genuinely interested in the love story. In contrast to the other translators, he supplements Guido with a summary (albeit brief) of the lovers' experiences before they must part, and he seems to grasp something of the comedy and tragedy of *Troilus*. He pretends to criticize Guido for blaming Criseyde's frailty, while in fact expanding the anti-feminist remarks in the *Historia* and adding a 'defence' that is really an attack in disguise.[10] The joke may be crude and is used elsewhere in the *Troy Book*, but it also suggests an awareness of both Chaucer's humour and his attitude of sympathy for Criseyde. Furthermore, Lydgate adds another passage that attributes the separation of the lovers to Fortune, a conventional explanation that nevertheless shows an attempt to treat the story as a medieval tragedy.[11]

As we have seen, Lydgate's interest in Troilus and Criseyde is exceptional among the English historians of Troy. The most striking avoidance of the love story in this tradition is to be found in the fifteenth-century prose *Sege of Troye*.[12] This brief redaction of the *Historia* knows and respects *Troilus and Criseyde* enough to draw on Chaucer, rather than Guido, for information about Calchas and his request that Antenor be exchanged for his daughter (who is called 'Criseide'). But even though both Troilus and Criseyde appear as historical characters in the prose *Sege*, their love affair is never once mentioned.

Later versions of the history of Troy continue to downplay the love of Troilus and Criseyde. The first book printed in English, Caxton's *The Recuyell of the Historyes of Troye* (c. 1474), a prose translation of Raoul Lefevre's compilation of Guido and other ancient stories, was an important source of Trojan material throughout the Renaissance.[13] Although Caxton knows or knows about Chaucer's poem, he never uses it to supplement the brief account of the love of Troilus and Criseyde in his source. He even goes so far as to use Lefevre's form of the heroine's name, though he is aware that 'Chaucer in his booke that he made of Troylus named her Creseyda'.[14] As elsewhere, we are urged to turn to *Troilus* for the

---

[10] Ibid., iii. 4201–20; iii. 4264–448.

[11] Ibid., iii. 4221–33.

[12] *The Sege of Troye*, ed. Nathaniel E. Griffin, *PMLA* 22 (1907), 157–200.

[13] William Caxton, *The Recuyell of the Historyes of Troye*, ed. H. Oskar Sommer, 2 vols. (London, 1894).

[14] Ibid., p. 601.

full story: 'who that lyste to here of alle theyr love, late hym rede the booke of Troyllus that Chawcer made; wherin he shall fynde the storye hooll, whiche were to longe to wryte here'.[15]

Over a hundred years later we find the same invitation in Thomas Heywood's *Troia Britanica*, a loose and fanciful poetic reworking of Caxton.[16] In the notes following canto XI, he explains why he has slighted the story of the Trojan lovers: 'The passages of love betwixt Troylus and Cressida, the reverent poet Chaucer hath sufficiently discourst, to whom I wholy refer you, having past it over with little circumstance'. In fact, Heywood gives no evidence of knowing Chaucer's poem, and his few references to the story are unprecedented: he invents a scene in which Diomede falls in love with Criseyde during a visit to Troy before the fighting begins, and blames her later desertion entirely on the persuasion of Calchas ('Shee's but a child, and must obey her father').[17] Although Heywood delights in retelling other amorous tales in the *Troia Britanica*, he continues the historical tradition of largely ignoring the love of Troilus and Criseyde.

Although the English historians of Troy are not especially interested in the love story of Troilus and Criseyde, its appearance in Guido gave the episode authenticity and it soon escaped into the general literary tradition. Today we know that the winning and losing of Criseyde was first invented in the twelfth century, but throughout the late Middle Ages and Renaissance the story was accepted as genuinely classical by a wide range of English authors. For instance, in Lydgate's 'A Wicked Tunge Wille Sey Amys', the 'love of Troylis' appears between citations of Hector and Caesar; in the next century David Lindsay's *Squyer Meldrum* (1550?) lists Troilus and Criseyde with Jason and Medea as examples of ancient stories told by Chaucer; and Surrey's 'The Lover Disceived' in the influential *Tottel's Miscellany* (1557) associates them with Ulysses and Penelope.[18]

[15] *The Recuyell of the Historyes of Troye*, p. 604.

[16] Thomas Heywood, *Troia Britanica* (London, 1609).

[17] Ibid., xi. 40–2; xiii. 16.

[18] John Lydgate, 'A Wicked Tunge Wille Sey Amys', *The Minor Poems*, ed. H. N. MacCracken, EETS os 192 (1934; rpt. London, 1961), ii. 839–44; David Lindsay, *Squyer Meldrum*, ed. James Kinsley (Edinburgh, 1959), 24–6; Henry Howard, Earl of Surrey, 'The Lover Deceived', *Tottel's Miscellany*, ed. Hyder E. Rollins, rev. edn. (Cambridge, Mass., 1966), i. 230–1.

In 'The Britlenesse of Thinges Mortall' (*c.* 1570) Thomas Howell asks:

> Where is faire Helines bewtie now be come,
> Or Cressed eke whom Troylus long time served,
> Where be the decked daintie Dame of Rome,
> That in Aurelius time so flourished?[19]

Such *ubi sunt* questions have didactic force only if Criseyde is thought to be a historical figure. Even the Renaissance rediscovery of the Homeric accounts of Troy did not immediately debunk Troilus and Criseyde. In a 1567 collection George Turberville reveals a knowledge of Criseyde's remote ancestors, Briseis and Chryseis ('The Lover Driven to Absent Him from his Ladie'), but in another poem in the same work includes a reworking of material from Chaucer and Henryson in 'The Lover in Utter Dispaire of His Ladies Returne'.[20]

As these examples suggest, the story of Troilus and Criseyde appears widely in the period, but often only in brief allusions. The lovers are commonly reduced to rather crude figures by both major and minor writers, with none of Chaucer's complexity and delicacy of characterization. In his *Troilus and Cressida*, Shakespeare has Pandarus, echoing a prediction already suggested in Chaucer, declare that if the couple are false to one another, 'Let all constant men be Troiluses, all false women Cressids, and all brokers-between Pandars!'[21] All three characters say 'amen', and it will indeed be so. Even before Shakespeare Pandar's name had become a common noun, one of those, as Sidney notes in *A Defence of Poetry*, 'we now use . . . to signify their trades'.[22] Because most uses of the love-story involve casual references rather than extended narration, the story is drastically simplified and Pandarus' role is often ignored entirely.

---

[19] Thomas Howell, 'The Britlenesse of Thinges Mortall', *New Sonets, and Pretie Pamphlets*, in *Occasional Issues of Unique or Very Rare Books*, ed. Alexander B. Grosart (privately printed, 1879), 121–2.

[20] George Turberville, 'The Lover Driven to Absent Him from his Ladie' and 'The Lover in Utter Dispaire of His Ladies Returne, in Eche Respect Compares His Estate with Troylus', *Epitaphes, Epigrams, Songs and Sonets* (London, 1567), fos. 125ʳ–127ʳ, 139ʳ–140ᵛ.

[21] *Troilus and Cressida*, III. ii. 202–4. All quotations from Shakespeare in my text are taken from *The Riverside Shakespeare* (Boston, 1974).

[22] Sir Philip Sidney, *A Defence of Poetry. Miscellaneous Prose Works of Sir Philip Sidney*, ed. K. Duncan-Jones and J. van Dorsten (Oxford, 1973), 86.

Troilus is seen primarily as a lover in this period, his prowess and sacrifice as a warrior largely (but not entirely) forgotten. As a lover he is a model of constancy and the only possible ideal among the three characters, as Shakespeare's Pandarus suggests. In Lydgate's 'On Gloucester's Approaching Marriage', the prospective groom is said to equal such as Hector (in hardiness), Caesar (in knighthood), and Troilus (in 'trouth of love').[23] At least two Englishmen were actually given the name 'Troilus' about 1600, and, helped by the alliteration, the Trojan prince is constantly referred to as 'true' or 'trusty'.[24] The (male) poet as lover often identifies with the nobility and suffering of Troilus, as two anonymous fifteenth-century works attest. The author of 'The Lover's Mass', thinking about his 'worthy bretheren and predecessours in love', calls first to mind 'the grete trouthe of Troylus', and the author of the lyric 'To His Mistress, Flower of Womanhood', calls himself a 'newe Troiles' because he loves without change.[25] Poets in the sixteenth century use the convention frequently to assert their faithfulness in contrast to the actions of their ladies, as we can see in many lyrics of Gascoigne, in an anonymous ballad 'Whan Cressyde came from Troye', and even in the titles of such poems as Turberville's 'The Lover in Utter Dispair of His Ladies Return'.[26]

Even noble Troilus may be lowered when divorced from the subtlety of Chaucer's extended characterization. Although he is always shown as a loyal lover, his unchanging fidelity makes him a

---

[23] John Lydgate, 'On Gloucester's Approaching Marriage', *The Minor Poems*, ed. H. N. MacCracken, EETS os 192 (1934; rpt. London, 1961), ii. 601–8 (quotation from l. 136).

[24] For the name 'Troilus' see Caroline F. E. Spurgeon's invaluable collection of early Chaucer citations, *Five Hundred Years Of Chaucer Criticism and Allusion* (1925; rpt. New York, 1960), iv. 53. In his important article, 'The Troilus-Cressida Story from Chaucer to Shakespeare', *PMLA* 32 (1917), 383–429, Hyder E. Rollins quotes the third edn. of Hutchins's *History and Antiquities of Dorset* to the effect that George Turberville, who often cites Troilus in his poetry, had a brother, cousins, and nephews called Troilus (p. 403 n.).

[25] 'The Lover's Mass', *English Verse between Chaucer and Surrey*, ed. Eleanor P. Hammond (Durham, NC, 1927), pp. 207–13, ll. 179–81; 'To His Mistress, Flower of Womanhood', *Secular Lyrics of the XIVth and XVth Centuries*, ed. Rossell H. Robbins (Oxford, 1952), pp. 190–1, l. 38.

[26] George Gascoigne, *The Posies: The Complete Works of George Gascoigne*, ed. John W. Cunliffe (Cambridge, 1907), vol. i; 'Whan Cresseyde came from Troye', *Tottel's Miscellany*, ed. Hyder E. Rollins, rev. edn. (Cambridge, Mass., 1966), ii. 294–5; George Turberville, *Epitaphes*, fos. 139^r–140^v.

static figure and somewhat of a fool (as cuckolds usually are). In her debunking speech in *As You Like It*, Rosalind cites him as 'one of the patterns of love', but notes that he died from a Greek club not a broken heart; and Petruchio in the *The Taming of the Shrew* names his spaniel Troilus.[27] In Lyly's *Euphues* (1578) Euphues woos Lucilla by asserting that 'though Aeneas were to[o] fickle to Dido, yet Troylus was to[o] faithfull to Craessida'.[28] His constancy has the potential to appear slightly ridiculous.

Criseyde is by far the most important and versatile of the three principal characters. Once the episode is removed from the general history of Troy and becomes only a love story she necessarily dominates. It is she who goes from Troy to the Greek camp, from Troilus to Diomede. Part of her interest is that of the pure villainess. In a pioneering study, Hyder Rollins suggested that Criseyde's debasement in the Renaissance was the result of Henryson's *Testament*, but Gretchen Mieszkowski has since shown that, except in Chaucer, Criseyde has a bad reputation from the twelfth to the fifteenth centuries, where she is consistently presented as 'a type of the fickle woman'.[29] Despite the relative sophistication and playfulness with which we saw Lydgate treat Criseyde in his *Troy Book*, his judgement in the later *Fall of Princes* is crudely reductive: he says she 'wilfulli forsook' worthy Troilus for Diomede and he can imagine her taking a third lover.[30] Similarly, the mid-fifteenth-century 'Chance of the Dice' presents Criseyde as a type of those lawless lovers who 'leve youre olde and taken newe and newe'.[31]

Henryson, as Anna Torti will show in her essay, does not fundamentally change this censorious tradition, though he offers a new vocabulary with which to blame Criseyde. The *Testament* was virtually unknown in England until Thynne printed it without attribution at the end of *Troilus and Criseyde* in his 1532 edition of

[27] *As You Like It*, IV. i. 99–100; *Taming of the Shrew*, IV. i. 150.

[28] John Lyly, *Euphues, The Descent of Euphues*, ed. James Winny (Cambridge, 1957), 35.

[29] See Rollins in n. 24; Gretchen Mieszkowski, 'The Reputation of Criseyde 1155–1500', *Transactions of the Connecticut Academy of Arts and Sciences*, 43 (1971), 78.

[30] John Lydgate, *Fall of Princes*, ed. Henry Bergen, EETS ES 121 (1924; rpt. London, 1967), i. 6014–20.

[31] 'The Chance of the Dice', ed. Eleanor P. Hammond, *Englische Studien*, 59 (1925), 1–16, l. 383.

Chaucer. The account of Criseyde's rejection by Diomede and pitiful death was generally accepted as Chaucer's own conclusion, and little distinction was made between the two narratives. Under the influence of the *Testament* sixteenth-century poets reduce Criseyde from a faithless woman to a prostitute and, as punishment for her sexual sins, a leper, but the subtlety and moral seriousness of Henryson's Criseyde is ignored by most later writers, even as they repeatedly echo the words he gives her when she finally accepts her guilt: 'Fy, fals Cresseid; O trew knicht Troylus!'[32]

If Troilus is sometimes patronized, Criseyde is regularly excoriated. To Alexander Craig she is simply 'the Trojan whore'.[33] Pistol in *Henry V* calls Doll Tearsheet a 'lazar kit of Cressid's kind',[34] and, aided by alliteration, like 'true Troilus', 'Cressid's kind' becomes a common term for a foul prostitute. In his 'Cressids Complaint' George Whetstone portrays Criseyde as unfaithful in both Troy and Greece and says he is using her as a symbol for all courtesans to warn men of his own time, 'for as much as Cressids heires in every corner live'.[35] Perhaps the ultimate degradation of Criseyde is found in the second part of Thomas Heywood's play *The Iron Age*.[36] In an apparent imitation and debasement of the scene in Shakespeare's *Troilus and Cressida* in which Troilus watches while Diomede seduces Criseyde, Heywood has the cynical Sinon tell an incredulous Diomede that even he can win Criseyde. Sinon proceeds to do so, with Diomede looking on, even though the famous betrayer makes his insincerity perfectly clear to Criseyde.

Mieszkowski argues that the virtually unanimous attitude toward Criseyde in this period is that of disparagement, but she is in fact a more complex figure even in the fifteenth century. As we have already seen, Lydgate's treatment varies between playful mock defence in the *Troy Book* and stern condemnation in the *Fall of Princes*. In the *Pastime of Pleasure* (first printed 1509), Hawes has a nasty dwarf call her 'so subtyll and so false of kynde', but the lover

[32] Robert Henryson, *The Testament of Cresseid*, in *The Poems of Robert Henryson*, ed. Denton Fox (Oxford, 1981), l. 560.

[33] Alexander Craig, 'To Lais', *The Amorose Songes, Sonets, and Elegies* (London, 1606; rpt. Huntarian Club, 1873), 83.

[34] *Henry V*, ii. i. 76.

[35] George Whetstone, 'Cressids Complaint', *The Rocke of Regard* (London, 1576), 17.

[36] *The Dramatic Works of Thomas Heywood* (London, 1874), iii. 363–5.

and his adviser earlier note her beauty and desirability.[37] Likewise, the author of the 'Chance of the Dyce' balances his later criticism with a description of the indescribable joy when 'Troylus wanne first Creseyde in Troye'.[38]

When we move slightly beyond Mieszkowski's time-limit of 1500 the range of possible ways of presenting Criseyde is clearer. John Skelton, for example, is censorious in one poem and neutral in another.[39] In 'Phyllyp Sparowe' he summarizes Chaucer's story in detail and finds Criseyde 'moch to blam', for 'Disparaged is her fame, | And blemysshed is her name, | In manner half with shame'.[40] Nevertheless, in the later 'Garlande or Chapelet of Laurell' (c. 1520) Lady Elizabeth Howard is compared to 'Goodly Creisseid, fayrer than Polexene' and said to be so beautiful that Troilus would have 'set his hole delight' on her if he had seen her.[41] Although the mention of Pandarus might make us suspect irony, the 'Garlande' is one of Skelton's most benign poems, and it is hard to imagine satire in praise of a girl of 'tender age' called 'plesaunt, demure, and sage', who may have been as young as five or six at the time.[42] As with Helen of Troy, Criseyde's beauty could be separated from her actions and admired for itself. Although somewhat surprised, Rollins notes that Criseyde 'was often glorified as the highest type of a sweetheart' in an important collection like *Tottel's Miscellany* (1557), which also has poems that present her unfavourably.[43] Despite the widespread attacks on her in English literature for more than two centuries, Criseyde could be portrayed as attractive at the conclusion of a 1612 poem by Richard Johnson addressed to his mistress:

> Troylus [did love?] withall his might,
> Cressed of Troy that was so bright:

[37] Stephen Hawes, *The Pastime of Pleasure*, ed. William E. Mead, EETS os 173 (London, 1928), ll. 3568; 1759, 1807–13.

[38] 'Chance of the Dyce', l. 140.

[39] John Skelton, *The Complete English Poems*, ed. John Scattergood (New Haven, 1983).

[40] 'Phyllyp Sparowe', ll. 677–723; 710–13.

[41] 'Garlande or Chapelet', ll. 871–7.

[42] See Eleanor P. Hammond, *English Verse between Chaucer and Surrey* (Durham, NC, 1927), 519, although others believe her to be another, older woman: see M. J. Tucker, *Renaissance Quarterly*, 22 (1969), 335.

[43] Rollins, p. 389.

And I do love as farre as he,
And ever shall untill I dye.[44]

Most references to Troilus and Criseyde in late medieval and Renaissance English literature are brief, as we have seen, but several minor writers examine the love story in more detail, producing a variety of perspectives. Moralizing, comedy, sympathy, and even approval are found, though tragedy is rare. Such treatments generally concentrate on the surface narration and ignore the deeper philosophical and religious questions raised by Chaucer and Henryson.

Moralization of the story as a conflict between truth and falsity in love drew inspiration from the gruesome details of the *Testament*, but such an interpretation existed in England even before Henryson was known, as can be seen by the three awkward rhyme-royal stanzas Wynkyn de Worde affixed to the end of the second edition of *Troilus* in 1517.[45] Under the title 'The auctour', Wynkyn draws a clear lesson from Chaucer's poem. Criseyde is the worst of women (though it is further suggested that no earthly woman 'can be trewe'), one who betrayed 'parfyte' Troilus, 'deflouryng his worthynes'. The knight is eulogized as the 'moste treuest lover that ever lady hadde', and the passage ends with a prayer that Christ will bring him to heaven.

The morality of Wynkyn's lines is entirely secular. Although Troilus is called a martyr worthy of heaven, his virtues have nothing to do with Christianity. Benoît and Guido were more orthodox; they blamed both lovers, and especially Troilus, for indulging in sensuality. In contrast, Wynkyn and most other writers in the Renaissance view Troilus' faithful sexual love as essential to his perfect worthiness.[46] The only sin is the amatory

---

[44] Richard Johnson, 'Lovers Song in Praise of His Mistress', *A Crowne-Garland of Goulden Roses* (London, 1612), fos. 7ᵛ–D8ʳ (D8ʳ).

[45] For text and discussion, see C. David Benson and David Rollman, 'Wynkyn de Worde and the Ending of Chaucer's *Troilus and Criseyde*', *Modern Philology*, 78 (1981), 275–9.

[46] Only rarely is the whole story found immoral, as in the comments of the Protestant martyr William Tyndale, who links the story with those of Robin Hood and Hercules as 'histories & fables of love & wantones & of rybaudry as fylthy as herte can thinke' (in Derek Brewer, *Chaucer: The Critical Heritage* (London, 1978), i. 87; see also the similar comments of Thomas Elyot in Brewer, i. 90). A stanza added to a moralized Scottish version of a popular ballad in praise of

deceit practised by Criseyde and potentially by all women. Wynkyn's edition was not itself very influential, but later poets frequently repeated his identification with Troilus and castigation of Criseyde. The result is not tragedy, but a powerful expression of the fear of women's infidelity and of men's helplessness before it: it is Wynkyn's Criseyde, after all, who is said to 'deflower' Troilus.

Such chauvinistic moralizing is common even in accomplished treatments of the story. The anonymous 'A New Dialogue betweene Troylus and Cressida', added to Thomas Deloney's *Strange Histories*, offers a careful redaction of the speeches in Book IV of Chaucer's *Troilus and Criseyde* when the lovers know they must part.[47] For all its skill and sensitivity, however, the dialogue ends abruptly with a harsh narrative judgement of Criseyde:

> But Cressida she brake her oath, she never came againe,
> But as she deserved, so God he rewarded her pride:
> For she full poore, from doore to doore,
> A loathsome Leper dy'de.

Although Renaissance English poets borrow details of Criseyde's punishment from the *Testament*, as the previous quotation shows, their use of the story largely ignores Henryson's serious concern with sin and punishment. The morality they offer is as secular, shallow, and self-interested as we saw in Wynkyn. Howell's 'The Britlenesse of Thinges Mortall' (*c.* 1570) dwells on the horror of Criseyde's decay ('Her comly corpes that Troylus did delight | All pust with plages full lothsomly there lay'), but the conclusion he draws is smug and practical: 'Lo here the end of wanton wicked life'.[48] In a revision a decade or so later, 'Ruine the Rewarde of Vice' (1581), Howell becomes even more self-righteous and unChristian as he denies Criseyde the possibility of mercy despite her repentance ('No sorrow then might salve her lewde offence... | Twas now to late to shunne the sheete of shame'), and he concludes

love does make the brief and unusual suggestion that Fortune punished Troilus for his enjoyment of Criseyde: 'Sic pleasoure bringis miserie, | As come to pas' (*A Compendious Book of Godly and Spiritual Songs*, ed. A. F. Mitchell. STS 1st ser. 39 (Edinburgh, 1897), 213).

[47] 'A New Dialogue betweene Troylus and Cressida', in Thomas Deloney, *Strange Histories* (London, 1612), fos. K2^v–L1^v.

[48] See n. 19 above.

with a mechanical and worldly lesson: 'For vice brings plagues, and vertue happy ende'.[49]

As in Howell's poems, the love story is often appropriated in the Renaissance to demonstrate the bitter earthly rewards of infidelity. Criseyde is the central figure in such works, though she usually appears only as a horrible *exemplum* with which the poet can threaten his lady or console himself when he has been played false. The real subject is not the ancient tale but the speaker's own love life. In one poem from his *Tragical Tales* (apparently published in 1575, though the first extant edition is 1587) George Turberville says that he is giving up his faithless Criseyde to a modern Diomede 'to glut his filthie lust' ('Finding His Mistress Untrue'), and in another ('To His Cruel Mistresse') he turns the story upside down, perhaps with deliberate wit, when he prays that his lady may be punished like Criseyde with plagues for *not* yielding to him (though, of course, the original punishment was for too much yielding).[50] This last 'moral' is a blatant expression of male selfishness, as is that of a stanza from J. Tomson's 'The Lover Complaineth the Losse of His Ladie' (printed in 1584), in which the author first hopes that Venus will grant him 'such happinesse' as Pandarus provided for Troilus through his niece, before switching gears entirely to take satisfaction in the punishment Criseyde received for finding happiness elsewhere:

> For she became so leprosie,
> That she did die in penurie:
> Because she did transgresse.
> Because she did transgresse.[51]

Although many authors approach the story moralistically it could also be told as comedy. A few in the Renaissance go even further, mocking the characters and presenting them as fools, a tradition of burlesquing the classical past found also in Shakespeare's *Troilus and Cressida*. In *Dan Bartholomew of Bath* (1573) George Gascoigne, who uses the love story frequently, calls Troilus a

---

[49] Thomas Howell, 'Ruine the Rewarde of Vice', *Howell's Devises*, ed. Walter Raleigh (Oxford, 1906).

[50] George Turberville, *Tragical Tales* (London, 1587), fos. 164[v], 182[v]–183[r].

[51] J. Tomson, 'The Lover Complaineth the Losse of His Ladie', *A Handful of Pleasant Delights*, ed. Hyder E. Rollins (Cambridge, Mass., 1924), 31–3 (ll. 870, 878–81).

'gemme of gentle deedes', but the Trojan knight's pursuit of Criseyde is made ridiculous:

> He bet about the bushe, whiles other caught the birds,
> Whome crafty Gresside mockt to muche, yet fede him still with
> > wordes.
> And god he knoweth not I, who pluckt hir first sprong rose,
> Since Lollius and Chaucer both, make doubt upon the glose.[52]

Even more reductive are the words in *The Rare Triumphes of Love and Fortune* that accompany the dumb show of Troilus and Criseyde, one of several classical scenes in the comedy. Presenting the lovers, Mercury says, 'Beholde how Troylus and Cresseda, | Cryes out on Love that framed their decay'; to which Vulcan replies, 'That was like the olde wife when her ale would not come, | Thrust a fire brand in the groute and scratcht her bum'.[53]

Other comic treatments of the story cleverly play off the expected moral. A short ballad summarizes the love affair indulgently ('They held sweet warr a winters night') before concluding with a 'moral' for young women: because loving one person soon cloys and grows dull, a lady should change men like her clothes: 'then chang love, with garments change, | & still the better take'.[54] Even more original is 'Furth ouer the mold at morrow as I ment', a poem in eight rhyme-royal stanzas from the Bannatyne Manuscript (1568) that again reveals the skill with which the Scots handled the theme of Troilus and Criseyde.[55] The narrator tells how he was out for a walk one morning and met a strange man in rich array who introduced himself as Pandarus, 'That sumtyme servit the gud knycht Troyelus'. Acknowledging him as an authority on love, the narrator asks Pandarus when ladies will be loyal to their lovers. He is told of a series of events that must happen first, such as the absence of poor people in Egypt or fish in the sea: 'And quhen the theivis thinkis schame to steill | Than ladyis to thair luvaris salbe leill'. In addition to the unusual prominence the poet gives to Pandarus, he creates a sophisticated twist in the conven-

[52] Gascoigne, *Complete Works*, i. 101.
[53] *The Rare Triumphes of Love and Fortune* (London, 1589), B1r.
[54] 'Cressus was the fairest of Troye', *Bishop Percy's Folio Manuscript*, ed. John W. Hales and Frederick J. Furnivall (London, 1868), iii. 301–2.
[55] 'Furth ouer the mold at morrow as I ment', *The Bannatyne Manuscript*, ed. W. Tod Ritchie, STS NS 26 (Edinburgh and London, 1930), iv. 40–2.

tion of Criseyde's faithlessness, which is never directly mentioned, reminiscent of Donne's 'Go and catch a falling star'.

In addition to moralistic and comic treatments of the story, a third group of poems presents the love of Troilus and Criseyde as delightful. The ballad that begins 'When Troylus dwelt in Troy towne' (1566?) has some of the humour of the poems just discussed, without their mockery.[56] The characters are hardly noble, but thoroughly enjoyed. The author knows Chaucer well and provides a hurried summary of the first three books of *Troilus and Criseyde*, ending with Pandarus' visit to Criseyde. The tone is light and approving, as in this description of Troilus falling in love:

> Tyll at the last he cam to churche
>   Where Cressyd sat and prayed a,
> Whose lookes gave Troylus such a lurche,
>   Hys hart was all dysmayde a.

The poem has no depth whatsoever and is all on the side of satisfied sexual love. Although the final lesson is 'The harder won, the greter joy', the poet only briefly mentions Troilus' long courtship, being more interested in the consummation. In contrast to Chaucer's hero, this Troilus does not faint when he comes into Criseyde's presence, though he is apparently cold—Criseyde lends him her 'nyght gowne', after which Pandarus suggests she warm him up in her bed. As befits the smirking male perspective, Troilus and Pandarus are the active characters. Except for a brief shriek when Troilus enters her bed, Criseyde says nothing until the next morning when she thanks her uncle for his pandering, 'Yow are a frend to trust a'. This prompts a laugh from Troilus: 'and wat yow why? | For he had what he lust a'.

A more substantial work that approves of the love of Troilus and Criseyde is 'A Comparison of His Love wyth the Faithful and Painful Love of Troylus to Creseide' from *Tottel's Miscellany* (1557), which balances other, more critical references in that influential collection.[57] Troilus' amorous sufferings are given at length,

[56] 'When Troylus dwelt in Troy towne', *Songs and Ballads, with other Short Poems; Chiefly of the Reign of Philip and Mary*, ed. Thomas Wright, Roxburghe Club (London, 1860), 195-7.

[57] 'A Comparison of His Love wyth the Faithfull and Painful Love of Troylus to Creseide', *Tottel's Miscellany*, ed. Hyder E. Rollins, rev. edn. (Cambridge, Mass., 1966), i. 183-5.

though Pandarus is not once mentioned. Troilus appears as a sincere lover whose devotion finally convinces Criseyde to become
'Phisicion to his wo' and makes him 'owner of her hart'. Thereafter
Criseyde shows herself to be everything a man could want in a
lover: 'From that day forth her study went, | To shew to love him
faithfully, | And his whole minde full to content'. The couple is
presented as ideal ('So happy a man at last was he, | And eke so
worthy a woman she'), and the poet concludes by urging his
beloved to imitate Criseyde: 'And set me in as happy case, | As
Troylus with his lady was'. For this poet, as later for Keats, the
Trojan love story could be used without irony or shadow by
simply ignoring the separation and betrayal.

A final tradition, which perhaps best reflects the achievements
of Chaucer and Henryson, acknowledges the unhappy ending of
the love story but is nevertheless sympathetic to the characters
themselves. The anonymous sixteenth-century *La conusaunce
damours* contains a four-stanza summary of *Troilus and Criseyde*,
as told by 'our ornate Chaucer', to whom the reader is referred for
the full story.[58] All the characters in this work are positive:
Criseyde is 'the goodly damosell' and 'fresshe may' and Pandarus is
Troilus' 'trusty frende'. As in Chaucer's poem, Troilus falls in love
from a wound by Cupid, and although the knight suffers for 'the
faire lady | Creseide' and eventually dies 'onely for her sake', no
criticism of her or of 'theyr great love' appears. This little-known
work offers one of the fullest treatments of Chaucer's poem since
Lydgate, and shows that it was possible to present the love of
Troilus and Criseyde as sentimental tragedy, similar to the story of
Pyramus and Thisbe with which the work begins. Like the author
of *La conusaunce damours*, George Peele almost a century later
combines reluctance to retell Chaucer's story with some recognition of its tragic effect. The second edition of his *Tale of Troy*
(1604), while recognizing Criseyde's fault, not only cites Chaucer's
poem, but also well describes its emotional power: Peele says
Troilus 'would tears exhale from eyes of iron mould'.[59]

A few works even present something of Criseyde's point of
view. After listing other faithless men, Sabina in the comedy *Common Conditions* (1576) answers Nomides' criticism of Criseyde by

[58] *La conusaunce damours* (London, [1525?]), C^r.
[59] George Peele, 'The Tale of Troy', *The Life and Minor Works of George Peele*,
ed. David H. Horne (New Haven, 1952), ll. 279–85.

picturing her caught between two men, honest Troilus and Diomede, who turns out to be untrue, and as the pitiful victim of bad
luck: 'And so betweene those twaine, and fortunes luckles hap, |
Shee was like Lazer faine to sit and beg with dish and clap'.[60] In *A
Poore Knight His Pallace of Private Pleasures* (1579), Criseyde is
finally condemned, but not before Diomede pleads on her behalf:

> And sayd that shee, had never broke the lawes:
> But yeelded there, where neede so strongly drawes,
> Doo what shee could, Perforce compeld her so:
> When shee was driven, from Troy to Greece to go.[61]

A dialogue in the third edition of *The Paradise of Dainty Devises*
(1580) also recognizes extenuating circumstances.[62] Whereas Troilus' 'Complaint' castigates 'Cressed in her gadding moode' for
going over to the Greeks in pursuit of novelty, her 'Replye' argues
that it was 'forced strife, | Compelled me retyre from Troy' and
that if only Troylus had married her 'No Diomede nor Greekish
wight, | Had sought my blame or his despight'. She concludes that
those who are noble-minded will not condemn her but 'will rue the
case and pittie mee'.

The most sympathetic treatment of Criseyde in the period is
'The Laste Epistle of Creseyd to Troyalus' (*c.* 1604), probably written by William Fowler.[63] The author is certainly Scots and, like his
countryman Henryson, invents a new episode, one in which
Criseyde writes a 300-line deathbed letter to her former lover
lamenting her fate and asking for forgiveness. The sensitive,
learned, though somewhat loose poem retells much of the love
story in a clever blend of *Troilus* and the *Testament*, while powerfully expressing the emotion Peele saw as the heart of Chaucer's
tale. Knowing that her 'rewfull race is ronne', Criseyde wishes that
she had died as a child before she had become, as we have seen, a
name for poets to blame and with which each lover can upbraid his

---

[60] *Common Conditions*, ed. Tucker Brooke, Elizabethan Club Reprints 1 (New Haven, 1915), ll. 822–3.

[61] *A Poore Knight His Pallace of Private Pleasures: Three Collections of English Poetry, of the Latter Part of the Sixteenth Century*, ed. Henry Ellis, Roxburghe Club (London, 1844), F.

[62] *The Paradise of Dainty Devises*, ed. Hyder E. Rollins (Cambridge, Mass., 1927), 117–19.

[63] William Fowler, 'The Laste Epistle of Creseyd to Troyalus', *The Works of William Fowler*, ed. Henry W. Meikle, STS, NS, 6 (Edinburgh, 1914), 379–87.

'fickle dame'.[64] She finds excuses for her infidelity in 'the fates, the froward fates', in Troilus' failure to stop Diomede from taking her away, and in her isolation among the Greeks, but she also acknowledges her own responsibility: 'I, reckless wight, to soone, allas! | Did hight him then my harte'.[65] After recounting her miserable life as a leper, Criseyde concludes by sending 'Troyalus deare' the ring he gave her on the night of their consummation and asking him to bury 'the corps | That of thyne armes hathe wynde'.[66]

With Fowler's remarkable poem we end our brief survey of Troilus and Criseyde as they appear in the minor English poetry of the fifteenth, sixteenth, and early seventeenth centuries. The love story continued to be retold, as in Dryden's sentimental play, but the *Canterbury Tales*, helped by Dryden himself, gradually overtook *Troilus and Criseyde* in popularity. In the 1630s *Troilus* was translated into both contemporary English, apparently by Jonathan Sidnam, and into Latin by Francis Kynaston (so that educated men would always be able to read it!).[67] *Troilus and Criseyde* would thenceforth be even more intimidating for later writers; it had become a classic.

[64] *The Works of William Fowler*, ll. 10, 29.
[65] Ibid., ll. 43, 235–6.   [66] Ibid., ll. 281, 303–4.
[67] For Sidnam's trans., see *A Seventeenth-Century Modernisation of the First Three Books of Chaucer's 'Troilus and Criseyde'*, ed. Herbert G. Wright (Bern, 1960); for Kynaston's *Amorum Troilii et Cresseidae*, only two books of which were published (in 1635), see Judith M. Newton, 'Chaucer's Troilus: Sir Francis Kynaston's Latin Translation', Ph.D. thesis, Univ. of Illinois, 1967.

9

From 'History' to 'Tragedy': The Story of Troilus and Criseyde in Lydgate's *Troy Book* and Henryson's *Testament of Cresseid*

ANNA TORTI

In the period between Chaucer's tale of the 'double sorwe of Troilus' and Shakespeare's *Troilus and Cressida* lie John Lydgate's and Robert Henryson's works on this story of love and war. These authors, however, develop certain elements that will appear again in later re-elaborations of the same story.[1]

The double problem that characterizes the story in the form in which it came down to the fifteenth century consists of Criseyde's infidelity and Troilus' death. Lydgate, respectful of this heritage, works the love story into the larger framework of the Trojan War. Henryson, instead, treats the terms of the problem as narrated by Chaucer with a reversal of emphasis: Troilus is overlooked and the consequences to herself of Criseyde's infidelity, and her end, become his chief concern. Henryson holds with the poet's not adhering strictly to historical 'truth', in favour of 'inuentioun',[2]

[1] On the evolution of the myth, see H. E. Rollins, 'The Troilus-Cressida Story from Chaucer to Shakespeare', *PMLA* 32 (1917), 383–429; G. Mieszkowski, 'The Reputation of Criseyde 1155–1500', *Transactions of the Connecticut Academy of Arts and Sciences* 43 (1971), 71–153; A. S. Miskimin, *The Renaissance Chaucer* (New Haven and London, 1975). On the historical tradition established by Guido delle Colonne's *Historia Destructionis Troiae*, and its impact on Middle English literature, see C. D. Benson, *The History of Troy in Middle English Literature* (Cambridge, 1980). On the transformations in Criseyde as a character from Benoît de Sainte-Maure to Shakespeare, see E. T. Donaldson, 'Briseis, Briseida, Criseyde, Cresseid, Cressid: Progress of a Heroine', in E. Vasta and Z. P. Thundy (eds.), *Chaucerian Problems and Perspectives: Essays Presented to Paul E. Blichner, C.S.C.* (Notre Dame and London, 1979), 3–12. See also Donaldson's *The Swan at the Well: Shakespeare Reading Chaucer* (New Haven and London, 1985), esp. chs. 4 and 5 which deal with the influence of *Troilus and Criseyde* on *Troilus and Cressida*; and A. Thompson, *Shakespeare's Chaucer* (Liverpool, 1978).

[2] *Testament*, l. 67. Quotations from Robert Henryson's *Testament of Cresseid* are taken from *The Poems of Robert Henryson*, ed. D. Fox (Oxford, 1981).

whereas in the Prologue to the *Troy Book*[3] Lydgate provides a clear, precise definition of the twofold function of the 'auctores'. They are the keepers of the truth of facts, and, by interpreting these facts, they make them clear to the audience.[4]

Lydgate's aim in setting to work to recount the facts of Troy and its heroes is manifest: commissioned by Prince Hal in 1412, the *Troy Book* is in the tradition of the *specula principum*[5] and the sources it draws on are by choice Latin rather than vernacular. Lydgate naturally takes up the commonplace of the historical reliability of Dares and Dictys, but he is especially laudatory of his main source, Guido delle Colonne:

> For he enlvmyneth by crafte & cadence
> This noble story with many fresche colour
> Of rethorik, and many riche flour
> Of eloquence to make it sownde bet.[6]

Lydgate is aiming—by means of a famous story from ancient times addressed to a prince desirous of imitating valorous men of the past and shunning the vices of other great men of antiquity—to try his prowess as a translator into English of Guido's *Historia*. The future Henry V is also interested in having the Trojan epic in circulation in the language of his country.

In addition to Guido, Lydgate has a model that cannot be left out of consideration. This is Chaucer's *Troilus and Criseyde*, to which he pays tribute in his treatment of the story of the two lovers in Books II and III. Just as Hoccleve had done in the *Regement of Princes*, Lydgate lauds Chaucer as a 'master of eloquence' and supremely skilful handler of the colours of rhetoric.

---

[3] The *Troy Book* quotations are taken from H. Bergen (ed.), *Lydgate's Troy Book*, EETS ES 97, 103, 106, 126 (1906–35).

[4] *Troy Book*, Prologue, ll. 149–53, 164–70.

[5] On the popularity of the genre in fifteenth-century English literature, see D. Bornstein, 'Reflections of Political Theory and Political Fact in Fifteenth-Century Mirrors for the Prince' in J. B. Bessinger, jun., and R. R. Raymo (eds.), *Medieval Studies: In Honor of Lillian Herlands Hornstein* (New York, 1976), 77–85. See also A. M. Kinghorn, *The Chorus of History: Literary-historical relations in Renaissance Britain* (London, 1971), ch. 11.

[6] *Troy Book*, Prologue, ll. 362–5. On Lydgate's treatment of the history of Troy in terms of medieval rhetoric, see D. Pearsall, *John Lydgate* (London, 1970), 122–51; L. A. Ebin, *John Lydgate* (Boston, 1985), 39–52, and esp. Benson, *The History of Troy*, ch. 5.

He proves himself an able imitator, thus inserting himself whole-heartedly into the Chaucerian tradition.[7]

The Troilus 'myth' is no longer, as in Chaucer, the particular story of Troilus' and Criseyde's sufferings against the background of the war between Trojans and Greeks, but a part of the history of mythical Troy from the quest of the Argonauts to Ulysses' adventures and death. The lovers are described along with other characters in Book II.[8] From the very beginning Criseyde's 'vnstedfastnes' and Troilus' being 'stedefast of corage' are emphasized.[9]

Their story is followed intermittently in Book III, which is mainly concerned with the battles fought by the two armies before the walls of Troy. Lydgate's handling of the narrative is very interesting: the first event to be mentioned is in fact the end of the love story—the lovers' parting. There follows Achilles' acceptance of Hector's challenge to end the war by a duel. At this point the Troilus and Criseyde episode is resumed[10] with the description of the lovers' sorrow at their parting, the mention of Chaucer and his *Troilus*, and a very brief summary of the love plot in it. The final acceptance of Diomedes' love by Criseyde is preceded by Lydgate's praise of Chaucer's language, his discussion of Guido's antifeminism, and his defence of women. The truce ends and Troilus fights with Hector against the Greeks. Diomedes unhorses Troilus and gives his steed to Criseyde, who accepts it.[11] From now on Troilus is described as a warrior. Criseyde plays with Diomedes' love.[12] Book III ends with Hector's death.

Book IV describes a long series of battles where Troilus is singled out for his valour. Calchas urges the Greeks to fight, since Troy must be destroyed.[13] Incensed by Diomedes' love for Criseyde, Troilus unhorses him.[14] Criseyde nurses Diomedes, thus definitely giving up Troilus and disappearing from the narrative.[15]

---

[7] On the inheritance of Chaucer in fifteenth-century literature, see A. C. Spearing, 'Chaucerian Authority and Inheritance', in P. Boitani and A. Torti (eds.), *Literature in Fourteenth-Century England* (Tübingen and Cambridge, 1983), 185–202, and, by the same author, *Medieval to Renaissance in English Poetry* (Cambridge, 1985).

[8] *Troy Book*, ii. 4677–762 (Criseyde), 282–92, 4861–95 (Troilus).

[9] Ibid., ii. 4761, 4875.

[10] Ibid., iii. 4077–448.

[11] Ibid., iii. 4620–59.

[12] Ibid., iii. 4820–69.

[13] Ibid., iv. 1978–2028.

[14] Ibid., iv. 2056–67.

[15] Ibid., iv. 2132–78.

The fire of war is renewed. Achilles decides to take vengeance on Troilus. He has the Myrmidons attack him *en masse*, and as the Trojan hero fights them without noticing him, he cuts off his head from behind. He then ties Troilus' body to his horse's tail.[16] Lydgate reproaches Homer for having exalted the treacherous Achilles.[17] The story ends with Priam's building of a rich tomb for his son.[18]

For the first time since Dares, Joseph of Exeter, and Benoît, Troilus' epic status is fully restored. His body, like Hector's in the *Iliad*, is dragged by Achilles around the field. Yet the treacherous manner in which the Greek butchers Troilus is a degraded version of all previous accounts and in fact paves the way for Shakespeare's staging of Hector's death. The emblematic finality of Troilus' funeral and tomb, which conclude the episode, stands in marked contrast to Chaucer's Epilogue, open to the ascent of Troilus' soul and to further mystery.

Lydgate's approach in offering his reinterpretation of the myth as macro-history (the History of Troy) and micro-history (the Troilus and Criseyde story) in imitation of his two 'auctores' Guido and Chaucer, often gives curious, subtly ambiguous results. As historian and as poet, in both roles bent on the moralization of History and history, the writer's task is 'To make a merour only to oure mynde, | To seen eche thing trewly as it was, | More bryȝt and clere þan in any glas'.[19] This means offering the reader a mental mirror where he can see the truth of things clearly and transparently. The mirror metaphor is therefore used in its positive connotation for didactic purposes.[20] These lines echo Chaucer's words in Book I of *Troilus* when, making 'a mirour of his mynde', Troilus falls madly in love with Criseyde after seeing her in the temple.[21]

If the two passages are carefully analysed, Lydgate's approach to

---

[16] *Troy Book*, iv. 2756–79.   [17] Ibid., iv. 2784–840.
[18] Ibid., iv. 3083–97.   [19] Ibid., Prologue, ll. 168–70.
[20] On mirrors in general, see J. Baltrušaitis, *Le Miroir* (Paris, 1978); on the use of the mirror metaphor in Middle English and Renaissance literature, see H. Grabes, *The Mutable Glass* (Cambridge, 1982). On the symbolic value of the mirror, see F. Goldin, *The Mirror of Narcissus in the Courtly Love Lyric* (Ithaca, NY, 1967), esp. the introd. On the relationship allegory/metaphor of the mirror, see J. I. Wimsatt, *Allegory and Mirror: Tradition and Structure in Middle English Literature* (New York, 1970).
[21] *Troilus*, i. 365–9.

the material in hand becomes clearer. Chaucer uses the mirror metaphor to represent Troilus' mind, which makes a mirror of itself[22] so as to be able to keep the image of Criseyde in loving memory. Lydgate instead radically transforms the metaphor, in that the literary work becomes the mirror—a mirror reflecting the memory of ancient heroes and their deeds—that is to be presented to the king and readers. The ambiguous meaning of the metaphor needs stressing: its significance is transferred from the individual to the social plane, but the profound negative value of the mirror remains unchanged. Troilus' love for Criseyde will have a disastrous outcome because of the woman's falseness: can it be that the story Lydgate is getting ready to translate has the seed of falsity in it? He makes haste, however, to confirm the veracity of what is written in books, using lexemes that leave no room for doubt: 'With-oute feynynge'; 'trouthe'.[23] The heroes' deeds need to be presented in high style enriched with the colours of rhetoric and eloquence. From the very beginning of the work the two motives that inform fifteenth-century narrative are thus brought out: truthfulness and eloquence.[24]

To achieve his aim of moralistic interpretation Lydgate proposes to keep 'as nyȝe as euer I may' to Guido.[25] His resolution may constitute a limitation, but it is also a challenge: he intends to deal with his subject with the detachment of a historian, but at the same time he intends to present it to his audience couched in the high style that 'This noble story' requires.[26] Just as Guido teaches,[27] so Lydgate faithfully reproduces, historical truth, enlarging on points where the *auctor*'s treatment of the subject is too succinct or obscure. It is precisely in virtue of the fidelity he so often lays claim to in the *Troy Book* that Lydgate glosses over the connection between the contemporary history of England and the history of

[22] On the Neo-Platonism inherent in the mirror metaphor, see H. Leisegang, 'La connaissance de Dieu au miroir de l'âme et de la nature', *Revue d'Histoire et de Philosophie Religieuses*, 2 (1937), 145–71. On the mirror metaphor in *Troilus*, see S. L. Clark and J. N. Wasserman, 'The Heart in *Troilus and Criseyde*: The Eye of the Breast, The Mirror of the Mind, The Jewel in Its Setting', *Chaucer Review*, 18 (1984), 316–28; and Sister M. C. Borthwick, FCSP, 'Antigone's Song as "Mirour" in Chaucer's *Troilus and Criseyde*', *Modern Language Quarterly*, 22 (1961), 227–35.
[23] *Troy Book*, Prologue, ll. 178, 180, 186, 194.
[24] Ebin, *John Lydgate*, pp. 41–4.
[25] *Troy Book*, Prologue, l. 375.
[26] Ibid., l. 363.   [27] Ibid., ll. 355–9.

mythical Troy, and introduces general moralizing on men's duty to practice virtue and shun vice.

Lydgate is consistently criticized for his verbosity in enlarging on his sources. In the case of the love story of Troilus and Criseyde, however, this criticism would be out of place, in that Lydgate's version is a drastically reduced one of his other *auctoritas*, Chaucer. When Criseyde is described in Book II, Lydgate recalls the loftiness of Chaucer's style in representing his heroine in *Troilus and Criseyde*. From it he learns a humbling lesson: 'Som goodly worde þer-in for to fynde, | To sette amonge þe crokid lynys rude | Whiche I do write'.[28] Criseyde's beauty is modelled on the description of her in the *Historia*, but the crude

Multos traxit propter suas illecebras amatores multosque dilexit, dum suis amatoribus animi constantiam non seruasset.

[Her charms brought her many suitors, and she granted her favour to many, but she did not remain constant in heart towards her lovers.][29]

is replaced by somewhat mitigating terms:

> And, as seiþ Guydo, in loue variable—
> Of tendre herte & vnstedfastnes
> He hir accuseth, and newfongilnes.[30]

Lydgate remains faithful to Guido, but he makes an effort to temper the harshness of his text with Chaucer's more diversified and mellower attitude to Criseyde.[31] Troilus too is characterized in the same book by his likeness to Chaucer's Troilus and in contrast to Criseyde:

> He was alwey feithful, iust, & stable,
> Perseueraunt, and of wil inmvtable
> Vp-on what þing he onys set his herte,
> þat doubilnes myзt hym nat peruerte.[32]

---

[28] *Troy Book*, ii. 4704–6.

[29] For the quotation from Guido, the edn. used is Guido delle Colonne, *Historia Destructionis Troiae*, ed. N. E. Griffin, Mediaeval Academy of America Publication 26 (Cambridge, Mass., 1936), 85; the English translation is in N. R. Havely, *Chaucer's Boccaccio* (Cambridge, 1980), 184.

[30] *Troy Book*, ii. 4760–2.

[31] On the influence of *Troilus and Criseyde*, and in particular on the narrator's influence in the *Troy Book*, see Mieszkowski, 'The Reputation of Criseyde', pp. 116–28.

[32] *Troy Book*, ii. 4879–82.

Lydgate puts more stress than Guido does on the young man's loyalty and steadfastness, and in so doing indirectly accentuates the negative elements in Criseyde. In Book III Lydgate makes a violent attack on Guido's anti-feminist tirade, but by enlarging on his source, with the introduction of the simile between women and serpents and other commonplaces, shows how he puts still more subtle and ambiguous emphasis on Criseyde's inconstancy.

Women 'han of kynde | To be double';[33] Criseyde too has to be excused for having so quickly forgotten Troilus for Diomedes:

> I can noon oþer excusacioun,
> But only kyndes transmutacioun,
> þat is appropred vn-to hir nature,
> Selde or neuer stable to endure,
> Be experience as men may ofte lere.[34]

In taking up Guido's polemic against women, Lydgate introduces the economic element that, as Jill Mann shows in her essay, will play such an important part in Shakespeare's *Troilus and Cressida*. The ambiguous anti-feminism of Book III gives way to the open anti-feminism of Book IV.

Among the various lexemes used to stress the inconstancy of women, the presence of the term *chaunge* is highly significant. This is gradually enriched by nuances of meaning in such a way that it covers the whole range of values from 'change' to 'exchange'. In Book III (3709) Calchas requests that his daughter 'With kyng Thoas she myȝt eschaunged be', and later on in the same Book *change* is associated with lexemes indicating the mutability of women in general. This association becomes more and more negative: 'And þus in chaunge al her loue is feired'.[35] Here the word 'chaunge' has the twofold meaning of *change* and *exchange*. The former is to be understood in the light of lines 4295-6, 'For vp-on chaunge and mutabilite | Stant hool her trust and her surete', which further stress women's doubleness. The latter meaning ('chaunge' as *exchange*) emerges three lines later: 'þe faire of chaunge lasteth ouer ȝere, | But it is foly for to byen to dere | þilke tresour, whiche harde is to possede'.[36] The progressive buildup of terms unquestionably allusive of women's putting themselves on sale is a foreshadowing of the theme of value that is central to Shakespeare's

---

[33] Ibid., iii. 4398-9.   [34] Ibid., iii. 4441-5.
[35] Ibid., iii. 4314.   [36] Ibid., iii. 4317-19.

Troilus and Cressida. Lydgate does not go into the existential/ essential issues of the theory of value:[37] by enlarging on Guido's references to the fickleness of women, however, he opens the way for Shakespeare. Guido's brief mention of women soliciting men[38] is taken by Lydgate as the opportunity for a realistic description of medieval life. If no 'chapman' is available,[39] women show themselves at the windows along every street in town, or make acquaintances favoured by pilgrimages or theatre shows, thus offering their wares in the hope of obtaining a customer: 'and al is for to selle'.[40] The wide range of meanings attributable to *chaunge* is synthesized by the verb *to selle.* Lydgate's thesis is at this point clear to the reader who already knows the story in Benoît's, Guido's, and Chaucer's versions: women go in search of customers, often more than one at a time; Criseyde, left without Troilus' support, offers herself to Diomedes, the best *chapman* available.

Lydgate goes ahead with his pseudo-censure of Guido on behalf of the many virtuous women, but before doing so he introduces the metaphorical analogy between the fickleness of women and the changeableness of the moon, the celestial orb that joins its evil influence to that of Saturn in determining the terrible fate which befalls Henryson's Cresseid. Whoever looks for faithfulness and steadfastness in women 'He shal hem fynde stedefaste as þe mone, | þat is in point for to chaunge sone'.[41] The introduction of the moon metaphor in its most negative interpretation is another proof of Lydgate's originality with regard to his source and suggests that considerable material re-elaborated in the *Testament of Cresseid* may derive from Lydgate. This supposition could perhaps gain support from the fact that Lydgate goes on to deal with natural feminine duplicity ('For ʒif wommen be double naturelly'[42]), and with Criseyde's fickleness, which he says is due only to 'kyndes transmutacioun, | þat is appropred vn-to hir nature'.[43] Nature is often assisted by the astrological influence of the moon in conferring this attribute of unsteadfastness on women.

Safely entrenched behind the example of his *auctoritas* Guido,

---

[37] See the pp. dealing with Shakespeare's *Troilus and Cressida* in T. Eagleton, *William Shakespeare* (Oxford, 1986), 57–63.

[38] *Historia Destructionis Troiae*, p. 164.

[39] *Troy Book*, iii. 4321. [40] Ibid., iii. 4329.

[41] Ibid., iii. 4337–8. [42] Ibid., iii. 4408. [43] Ibid., iii. 4442–3.

Lydgate tends to excuse Criseyde because he can see a natural characteristic in her changeableness. This works only on the surface, however, because deep down the amplification of the anti-feminist satire and the play on the various meanings of *chaunge* show that, unlike Chaucer, Lydgate is fully in agreement with the condemnation of Criseyde. Setting aside the frequently repeated 'But Guydo seith'[44] that had served his purpose in attenuating the crudity of Criseyde's hasty betrayal of Troilus, Lydgate uses the *chaunge* metaphor again and on this occasion with an explicit reference. Chaucer's emphasis on Criseyde's fear and psychological frailty,[45] and on Diomedes' verbal persuasiveness, is hurriedly liquidated by Lydgate before he resumes the commercial metaphor. Criseyde 'þouȝt she wolde for no þing be vnsure | Of puruyaunce, nor with-oute stoor',[46] and so she entrusts her heart to Diomedes, deserting Troilus forever. Commercial terms such as *puruyaunce* and *stoor* amplify the anti-feminism of Book III in tones similar to Shakespeare's:

> þe change is nat so redy for to make
> In Lombard Strete of crowne nor doket—
> Al paie is good, be so þe prente be set:
> Her lettre of change doth no man abide![47]

The bitter irony is increased by the final comment on the episode of Criseyde's yielding:

> For leuere she had chaunge & variaunce
> Were founde in hir þanne lak of pite,
> As sittyng is to femynyte,
> Of nature nat to be vengable,
> For feith nor oþe, but raþer mercyable
> Of mannys lyf stondyng in distresse.[48]

The allusion to Criseyde's positive qualities is a heritage of Chaucer's favourable attitude, but the general effect of the passage is created by the two lexemes, *chaunge* and *variaunce*, which are essential for an understanding of later versions of the myth.

But how does the story of Troilus' and Criseyde's love, concise

[44] Ibid., iii. 4435.
[45] On Criseyde, 'the ferfulleste wight that myghte be', see A. J. Minnis, *Chaucer and Pagan Antiquity* (Cambridge, 1982), 83–93.
[46] *Troy Book*, iv. 2144–5. [47] Ibid., iv. 2154–7.
[48] Ibid., iv. 2172–7.

though it is, fit into the history of the Trojan War? Lydgate's attitude to the micro-history is similar to Guido's: it is one of many
episodes worth recounting and, as such, it is broken up so as to act
as a chronological and moralistic counterpoint to the stages of the
war being waged. Lydgate's interest is in fact concentrated on the
war and its futility. Benson states that in Lydgate the horror of the
war is toned down by comparison with the *Historia*, where the
dominant note is pessimism before a menacing Fate that makes
vain men's plans.[49] If this is true, it is also true that even in the love
story of Troilus and Criseyde he gives most of his attention to
what surrounds the story—the war, the heroes—and, therefore, of
the two lovers he favours Troilus. His moralizing on the unstead-
fastness and changeableness of women—and of Criseyde in particular—serves as a microcosm, as a reductive mirror of the
instability and the continual transformations wrought by the war.

The parallels Chaucer draws in *Troilus and Criseyde* between love
and war—fortune and misfortune in love and war[50]—have their
counterpart in the method chosen by Lydgate to deal with the story
of the two lovers. The initial opposition between Criseyde's moral
frailty and Troilus' determination and loyalty is then developed in
the following episodes of the love story. When Priam decides in
Book III to let Criseyde go to the Greek camp, it is pointed out that
much grief will result from her departure. Between Priam's decision
and the lovers' painful separation Lydgate inserts Hector's challenge
to Achilles to put an end to the war. Hector's speech (and quite deliberately Troilus is repeatedly called 'þe secunde Ector') is rich in allusion and explicit references to the parallel nature of love and war:

> For of werre may no frendlyhede,
> Nor of debate loue a-riȝt procede;
> For, sothly, loue, moste in special,
> Of feithfulnes hath his original.[51]

[49] Benson, *The History of Troy*, pp. 118–20.

[50] On parallelism between love and war, see J. P. McCall, 'The Trojan Scene in
Chaucer's *Troilus*', *English Literary History*, 29 (1962), 263–75; M. Storm, 'Troilus,
Mars, and Late Medieval Chivalry', *Journal of Medieval and Renaissance Studies*, 12
(1982), 45–65; W. H. Brown, jun., 'A Separate Peace: Chaucer and the Troilus of
Tradition', *Journal of English and Germanic Philology*, 83 (1984), 492–508. On love
as war, see E. Vance, *Mervelous Signals: Poetics and Sign Theory in the Middle Ages*
(Lincoln and London, 1986), ch. 9: 'Mervelous Signals: Sign Theory and the Politics of Metaphor in Chaucer's *Troilus and Criseyde*', esp. pp. 287–301.

[51] *Troy Book*, iii. 3899–902.

He points out that love is complete agreement that leaves no room for duplicity. Everything else, according to Hector, is hatred, rancour, slaughter, war. War is not then limited to great battles: it is also unfaithfulness, unlovingness, which begins between individuals and then spreads to society as a whole, in this case the Greeks and the Trojans. And does not this war, which involves so many men, offer numerous examples within the Greek camp and within the Trojan walls, of infidelity and hatred?[52] There is the rape of Helen, the cause of the war; and is not Calchas' treachery in going over to the enemy the symbol of double-dealing and breach of loyalty to one's homeland? Hector in his magnanimity endeavours to reduce the conflict to less cosmic, more human, dimensions, so as to save the two peoples from the final slaughter.

After Achilles' acceptance of Hector's challenge, Lydgate inserts an apostrophe to Fortune, represented by the wheel that turns to Troilus' disadvantage.[53] The fact that the complaint against Fortune is placed between the episode of the Hector–Achilles challenge and the account of Criseyde's departure from the city of Troy has an extremely clear meaning: the bloodless outcome of the war that the Hector–Achilles duel is aimed at achieving is shown to be unattainable, since even Troilus' and Criseyde's love will come to a sad end because of the woman's infidelity. Hector's words, 'For where loue is, it contuneth euere', are echoed in the narrator's words with reference to Troilus' love; 'And so contuneth by certeyn ȝeris space'.[54] But Fortune as irrational Fate is always lying in wait: Criseyde must go, and before nightfall she has lost her heart to Diomedes. Treachery on the part of the traitor Calchas' daughter reminds the reader that Hector will never succeed in defeating the Greeks if betrayal is not limited to the battlefield, but strikes where sentiments are strongest and dearest. To Hector's wounding corresponds Criseyde's acceptance of Troilus' steed when he is unhorsed by Diomedes.[55] And is not the horse the symbol of Troy's fall? To Criseyde's frivolous behaviour in keeping Diomedes on a string, so as to tie him more tightly to her, is opposed the description of faithful Andromache's dream. Against his wife's

---

[52] On the war outside and inside the walls of Troy, see Vance, *Mervelous Signals*, pp. 264–70.

[53] On the role of Fortune in the *Troy Book*, see Benson, *The History of Troy*, pp. 120–4.

[54] *Troy Book*, iii. 3908; iii. 4220.

[55] Ibid., iii. 4625–52.

will Hector goes out to fight, and the lack of accord between them may be the cause of Hector's act of covetousness (his taking the armour off the body of a dead Greek king) and of his death. When Criseyde gives herself wholly to Diomedes the war takes on new impetus: Achilles agrees to throw his Myrmidons into the fray, and the fate of noble Troilus is sealed. The exaltation of Troilus and the denigration of Achilles conclude Troilus' earthly life; he has of necessity been betrayed by Criseyde but also, it could be added, by Hector. The act of covetousness that causes Hector's death and thus obliges Troilus to take his place is analogous to Criseyde's acceptance of Diomedes' love for fear of being left without material support, and this analogy is tangibly and ironically exemplified by the gift of Troilus' horse that Diomedes makes and Criseyde accepts.

Troilus' and Criseyde's love story offers a further opportunity to moralize and at the same time to give an example of a historical approach to the subject. Lydgate's continually repeated references to Guido and Chaucer bear witness to his intention of both faithfully adapting the sources at his disposal and of proposing himself as the direct, authoritative heir to their work. It is Chaucer of course who is the authority *par excellence* for this episode,[56] but the frequent use of the term 'translacioun' stresses how much Lydgate has relied on Guido for the plan of the work in general and the individual episodes in particular. Lydgate does not trouble himself much about the conclusion of the love story, unlike Chaucer who had offered a multiplicity of possible endings to the story.[57] Troilus' death in battle is what is important, seeing that Criseyde's end is implicit in the way she is presented. It is true that the confirmation given by the *auctoritas* functions in the *Troy Book* somewhat as the narrator in *Troilus and Criseyde* does,[58] but it should also be noted that the various arguments that Lydgate puts forward in Criseyde's defence are pseudo-arguments which, instead of presenting her to advantage, introduce new elements to her

---

[56] For Lydgate Chaucer is a model of eloquence: see R. O. Payne, 'Late Medieval Images and Self-Images of the Poet: Chaucer, Gower, Lydgate, Henryson, Dunbar', pp. 255–7; and L. Ebin, 'Poetics and Style in Late Medieval Literature', pp. 268–73, both in L. Ebin (ed.), *Vernacular Poetics in the Middle Ages*, Studies in Medieval Culture, 16 (Kalamazoo, Mich., 1984).

[57] On the question of genre in *Troilus*, see M. E. McAlpine, *The Genre of Troilus and Criseyde* (Ithaca and London, 1978).

[58] Mieszkowski, 'The Reputation of Criseyde', pp. 124–5.

detriment. Troilus is a mirror of faithfulness, an ideal lover; Criseyde, while tender, sympathetic, and pardonable because she is a woman, is an example of variability and changeableness. Criseyde is in any case to be condemned as inconstant and unfaithful, as all—or almost all—women are. Lydgate crystallizes his attitude to the question of female characters by providing us with an archetype in the story of Medea and Jason. Already in this episode Lydgate amplifies the source, by introducing digressions about women's changeableness and using the metaphor of the serpent. And here as well Lydgate makes a point of distinguishing his position from Guido's, that men are to blame if women change lovers. From the analogy between the two episodes and their two central female figures, Medea and Criseyde, it can be noted how Lydgate's approach to the question of women's nature is always the same: he denigrates and then defends by attributing to Guido the blame for the denigration of which he in reality approves. The meaning of the two episodes is the same: both heroines create their own unhappiness and that of those around them in circumstances determined by a male will in a cause which goes far beyond their individual spheres. In Medea's case, Jason's enterprise must be brought to a successful end; in Criseyde's case, Troilus' death is inevitable, just as Troy's destruction is inescapable. Ashes will not be all that remains from the destruction of Troy, because 'Ful many cite was I-bilt and wrou3t, | And many lond and may riche tovn | Was edified by thocasioun | Of þis werre, as 3e han herde me telle'.[59] Even the worst evil, war, can bring wealth and power in its train, but Lydgate, hoping for a period of peace from the marriage of Henry V and Catherine of France, seems quite obviously to prefer peace and prosperity.

The love-story of Troilus and Criseyde is described by Lydgate with strict adherence to the source and in high style. At various points in the narration of the episode he cites Chaucer, praising him as a master of eloquence and using metaphors connected with precious stones and gold. To Lydgate's mind the poet's task is to conserve the 'substance' of the source, ornamenting it with rhetorical figures. In Lydgate, then, as in other poets of the late Middle Ages, there is a tendency to speculate on the role of the poet and on the expressive possibilities of the English language. This is

<hr />

[59] *Troy Book*, i. 914–17.

particularly significant in a work like the *Troy Book*, which is *par excellence* the epic that *must* be made known in an English version at a time when the foundations of English national identity are being strengthened and there is an endeavour to bring the war against France to a close. The high style predominates in the descriptions of the great battles and the deeds of the most famous heroes, like Troilus and Hector, and reflects the effort, uneven though it may be, to confer on English the status Latin enjoyed.

In conclusion, the Troilus and Criseyde story in the *Troy Book* reinforces the dichotomy, already present in Guido and in Chaucer, between Troilus' nobility and Criseyde's inconstancy. Her doubleness, according to the poet, has a justification: it is unavoidable because woman is changeable by nature and because Fortune, in its variability, helps reverse the destinies of peoples and also of individuals.[60]

If we now turn to an examination of Robert Henryson's *Testament of Cresseid* as a further development and transformation of the story a little less than a century after the *Troy Book*, we will notice that the compression of the narrative Lydgate achieved is accentuated and improved upon. The most notable differences between the two types of approach are the autonomy of the love story in relation to the general Trojan frame, and Criseyde's illness and death along with the author's indifference about Troilus' end. The innovations are recognizable not only thematically but structurally as well: unlike Lydgate, Henryson ascribes a fundamental role to the narrator, as Chaucer had done.

The series of analogical oppositions on which the double story of love and war is based in Chaucer[61] and Lydgate—Troy–Greece, Troilus–Criseyde, Man–Fortune—becomes in Henryson a paradigm of inner conflict rather than an inner–outer pattern. Although Chaucer's interest is focused principally on the love story, the love–war relationship remains constant in his *Troilus*, thanks to the parallelism between the love plot and the events of war. Lydgate renders this parallelism more obvious both themati-

---

[60] Among the many descriptions of Fortune that Lydgate gives us in the *Troy Book*, his characterization of her at the beginning of Book II is especially significant, as in it he states in advance the characteristics of women in general and of Criseyde in particular (1–6).

[61] For this analogy see Vance, *Mervelous Signals*, pp. 286–7.

cally and structurally by breaking the love story up into various episodes and inserting these as highlights illuminating the various phases of the war. In both authors, then, there is a dense interweaving of references, from war to love and from love to war; the weave is more complex in *Troilus* thanks to the various points of view succeeding one another, and simpler, although just as close, in Lydgate.

The war does not disappear from Henryson's version. In order to understand the development of the love story readers are supposed to know the history of the conflict between Troy and Greece, just as, in order to understand the fate Henryson reserves to Cresseid, they are supposed to be familiar with the love-and-betrayal plot in Chaucer's poem.[62] The references remain indirect: Cresseid is called 'the flour and A per se | Of Troy and Grece'; Troilus appears at the head 'of Troy the garnisoun' after vanquishing numerous 'Knichtis of Grece'.[63] The emphasis in the *Testament of Cresseid* is not on the alternate developments in love and war, nor on the two lovers' grief at their separation—because this had already been dealt with by Chaucer and later by Lydgate—but on the 'fatall destenie | Of fair Cresseid, that endit wretchitlie'.[64]

The most suitable genre for a tale of this kind is of course tragedy, and Henryson does in fact define his poem as a 'tragedie' right from the beginning.[65] This term is to be understood according to the meaning it has in the *Monk's Prologue*,[66] words Henryson echoes at line 63—and in Book II of the *Troy Book*. When Lydgate describes the sports and amusements that are common in New Troy, among the latter he deals with comedies and tragedies:

> But tragidie, who so list to knowe,
> It begynneth in prosperite,
> And endeth euer in aduersite;

[62] On how history is dealt with in the *Testament of Cresseid*, see Benson, *The History of Troy*, pp. 143–50; on the influence of *Troilus and Criseyde*, see G. Kratzmann, *Anglo-Scottish Literary Relations 1430-1550* (Cambridge, 1980), 63–86; and J. A. W. Bennett, 'Henryson's *Testament*: A Flawed Masterpiece', in his *The Humane Medievalist*, ed. P. Boitani (Rome, 1982), 89–103.

[63] *Testament*, ll. 78–9; 484, 487.   [64] Ibid., ll. 62–3.

[65] Ibid., l. 4. For a discussion of the various ways of understanding the genre 'tragedy', see again McAlpine, *The Genre of Troilus*; on the *Testament of Cresseid* in general and as an example of Senecan tragedy, see the excellent ch. 5 in D. Gray, *Robert Henryson* (Leiden, 1979). See also A. Clough, 'Medieval Tragedy and the Genre of *Troilus and Criseyde, Medievalia et Humanistica*', 11 (1982), 211–27.

[66] *Monk's Prologue*, ll. 1973–7.

> And it also doth þe conquest trete
> Of riche kynges and of lordys grete,
> Of my3ty men and olde conquerouris,
> Whiche by fraude of Fortunys schowris
> Ben ouercast & whelmed from her glorie.[67]

Both these definitions can be applied to the *Testament of Cresseid* because—although it imitates expressive modes such as the dream-vision and the tradition of the testament or last will[68]—it remains the account of the terrible end of the once lovely, rich, and beloved Cresseid. Furthermore, Troilus himself has a fatal destiny in store. Since at the beginning of the poem we are reminded that the author is reading Chaucer's *Troilus*, the death of the hero at Achilles' hands may be indirectly assumed to be forthcoming. By means of intertextuality the *Testament* would thus present itself not as a continuation but as a complement to the *Troilus*, narrating events that would take place in Book V of Chaucer's poem between Troilus' recognition of Criseyde's betrayal and his sub-sequent complaint, on the one hand, and his death in battle, on the other.[69] Henryson's poem would then appear to be a parenthesis within Chaucer's narrative—an analepsis based on the 'vther quair' he maintains to have resort to for his account.[70]

Troilus' death, however, is never mentioned in the *Testament*, where he is still alive and Cresseid, who has become a prostitute after Diomedes' desertion of her, returns to her father Calchas—who in this version of the story has been made a priest of Venus. Cresseid curses the gods Venus and Cupid for causing her ruin and straightway has the vision of the seven planets who, assembled by Cupid, descend in order to judge and find her guilty. Saturn and Lady Cynthia sentence her to become a leper, and in fact when Cresseid wakes she is fatally ill. One day, as she is out begging with other lepers, she meets Troilus riding back into Troy. Neither recognizes the other, but the sight of her brings back to his mind the image of his beloved and he throws a generous offering into her lap. When she learns that the knight was Troilus, Cresseid, over-come by her guilt, dies (having just sent Troilus a ring). No longer

---

[67] *Troy Book*, ii. 852–9.

[68] On the use of the dream-vision device, see J. MacQueen, *Robert Henryson: A Study of the Major Narrative Poems* (Oxford, 1967), 65–81.

[69] *Troilus*, v. 1646–750, *Testament*, ll. 43–60; *Troilus*, v. 1751–806.

[70] *Testament*, l. 61.

ignorant of Cresseid's painful story, Troilus has a fine tomb made ready for her.

The finality of Cresseid's death is so strong, the tomb and the inscription are so emblematic of the 'sense of an ending' the author wants to convey, that any reader would at this point forget that Troilus' death is 'intertextually' still to come. In other words, the connection between the *Testament* and *Troilus and Criseyde* is severed by the end of Henryson's poem. The *Testament* is no longer an ideal parenthesis of the *Troilus*, but a variation on it—a 'continuation' which radically changes its source's narrative sequence and meaning.

The most novel element in the presentation of Cresseid is not so much the leprosy—which represents just punishment for her inconstancy[71]—as her final self-awareness in acknowledging her guilt. Henryson makes his contribution to the tradition of Cresseid's guilt by presenting her as a prostitute after Diomedes, for whom she was probably only one of many lovers, has abandoned her: 'Than desolait scho walkit vp and doun, | And sum men sayis, into the court, commoun'.[72] Even when the narrator seems to make excuses for her, describing her as 'fortunait'[73]—persecuted by Fortune—in reality he stresses her 'filth', her 'spots', and above all her stooping to sin:

> O fair Creisseid, the flour and A per se
> Of Troy and Grece, how was thow fortunait
> To change in filth all thy feminitie,
> And be with fleschelie lust sa maculait,
> And go amang the Greikis air and lait,

---

[71] Leprosy is seen as the disease which best befits Cresseid's punishment: cf. Fox, *The Poems of Robert Henryson*, pp. lxxxiv–xciii. Among the critics who justify Cresseid's punishment from a theological point of view, see M. W. Stearns, *Robert Henryson* (New York, 1949); E. M. W. Tillyard, *Five Poems, 1470-1870* (London, 1948) who sees the sins of pride and anger exemplified in Cresseid; and the introd. to C. Elliott, *Robert Henryson: Poems* (Oxford, 1974). The role of Cresseid's blasphemy is stressed by MacQueen, *Robert Henryson*, and by E. D. Aswell, 'The Role of Fortune in *The Testament of Cresseid*', *Philological Quarterly*, 46 (1967), 471–87. The debate between paganism and Christianity is treated by L. W. Patterson, 'Christian and Pagan in *The Testament of Cresseid*', *Philological Quarterly*, 52 (1973), 696–714, while the paganism of the *Testament* is pointed out in Benson, *The History of Troy*, pp. 148–50.

[72] *Testament*, ll. 76–7.

[73] Ibid., l. 79.

Sa giglotlike takand thy foull plesance!
I haue pietie thow suld fall sic mischance![74]

The *change* ascribed to Cresseid by Henryson is much more
drastic than the *change* in the *Troy Book*, because it is endowed
with a value of *moralitas*: it is not a question of a generic changeableness but of a transformation from purity ('feminitie') into dirt
('filth'). Like Chaucer and Lydgate, Henryson is conscious of the
bad reputation attached to Cresseid and makes an effort to justify
her by attributing the reason for her change to Fortune:

> 3it neuertheles, quhat euer men deme or say
> In scornefull langage of thy brukkilnes,
> I sall excuse als far furth as I may
> Thy womanheid, thy wisdome and fairnes,
> The quhilk fortoun hes put to sic distres
> As hir pleisit, and nathing throw the gilt
> Of the—throw wickit langage to be spilt![75]

The narrator's words are ambiguous because they make a distinction between moral 'brukkilnes' and the secular qualities
'womanheid', 'wisdome', and 'fairnes',[76] which alone seem to be
upset by the erratic turns of Fortune. The two stanzas quoted anticipate Cresseid's fate: 'filth' and 'maculait' are terms that should
not be understood only in their moral sense but also as a fore-
shadowing of the physical ravages leprosy will inflict on the
woman's body. On the other hand disease was considered in the
Middle Ages as God's punishment to remove guilt and expiate
sin—and this explains the connection between the two kinds of
spot. The references to the 'scornefull' and 'wickit' language that
men will use to describe Cresseid also foreshadow the kind of language the woman will adopt later on with regard to the gods.

By way of parallels and repetitions of the same lexemes Henryson seems to proceed by linked stanzas that both recall what has
already been said and anticipate what is to come. Thus, the 'excludit' and 'desolait' at the moment of Diomedes' desertion are
repeated in the 'outwaill' and 'excludit' of Cresseid's apostrophe to
the gods.[77] They quite clearly prelude the final social exclusion she
will be subjected to from her father and all other men. Perhaps

---

[74] *Testament*, ll. 78–84.   [75] Ibid., ll. 85–91.
[76] Elliott, *Robert Henryson*, p. 165.
[77] *Testament*, ll. 75, 76, 129, 133.

by the law of retaliation the once 'commoun'[78] Cresseid is first excluded by Troilus and Diomedes, and then, because of her leprosy, by society. In the *Troy Book* the influence of fickle Fortune plays its part in Criseyde's moral changes with regard to Troilus; here not only Fortune but above all the astrological influence of the seven planets accelerate Cresseid's external transformation, bringing about her final exclusion from the world.

The further re-elaboration of a classical story involves a process of inclusion and exclusion: the author includes certain 'historical' details—often taken over from Chaucer—and almost completely excludes noble Troilus, and the history of the war, in order to concentrate on Cresseid's 'shame and guilt'.[79] All the changes indicated in the *Testament* are irreversible: joy turns into grief, the once-green seed of love is slain by the frost. Her doom as a leper does not however seem—at least until her meeting with Troilus—to be due to the fickleness of which Guido, Chaucer, and Lydgate accused her, but to her blasphemy against the divinity of Venus and Cupid. As partial justification of Cresseid Henryson presents to us an extremely ambiguous Venus who embodies both the positive and the negative qualities ascribed to women.[80] Venus is lovely, but the description of her is entirely based on a series of oppositions that can better be understood if the characteristics that Lydgate in his translation of Guido inflicts on women in general and Criseyde in particular are borne in mind. The hues of Venus' raiment are green and black, her hair is drawn back like Criseyde's in the *Troy Book* and her inconstancy is reiterated: 'Bot in hir face semit greit variance, | Quhyles perfyte treuth and quhyles inconstance'; 'Thus variant scho was, quha list tak keip'; 'Richt vnstabill and full of variance'.[81] In the three stanzas describing *Venus* we find all the reasons for the fault for which *Cresseid* should be condemned. Only after the appearance of Troilus, towards the end of the poem, does Cresseid acknowledge her guilt and seal her new self-awareness with the refrain 'fals Cresseid' | 'trew knicht Troylus'.

We might ask ourselves at this point why Henryson represents Venus in such an ambiguous way and why he postpones recourse

---

[78] Ibid., l. 77.   [79] Gray, *Robert Henryson*, pp. 204–5.
[80] On the ambiguity of Venus' characterization, see Aswell, 'The Role of Fortune'; Gray, *Robert Henryson*, pp. 185–7. On the iconographic representation of Venus, see M. Twycross, *The Medieval Anadyomene* (Oxford, 1972).
[81] *Testament*, ll. 223–4; 230; 235.

to Criseyde's traditional attributes until the very last. We need to
discuss here the sources of the *Testament* and the role of the narrator. Henryson immediately presents himself in the guise of the
author of the poem: 'Richt sa it wes quhen I began to wryte | This
tragedie'.[82] The astronomical setting the narrative unfolds in is
typical of late medieval dream poems (Lydgate's *Temple of Glas* is a
case in point). The weather is mild enough, but the sky is threatening in the north. The cold that obliges the poet to retire indoors
and the impossible opposition of Venus and the Sun emphasize the
threat that hangs over the scene. If by tragedy we are meant to
understand the fall from prosperity to ruin, then the astronomical
notations are appropriate: the wind has swept the clouds away, but
its freezing blasts counteract the warmth of the sun's rays shining
through the windowpanes. And it is here that the play of mirror-
ings on which the poem is based begins. The poet is old: he would
like to pray to Venus to revive his capacity to love, but he gives up
the idea because of the cold. The contrast between warmth and
cold, the hot blood of youth and the inertia of old age, connects the
narrator's story with Cresseid's by anticipating it; it also stresses
the 'comic' aspect of the poem—represented by the poet reading
by the fire and who, as narrator, recounts the story. The 'tragic'
aspect of his work is embodied in Cresseid's cruel destiny. As far as
the sources and Henryson's approach to them are concerned, it
should be noted that the poet, in the best Chaucerian tradition,
picks up a book to make the hours of night pass more rapidly: it is
the 'quair' of the famous story of *Troilus and Criseyde*. After paying
his tribute to Chaucer—whose style is summed up in the line 'In
gudelie termis and in ioly veirs'[83]—by offering a brief résumé of
Troilus, he turns to another 'quair' containing the unhappy end of
the heroine.

Like Lydgate, Henryson has two sources—Chaucer and an
unknown author—but unlike Lydgate he does not translate any
given text, even though he often plunders *Troilus*. On the contrary,
he asks himself the question:

> Quha wait gif all that Chauceir wrait was trew?
> Nor I wait nocht gif this narratioun
> Be authoreist, or fenȝeit of the new
> Be sum poeit, throw his inuentioun

[82] *Testament*, ll. 3–4.   [83] Ibid., l. 59.

Maid to report the lamentatioun
And wofull end of this lustie Creisseid,
And quhat distres scho thoillit, and quhat deid.[84]

This stanza undoubtedly marks a milestone in the passage from
the Middle Ages to the Renaissance in terms of their conceptions
of poetry. The contraposition between *auctoritas* and poetic
creativity is clearly demonstrated in the chiastic structure of lines
66–7, where the correspondence *fenȝeit of the new-poeit* is played
off against the apparent opposition *authoreist-inuentioun*. The
chiastic structure is able to recompose the latter opposition, denying its literal value in virtue of a new conception of poetry where
even the 'auctores' invent their stories. This is confirmed by line 64,
where the truthfulness of the story told in *Troilus* is not ques-
tioned, but where the creative capacity of poets, and in particular
of the great master Chaucer, is asserted.

On the other hand Henryson assumes from the start the role of
author—a court poet, as the final invitation to 'worthie wemen'
indicates.[85] He takes Chaucer and another author as his sources,
but he also invents a new story on a traditional theme. As we have
seen, the history of Troy and the personal story of Troilus have
only a marginal collocation in the *Testament*, which is centred on
Cresseid and the poet-narrator. Just as the poet retires to his room
in the uncertain spring weather, so Cresseid, alone and abandoned,
takes refuge in a 'secreit orature',[86] where she falls on her knees not
to pray, but to upbraid and throw the blame on Venus and Cupid
for her unhappy state as a rejected woman. The poet's attitude to
Venus is analogous to Cresseid's. The Venus 'luifis quene' to whom
the poet thinks of applying for the enjoyment of love as he had
known it in his youth, is the same 'of lufe the blind goddes' who
was to keep forever green the seed of love on Cresseid's face.[87] This
Venus, represented like Fortune and therefore fickle, was once
benevolent towards the poet and Cresseid, but no longer grants
them her favours. This does not justify Cresseid's blasphemy, but it
does lessen its extent.

Henryson's most remarkable invention is the assembly of the
seven planets. These are presented in both their astrological and
their symbolic significance and divided into malevolent (Saturn,

[84] Ibid., ll. 64–70.   [85] Ibid., l. 610.
[86] Ibid., l. 120.   [87] Ibid., ll. 22; 135.

Mars, Venus), benevolent (Jupiter, Phoebus, Mercury), and neutral (Lady Cynthia). Mercury, who chooses Saturn and Cynthia to deliver the sentence, turns out to be malevolent. He is seen as the god of poetry—'Lyke to ane poeit of the auld fassoun'[88]—and it is he who sanctions the penalty inflicted on Cresseid. His prerogatives—eloquence, rhetoric, and skill in writing and in using the terms of the aureate style—reflect those of Chaucer and of the poet-narrator who is recounting the tragic story of Cresseid. Like the poet, however, Mercury cannot refrain from acting in the interests of justice, and so he condemns Cresseid for being blasphemous. Henryson may invent a different ending from Chaucer's, but this ending must once more be tragic. Cresseid must die because she is guilty. The gods must punish her or run the risk of their authority's being derided. Henryson must create a tragic destiny or risk his credibility as a poet in line with the 'auctores'. After Chaucer's 'litel tragedye' only another tragedy can follow.

'To be foirspeikar in the parliament', Mercury is chosen for his gifts as a rhetorician: 'His facound toung and termis exquisite, | Of rethorick the prettick he micht leir, | In brief sermone ane pregnant sentence wryte'.[89] This is an appropriate choice both because Mercury is the god of eloquence and because his rhetorical skill corresponds to those ideals of conciseness to which the literature of the Middle Ages aspires.[90] Henryson manages to construct a *sententia* in just 616 lines: if at all, there may be a touch of irony in the emphasis on *abbreviatio* within the longest episode in the poem, where the poet exploits the aureate style. There certainly is irony in the description of the stock of medicines that will not serve to cure Cresseid's disease and in the qualities of honesty attributed to the god, 'Honest and gude, and not ane word culd lie'.[91] In mythology Mercury is accused of various thefts from

[88] *Testament*, l. 245. On the description of Mercury as a poet, see P. Bawcutt, 'Henryson's "Poeit of the Auld Fassoun"', *Review of English Studies*, NS, 32 (1981), 429–34.

[89] *Testament*, ll. 266; 268–70.

[90] A. C. Spearing, in his 'Conciseness and *The Testament of Cresseid*' in *Criticism and Medieval Poetry* (London, 1964), 118–44, proves that the 'high concise style' of the *Testament* derives from a precise literary theory that was widespread in the late Middle Ages. On the contribution of rhetoric to the structure of the *Testament*, cf. L. M. Sklute, 'Phoebus Descending: Rhetoric and Moral Vision in Henryson's *Testament of Cresseid*', *English Literary History*, 44 (1977), 189–204.

[91] *Testament*, l. 252.

Apollo, Neptune, and Venus, and he is particularly dear to thieves and rascals. But here the verb 'lie' refers us back to the isotopy of falseness, pretence, and treachery that makes Fortune, Venus, Diomedes, Cresseid, and the narrator all alike.

The detailed description of the gods' prerogatives answers the need to stress the power and irrevocability of the decisions of pagan deities. The seven planets are indeed defined as 'Quhilk hes power of all thing generabill, | To reull and steir be thair greit influence | Wedder and wind, and coursis variabill'.[92] All begotten things are subject to change: the poet on the threshold of old age changes, as does Cresseid, who in the flower of her youth is doomed to a cruel fate. Only the gods, in disagreement among themselves though they may be, remain fixed in their pre-Christian justice; this is a justice not tempered by mercy, which metes out the appropriate reward for the insult to their divine essence. The narrator's apostrophe to cruel Saturn is in itself a reinforcement, by contrast, of man's powerlessness. Here Guido's pessimism, which both Chaucer and Lydgate also display, is predominant.

When the dream vanishes, the timeless time of the vision suddenly becomes reality, a time which flies towards its earthly annihilation at death's hands.[93] The first object Cresseid touches is a 'poleist glas' in which to see her reflection, 'hir schaddow'.[94] After dwelling on the details of Cresseid's physical transformation, which is foretold in her dream, Henryson inserts a telling couplet that sums up her grief:

> And quhen scho saw hir face sa deformait,
> Gif scho in hart was wa aneuch, God wait![95]

From this moment on Cresseid is a *speculum* and an *exemplum*: Henryson the moralizer takes over.

According to modern methods of analysis, taking up a mirror implies the recognition of a division of the ego, of a tension within the individual due to social ties and language acts. The brief *planctus* that follows seems to suggest precisely this, but it also indicates, according to the Neo-Platonic conception, a first step

[92] Ibid., ll. 148–50.
[93] On the theme of time, cf. J. M. Ganim, 'The Limits of Vision in Henryson's *Testament of Cresseid*', in *Style and Consciousness in Middle English Narrative* (Princeton, NJ., 1983), 123–41.
[94] Ibid., l. 348.   [95] Ibid., ll. 349–50.

towards knowledge of oneself. Finally, in the 'schaddow' Cresseid glimpses in the mirror, in that individual disfigurement and ruin, we might symbolically see the compression and synthesis of that greater, collective ruin that is war—which is also the ultimate cause of the onset of her change. Even if the war is not present, the reader has firmly in mind the context from which the text originates. It was the war that left her bereft of her guide, Troilus; it was the war that made her betray Troilus with Diomedes.

Immediately after the brief, realistic episode of the boy who calls Cresseid to dinner come the two stanzas in which Calchas recognizes the signs of his daughter's illness. A glance at Cresseid's face is enough for her father to see the horrible truth of leprosy and to realize that a cure is impossible. From the moment Cresseid sees confirmed in her mirror the sentence pronounced on her by the gods, there is a proliferation of terms referring to seeing, observing, and knowing. This accentuates the irony of a fate that makes it impossible for other people to know her and in any case separates her from the rest of society: 'scho saw', 'sa is sene on me', 'He luikit', 'he knew weill', 'Sum knew hir weill, and sum had na knawledge'.[96] In the long complaint that follows, Cresseid passes from a recognition of the lost joys of life to regret and grief at her present miserable condition. The *moralitas* is suggested by Cresseid herself; she identifies with the narrator in holding herself up as an example to Greek and Trojan women:

> Be war in tyme, approchis neir the end,
> And in ʒour mynd ane mirrour mak of me:
> As I am now, peraduenture that ʒe
> For all ʒour micht may cum to that same end,
>
> Exempill mak of me in ʒour memour
> Quhilk of sic thingis wofull witnes beiris.[97]

Like Lydgate, Henryson imitates the line from Chaucer's *Troilus*, and once again changes its meaning. In this context the metaphor takes on a negative connotation: let the women of Greece and Troy keep firmly in mind the memory of Cresseid's fate to escape ruining themselves the way she did. Everything is doomed to fall prey to time, because 'Fortoun is fikkill'.[98] Against the power of the gods, against their way of ruling the world,

---

[96] *Testament of Cresseid*, ll. 349; 353; 372; 376; 393.
[97] Ibid., ll. 456–9; 465–6.   [98] Ibid., l. 469.

nothing can be done: the only suggestions that may avail is that of a 'lipper lady'—'I counsall the mak vertew of ane neid'.[99]

In this pessimistic vision of the sublunary world a part of her past comes before Cresseid: a conquering hero after a battle against the Greeks, Troilus passes by the lepers without recognizing the woman. The stanza that follows,

> Than vpon him scho kest vp baith hir ene,
> And with ane blenk it come into his thocht
> That he sumtime hir face befoir had sene,
> Bot scho was in sic plye he knew hir nocht;
> 3it than hir luik into his mynd it brocht
> The sweit visage and amorous blenking
> Of fair Cresseid, sumtyme his awin darling,[100]

is undoubtedly one of the most perfectly constructed of the poem, wholly based as it is on terms referring to sight and thought. For five lines the narrator stresses Troilus' effort to remember that face with lexemes, 'hir ene', 'his thocht', 'befoir had sene', 'he knew hir nocht', 'hir luik into his mynd it brocht', until what has en- gendered that agonizing recollection comes back to him: 'The sweit visage and amorous blenking | Of fair Cresseid'. To provide relief from the pathos of Troilus' failure to recognize Cresseid the poet inserts an explanation of Troilus' mental processes in terms of Aristotelian psychology.[101] The 'idole'[102] impressed on Troilus' imagination, which makes him see Cresseid in the 'lipper' woman, stands before him in the flesh. In remembrance of past love, Troilus throws gold and jewels into her lap. It is Troilus the knight, with his pomp and wealth, who introduces here the theme of *change/ exchange* that was already present in the *Troy Book*. The memory of Cresseid makes Troilus suffer now and almost die 'for wo' later, when he learns that Cresseid is dead.[103]

---

[99] Ibid., l. 478. An echo of Chaucer's *Knight's Tale*, 'To maken vertu of neces- sitee' (l. 3042). On the philosophy expressed in the *Knight's Tale*, see Minnis, *Chaucer and Pagan Antiquity*, pp. 121–31.

[100] *Testament*, ll. 498–504.

[101] The cognitive process Henryson refers to may be ascribed to a tradition that passes through Aristotle's *De Anima*, Plutarch, and Augustine's *De Trinitate*: see Stearns, *Robert Henryson*, pp. 97–105; for a less positive interpretation of the non-recognition of Cresseid by Troilus, who allows himself to be carried away by a false imagination, cf. Benson, *The History of Troy*, pp. 146–7.

[102] *Testament*, l. 507.   [103] Ibid., ll. 512–25; 596–602.

When Cresseid is told that the generous knight was Troilus she collapses from grief and finally admits her guilt: 'O fals Cresseid and trew knicht Troylus'.[104] The succeeding four stanzas are a variation on the theme of inconstancy that can be summed up in the line, 'Als vnconstant, and als vntrew of fay'.[105] Troilus' failure to recognize her has the beneficial effect of starting Cresseid along the way towards acknowledgement of her guilt and disdain of earthly riches. In this late medieval 'tragedy', then, we have a highly pathetic progress from mutual misrecognition to separate knowledge, and finally to individual self-recognition and confession. With supreme tragic irony, Troilus, unaware of Cresseid's repentance, builds for her a marble tomb, but lends further weight to her bad reputation with his final 'Scho was vntrew and wo is me thairfoir'.[106] The narrator's moral is analogous: 'Ming not ʒour lufe with fals deceptioun'.[107]

Before her disparagers (Troilus and the narrator included) Cresseid acknowledges her guilt and the evil she has done her lovers by her fickleness. She blames no one but herself for her ruin. It is Henryson's aim, without offering Christian interpretations, to stress that this woman—an archetype of inconstancy—contrasts present and past and does not condemn earthly love: on the contrary, she finds in it a means of expiation. Cresseid insists on the need for faithfulness, even if this is difficult to maintain. For Henryson, then, Cresseid must pay the penalty of her fault, she must acknowledge her sin, and die:

> Sen scho is deid I speik of hir no moir.[108]

In conclusion, the love story of Troilus and Criseyde remains the same in Lydgate and Henryson in that it is based on the opposition soon (as David Benson shows) to become paradigmatic, between *double Criseyde* and *worthy Troilus*, between *fals Cresseid* and *trew Troylus*. This opposition is already present in Chaucer, but it is less clearly defined there because the narrator delays revealing in full the difference in behaviour between Troilus and Criseyde until the ending. In the *Troy Book* the opposition is pre-eminent, even though the love story is reduced to a series of brief episodes within the framework of the history of the conflict between Troy and Greece. The *Testament of Cresseid* re-establishes

---

[104] *Testament*, l. 546.   [105] Ibid., l. 571.
[106] Ibid., l. 602.   [107] Ibid., l. 613.   [108] Ibid., l. 616.

the independence of the love story that Lydgate had treated 'historically', and has the temerity to assert its 'fictional' character. The poet's opportunity to create anew a tragic ending tacked on to the traditional 'mater' and his skill in doing so are anticipations of the Renaissance conception of poetry. Although subject to limitations that a late medieval poet could not yet overcome, Henryson does make an attempt to break down certain barriers to individual expression.

It may then be interesting to see how, but a hundred years later, the old dichotomy between Criseyde's unfaithfulness and Troilus' 'truth' becomes a contrast between the real and the ideal, between deeds and words. This, the new mark of dramatic expression, is the gap Shakespeare is interested in:

> Words, words, mere words, no matter from the heart;
> Th'effect doth operate another way.
> Go, wind, to wind: there turn and change together.
> My love with words and errors still she feeds,
> But edifies another with her deeds.[109]

[109] *Troilus and Cressida*, v. iii. 108–12.

10

Fragments and Scraps: Shakespeare's
Troilus and Cressida

AGOSTINO LOMBARDO

The Prologue of *Troilus and Cressida* seems the product of contingency—an ironic answer to the Prologue 'in armour' with which Ben Jonson in 1601 began his *Poetaster*. Explicitly entering the lists of the 'war of the theatres', Jonson writes:

> If any muse why I salute the stage,
> An armed Prologue; know, 'tis a dangerous age:
> Wherein who writes, has need present his scenes
> Forty-fold proof against the conjuring means
> Of base detractors, and illiterate apes,
> That fill up rooms in fair and formal shapes.
> 'Gainst these, have we put on this forced defense.[1]

Shakespeare similarly opens his play, some time after, with a 'Prologue in armour'; but, while this can be considered one of several nods in his friend and rival's direction ('. . . and hither am I come | A Prologue armed, but not in confidence | Of author's pen or actor's voice'), it also serves to take us straight into *Troilus and Cressida*, providing the background to the action:

> In Troy there lies the scene. From Isles of Greece
> The princes orgulous, their high blood chaf'd,
> Have to the port of Athens sent their ships
> Fraught with the ministers and instruments
> Of cruel war[2]

and stating its limits as regards the Trojan War:

> our play
> Leaps o'er the vaunt and firstlings of these broils,

[1] *The Complete Plays of Ben Jonson* (London, 1946), 235.
[2] *Troilus and Cressida*, Prologue, 1–5.

Beginning in the middle, starting thence away
To what may be digested in a play.[3]

But it is a lead-in to the play in a far more significant sense too; in its desecration of epic language, adopting a sarcastically reductive point of view regarding the mythical war and its causes ('. . . and their vow is made | To ransack Troy, within whose strong immures | The ravish'd Helen, Menelaus' queen, | With wanton Paris sleeps—and that's the quarrel'[4]), and its use of images of chance and uncertainty, it encapsulates the actual nature of the play which follows, a play which, like its near-contemporaries *All's Well* and *Measure for Measure*, is not to be considered a comedy, having nothing of the comic and of the 'light fantastic' which Shakespeare's other comedies possess. Yet, neither is the play a tragedy, its world lacking the stable values and points of reference which make tragedy possible; even death, ever-present to freeze the smile of comedy, fails to bring about tragic catharsis. It represents no value or vital experience, but simply death: the end. A *dark comedy*, then; a disquieting and problematic, lacerated and ambiguous work, which is also, and for this reason, a crucial moment in the development of Shakespeare and of modern theatre.

Thus, in what the title announces as a love story (but which the Elizabethan public, from Chaucer and other sources, would immediately read in a different light), love is the first 'value' whose fragility is traced and represented. Initially it appears to bud and blossom in spite of everything: Troy has been at war for seven years, blood and destruction are the norm, but the young Troilus, son of Priam, is in love with Cressida, daughter of Calchas; and Cressida, in her turn, is in love with him. In reality one detail is already warning us to be on our guard: the fact that their love is mediated through Cressida's uncle, pander in name and nature, and in Shakespeare not merely a comic figure but a corrupter whose vulgarity and sensuality belittle and degrade all he touches. This emerges in his very first exchange with Troilus (and the use of prose is far from incidental), when he describes love in the extended metaphor of making a cake, giving rise to the series of food images which communicate more concretely than anything else in the play the material and corruptible nature of the real:

[3] *Troilus and Cressida*, ll. 26–9.   [4] Ibid., ll. 7–10.

PANDARUS. . . . He that will have a cake out of the wheat must tarry the grinding.

TROILUS. Have I not tarried?

. . . .

PANDARUS. Ay, to the leavening; but here's yet in the word 'hereafter' the kneading, the making of the cake, the heating of the oven, and the baking: nay, you must stay the cooling too, or you may chance burn your lips.[5]

There is a similar vulgarity underlying his first exchange with Cressida, when his eulogy of Troilus degenerates from a portrait of the complete Renaissance man into an image of food:

Well, well? Have you any discretion? Have you any eyes? Do you know what a man is? Is not birth, beauty, good shape, discourse, manhood, learning, gentleness, virtue, youth, liberality and such like, the spice and salt that seasons a man?[6]

Cressida, it will be remembered, conceals her love for Troilus both out of coyness and a refusal of Pandarus' corrupting mediation,[7] but also because, in her female realism and condition as a child of the war (perceptively focused by Ian Kott)[8] she is so much more aware than Troilus of its precarious and incongruous nature. Their love can only be realized in the third act. The scene in the garden (which glances at, while diverging substantially from, that of *Romeo and Juliet*), in which the two can finally express their feelings, and Cressida finally throw down her 'mask',[9] owes its anguished dramatic intensity precisely to its long delay through so many scenes treating its opposite theme, war, in both the Greek and Trojan camps. Furthermore, the presence of Pandarus during their meeting quietly points to this realization as being as precarious as it is ambiguous; love, in such a context, both general and particular, is rotten before ripening, and over before it has begun. It comes as less of a surprise therefore that as they retire for their one night of love (but under Pandarus' roof) Cressida's father, the soothsayer Calchas, prisoner of the Greeks, requests that his daughter be exchanged for the Trojan Antenor; or that their awakening coincides with the brusque irruption of the outside world, and reason of state. There is no place in the world of the

[5] Ibid., I. i. 14–26. [6] Ibid., I. ii. 255–60.
[7] Ibid., I. i. 289–90. [8] *Shakespeare Our Contemporary* (New York, 1964).
[9] *Troilus and Cressida*, III. ii. 112–14.

play for individual emotions, and Pandarus' house becomes a
bargaining-place for 'the exchange of Cressida for Antenor. The
two lovers, after vain resistance, must finally bow to superior
forces, and Cressida, in a highly symbolic scene,[10] is given to
Diomedes. Their parting takes place among repeated vows of
mutual faithfulness and exchange of love-tokens, but it is in parting
and distance that their love ends. For all her exclaiming:

> O you gods divine,
> Make Cressid's name the very crown of falsehood
> If ever she leave Troilus![11]

Cressida reacts to the gods' brutality by replacing her mask and
rejecting all illusion; she accepts not merely the kisses and pleasan-
tries of the Greek commanders, but equally the advances of her
new lord. The garden scene is juxtaposed with the painful,
poignant scene in the Greek camp[12] (an anticipation, albeit
inverted, of the Bianca scene in *Othello*),[13] in which Troilus, unseen
and accompanied by Ulysses and Thersites, observes the tender
exchanges between Cressida and Diomedes, and her gift to him of
Troilus' love-token. Cressida, unaware that she is overheard
(although everyone is overheard in *Troilus and Cressida*, a play
admitting no privacy), takes her clear-sighted farewell:

> Troilus, farewell! One eye yet looks on thee,
> But with my heart the other eye doth see.
> Ah, poor our sex! this fault in us I find:
> The error of our eye directs our mind.
> What error leads must err; O, then conclude,
> Minds sway'd by eyes are full of turpitude.[14]

Troilus' world collapses, and he can only cling to the hope that
appearance and reality have changed places, and that *his* Cressida
is still faithful:

> This she?—No, this is Diomed's Cressida.
> If beauty have a soul, this is not she;
> If souls guide vows, if vows be sanctimonies,
> If sanctimony be the gods' delight,

---

[10] *Troilus and Cressida*, IV. iv.   [11] Ibid., IV. ii. 102–4.   [12] Ibid., V. ii.
[13] *Othello*, III. iv. 'Inverted' in that what Othello 'sees' is false, while Troilus
witnesses the truth.
[14] *Troilus and Cressida*, V. ii. 106–11.

If there be rule in unity itself,
This is not she.[15]

In the world in which they are forced to exist, however, no such conditions obtain; much as he exclaims 'Cressid is mine, tied with the bonds of heaven',[16] he himself recognizes immediately afterwards—and in images which project the particular into a far more general sphere, and into the imagery scheme of the whole play— that these bonds have come untied:

> The bonds of heaven are slipp'd, dissolv'd, and loos'd;
> And with another knot, five-finger-tied,
> The fractions of her faith, orts of her love,
> The fragments, scraps, the bits, and greasy relics
> Of her o'er-eaten faith are given to Diomed.[17]

All illusion spent, his only course is action: to act his part in the general blood-bath—he who had opened the play by taking off his armour (in ironic contrast to the Prologue 'in armour') to pursue his love for Cressida and, rejecting the 'ungracious clamours' and 'rude sounds' of war, had, in the light of his love, recognized its senselessness for Trojans and Greeks alike:

> Fools on both sides, Helen must needs be fair
> When with your blood you daily paint her thus.[18]

He who had attempted to reconcile the ideals of love and knightly conduct, defending, in the discussion among the Trojan commanders, the continuation of the conflict, and resuming his place in the fight, now realizes that no such reconciliation is possible; only action remains. At the end of the play he is seen thirsting for Diomedes' blood—vainly, however, since *Troilus and Cressida* is a play without conclusions, and even this final confrontation with Diomedes will be denied him. His words, as he withdraws after Hector's death, vow revenge; insulting Pandarus, they are in effect submerged by Pandarus' parting comment:

O world, world, world! Thus is the poor agent despised. O traitors and bawds, how earnestly are you set awork, and how ill requited. Why should our endeavour be so loved and the performance so loathed?[19]

[15] Ibid., v. ii. 126–41. [16] Ibid., v. ii. 153. [17] Ibid., v. ii. 155–9.
[18] Ibid., I. i. 89; I. ii. 90–1. [19] Ibid., v. x. 36–40.

It is not without significance that the last figure on the stage is Pandarus, and that the Epilogue is assigned to him. He is the tangible sign of the impossibility in the world of *Troilus and Cressida* (as in that of *Hamlet*, *All's Well*, and *Measure for Measure*) both of love and of heroism. Shakespeare had already started on a process of 'de-heroicization' in 1599, in *Julius Caesar*, where the 'heroes', from Caesar to Brutus, are represented chiefly in their weakness and fragility; but this arose less from a negative and desecrating intention than from a need both to represent the characters' human dimension and to pronounce a basically relative judgement in the face of a mysterious and near-indecipherable reality. The intention in *Troilus and Cressida* is different; here the heroes (and the traditions which mythicize them) are mocked and emptied of substance. A significant scene is that in which the Trojan warriors march past the battlements and Pandarus, using the parade to further Troilus' cause with Cressida, illustrates each man's qualities in a tone which belittles while seeming to exhalt:

That's Aeneas, is not that a brave man? He's one of the flowers of Troy, I can tell you. But mark Troilus; you shall see anon.... That's Hector, that, that, look you, that; there's a fellow! Go thy way, Hector—there's a brave man, niece—O brave Hector! Look how he looks, there's a countenance: is't not a brave man?... It does a man's heart good. Look you what hacks are on his helmet—look you yonder, do you see? Look you there: there's no jesting, there's laying on. Take off who will, as they say: there be hacks.[20]

And if this process of 'reduction', already underway before Pandarus speaks,[21] takes place in the Trojan camp, which, as Coleridge observes, represents a world still bent on nurturing ideals,[22] in the

[20]   *Troilus and Cressida*, I. ii. 188 ff.

[21]   See also the conversation between Cressida and Alexander before Pandarus appears, for its presentation both of Ajax's animalesque nature and of Hector's distinctly unheroic churlishness towards Andromache, in reaction to being discomfited by Ajax in battle: 'This man, lady, hath robbed many beasts of their particular additions: he is as valiant as the lion, churlish as the bear, slow as the elephant ...'; and 'They say he yesterday coped Hector in the battle and struck him down, the disdain and shame whereof hath ever since kept Hector fasting and waking' (I. ii).

[22]   Coleridge sees in the play an opposition between 'The inferior civilization but purer morals of the Trojans' and 'The refinements, deep policy, but duplicity and sensual corruptions of the Greeks', *Coleridge on Shakespeare*, ed. T. Hawkes (Harmondsworth, 1969), 272. His observations are, as always, of great interest.

Greek camp it assumes grotesque proportions, not least because the 'heroes'—if such a term is appropriate—are all refracted through the deforming glass of Thersites, Pandarus' counterpart on whom the theme of war is centred, just as that of love is centred on Pandarus. Obscene, repulsive, and as deformed in mind as in body, Thersites is of a piece with the disharmonious world of the action, its symbol and faithful interpreter, underscoring—and behind this 'denigratory chorus' lies, of course, both the Medieval Vice and the bitter satire of a Marston—all its evil and corruption. Thus refracted (Casca's role in *Julius Caesar* is not dissimilar), men are seen at their vilest, with all their ills and weaknesses; ills which through the figure of Thersites assume a terrible concreteness (the imagery here plays an essential role) as the diseased rottenness of the world. The heroes are made more grotesque than ridiculous, transformed by this new Circe into hideous animals, with much of the Swiftian Yahoo:

Here's Agamemnon: an honest fellow enough, and one that loves quails, but he has not so much brain as ear-wax; and the goodly transformation of Jupiter there, his brother the bull, the primitive statue and oblique memorial of cuckolds, a thrifty shoeing-horn in a chain at his brother's leg: to what form but that he is, should wit larded with malice and malice forced with wit turn him to? To an ass were nothing: he is both ass and ox.[23]

War is a grotesque pantomime, and the 'sleeve' itself, which in the Troilus tradition represents the dramatic token of unfaithfulness and the cause of Troilus' relentless hatred for Diomedes, is reduced to the object of a worthless 'errand', the mere symbol of a 'dissembling luxurious drab':

Now they are clapper-clawing one another, I'll go look on. That dissembling abominable varlet Diomed has got that same scurvy, doting, foolish knave's sleeve of Troy there in his helm. I would fain see them meet, that that same young Trojan ass, that loves the whore there, might send that Greekish whoremaster villain with the sleeve back to the dissembling luxurious drab of a sleeveless errand. O'th'other side, the policy of those crafty swearing rascals—that stale old mouse-eaten dry cheese Nestor, and that same dog-fox Ulysses—is not proved worth a blackberry.[24]

Life and death, love and pain, and all human thoughts and feelings

Thersites, for example, is the 'Caliban of demagogues' life—The admirable portrait of intellectual power deserted by all grace, all moral principle' (p. 272).

[23] *Troilus and Cressida*, v. i. 50-9.   [24] Ibid., v. iv. 1-11.

form, as in Pope's *Dunciad*, one leering image of universal degradation:

Here is such patchery, such juggling, and such knavery! All the argument is a whore and a cuckold: a good quarrel to draw emulous factions, and bleed to death upon. Now the dry serpigo on the subject, and war and lechery confound all!

Lechery, lechery, still wars and lechery! Nothing else hold fashion. A burning devil take them![25]

On the other hand, if satire in Thersites' mouth is ruthlessly pitiless, thus removing from him and his language any elements he may otherwise have shared with the fool, the satire Shakespeare operates directly is less deforming but no less destructive or ruthless. To take examples from the Greek camp (although, as indicated above, the same is true, in milder and different ways, of the Trojan camp too), ample emphasis is given to the abstraction and rhetoric of Agamemnon and Nestor,[26] both vainly inflated. The first lines of their first speeches will suffice:

AGAMEMNON.   Princes,
   What grief hath set these jaundies on your cheeks?
   The ample proposition that hope makes
   In all designs begun on earth below
   Fails in the promis'd largeness

NESTOR. With due observance of thy godlike seat,
   Great Agamemnon, Nestor shall apply
   Thy latest words. In the reproof of chance
   Lies the true proof of men. The sea being smooth,
   How many shallow bauble boats dare sail
   Upon her patient breast, making their way
   With those of nobler bulk[27]

Diomedes, Menelaus, and Patroclus are all subjected to Thersites' accusations and pointed satire—and Shakespeare's too. This is even truer of Ajax, an ironic portrait of brute force even in Homer, and on whom Shakespeare, adding the fact of his being 'half Trojan and half Greek', launches a threefold attack: the continual invective of

[25] *Troilus and Cressida*, II. iii. 73–7; v. ii. 93–5.
[26] Not for nothing is the second episode in Joyce's *Ulysses*—a novel which reveals the clear influence of *Troilus and Cressida* if only in its attitude to classical myth—entitled 'Nestor'.
[27] *Troilus and Cressida*, I. iii. 1–5; I. iii.31–7.

Thersites, the irony and sarcasm of his fellow-soldiers, and direct exposition.[28] Achilles, the hero by definition, is spared some severity, but if the intellectual acumen, force of personality, and forthrightness which distinguish him from the others are all duly presented, so are his vanity, his passion for Patroclus, and his immaturity. His traditional 'direful wrath' is reduced to puerile hysteria, and his part in the action ends with the vile and base way he kills Hector—or has him killed. In the thick of the battle, in the last act, when Hector and Achilles meet, Achilles is spared, and allowed a respite. They meet again, and the situation is reversed: Hector is resting, exhausted by the fighting and appalled by the blood he has been forced to shed:

> Most putrefied core, so fair without,
> Thy goodly armour thus hath cost thy life.
> Now is my day's work done: I'll take my breath.
> Rest, sword; thou hast thy fill of blood and death.[29]

While Hector rests, unarmed, Achilles returns, now accompanied by the Myrmidons, who have already received instructions:

ACHILLES. Look, Hector, how the sun begins to set,
  How ugly night comes breathing at his heels;
  Even with the vail and dark'ning of the sun
  To close the day up, Hector's life is done.
HECTOR. I am unarm'd: forego this vantage, Greek.
ACHILLES. Strike, fellows, strike: this is the man I seek.

  [Hector falls

> So, Ilion, fall thou next! Come, Troy, sink down!
> Here lies thy heart, thy sinews, and thy bone.
> On, Myrmidons, and cry you all amain
> 'Achilles hath the mighty Hector slain'.[30]

The scene is an important one, an access-key to a problematic play. Fundamental in elaborating the theme of betrayal which is central to Shakespeare's work in this period (for instance, in *Measure for Measure* and, shortly after, *Othello*), it is also vital in marking, through Achilles' baseness, the death of Hector's illusions. A world which precludes love also precludes the ideals of chivalry; Hector's death is a tragic emblem of this. Just as Troilus believed

---

[28] Ibid., IV. v. 1–11. [29] Ibid., v. viii. 1–4.
[30] Ibid., v. viii. 5–14.

love could survive blood and destruction, so Hector tried to keep faith to an extinct code; and as Troilus had to abandon love for action, so Hector is killed through treachery, and his body dragged like an animal's carcass, as Troilus himself observes: 'He's dead, and at the murderer's horse's tail | In beastly sort dragg'd through the shameful field'.[31]

Yet, Hector had had no illusions as to the nature of the war he so valiantly fought. Indeed—and it is this which makes him the most fascinating character in the whole play—he was as aware as Thersites, in all other respects his opposite, that it was a vile and senseless war. Of significance here is the scene in Act II in which, in perfect parallelism to the meeting among the Greek leaders, Priam and his sons consider whether to restore Helen and end the conflict. In the passionately argued debate (an example of the rational, analytical density of the whole play), it is Hector who recognizes that, as Thersites has said, this is a war about 'a whore and a cuckold': 'She is not worth what she doth cost the keeping'.[32] Familiar with war and death, he knows that the lives of the slaughtered soldiers are worth more than Helen's:

> Let Helen go.
> Since the first sword was drawn about this question
> Every tithe soul 'mongst many thousand dismes
> Hath been as dear as Helen—I mean, of ours.
> If we have lost so many tenths of ours
> To guard a thing not ours nor worth to us
> (Had it our name) the value of one ten,
> What merit's in that reason which denies
> The yielding of her up?[33]

It is he, however, who at the end of the discussion, despite Cassandra's irruption and prophecies of destruction,[34] decides to keep Helen:

> yet ne'ertheless,
> My sprightly brethren, I propend to you
> In resolution to keep Helen still;[35]

---

[31] *Troilus and Cressida*, v. x. 4–5.
[32] Ibid., ii. ii. 52.
[33] Ibid., ii. ii. 17–24.
[34] 'Cry, cry! Troy burns, or else let Helen go' (113).
[35] Ibid., ii. ii. 190–3.

giving as his reason

> For 'tis a cause that hath no mean dependence
> Upon our joint and several dignities.[36]

Hector despises Helen, whom he knows well and of whom Shakespeare too is fiercely denigratory;[37] he knows that the Trojan position is morally untenable, and he is too expert a warrior not to realize that the superiority of their enemy makes victory impossible, and death inevitable. When he leaves for his final battle, his doom is announced in chorus: his wife Andromache has dreamt of death, his sister Cassandra has prophesied it, and everyone, including Priam, urges him to remain safely within the walls. But he keeps to his vow:

> Hold you still, I say.
> Mine honour keeps the weather of my fate:
> Life every man holds dear, but the dear man
> Holds honour far more precious-dear than life.[38]

This is the illusion for which Hector lives and dies, the Utopia which reality destroys. He believes it to be a world in which honour still has meaning, and values survive; a fantasy which is given short shrift by Troilus:

TROILUS. Brother, you have a vice of mercy in you,
  Which better fits a lion than a man.
HECTOR. What vice is that? Good Troilus, chide me for it.
TROILUS. When many times the captive Grecian falls
  Even in the fan and wind of your fair sword,
  You bid them rise, and live.
HECTOR.   O, 'tis fair play.
TROILUS. Fool's play, by heaven, Hector.[39]

Troilus, in whom idealism and realism coexist, is here more perceptive, more free of illusion—more realistic—than Hector.[40] In

---

[36] Ibid., 194–5.
[37] See the first scene in Act III, showing Paris and his 'Nell'.
[38] Ibid., v. iii. 25–8.,   [39] Ibid., v. iii. 37–43.
[40] It is almost certainly not incidental that Troilus, like the Greeks, uses mercantile images: 'Her bed is India; there she lies, a pearl. | Between our Ilium and where she resides, | Let it be call'd the wild and wandering flood, | Ourself the merchant, and this sailing Pandar | Our doubtful hope, our convoy and our bark' (i. i. 100–4). The image runs through the discussion among the Trojans: 'We turn not back the silks upon the merchant | When we have soil'd them . . .'; 'Why, she

their universe, war is precisely that: a fight to the death, without loyalty and the 'vice of mercy'. There is no room for abstract ideals or traditional values: if refusing to fight his cousin Ajax was a mistake, ('Cousin, all honour to thee!'[41]), sparing Achilles was a fatal error which bought him a treacherous, merciless death. His funeral is as 'beastly' as his killing: neither a rite nor a symbol, for here death is not greatness, but simply destruction. Reality is very different from the idealized portrait Hector draws in his imagination; it is as Thersites sees it, and as Shakespeare suggests it to be through the language and action of the whole play: brutal, material, and imprisoned by the present. Man must aim at the concrete and the utilitarian and can survive and exert some control over reality only by resisting emotion and the cult of ideals. This is the mistake made by Hector, the anachronistic hero of a lost world who, like Don Quixote, is the champion of illusions, not of reality: a man of the past in a world in which time and the past hold no surety for the present. This is basically Ulysses' point to Achilles in one of his great and seminal speeches. When Achilles complains of the Greek neglect which Ulysses has made him aware of, and asks if all his past deeds are similarly forgotten, he is urged not to live off past glory, since

> Time hath, my lord, a wallet at his back
> Wherein he puts alms for oblivion,
> A great-sized monster of ingratitudes.
> Those scraps are good deeds past, which are devour'd
> As fast as they are made, forgot as soon
> As done. Perseverance, my dear lord,
> Keeps honour bright: to have done is to hang
> Quite out of fashion, like a rusty mail
> In monumental mockery.[42]

As he later puts it, 'The present eye praises the present object',[43] enunciating a conception of life which Hector is unable to accept or understand. In his unequal fight with reality he is inevitably destroyed, as Troy itself will be.

is a pearl | Whose price hath launched above a thousand ships | And turn'd crown'd kings to merchants'. (II. ii. 70–1; 82–4.) And see Jill Mann's essay in the present volume.

[41] Ibid., IV. v. 137.
[42] Ibid., III. iii. 144; III. iii. 145–53. See also III. iii. 165–74.
[43] Ibid., III. iii. 180.

The instrument of Troy's destruction is, of course, Ulysses, in a sphere of action which lies outside that of *Troilus and Cressida.* Here too, however, he is portrayed as the character most capable of deciphering and facing reality, and thus as Hector's true rival, although the two men belong to the same system of values, as Ulysses demonstrates in his most celebrated speech, the 'degree' speech which dominates the first act:

> The heavens themselves, the planets, and this centre
> Observe degree, priority, and place . . .[44]

After the initial scenes dealing with Troilus' love for Cressida and introducing the Trojan 'heroes' as they march past, observed by Pandarus, we move to the Greek camp. First Agamemnon then Nestor, each in the language consonant to him, deplores the state of crisis in the Greek camp. Ulysses then asks to speak and, having reminded them that Troy resists only because the Greeks persist in ignoring the 'specialty of rule', he launches into his harangue, powerfully evoking the fabric of both the cosmos and of human society. 'Degree' holds them together, is 'the ladder to all high designs'. 'Take but degree away, untune that string', Ulysses says, 'And hark what discord follows'—'when degree is suffocate', chaos 'follows the choking'.[45] The speech has been frequently analysed, and is too often considered a set piece, devoid of context: a memorable synthesis—which it is—of a 'hierarchic' vision of reality. But in drama no speech can be completely understood without relating it to the concomitant elements of the specific theatrical image it is part of, the particular and general situation represented, the nature of the speaker, and its functions and the actions which precede and succeed it. Thus considered, it should be clear that the speech is not proposing the apostrophized 'order' as a state to be restored. The harmonious vision Ulysses presents to us and to the Greek commanders is actually as remote as the world of abstract ideals Hector aspires to. It has been banished by disorder, chaos, and an impetus of individual and collective forces which have broken the geometrical regularity of 'degree'; and while Ulysses is undoubtedly nostalgic for it, and passionately desires its return, as

[44] Ibid., i. iii. 85–6.
[45] Ibid., i. iii. 85–137. It may be worth noting that in Chaucer's poem the place Ulysses assigns to 'degree' was taken by the very different concept of universal love. See Troilus' Boethian hymn in *Troilus and Criseyde*, iii. 1744–72.

his language makes clear, he is also painfully and perceptively aware that his desire will be unfulfilled, and that universal hierarchy has definitively disappeared. Unlike Hector, he cherishes no illusions as to present reality; reality is the chaos he describes with such vivid horror. But, again unlike Hector, he accepts it, and faces it squarely; not with the inadequate aid of an abstract faith in 'universal order', the unchanging correspondence between earth and heaven which supported Dante's world and which is certainly present as a concept in Ulysses' speech, but with the only resources available to man, fragile as he is: those of experience, political realism, and intellectual acumen. His subsequent actions confirm this reading. The speech—and it is easy to overlook this— is an integral part of his action, both as an act of self-awareness, and self-accusation, and as an accusation of Agamemnon and Nestor. The reproach is repeated, indirectly, in the lines which follow, mocking Achilles and Patroclus:

> Sometime, great Agamemnon,
> Thy topless deputation he [Patroclus] puts on,
> And like a strutting player, whose conceit
> Lies in his hamstring and doth think it rich
> To hear the wooden dialogue and sound
> 'Twixt his stretch'd footing and the scaffoldage,
> Such to-be-pitied and o'er-wrested seeming
> He acts thy greatness in; and when he speaks,
> 'Tis like a chime a-mending, with terms unsquar'd,
> Which, from the tongue of roaring Typhon dropp'd,
> Would seem hyperboles.[46]

Ulysses' astuteness and realism are amply displayed in this extraordinary 'play within the play', and even more in the action which follows: in his suggestion that Ajax be made to accept Hector's challenge to Achilles, to provoke the hero's resentment;[47] in persuading Ajax to accept, by appealing to his vanity; in his advice to the Greek leaders to ignore Achilles, to undermine his faith in his own greatness; in his exchanges with Achilles, when, to urge him to resume his duties, he first underlines the importance of public opinion and reputation, going so far as to identify the real self with what others see and judge:

[46] *Troilus and Cressida*, I. iii. 151–61.
[47] Ibid., I. iii. 374–86.

> no man is the lord of anything,
> Though in and of him there be much consisting,
> Till he communicate his parts to others;
> Nor doth he of himself know them for aught,
> Till he behold them form'd in the applause
> Where th'are extended; who, like an arch, reverb'rate
> The voice again[48]

then developing, as noted above, the theme of 'envious and calumniating Time',[49] and finally, in introducing Achilles' love for the Trojan Polixena, Priam's daughter, and contrasting his 'privacy' with the 'reasons . . . more potent and heroical' which should urge him to fight.

If Ulysses' action then falls short of its aim (Achilles seems initially convinced, only to renounce the field once more on receiving a message from Polixena,[50] and he returns to battle only after the death of Patroclus), it has however served to recharge the mechanism of war. It has also demonstrated that the magma of reality can only be faced by the exercise of reason.

It is this rationalizing tendency above all which, within the structure of the play, makes Ulysses Hector's antagonist, and which gives this work aspects and tones which are less univocal than they may appear. *Troilus and Cressida* is a problematic play, permeated by a sustained note of disquietude which borders on desperation (giving it much in common with *Timon of Athens*); a bitter, 'dark' play which contains and communicates anguish. It is clearly rooted in the crisis in English society the historical and political emblem of which is James I's succession to Queen Elizabeth, the Stuarts to the Tudors, although its wider context is of course the decline of the aristocracy, the rise of the merchant class and the bourgeoisie, the explosion of religious tensions and the beginnings of a new science and philosophy. Shakespeare's awareness of the change is apparent both in *Julius Caesar* and, even more, in *Hamlet*, where at the centre of action is man and the Elizabethan intellectual, faced with an 'out of joint' universe to decipher and grapple with. *Troilus and Cressida* (written shortly before James I's accession, in 1603, focused the changes even more clearly) embodies all the elements of 'the new philosophy' which

---

[48] Ibid., III. iii. 111–21. [49] Ibid., III. iii. 180–4.
[50] 'Fall, Greeks; fail, fame; honour, or go or stay; | My major vow lies here, this I'll obey' (v. i. 42–3).

so perturbed and disorientated the period. If, as commentators have frequently and rightly observed, the 'degree' speech is a summary of the ideology underlying Elizabethan society, the Tudor period, and Shakespeare's plays (the histories in particular) up until the end of the sixteenth century, the contextual reading suggested above posits it not as a positive ideological and political proposal on the part of Shakespeare (and Ulysses), but rather as an elegy for a vanished world, an acceptance that the Middle Ages are over and that the Elizabethan synthesis of the medieval and the Renaissance is no longer possible. It is a statement of awareness of crisis, and as such essentially similar to Donne's violent and anguished vision, in his *Anatomy of the World*, of a universe reduced to 'atoms'.

His awareness of the Greek situation is for Ulysses the start of a search for cogent action; Shakespeare's awareness of the Elizabethan crisis leads to the tentative and tormented search which is begun in *Troilus and Cressida*. The search is for a means whereby the new man, whose features Hamlet had already sketched in, can operate in the modern world. This will no longer be based, like that of the Middle Ages, on the solid pillars of religion and hierarchy, but on the fragile foundations of a society and culture in transformation.

This is chiefly effected through Ulysses, a man of the past able to face the present, and who, unlike Hector, can relinquish his fideistic vision of the universe and the providential conception of history implicit in the 'degree' speech, and contemplate reality with the scientific rationalism of the philosophy of experience of a Bacon, and the politics of realism of a Guicciardini or a Machiavelli. The search is furthered by Troilus, who, in his doubts and torments, has more in common with Hamlet than with Romeo,[51] and whose experience of love is a sequel of initiation, the painful and often traumatic passage from illusion to reality, or the slow and painstaking entry into the new world in which, as a young prince, he will be called to play a major role (significantly, Shakespeare diverges sharply from his sources and spares Troilus at the end of the play). But it is also—perhaps especially—embodied in Cressida, here not the traditional symbol of 'frailty', but a woman whose female condition of subordination and humiliation has created a robust sense of the real, and who will rip away any veil of illusion

[51] At several points in the first scene his questions seem to be echoing Hamlet's: 'Tell me, Apollo . . . | What Cressid is, what Pandar, and what we?' (98-9).

obstructing her vision. In this sense her gift to Diomedes of Troilus' love-token is not a theatrical sign of fickleness and inconstancy, but represents the painful awareness that the 'sleeve' is an illusory token of an impossible love, and that survival requires a rational and more clear-sighted acceptance of reality.

Of course, one need only look at the play's conclusion, or rather non-conclusion, with the words of Pandarus against a background of physical and moral devastation, to realize that any search can only be embryonic, tentative, and contradictory. The only certainty is Hector's death and the end of a past to which no alternative has yet been found by those able to face the present. They can see no pattern in a world which is still that described by Thersites, and which they regard with fear and dismay. Ulysses, Troilus, and Cressida, like all the other characters, leave the scene with no certainty beyond Hector's inhuman, 'beastly' funeral. Unlike the others, however, either as a result of their political astuteness, as in Ulysses' case, or on account of an experience of unhappy love, as in Troilus' and Cressida's (and in this light the play's title seems less incongruous), they have at least acquired awareness. They know, if nothing else, that survival in the new world means shedding illusions, myths, and false certainties, and trusting, as Hamlet had come to realize, in truth, experience, and reason. Once again Ulysses' words are emblematic, the more so in coming immediately after the 'degree' speech:

> They tax our policy and call it cowardice,
> Count wisdom as no member of the war,
> Forestall prescience, and esteem no act
> But that of hand. The still and mental parts,
> That do contrive how many hands shall strike
> When fitness calls them on and know by measure
> Of their observant toil the enemy's weight—
> Why, this hath not a finger's dignity.
> They call this bed-work, mapp'ry, closet-war;
> So that the ram that batters down the wall,
> For the great swinge and rudeness of his poise,
> They place before his hand that made the engine,
> Or those that with the fineness of their souls
> By reason guide his execution.[52]

This search to know the features of the new world would have

[52] Ibid., I. iii. 197–210.

been impossible without a new kind of language, and this too begins to emerge in *Troilus and Cressida*. That the language of the past had become 'false' and inadequate to represent the complexity and ambiguity of the present Shakespeare had already realized in *Julius Caesar*, where the precarious link between words and things is frequently underlined. In *Hamlet* it is stated explicitly, with the sharp distinction between the language of being, Hamlet's, and the language of seeming and deceit adopted by Claudius and the courtiers, Polonius and the Queen. In *Troilus and Cressida*, however, there is total awareness that the crisis of reality is a crisis of language, and the lesson of *Hamlet* has been learnt so well that the play presents what is to all effects a *tabula rasa*. The rejection and deconsecration of the myths of the past is paralleled (as in Sterne's *Tristram Shandy*, and even more so in Joyce's *Ulysses*) by the demystification of the forms used to construct and celebrate those myths. Classical and romantic epics, Petrarchan and Elizabethan poetry all undergo the process of unmasking and destruction to which past heroes and 'values', anachronistic and therefore false, are also subjected. This is even more true of the theatre, and not only that of preceding and contemporary playwrights, but of Shakespeare himself. The recurring echoes of his other plays— from *Romeo and Juliet* to the histories and comedies—is no self-congratulatory or nostalgic use of quotation, but ironic allusion to a language no longer viable in the theatre. Accompanying this is a freer use of previously tried devices which were the hallmarks of the exuberance and openness of the Elizabethan stage, and which in *Troilus and Cressida* are carried to their extremes: not merely a mixture of tragedy and comedy, but pastiche; not merely a flexibility of action, but its continual interruption; not merely freedom with, but an overlapping of space and time; not merely a varied and changing linguistic fabric, but a protean mass of language which is tragic and comic, grotesque and obscene, philosophical and colloquial, lyrical and prosaic, elegiacal and satirical. The result, reached by a process which is quite the reverse of the slackness denounced by those critics who have misunderstood the mechanism in action, is twofold. On the one hand, it creates a work whose form re-enacts at all levels, from the metre to the imagery and action, the tensions, lacerations, and ambiguities of the problematic reality which produced it. On the other, it destroys the illusion that the theatrical language of even the recent past was in any way able to represent it. The play thus takes its part in the 'war of the theatres', but in such a way as to take it beyond local in-fighting to something of extreme and far-reaching importance. It was not simply a question of opposing the theatre hacks and arguing, seriously or otherwise, with friends and rivals; of winning over a wider public; of practising any kind of 'trick'.[53] It was a question of reshuffling the cards completely and exploding previous language,[54] to pave the way for a language of being and not of seeming, as desired by Hamlet. And this is what happens. If *Troilus and Cressida* occupies a position of prominence in Shakespeare's development as an admirably resolute image of a world in crisis (compounded rather than undermined by the continual sense of precariousness in the very form of the play), its definitive eminence is due to that radical and ruthless experimentalism which took the language of crisis to its extreme, thus making possible the world and the linguistic achievement of the great tragedies.

[53] See Ben Jonson in *The Case is Altered* (1601).

[54] Jonson had already pointed the way in his *Poetaster*, as in the finale when the bad poet Crispin (Dekker) is forced to vomit up all words no longer in use: 'retrograde ... reciprocal ... incubus ... glibbery ... lubrical ... defunct ... Magnificate ... spurious ... snotteries ...', etc.

11

Shakespeare and Chaucer: 'What is Criseyde worth?'

JILL MANN

Chaucer's *Troilus and Criseyde* is a supremely *dramatic* poem. It is, indeed, a brilliant example of that ability to suggest a living, fluctuating personality behind the surface manifestations of speech, look, and gesture, which we think of as characteristically 'Shakespearean', and its influence on Shakespeare could therefore be traced far beyond the confines of a single play. Yet, if we do narrow the basis of comparison to the two versions of the Troilus story, a rather curious paradox emerges: in the presentation of Criseyde, Chaucer is more 'Shakespearean' than Shakespeare—that is, his heroine has a depth of life denied to her stage counterpart. It is both the hows and the whys of this difference that I wish to examine.[1]

It is obvious at first glance that *Troilus and Criseyde* contains large stretches of dialogue; but it is not only the dialogue, vivid as it is, that constitutes the 'dramatic' quality of the poem. Even more significant is the fact that Chaucer constantly writes in 'stage directions'—minute indications of physical location, gesture, look, appearance.[2] A few—very few—of these indications he found already present in his own source, the *Filostrato* of Boccaccio, but

---

[1] For more general comparisons of Chaucer's poem and Shakespeare's play, see Muriel C. Bradbrook, 'What Shakespeare did to Chaucer's *Troilus and Criseyde*', *Shakespeare Quarterly*, 9 (1958), 311–19, repr. in her *The Artist and Society in Shakespeare's England* (Brighton, Sussex, and Totowa, NJ, 1982), 133–43; Ann Thompson, *Shakespeare's Chaucer* (Liverpool, 1978), 111–65; E. Talbot Donaldson, *The Swan at the Well: Shakespeare Reading Chaucer* (New Haven and London, 1985), 74–118, 148–57.

[2] On Chaucer's use of gesture, see Barry Windeatt, 'Gesture in Chaucer', *Medievalia et Humanistica*, 9 (1979), 143–61; Robert D. G. Benson, *Medieval Body Language: A Study of the Use of Gesture in Chaucer's Poetry*, Anglistica, 21 (Copenhagen, 1980); John P. Hermann, 'Gesture and Seduction in *Troilus and Criseyde*', *Studies in the Age of Chaucer*, 7 (1985), 107–35.

he gave them a quite different role and meaning through his own additions and expansions. For example, in the opening scene in the temple, Boccaccio describes Criseida as standing near the temple door, 'self-confident, gracious, and amiable' ('negli atti altiera, piacente ed accorta').[3] In taking over these details, Chaucer makes them dramatically meaningful by relating them to Criseyde's present situation, turning them into a dialectical articulation of her consciousness of herself and her relation to other people. The dialectic begins to make itself felt in the 'And yet' with which he follows his description of her beauty:

> And yet she stood ful lowe and stille alone,
> Byhynden other folk, in litel brede,
> And neigh the dore, ay undre shames drede,
> Simple of atir and debonaire of chere,
> With ful assured lokyng and manere.[4]

Criseyde is sensitive to 'shames drede' because she is the daughter of a traitor who has abandoned the city of Troy in the midst of a war; allowed by the generous patronage of Hector to live on unmolested in Troy, her humble attire and meek appearance signal an acknowledgement of the precariousness of her position and her wish to avoid offence by obtruding herself. This is also why she takes up a humble position near the door and 'Byhynden other folk'. But, at the same time, her assurance and dignity of manner indicate that her father's guilt is not her own, and she will therefore defend her right to the 'litel brede' in which she stands, in the face of any public expression of hostility. The features of this description are not, that is, to be interpreted as a simple reflex of her character or her temperament; they are, rather, the result of what we may call 'arranged behaviour'. It is only by interpreting the semiotics of this 'arranged behaviour' that we arrive at any understanding of Criseyde's inner self, of her sense of right and propriety and her ability to behave with poise and tact.

Troilus too 'arranges' his behaviour with an eye to its effect on the beholder. After reporting Troilus' speech of contempt for the 'blynde' lovers who cannot 'war by other be', Chaucer adds an expressive facial gesture which has no counterpart in Boccaccio:

[3] *Filostrato*, i. xix. 8.
[4] *Troilus*, i. 178–82.

> —with that word he gan caste up the browe,
> Ascaunces, 'Loo! is this naught wisely spoken?'[5]

The casting up of the brow, which Chaucer glosses for us, gives an 'illocutionary force', in Austin's terms, to Troilus' statement, and provides us with the key to its tone (it is a young man's high spirits, rather than, for example, a gloomy philosophical profundity).

Troilus' gaze, ranging idly through the crowd, 'smites' on Criseyde and is suddenly fixed there. When he recollects himself, he returns to 'his firste pleyinge chere',[6] 'arranged behaviour' becoming evident again as we contrast his outward manner with his inward confusion. Criseyde's glance too plays a part in this first contact between them, and Chaucer devotes two whole stanzas to describing it and its effect on Troilus:

> To Troilus right wonder wel with alle
> Gan for to like hire mevynge and hire chere,
> Which somdel deignous was, for she let falle
> Hire look a lite aside in swich manere,
> Ascaunces, 'What! may I nat stonden here?'
> And after that hir lokynge gan she lighte,
> That nevere thoughte hym seen so good a syghte.

> And of hire look in him ther gan to quyken
> So gret desir and such affeccioun,
> That in his hertes botme gan to stiken
> Of hir his fixe and depe impressioun.
> And though he erst hadde poured up and down,
> He was tho glad his hornes in to shrinke:
> Unnethes wiste he how to loke or wynke.[7]

The account of Criseyde 'lightening' her expression is Chaucer's own addition to Boccaccio's description of her slightly disdainful ('sdegnosetto') glance and gesture.[8] The effect of the extra detail is not merely arithmetical—to suggest two character traits instead of one; it changes the whole meaning of Criseyde's glance. For, in Chaucer's presentation it is clear that her first disdainful look is a reaction to her consciousness of Troilus' gaze; she interprets the fixity of his attention to her as a sign that he is critical of her presence, and responds first with self-defensiveness, and then with a placatory softening that indicates it is not to be taken as brazen

---

[5] Ibid., i. 204-5.   [6] Ibid., i. 280.   [7] Ibid., i. 288-301.
[8] *Filostrato*, i. xxviii. 2.

aggressiveness. This first encounter between Troilus and Criseyde is thus conducted in the 'language of looks', not of words; what is important is not only that we learn to decode the 'language of looks' but that this decoding leads us into a vivid awareness of the constant trafficking between a world of formed, coded, outer speech and behaviour, and an inner world of spontaneous thought and feeling. This interaction between the inner and the outer, between private reaction and social behaviour, interests Chaucer as much as or more than Criseyde's individual character.

It is this interest that leads to Chaucer's considerable expansion of Boccaccio's narrative in Book II of his poem, which recounts the wooing of Criseyde, and that gives it its dramatic quality. A few representative moments will serve as illustration. The first is the moment of Pandarus' arrival at Criseyde's house:

> Quod Pandarus, 'Madame, God yow see,
> With youre book and all the compaignie!'
> 'Ey, uncle myn, welcome iwys,' quod she;
> And up she roos, and by the hond in hye
> She took hym faste, and seyde, 'This nyght thrie,
> To goode mot it turne, of yow I mette.'
> And with that word she doun on bench hym sette.
>
> 'Ye, nece, yee shal faren wel the bet,
> If God wol, al this yeer,' quod Pandarus;
> 'But I am sory that I have yow let
> To herken of youre book ye preysen thus.
> For Goddes love, what seith it? telle it us!
> Is it of love? O, som good ye me leere!'
> 'Uncle,' quod she, 'youre maistresse is nat here.'
>
> With that thei gonnen laughe . . .'[9]

We know, without prompting from Chaucer, that Pandarus is deliberately using any pretext to introduce the subject of love, and so to encourage thoughts of it in Criseyde's mind. We make this deduction instantaneously, 'glossing' Pandarus' speech in the light of our knowledge of his concealed intention just as we should do if we were watching an actor in a play. But, over and above this, Pandarus' speech in another sense *proclaims* an insincerity of a less specific sort; the 'high-flown', exaggerated earnestness in his request makes it obvious that 'he doesn't really mean it'. Criseyde

[9] *Troilus*, ii. 85–99.

deflates her uncle's mock solemnity, not by direct comment but by a joke. Skilled in the 'language of looks', she is also adept in the art of civilized discourse, in the ability to use speech not as a transparent register of feeling but as an instrument which can be made to create relations of ease and frankness. The joking imputation of a concealed motive breaks through the surface of language only in order to flatter Pandarus with the implication that he too is adept in these arts, and will therefore relish this acknowledgement of the gap between its 'arranged' surface and the private motives which are screened behind it.

Now it is *because* Pandarus really does have a concealed intention of a very specific sort, while Criseyde does not, that we can measure the difference between 'hypocrisy' or 'deception', and what I have called 'arranged behaviour'. Criseyde's behaviour is 'arranged', not because she is playing a hidden game, but because any speech or action of hers represents a *selection* from a vast reservoir of thoughts and feelings that lie behind these surface manifestations—a selection in which a sense of propriety and a response to others will play as large a part as her own impulses. The more sophisticated her speech, that is, the more we have a sense of Criseyde *thinking behind* her speech, not expressing everything that is in her mind, nor thinking only what she expresses.

In what follows, we are continually aware of this reservoir of thought and feeling, because it is to it that Pandarus covertly addresses himself. His tantalizing hints of a splendid piece of news, which must nevertheless be withheld from his niece, aim to arouse her curiosity, and he keeps it aroused by commanding her not to question him further. Criseyde dutifully obeys, but when, after another hundred lines, Pandarus mentions her 'faire aventure' again, her curiosity, welling up behind the barrier of her obedience like water behind a dam, at once breaks out through this offered chink:

> 'A! wel bithought! For love of God,' quod she,
> 'Shal I nat witen what ye meene of this?'[10]

By leaving a gap between Pandarus' two references to Criseyde's 'faire aventure' Chaucer does more than increase suspense (in Criseyde and the reader); the suppressed remembrance of the

[10] Ibid., ii. 225–6.

earlier exchange, which we share with Criseyde, instructs us in the *continuing* existence of a half-conscious mental life into which ideas and impressions are absorbed and from which they can surface into speech or action as occasion calls them forth. Pandarus' elaborate manœuvring aims at making the fact of Troilus' love part of Criseyde's 'mental furniture' in this way, so that it can be left to have its own effect. We can see it doing just that when, after the initial storms that greet Pandarus' revelation of the truth have subsided into Criseyde's agreement to offer Troilus 'good chere' but nothing more, Criseyde introduces into their cheerful talk of other matters an apparently casual question:

> Tho fellen they in other tales glade,
> Tyl at the laste, 'O good em,' quod she tho,
> 'For his love, that us bothe made,
> Tel me how first ye wisten of his wo.
> Woot noon of it but ye?' He seyde, 'No.'
> 'Kan he wel speke of love?' quod she; 'I preye
> Tel me, for I the bet me shal purveye.'
>
> Tho Pandarus a litel gan to smyle[11]

Pandarus smiles because he can see that the idea he has introduced into Criseyde's mind is working in it with the silent but ceaseless action of yeast; his first task is done.

Among the facial expressions—such as the smile—which translate inner states into public signals (or, to put it the other way round, which offer a clue to the spontaneous responses within), the blush has a particularly important and interesting place, because it is involuntary.[12] It is given a key role in the scene that follows, when Criseyde, finally left alone by Pandarus, sits down to formulate the unformulated impressions she has received, but finds that there is yet another to add to them, for at that moment Troilus by chance rides past her window. The people admiringly hail the brave young defender of the city, and Troilus blushes in response. The blush in turn calls forth a spontaneous response in the watching Criseyde, and as she becomes conscious of this response she too blushes.[13]

[11] *Troilus*, ii. 498–505.

[12] Although Diomede seems able to blush at will, as he *mimics* the behaviour of the embarrassed lover (v. 925–9).

[13] This scene is invented by Chaucer; in the later window scene, which corresponds more closely to Boccaccio, the two lovers again blush (ii. 1256–8), whereas

For which he wex a litel reed for shame
When he the peple upon hym herde cryen,
That to byholde it was a noble game
How sobrelich he caste down his yën.
Criseÿda gan al his chere aspien,
And leet it so softe in hire herte synke,
That to hireself she seyde, 'Who yaf me drynke?'

For of hire owen thought she wex al reed,
Remembryng hire right thus, 'Lo, this is he
Which that myn uncle swerith he moot be deed,
But I on hym have mercy and pitee.'
And with that thought, for pure ashamed, she
Gan in hire hed to pulle, and that as faste,
Whil he and alle the peple forby paste[14]

The blush in each case represents an inward response to an image of the self offered from outside. Both Troilus and Criseyde suddenly perceive how they appear (or may appear) to others; Troilus sees himself reflected in the people's acclaim as the brave defender of Troy, Criseyde sees herself as the beloved of this young hero (and also sees that her own gaze might be attributed to her desire to assess his suitability as a lover). Because the blush is spontaneous and uncontrollable, it is the sincerest of testimonies to the inner being that it manifests.[15] Troilus' blush testifies to his modesty; it rebuts the possible accusation of vanity at his acclaim by very virtue of the fact that it acknowledges his consciousness of its possibility. Criseyde's blush rebuts the accusation of brazenness in the same way. The blush is a direct road of access to the heart and mind, a means of penetrating to the most instinctive movements of the inner self. It mediates between public and private; the public gaze is internalized within the mind, private impulses are laid bare to the outside world. Taking its origin in intimate and secret thoughts, the blush comes to birth as the thinker, suddenly taking the position of an outward observer, becomes conscious of those thoughts, and responds again to that consciousness with an instinctive emotion which instantaneously translates itself into an outward signal.

in the *Filostrato* they gaze at each other with unembarrassed complaisance (ii. lxxxii–lxxxiii).

[14] *Troilus*, ii. 645–58.
[15] See Windeatt, 'Gesture', pp. 151–3 and, on blushing generally, Christopher Ricks, *Keats and Embarrassment* (Oxford, 1974), esp. chs. 2–3.

It is through this sense of the constant dialectic between an inner world of unformulated thought and emotion and an outer world of speech and behaviour that Chaucer convinces us of the existence of Criseyde's inner reservoir of thought and enlightens us as to its nature. When therefore she finally sits down to reflect once more and we are led deep into the private world of her thoughts and feelings, we are ready to see her reflections for what they are—not an insight into her 'character', but a glimpse into that whole restless world of impulsive movement and response from which decisions and actions arise by a process as mysterious as the birth of Venus from the sea. We can understand, finally, how within this fluctuating process the idea that Pandarus has introduced into her mind begins to take hold and to grow in it, how it can be encouraged and nourished by following events, until it has become an acknowledged part of her willed behaviour. And we can see how, ultimately, the idea of betraying Troilus and giving herself to Diomede can gradually lodge itself in her mind by the same process.

We take for granted the dramatic life of *Troilus and Criseyde*, performing instinctively and immediately the interpretative acts I have had to trace so laboriously. But we take it for granted, I think, largely *because* we are early accustomed to it by our familiarity with Shakespeare.[16] The sense of a whole world of emotional response and unspoken thought which is only partially and tangentially reproduced in dialogue, is one of the great strengths and pleasures of Shakespeare's plays; in the works of lesser dramatists we find all too often that what is said can be taken to be coextensive with what is thought. To take an example somewhat akin to the Chaucerian passages I have discussed, in the scene on the quay in *Othello* we can sense Desdemona's tension and anxiety— betrayed in her quick question 'there's one gone to the harbour?'— lying behind her cheerful badinage with Iago, without needing her own gloss: 'I am not merry, but I do beguile | The thing I am, by seeming otherwise'.[17] But this only makes it the more surprising that when Shakespeare, in his turn, comes to represent Cressida, he carefully *suppresses* all that sense of a living human responsiveness

[16] 'In the free flow of Shakespeare's world, motivation is never analysed or presented for inspection, but inferred by us instinctively, as we might infer that of real people around us'; John Bayley, *Shakespeare and Tragedy* (London, 1981), p. 106.   [17] *Othello*, II. i. 122-3.

lying behind speech by means of which we could make meaningful sense of dialogue and action. The few speeches she is given—and they are surprisingly few[18]—offer disconcertingly contradictory impressions of her.[19] Some critics interpret her early banter with Pandarus, which constitutes her most extended series of utterances, as evidence of shallowness or wantonness; others point out that it could as well come from one of Shakespeare's romantic heroines, from Beatrice or Rosalind.[20] But we are not, as we are with Beatrice or Rosalind, allowed a secure sense of a serious centre of being lying behind the verbal flippancy. For one thing, Cressida has no female friends or relatives, as they do, with whom she might reveal a more intimate self, and her witty exchanges with Pandarus keep both him and us at arm's length. We wait for this lone heroine to speak directly to the audience—as does Viola, say— but in the brief soliloquy in which she reveals that she values Troilus even higher than Pandarus' praise, and yet holds off, since 'Things won are done', we are still left in suspense to know how to resolve the apparent contradiction between her passionate admiration and her cool calculation.[21] No sooner is the sincerity of her love for Troilus witnessed by the passionate outburst in which she voices her agony at parting from him and protests her eternal loyalty,[22] than we see her in the Greek camp accepting Diomedes' advances—and even here the resurgence of tender memories of Troilus at a time when a whore or a sexual politician would have nothing to gain from them runs counter to the inference that might be drawn from her rapid transfer to the Greek's protection. Most important of all, the fact that we 'eavesdrop' on this scene with Ulysses and Troilus, and hear only snatches of Cressida's conversation with Diomedes, means that we gain no inkling of what has brought about this devastatingly sudden change in her. We observe it from without, as uncomprehending as Troilus. It is as if the new context automatically produces a new Cressida; she changes with her changing environment.

[18] Donaldson, *The Swan at the Well*, p. 86, notes that 'her speaking role in the play is small: she speaks only 152 times, and 128 of her speeches are of less than twenty words, 93 of less than ten.'

[19] For Bayley Cressida is 'discontinuous with any idea of personality' ('Time and the Trojans', *Essays in Criticism*, 25 (1975), 61).

[20] Bayley, *Shakespeare and Tragedy*, p. 103; cf. Donaldson, *The Swan at the Well*, p. 87.

[21] *Troilus and Cressida*, I. ii. 289–300.   [22] Ibid., IV. ii. 99–108.

I want to suggest that the reasons why Shakespeare denies us access to Cressida's inner life lie in her crucial role in relation to a central theme of the play, the problem of value.[23] It is in making this theme the centre of his conception of the Troilus and Cressida story that Shakespeare departs most obviously from Chaucer, and an exploration of it will result in a sharper sense of the instructive differences between the two writers. But I shall suggest in conclusion the ways in which Chaucer's poem nevertheless contains the seeds from which Shakespeare's new interpretation could have germinated.

In response to Troilus' threatening insistence that the Greeks treat Cressida well, Diomedes gives the sober reply: 'to her own worth | She shall be priz'd'.[24] Coming as they do at the moment of Cressida's transition from Trojans to Greeks, from passionately committed lover to fickle mistress, Diomedes' words raise in acute form the question: What is Cressida's 'own worth'? On which of

[23] On the theme of value, see: Winifred M. T. Nowottny, '"Opinion" and "Value" in *Troilus and Cressida*', *Essays in Criticism*, 4 (1954), 282–96; Frank Kermode, 'Opinion, Truth, and Value', *Essays in Criticism*, 5 (1955), 181–7; I. A. Richards, *Speculative Instruments* (London, 1955), 201–2; A. P. Rossiter, *Angel with Horns and other Shakespeare Lectures*, ed. Graham Storey (London, 1961), 141–5; Terry Eagleton, *Shakespeare and Society* (London, 1970), 14–38; R. A. Yoder, '"Sons and Daughters of the Game": An Essay on Shakespeare's "Troilus and Cressida"', *Shakespeare Survey*, 25 (1972), 16–19; Douglas B. Wilson, 'The Commerce of Desire: Freudian Narcissism in Chaucer's *Troilus and Criseyde* and Shakespeare's *Troilus and Cressida*', *English Language Notes*, 21 (1983), 11–22; Kermode, '"Opinion" in *Troilus and Cressida*', *Teaching the Text*, ed. Susanne Kappeler and Norman Bryson (London, Boston, Melbourne, and Henley, 1983), 164–79. None of these critics makes any attempt to relate the problem of value to philosophical/economic thinking on the subject; although the definition of 'true worth' varies from critic to critic, its 'objective' status is always assumed, not regarded as problematic. An exception is the article by Gayle Greene, 'Shakespeare's Cressida: "A kind of self"', pp. 133–49 in *The Woman's Part: Feminist Criticism of Shakespeare*, ed. Carolyn Ruth Swift Lenz, Gayle Greene, and Carol Thomas Neely (Urbana, Chicago, and London, 1980), who follows Elton (see n. 30 below) in recognizing the subjective nature of value, and links this with the change in Cressida ('as opinion changes, so does she'), but follows him also in assuming that this subjectivity represents 'the breakdown of an ordered, hierarchical notion of reality' reflecting 'the transition in conceptions of value that was occurring in the Renaissance' (p. 147 n. 4), and so both sentimentalizing and misrepresenting the medieval thinking on price and value. It is *because* we cannot pin the blame for the play's theory of value on 'the spirit of capitalism' characteristic of the modern world (p. 137) that it is so challenging and disturbing. See also n. 29.   [24] *Troilus and Cressida*, IV. iv. 131–2.

her two selves are we to base our estimate of her? It is here that our lack of access to her inner thoughts and feelings becomes crucially important, for only through such access would we feel confident in identifying the 'real Cressida' as (say) a calculating siren, a fickle whore, or a helpless victim of circumstance. By denying us this possibility Shakespeare frees us to notice that the question 'what is Cressida worth?' has two problematic aspects, not one. Cressida is one element in the problem, the question of what constitutes worth is another.

This question runs through the whole play, and both Greeks and Trojans are confronted by it. On the Greek side, it is presented in male terms: it is the question of Achilles' worth. Achilles' estimate of his own worth becomes inflated; he overvalues himself, 'grows dainty of his worth', as Ulysses tells the Greek council; 'Imagin'd worth' disturbs his judgement.[25] Overvaluing himself naturally leads Achilles to undervalue others—in particular, Agamemnon, who complains to Patroclus about the consequent derangement in the hierarchy which reflects and regulates relative worth: Achilles 'overholds his price', and forces those 'worthier than himself' to dance attendance on him and humble themselves to his whims.[26] This blurring of relative value underlies the annihilation of degree vividly imagined in Ulysses' famous speech; degree is obscured when 'th'unworthiest' are not distinguished from their betters.[27]

Ulysses' plan to bring Achilles to his senses is of course to exalt the worth of Ajax in such a way as to devalue Achilles. Ulysses, that is, teaches Achilles a very valuable lesson in economics—that value is 'subjective' rather than 'objective'. The value of an object is set by the level of desire for it in its potential buyers; it is not an inalienable property of the object itself. If gold ceased to be prized, it would cease to be valuable; if changes in human society create a new demand for a commodity (oil, for example), its value will rise. Similarly, a man's worth is set by the value placed on him by others, as Ulysses explains:

> no man is the lord of anything
> Though in and of him there be much consisting,
> Till he communicate his parts to others;

[25] Ibid., I. iii. 145; II. iii. 173–7.
[26] Ibid., II. iii. 135, 124–31. [27] Ibid., I. iii. 83–4.

> Nor doth he of himself know them for aught,
> Till he behold them form'd in the applause
> Where th'are extended[28]

It must be grasped that what Ulysses is talking about is not simply the *recognition* of worth, but its very constitution. A man's qualities only become valuable in so far as others concur in so defining them; it is not that his worth is scorned, it is that it does not exist outside the applause of others. Thus, even he himself can only gauge his own worth by the measure of others' praise. Diomedes' suggestion that Cressida's 'own worth' is intrinsic to her is therefore misleading; her value will depend not only on the qualities she possesses but on the qualities admired by her valuers. In economic terms, it is consumer demand that creates value in commodities.

Ulysses' notion that value is determined by the valuer rather than the object of valuation is neither original nor idiosyncratic, nor does it represent (as some critics assume) a cynical rejection of medieval idealism.[29] On the contrary, it is entirely in line with the orthodoxies of medieval economic thinking, as it developed in a series of commentaries on Aristotle.[30] The starting-point for

[28] *Troilus and Cressida*, III. iii. 115-20.

[29] This is the line taken by Rossiter, who considers the 'practical "realist" argument' in this speech, which 'denies the "estimate and dignity" of intrinsic merit', to be in contradiction with the 'universal, eternal values' asserted in Ulysses' speech on degree (*Angel with Horns*, p. 145); cf. his further remarks on 'the questioning of values in [a] new and sceptical atmosphere', and the dismissal of 'the old stable Medieval universals' (p. 148). Ulysses' speech on degree is not however at odds with this theory of value. It is precisely because worth is established by general consensus that the undervaluing of Agamemnon instigated by Achilles is to be taken so seriously.

[30] On this commentary tradition, which arose in the wake of Robert Grosseteste's translation of the *Ethics* into Latin in the mid-thirteenth century and continued into the Renaissance, see the excellent study by Odd Langholm, *Price and Value in the Aristotelian Tradition* (Bergen, Oslo, and Tromsø, 1979), esp. pp. 18-20; Grosseteste's translation was 'gradually superseded by the Renaissance translations of Aretinus and Argyropulus; after 1530 there is a whole host of new ones' (Langholm, p. 16). In following nn. I give references to Langholm's survey to save space; I have however consulted Buridan's work at first hand. W. R. Elton, 'Shakespeare's Ulysses and the Problem of Value', *Shakespeare Studies*, 2 (1966), 95-111, interprets the value-theory in the play on lines broadly similar to my own, but uses as a basis of comparison Hobbes's views on value-relativism, which are too late to have influenced the play and therefore less relevant to it than the mainstream Aristotelian tradition outlined here. Neither Elton nor any of the

medieval discussions of the 'just price' and the determination of value was Book V, chapter 5 of the *Nicomachean Ethics*, a text translated by Robert Grosseteste and thereafter interpreted by a series of medieval commentators. In this short passage Aristotle discusses justice in exchange as a subcategory of commutative justice. If a shoemaker and a builder are to make a just exchange of the goods they produce, the relative value of shoes to house must be established. Their monetary price is the conventional notation of this relative value, but money is only an index of worth, not its determiner. What in fact determines worth, for Aristotle, is need (the Greek word is *chreia*, which the medieval Latin translators and commentators render by *opus*, *necessitas*, or *indigentia*—all meaning 'need'); it is the relative level of need for shoes as against a house in the parties making the exchange that will determine the relative value of the commodities. This 'need' is not however to be identified with physical deprivation; the famous fourteenth-century philosopher John Buridan, recognizing that most objects of exchange are not needed in the sense of being essential to survival, interpreted *indigentia* as any consciousness of insufficiency, any sense of lack on the part of the consumer. Thus, we can say that rich men 'need' luxuries because they demonstrate that need in their willingness to exchange other goods or money for them.[31] In Buridan's hands, 'need' thus becomes virtually indistinguishable from the modern English 'demand', and this emphasis on demand constitutes a recognition of the subjective desires of the consumer as the true determinant of value. 'Objective' value is a chimera of the imagination in economic terms, since the objective utility of a commodity exists only in its usefulness to the consumer[32]—and 'utility' must be defined not with reference to that which is necessary for survival, but as whatever men deem critics cited in n. 23 notices the connection between value-theory and the exchange of Cressida.

[31] Langholm, *Price and Value*, pp. 123–7. Buridan's work was highly influential, and his *Quaestiones* on the *Ethics* were printed in 1489, 1513, and 1637; his ideas were also 'kept alive in a number of summaries and paraphrases' from the fifteenth to the seventeenth centuries (ibid., pp. 141–2).

[32] Subjective value (*complacibilitas*) and objective value (*virtuositas*) are distinguished in the branch of value-theory represented by San Bernardino of Siena (1380–1444); see Raymond de Roover, *San Bernardino of Siena and Sant'Antonino of Florence: The Two Great Economic Thinkers of the Middle Ages* (Boston, Mass., 1967), 16–23; and for the misleading nature of the distinction, Langholm, *Price and Value*, p. 115.

necessary for their existence. 'Res valet quantum vendi potest' ('a thing is worth what it can be sold for'), as the medieval canon lawyers put it, in a quite uncynical spirit.[33] Value is not determined by idealizing theories;[34] it is market value, determined by aggregate demand, and settled in the everyday operations of market exchange.

The influence of the *Nicomachean Ethics* on Shakespeare's *Troilus and Cressida* has been claimed by the Arden editor,[35] but neither he nor (as far as I know) anyone else has recognized the fundamental importance of the *Ethics* to the play's exploration of the question of value. Ulysses, as we have seen, aims to teach Achilles the importance of demand in creating worth. Among the Trojans, Troilus too recognizes the crucial role of demand, the subjective desire of the consumer. 'What's aught but as 'tis valued?'[36] is how he answers Hector's argument that Helen 'is not worth what she doth cost the keeping'—the cost being the 'many thousand' Trojans who have died 'To guard a thing not ours nor worth to us | . . . the value of one ten'.[37] For Troilus, the many thousand Trojan deaths *prove* Helen's value, since they measure the level of desire for her possession. Hector vainly appeals to a notion of intrinsic value which will justify the subjective estimate:

> But value dwells not in particular will:
> It holds its estimate and dignity
> As well wherein 'tis precious of itself
> As in the prizer. 'Tis mad idolatry
> To make the service greater than the god;
> And the will dotes that is attributive
> To what infectiously itself affects,
> Without some image of th'affected merit.[38]

Hector, like the average layman reacting to the astronomical price fetched by a Picasso, indignantly tries to assert the idea of an inherent worth which is somehow to be defined by common sense.

[33] *Price and Value*, pp. 130–1.

[34] Thus Aquinas, following St Augustine, pointed out that in economic terms a pearl is more valuable than a mouse, although the mouse, as a living creature, has a higher status in the scale of being (Langholm, *Price and Value*, p. 87).

[35] In particular he sees it as a source for Hector's speech, with its reference to Aristotle, in the Trojan council; see his introd., pp. 48–9, and app. iii, pp. 311–20.

[36] *Troilus and Cressida*, II. ii. 53.

[37] Ibid., II. ii. 52; 18–25.   [38] Ibid., II. ii. 54–61.

Many modern critics align themselves with this view, but economi-
cally speaking his view is untenable by the standards of medieval
and Renaissance thinking. Hector's insistence on objective worth
would hold good only in cases of counterfeit—in cases, that is,
where a gullible fool allows himself to believe a glittering metal is
gold; in such a case, the commodity does not have the attributes
that are agreed to constitute preciousness. But gold itself—real
gold—is not 'precious of itself'; it is precious *because* its human
prizers agree in attributing value to it. (One could imagine a society
in which it had no value at all.) Troilus answers Hector's charge of
whimsical subjectivity by appealing to mercantile realities as proof
that the subjective estimate of value becomes *binding*; there is no
going back on the bargain once it is struck. Value may be determined by subjective desire, but it does not subsequently fluctuate
with a change in the desiring subject, since the realities of the
market fix it in the act of purchase.

> We turn not back the silks upon the merchant
> When we have soil'd them, nor the remainder viands
> We do not throw in unrespective sieve
> Because we now are full.[39]

Helen is 'a pearl | Whose price hath launch'd above a thousand
ships'; if the Trojans judged her 'Inestimable' when Paris brought
her home, they cannot now 'Beggar the estimation which [they]
priz'd | Richer than sea and land'.[40] The realities of commerce
become one with the idealism of chivalry: since value is fixed by
the commitment of the valuer to the prized object, to change one's
estimate of value is to lose honour through the abandoning of that
commitment. And the greater one's 'bank' of honourable commitment, the higher the potential rise in value of the object on which it
is expended. In response to Hector's first sober appraisal of the
cost of keeping Helen Troilus protests not her worth but Priam's:

> Fie, fie, my brother:
> Weigh you the worth and honour of a king
> So great as our dread father's in a scale
> Of common ounces? Will you with counters sum
> The past proportion of his infinite,
> And buckle in a waist most fathomless

[39] Ibid., ii. ii. 70–3.   [40] Ibid., ii. ii. 82–93.

With spans ånd inches so diminutive
As fears and reasons? Fie for godly shame![41]

Helen's 'inestimable' value is guaranteed by Priam's 'fathomless' worth; to count the cost of keeping her is to make of Priam a penny-pinching millionaire. Female worth and male worth thus enjoy a symbiotic relationship; the valuable object testifies to the wealth of the buyer, just as that very wealth raises the price of the object. The cautious buyer, on the other hand, depresses the price of the commodity. Just as Diomedes differs from Troilus as to how Cressida's worth is to be measured, so he 'weighs up' the worth of Helen in exactly the calculating way that Troilus rejects:

> For every false drop in her bawdy veins
> A Grecian's life hath sunk; for every scruple
> Of her contaminated carrion weight
> A Trojan hath been slain. Since she could speak,
> She hath not given so many good words breath
> As for her Greeks and Trojans suffer'd death.[42]

Paris treats this as 'sales talk' designed to disguise the real value attached to the object; the Greeks show what Helen is worth to them in their continued commitment to the cause of recovering her.

Cressida is as acutely aware as Troilus and Ulysses that value resides in the estimation of the valuer, as we see from her first soliloquy.

> Women are angels, wooing:
> Things won are done; joy's soul lies in the doing.
> That she belov'd knows naught that knows not this:
> Men prize the thing ungain'd more than it is.[43]

The point of this soliloquy is not to expose feminine coquetry, but to make it clear that in the world of the Trojans as in the world of the Greeks the value of women is determined by men. Hector's challenge to the Greeks is a prime illustration of this unromantic truth, for all its apparent evocation of an outdated world of chivalric gallantry: the superior worth of Andromache over the women of Greece is to be proved, not by reference to the women themselves, but by male valour. If no Greek accepts the challenge, it will

---

[41] *Troilus and Cressida*, II. ii. 25–32.   [42] Ibid., IV. i. 70–5.
[43] Ibid., I. ii. 291–4.

be proved that 'The Grecian dames are sunburnt and not worth | The splinter of a lance'.[44]

Like the other women in this play, Cressida is a blank cheque on which men write their own estimates of value. For Troilus she is, like Helen, 'a pearl', and he himself a merchant using Pandarus as 'convoy'.[45] For Diomedes, as we have seen, she is more coolly appraised. What is interesting here is that all the 'language of looks' which in Chaucer's *Troilus and Criseyde* acts as a passport to the inner heart, revealing it in its interaction with the outer world, here becomes a series of external signs appraised by men in their determination of female value. Instead of seeing Cressida blushing on stage, we have Pandarus giving Troilus an account of her blushes and short breathing; the effect is to raise her erotic appeal for her lover—to raise the value of the commodity—rather than to give us direct access to her emotions.[46] In the Greek camp, when the Greek leaders kiss Cressida in turn, Ulysses perversely takes the kissing as indicative of *her* licentiousness, rather than that of the men, although it was in fact his own suggestion, and Cressida's only contribution to the scene is a witty refusal to kiss both him and Menelaus. Apparently out of pique, Ulysses then instantly interprets her looks and gestures as unmistakable signals of wantonness. The 'language of looks' is not so much decoded as constructed by the observer.[47]

> Fie, fie upon her!
> There's language in her eye, her cheek, her lip—

[44] Ibid., I. iii. 281-2.   [45] Ibid., I. i. 100-4.   [46] Ibid., III. ii. 28-39, 99.

[47] Everything depends of course on how the scene is acted, but there is nothing elsewhere in the text to justify Ulysses' speech and a fair amount to suggest that the Greeks' coarse notions of 'courtesy' are unpleasant to Cressida. In so far as we can check Ulysses' description against the text (e.g. on Cressida's readiness to 'give accosting welcome ere it comes') it is inaccurate. Donaldson, *The Swan at the Well*, pp. 112-13, comments: 'It seems clear that a pretty young woman should not defeat a middle-aged self-proclaimed thinker in a small battle of wits, or deny him a kiss that others have received. Sour are the grapes of his wrath'. As elsewhere in Renaissance drama, female sharpness of tongue is taken as a sign of licentiousness (see Lisa Jardine, *Still Harping on Daughters: Women and Drama in the Age of Shakespeare* (Brighton, Sussex, and Totowa, NJ, 1983), ch. 4. Cressida's vulnerability to male interpretations of her words and actions has already given rise to some uneasy moments in an earlier scene with Troilus, when he imputes a *double entendre* to her invitation 'come you again into my chamber' (IV. ii. 377): see Donaldson, p. 94.

Nay, her foot speaks; her wanton spirits look out
At every joint and motive of her body.[48]

Ulysses' speech is immediately followed by the general cry 'The
Trojan's trumpet' (referring to the arrival of Hector); the punning
alternative 'The Trojan strumpet' has been noted since Rossiter,[49]
but what critics fail to comment on is the irony in the fact that the
trumpet announces Hector's arrival for the single combat which is,
theoretically, to uphold the worth of Trojan womanhood (significantly, there is not a word of reference to this in the actual combat
scene). Creating female worth with one hand, these battling men
destroy it with the other.

Throughout the play, there is a strong sense of the separation
between a man's world and a woman's world. We feel this instantly
in the very first scene as Troilus is transformed from a languishing
introspective lover into a brisk comrade-in-arms by the entry of
Aeneas; dropping his flights of rhetoric, he takes on the brusque
laconicism of the club or the locker-room. The putting away of the
woman's world appears in his answer to Aeneas' enquiry as to the
reason for his absence from the battlefield: 'Because not there. This
woman's answer sorts, | For womanish it is to be from thence'.[50] (In
Chaucer's poem, where the war is kept very much out of sight,
there is none of this sense of 'men's talk', in the scenes between
Troilus and Pandarus.) Male solidarity expresses itself also in willingness to 'guarantee' the worth of other men and to interpret
their outward behaviour as a sign of it. In the same scene in which
he produces his hostile reading of Cressida's 'body language',
Ulysses represents Diomedes' gait as a sign of his 'aspiration', and
willingly passes on Aeneas' 'translation' (as he calls it) of Troilus'
nature to his fellow Greeks.[51] Aeneas interprets Hector's actions
for the benefit of Achilles, the one figure who breaks this male
solidarity by his willingness to sneer at enemies and friends alike.[52]
In contrast, Cressida, like the other women in the play, stands
alone, bereft of interpreters of her own sex and open to the construction the men put on her.[53]

[48]   *Troilus and Cressida*, IV. v. 54–7.
[49]   *Angel with Horns*, p. 133.
[50]   *Troilus and Cressida*, I. i. 106–7.
[51]   Ibid., IV. v. 14–16; 96–112.   [52] Ibid., IV. v. 77–86.
[53]   Donaldson, *The Swan at the Well*, pp. 84–5, notes that 'Cressida is one of
Shakespeare's few unmarried women without a confidante'.

One could trace the separation of the male and female worlds throughout the whole play, but it is most clearly realized in Hector's parting from Andromache. Its ultimate source, in Book VI of the *Iliad*,[54] is a scene of great beauty and tenderness. Although Hector refuses Andromache's plea that he stay at home, he does so with a sense of tragic necessity, sorrowfully foreseeing her future capture and thraldom. He offers to kiss his baby son Astyanax, but the boy shrinks back into his nurse's arms, terrified by his father's helmet with its nodding crest; both father and mother laugh at the childish terror and Hector lays aside his helm to kiss the boy before turning back to his mother, smiling amid her tears. The hero seems all the more heroic for this touch of domestic tenderness. Shakespeare must have known this original version of the scene, if not from Chapman (whose first selection from the *Iliad* did not include Book VI), then from one of the earlier Renaissance translations of Homer,[55] but he preferred to follow the tradition established by Dares' Latin version of the *Iliad*, in which Andromache's pleas are fused with the much later appeals of Priam and Hecuba, addressed to Hector as he is about to fight Achilles.[56] In this medieval tradition, Hector angrily scorns Andromache and the womanish fears created in her by a dream.[57] The medieval authors vary in the degree of harshness they attribute to Hector's rejection of Andromache, but the underlying point—the manly refusal to be cowed by womanish words (*muliebria verba*)—remains the same.[58] And so it does in

[54] *Iliad*, vi. 390–493.

[55] See the list of translations of the *Iliad* available to Shakespeare in J. S. P. Tatlock, 'The Siege of Troy in Elizabethan Literature: Especially in Shakespeare and Heywood', *PMLA* 30 (1915), 742.   [56] *Iliad*, xxii. 25–89.

[57] *Daretis Phrygii De Excidio Troiae Historia*, ed. Ferdinand Meister (Leipzig, 1873), pp. 28–9. The *Ilias Latina* (ed. Emil Baehrens, *Poetae Latini Minores*, iii (Leipzig, 1881), 564–74) follows Homer, but later writers took their cue from Benoît and Joseph of Exeter, who follow Dares. See Benoît de Sainte-Maure, *Le Roman de Troie*, ed. Léopold Constans, SATF, 6 vols. (Paris, 1904–12), 15263–599; Joseph of Exeter, *Frigii Daretis Yliados Libri Sex*, ed. Ludwig Gompf (Leiden and Cologne, 1970), 425–66; Guido delle Colonne, *Historia Destructionis Troiae*, ed. Nathaniel E. Griffin (Cambridge, Mass., 1936), pp. 172–3; John Lydgate, *Troy Book*, ed. Henry Bergen, pt. ii, EETS E.S. 103 (London, 1908), iii. 4896–5143; William Caxton, *The Recuyell of the Historyes of Troy*, ed. H. Oskar Sommer, 2 vols. (London, 1894), ii. 610–12.

[58] 'At ubi tempus pugnae supervenit, Andromacha uxor Hectoris in somnis vidit Hectorem non debere in pugnam procedere; et cum ad eum visum referret, Hector muliebria verba abicit. Andromacha maesta misit ad Priamum, ut ille prohiberet, ne ea die pugnaret. Priamus Alexandrum Helenum Troilum et Aenean in pugnam

Shakespeare; although not harsh in itself, Hector's rejection of his wife has a shocking effect precisely because it comes from the gentle Hector.

> Andromache, I am offended with you:
> Upon the love you bear me, get you in.[59]

This, be it remembered, is the wife whose worth Hector earlier fought for; her husband determines her value, but she is not to determine his fate.

It is thus the men who finally fix Cressida's worth; yet they do so not by verbal assessment, but by the same mechanism which determines market value. For, Aristotle makes clear that it is by *exchange* that value is determined, since there must be a 'proportionate equivalence' between the goods exchanged.[60] The exchange of three apples for two pears establishes an equivalence of worth between the two sets of items, despite their disparity in nature and number. It is thus no accident that Shakespeare chose to articulate the question of value in a play that culminates in an exchange. The exchange of Cressida for Antenor functions in the imaginative fabric of the play as the point at which the Trojans fix her worth. Antenor appears on stage several times, but he never speaks. A. P. Rossiter romanticized this wordless bystander into an imaginative picture of Antenor as 'Shakespeare's one strong silent man', the 'one character [who] comes out of it without a scratch', the plain man of goodwill and limited comprehension caught up willy-nilly in the fortunes of war.[61] Rossiter's fanciful picture is either ignorant or wilful; for to anyone at all acquainted with the

---

misit. Hector ut ista audivit, multa increpans Andromacham arma ut proferret poposcit nec retineri ullo modo potuit. maesta Andromacha summissis capillis Astyanactem filium protendens ante pedes Hectoris eum revocare non potuit. tunc planctu femineo oppidum concitat . . .' (Dares, ed. Meister, xxiv, pp. 28–9). Shakespeare's picture of Hector chiding Andromache when out of temper because he has been worsted by Ajax (I. ii. 4–6) is probably also inspired by this scene.

[59] *Troilus and Cressida*, v. iii. 76–7.

[60] 'Contrapassum secundum proportionalitatem, et non secundum aequalitatem'; Langholm, *Price and Value*, p. 167. Agamemnon's implied comparison between the testing of metal and the trial of human worth in adversity (i. iii. 19–23) invokes the idea of settling worth by 'assay', but assay only fixes worth on a scale of values already determined by market forces.

[61] *Angel with Horns*, p. 151.

story of Troy in the Middle Ages and Renaissance, Antenor was notorious as the man by whom Troy was finally betrayed.[62] Chaucer, for example, exclaims at length upon the irony that the Trojans build their own destruction by exchanging Criseyde for the man who is to destroy them.[63] (When Shakespeare's Pandarus speaks approvingly of Antenor as 'one o'th'soundest judgements in Troy whosoever, and a proper man of person',[64] the audience would have been conscious of a similar irony.) The exchange fixes Cressida's value as equivalent to the value of that for which she is exchanged—that is, as the value of a traitor. Troilus' assertions of her unquantifiable worth are irrelevant;[65] she is valued by the market process that equates her worth with that of Antenor. His future treachery is balanced by hers.

We can see therefore why Shakespeare 'externalizes' his presentation of Cressida; her value is brought to her from outside, without reference to her inner being. Chaucer conceives her shift from true lover to faithless mistress from within; although briefly presented, it is nevertheless shown to be the result of a slow erosion of her former self, her old allegiances and habits of mind fading gradually under the influence of new surroundings. We are emotionally distanced from the new Criseyde, but we are not debarred access to understanding her. In Shakespeare the change is accomplished instantly and from without, with the shift from Troilus' romantic rhetoric to Ulysses' anti-feminist scorn. It is tempting to moralize on Troilus' bitter disillusionment—tempting, that is, to say that here we do have a case of counterfeit: he took glittering metal for gold. But to do so involves constructing precisely that definition of the 'real Cressida' that the play, as I have argued, withholds from us. If Shakespeare's Cressida is unlike Chaucer's Criseyde, Shakespeare nevertheless resembles Chaucer in refusing to take the easiest and most popular way of accounting for her defection by depicting her as a deceitful whore from the start.[66] What is fundamental for him as for Chaucer

---

[62] See Guido's *Historia*, bks. xxix–xxx.   [63] *Troilus*, IV. 197–210.
[64] *Troilus and Cressida*, I. ii. 193–4.   [65] Ibid., IV. iv. 122–3.
[66] For evidence of the predominance of this view of Cressida in both medieval and Renaissance literature, see Gretchen Mieszkowski, 'The Reputation of Criseyde 1155–1500', *Transactions of the Connecticut Academy of Arts and Sciences*, 43 (1971), 71–153, and Hyder E. Rollins, 'The Troilus-Cressida Story from Chaucer to Shakespeare', *PMLA* 32 (1917), 383–429. Rollins comments (pp. 427–8) that in comparison with his immediate predecessors and contemporaries Shakespeare treats Cressida gently.

is the conception that her shift from Troilus to Diomedes is a *change*, rather than the dropping of a mask. Under the pressure of external events a new self comes into being. Chaucer shows how the noble and generous elements in Criseyde blossom in the association with Troilus; under the influence of Diomede another self, which is capable of cheapness and dishonesty, gradually takes shape. In Shakespeare the range of potentialities suggested is narrower, but it remains true that the transfer of allegiance to Diomedes is profoundly disturbing precisely because we cannot relate it to the old Cressida. 'This is, and is not, Cressid'. What Criseyde/ Cressida stands for is not sensuality but change—the change which is indelibly rooted in human beings. 'Men loven of propre kynde newefangelnesse'[67] is Chaucer's deep-held belief, and Shakespeare is clearly echoing Chaucer in Ulysses' similar identification of 'newefangelnesse' as a fundamental trait of human nature:

> One touch of nature makes the whole world kin—
> That all with one consent praise new-born gauds.[68]

It is the propensity to change that makes the valuation of human beings even more hazardous than the valuation of commodities. What we ought to deduce from Troilus' appeal to the mercantile bargain as a model for knightly honour is the *riskiness* in the commitment to value—the risk that the merchant, piloting his convoy between 'dangerous shores', has to accept as whole-heartedly as any chivalric warrior facing 'the chance of war'. The risk increases when the commodities bargained for are human beings. The attributes of gold may cease to be valuable if the social consensus alters, but they do not cease to exist. In human affairs, a change in the valuer can effect a change in the object valued; demand creates supply. 'This is Diomed's Cressida'; the self is transmuted into the forms the market requires. To set Cressida down as 'a daughter of the game' from the outset is to obliterate this significant process of change.[69] Shakespeare, like Chaucer, sees the importance of context

---

[67] *Squire's Tale*, 610.   [68] *Troilus and Cressida*, III. iii. 175–6.

[69] Cf. Donaldson, *The Swan at the Well*, p. 118: 'for us to see from the beginning of the play no potentiality in Cressida for a future better than the one we know she will have . . . is to reduce the play's vision to that of Thersites'. For changing critical attitudes to Shakespeare's Cressida, see the excellent summary by Donaldson, pp. 149–51 n. 13, which shows that the older view of her as shallow and vulgar has been replaced in recent criticism by more careful and discriminating appraisals.

in creating the wholeness of a person—the coalescence of inner and outer that makes up their 'worth'. 'What is Criseyde worth, from Troilus?'[70] is Criseyde's anguished question as she contemplates leaving Troy. Away from Troilus, she loses the esteem that constitutes her worth as a person.

This moment in Chaucer's poem is, however, an isolated one. We must look elsewhere in medieval literature—in the works of the *Gawain*-poet, for example—to find a literary exploration of the theme of value which has the same Aristotelian background as Shakespeare's, and is equally ingenious in giving it imaginative expression.[71] In Chaucer, the theme of value is confined to a few hints, and behind them we can sense a tradition quite different from the Aristotelian one. Chaucer's version of the consummation scene picks up Boccaccio's use of the word 'valore' in his coy description of the physical union of the two lovers ('d'amor sentiron l'ultimo valore'—'they experienced love's utmost pleasure') and transforms its meaning:

> I kan namore, but thus thise ilke tweye
> That nyght, bitwixen drede and sikernesse,
> Felten in love the grete worthynesse.
>
> O blisful nyght, of hem so longe isought,
> How blithe unto hem bothe two thow weere!
> Why nad I swich oon with my soule ybought,
> Ye, or the leeste joie that was theere?[72]

Not only does Chaucer's 'grete worthynesse' have an emotional resonance that goes far beyond Boccaccio's notion of physical rapture, but the meaning of the word is fully activated by the subsequent use of the metaphor of 'buying' such joys at the cost of one's soul. The extravagant language might well prompt a censorious reader to conclude that we are here to see Troilus as making a 'bad bargain', as the epilogue to the poem invites us to lament the waste of 'his grete worthynesse' in devotion to an unworthy object. Yet, in this same epilogue the metaphor of buying surfaces again, and this time it shows us a God who made

[70] *Troilus*, iv. 766.
[71] See Jill Mann, 'Price and Value in *Sir Gawain and the Green Knight*', *Essays in Criticism*, 36 (1986), 294-318.
[72] *Filostrato*, iii. xxxii. 8; *Troilus*, iii. 1314-20.

what prudence might consider a 'bad exchange', from a similarly uncalculating devotion to the unworthy:

> —loveth hym the which that right for love
> Upon a crois, oure soules for to beye,
> First starf, and roos, and sit in hevene above.[73]

Chaucer, in other words, links the question of value with the language of redemption ('buying back'), in keeping with his poem's exploration of the divine as an aspect of the human. Shakespeare conceives the buying and selling of human lives—in this play—in human, not divine, terms, and ties the problem much more closely to the complexities of late medieval and Renaissance economic thought. Nevertheless, if we look back to Chaucer's poem with Shakespeare's dramatization of the male valuation of women in mind, one striking line leaps into sudden prominence. It is the climax of Hector's response to the embassy that comes to request the exchange of Criseyde for Antenor—a response that acquires a depth of significance not only because of the manly dignity with which it affirms female dignity, but also because it seems to lie quite outside the mental world of the men of Shakespeare's play:

> 'Syres, she nys no prisonere,' he seyde;
> 'I not on yow who that this charge leyde,
> But, on my part, ye may eftsone hem telle,
> We usen here no wommen for to selle.'[74]

---

[73] *Troilus*, v. 1842–4.   [74] Ibid., iv. 179–82.

12

'To Make that Maxim Good': Dryden's Shakespeare

SERGIO RUFINI

In *Truth Found Too Late*, Dryden's rewriting of Shakespeare's *Troilus and Cressida*, Cressida's yielding to Diomedes (V. ii),[1] which in the new plan devised by Dryden takes place in IV. ii, is presented by him as a pretence, to which she resorts with the sole purpose of ingratiating herself with the Greek leader, thus securing her return to Troy and to the arms of Troilus whom she has never really betrayed. But Troilus (who, as in Shakespeare, is watching the scene unnoticed), misunderstands, and continues to do so later when, at the end of Act V, which was completely rewritten by Dryden, Cressida intervenes between him and Diomedes in order to prevent the killing of one or the other from frustrating her plan in any way. At this point it is of no avail to her to reveal her true intentions to the two rivals. While Diomedes treacherously contradicts her, boasting of favours granted, Troilus, ever more blinded by jealousy, spurns her indignantly. To establish the truth, all that remains for Cressida is the drastic gesture of suicide. Deeply moved and enraged, Troilus then hurls himself on Diomedes, but does not succeed in ending the duel before, amid the renewed hostilities between the Greeks and Trojans, he himself is slain by Achilles, who has entered with his Myrmidons. Apart from this last detail, one cannot imagine a more sensational overturning of the plot, not only with respect to Shakespeare's text, but also to the story of Troilus and Cressida in general. If there is one thing which is constant throughout Cressida's fortune, it is precisely the emphasis placed on her inconstancy.[2]

[1] The text I use for quotation and reference is vol. xiii of the California edn. of *The Works of J. Dryden*, ed. M. E. Novak, G. R. Guffey, and A. Roper (Berkeley, Los Angeles, and London, 1984).

[2] See G. Mieszkowsky, 'The Reputation of Criseyde, 1155–1500', *Transactions of the Connecticut Academy of Arts and Sciences*, 43 (New Haven, 1971).

Curiously, in the Prologue to the play, Dryden tends to play down this aspect, through the words of the 'Ghost' of Shakespeare himself. The latter, addressing the audience in the guise of a sort of 'noble savage', informs them that his reviser will limit himself to the formal aspects of the play, the fruit of a genius as powerful as it was, alas, disorderly:

> *Untaught, unpractis'd, in a barbarous Age,*
> *I found not, but created first the Stage*
> *And, if I drain'd no* Greek *or* Latin *store,*
> *'Twas, that my own abundance gave me more.*
> *On foreign trade I needed not rely,*
> *Like fruitful* Britain, *rich without supply.*
> *In this my rough-drawn Play, you shall behold*
> *Some Master-strokes, so manly and so bold,*
> *That he, who meant to alter, found 'em such,*
> *He shook, and thought it Sacrilege to touch.*[3]

And in fact, up to IV. ii *Troilus and Cressida* gives the impression of the most conservative Shakespearian adaptation ever attempted by Dryden. Admittedly he alters the order of the scenes, in an effort to obviate, by at least a more symmetrical arrangement, what in the Preface to the play is pointed out by him as an original flaw in the plot, and one which cannot even be ascribed to Shakespeare's ignorance of the rules: its necessary *'leaping from* Troy *to the* Grecian Tents, *and thence back again in the same Act.'*[4]

But as to the rest, Dryden's Preface repeatedly encourages the opinion that his is mainly the completion and refinement of a text which he considers perhaps the most imperfect in the canon, written and left unfinished by Shakespeare when he must, perforce,

---

[3] *Truth*, Prologue, 7–16.

[4] If *A* is the Greek camp and *B* Troy, this reordering can be seen in the sequence of the five acts, thus:

	I	II	III	IV	V	
Shakespeare:	BBA	ABA	BBA	BBBBA	AAB	(. . . No man's land)
Dryden:	AB	BBA	AB	BA	BA	

Not only does each act, except the second, consist of two scenes, but each begins in the same place in which the preceding one ended. The fact that Act V does not respect this rule allows for a circular close to the play, bringing it back to where it began rather than leaving it, as in Shakespeare, in the middle of a no man's land, with the action reduced to '*nothing but a confusion of Drums and Trumpets, Excursions and Alarms*'.

have been at the very beginning of his career. So much so that for about half the material which comprises the first four acts Dryden's text does not depart from Shakespeare's. All seems reduced to a matter of cutting and pasting and, where necessary, of correction and translation, according to very predictable linguistic principles. Disturbed by Shakespeare's 'scarce intelligible', 'ungrammatical', over-'figurative' elocution, Dryden tends on the whole to style himself as a conscientious restorer who merely 'undertook to remove that heap of Rubbish, under which many excellent thoughts lay wholly bury'd'.

Even the 'wholly new' parts interpolated between those that Dryden simply refines or leaves untouched seem to be inspired by a desire for complete continuity, rather than for radical alteration. Such is the case with the most substantial addition, the one of which Dryden is proudest, although he confesses that he came to it almost by chance, at the suggestion of Mr Betterton, the actor who first played his Troilus.[5] This addition, the dispute between Hector and Troilus over the exchange of Cressida for Antenor, though placing the issue in a more articulate context, does not alter the usual course of events: Cressida is, in any case, exchanged.

Finally, it is the one direct reference in the Preface to the unsatisfactoriness of Shakespeare's ending that turns out to be quite misleading. Incapable, for obvious reasons, of seeing the hybrid nature of *Troilus and Cressida* as a subtle stylistic feature of what critics have re-evaluated as Shakespeare's 'problematic' phase, Dryden is convinced, as I have said, that he is dealing with something which is incomplete: a tragedy which was interrupted prematurely, before the two principal characters could die, as they should have done according to Aristotelian convention. But what seems most unjust, to Dryden, is that the heroine, though faithless, gets away scot-free, slipping off into the wings when her misdeeds

---

[5] The actor must have considered the few protests which Troilus makes at such a crucial point in his life insufficient for the characterization of his role. And since he had played several times in *Julius Caesar* it cannot be ruled out that it was he who suggested to Dryden the model for a scene that might test his histrionic powers more fully: the dispute between Cassius and Brutus in Act IV. Dryden does not deny that the clash between Hector and Troilus may have points in common with this scene. Although, as if to reclaim the choice for himself, and to distance it from the contingencies of the stage, he informs us that his model was in fact another solemn dispute between brothers: that of Agamemnon and Menelaus in Euripides' *Iphigenia in Aulis*.

are done: 'Cressida is false and is not punished'. As for Troilus, these observations allow us to foresee the end which Dryden allots him, that is his condemnation to a violent, heroic death, in keeping with the tradition. For Cressida, at best we expect a tragic conclusion in an expiatory sense, along the lines of Henryson's continuation of Chaucer's *Troilus and Criseyde.* Of course the theatrical conventions of the Restoration were not such as to allow the depiction of a leper colony, with the heroine redeeming herself by dying in hardship among the plague victims. But how could one expect as the only possible alternative the one which Dryden has in store for his audience?

These reactions are naturally those of a first, cursory reading, one, furthermore, which allows itself to be influenced too much by Dryden's tactics of understatement in the Prologue and the Preface. As W. W. Bernhardt noted in an article of about twenty years ago, the unexpected conclusion is by no means 'a rude sort of poetic justice' which Dryden 'introduced . . . at the eleventh hour'.[6] Through a closer examination of his conservative revisions and additions we can see how, in fact, they carefully prepare it. In Bernhardt's view, Shakespeare chose the age-old story of Troilus and Cressida chiefly as a pretext for portraying the confusion of the adolescent phase, for outlining the archetype of the hero as a young man. The result was a skilful blend of the comic and the heroic which was taken by Dryden for a serious error. He blamed the undisciplined youthfulness of the author for what was intended to be the multi-faceted portrait of a youth. And he could not have reacted otherwise, considering the principles of dramatic composition and for the construction of the tragic character propounded in his essay *The Grounds of Criticism in Tragedy*, perhaps his most rigid in Aristotelian and neo-classical terms, which was inserted between the Preface and the text in the edition of this adaptation. Thus, he proceeded to reform Troilus' character: on the one hand, highlighting everything which could serve to support his virile, heroic, stature; on the other hand, minimizing as far as possible whatever threatened to contradict it, diverting on to the others (e.g. Pandarus) any hint of satire.

A certain amount has been written also on the historical reasons which may have induced Dryden to carry out this reform. The play

---

[6] W. W. Bernhardt, 'Shakespeare's *Troilus and Cressida* and Dryden's *Truth Found too Late*', *Shakespeare Quarterly*, 20 (1969), 134.

saw the light in 1679, with the background of the Popish Plot and the beginning of the Exclusion Crisis. This would explain not only the numerous clerical broadsides which Dryden takes the opportunity to insert, but also, and especially, the transformation of Calchas into the *deus ex machina* who brings about the ruin of the two main characters.[7] More precisely, the whole affair, suitably restructured, would allow Dryden to build an allegory on the power of the monarchy. The Trojan War, the Greek and Trojan commanders alternatively, became the occasion for allusions to contemporary disputes, events, and characters, to whatever could undermine or reinforce the moral, political, and religious unity of the nation; although in the end it is with the Trojans as forefathers of the ancient Britons that Dryden's sympathies principally lie, as the 'Ghost' of Shakespeare admits in the Prologue, apologizing to that of Homer. In this sense Hector, more than Troilus, emerges as a fully heroic figure, stripped of that aura of inconclusiveness which not even he was spared by Shakespeare.[8]

The main shortcoming of all these approaches is, in my opinion, that they are too exclusively centred on Troilus and, by reflection, on Hector, assigning only a peripheral relevance to what is, after all, the most conspicuous change in the play: the new ending, the complete overturning of Cressida's reputation that it entails.[9] But as I have already hinted, the restoration in Dryden's rewriting of Hector and Troilus to a more constant level of heroism, and the consequent return to a climate of nobility on both the Greek and Trojan sides, could be necessary conditions only, not sufficient ones, to transform Cressida into the epitome of constancy. Therefore, we cannot exclude the hypothesis that, apart from the rather obvious possibility of reshaping Troilus (Hector) according to the

[7] See G. D. Atkins, 'The Function and Significance of the Priest in Dryden's *Troilus and Cressida*', *Texas Studies in Literature and Language*, 13 (1971–2), 29–37.

[8] See L. D. Moore, 'For King and Country: John Dryden's *Troilus and Cressida*', *College Language Association Journal*, 26 (1982–3), 98–111.

[9] Bernhardt, for instance, in spite of his premises, hardly dwells upon it, and only to make it a natural consequence of Troilus' reshaping: 'With the moral lines of the play thus clearly drawn, there is no . . . opportunity to suspect that Cressida is no better than she should be. Her speeches, in accordance with her new character, are considerably chastened and brought into conformity with those of Troilus. Indeed, Dryden is able to make her a considerably more savoury character than Bowdler, in his expurgated *Family Shakespeare*, was later able to do' (p. 135).

rules, the whole operation may have arisen also from the much more striking one of redeeming Cressida. Might not Dryden's undoubted theatrical genius have glimpsed this second possibility in the peculiar ways to which Shakespeare had resorted when re-staging her betrayal? Before we ask ourselves why Dryden, after an initially rather conservative treatment of the original, decided on such a sharp turn, we should look at how it is put into practice and at what there was in Shakespeare's text to make it, with relatively few changes, so surprisingly possible.

For, in Shakespeare's play Troilus is far from being the only character in constant conflict with himself. Nor can his inherent contradictions be ascribed solely to his age, to his premature hero-ism. That Shakespeare intended to write a sort of precursor of the *Bildungsroman* is still one of the slowest clichés to disappear. Nor is this surprising when we consider that even E. M. W. Tillyard, one of the first and most perspicacious critics to re-evaluate the Problem Plays, ran into trouble on this point. Indeed, in his opinion, already by Act III, at the moment of his separation from Cressida, 'Troilus behaves with dignity, already an *older* man than the youth of the play's opening scene: a clear analogy with Ham-let'.[10] But we need only compare the fluctuations between oppo-sites, the irreconcilable impulses which characterize this scene, with the identical ones found in his every appearance from first to last, to realize that at no point in the play does he show any signs of even the slightest progress, or of any greater uniformity of vision.

In short, independently of his status as a hero *in fieri*, as an immature Hector, Shakespeare's Troilus shares in a more radical dichotomy also found in every other character in the play—includ-ing Cressida, with the thorny question of her inconstancy. This is so methodical, whether consciously so or not, that it prevents the clear emergence of a *Bildung* of any sort.

We are faced here not with a *Bildungsroman* but with the sys-tematic dismantling of the very concept of formation. Indeed, we get the distinct impression that when, in the most problematic phase of his career, Shakespeare turned to this story, what attracted him, apart from its great popularity, was the wealth of paradoxical material it could offer. Not that his *Troilus and Cressida* openly contradicts the reputation of the two principal characters as archetypes, respectively, of the 'faithful lover' and of

[10] E. M. W. Tillyard, *Shakespeare's Problem Plays* (London, 1965), 76.

'female inconstancy'. On the contrary, in a way it underlines it with a neatness unprecedented in earlier versions of the story. But along with the simple reiteration of the two models in all their dogmatic fixity (Shakespeare even puts it in inverted commas: 'As true as Troilus'; 'As false as Cressida'), there is, schizophrenically, a reconsideration of their case and of the background against which they move, open to doubts and uncertainties which had always lurked in the shadows. Shakespeare does not answer these questions. He merely poses them, through a subtle technique of contrasts which opposes and interweaves each potential meaning with its precise opposite. To this end he makes use of every possible device, from the skilful manipulation of his sources to the illusory resources of the theatrical medium, to the duplicity of language, even of the single letter: consider the cry of the Greek commanders after Cressida has just been handed over to them and they have all kissed her in turn ('The Trojan(s) trumpet'). Here, depending on where the 's' is placed, the listener may hear a simple reference to the trumpet which sounds at that moment to announce the beginning of the duel between Hector and Ajax, or a sarcastic comment ('strumpet') on the woman whom they have all just kissed.[11]

Or consider the mysterious 'Ariachne', a neologism introduced by Troilus to describe the feeling of love/hate, of absolute laceration mixed with an enduring, unshakeable attachment, which he experiences on seeing Cressida's change of loyalty. This strange symbiosis of the mythical 'Ariadne' and 'Arachne', usually attributed to an error on the part of the uneducated printers, has also been pointed out by J. Hillis Miller as clear evidence of the shifting texture of the play, which is scattered throughout with two-headed monsters, with self-negating images.[12]

In short, this writing is anything but chaotic, showing great affinities with that of the contemporary metaphysical poets, with their ingenious games of anamorphosis and 'curious perspective'.[13] There is perhaps no theatrical text of the period, or in the entire Shakespearian canon, which in my opinion is more homologous with the style of the *Songs and Sonets* or the *Paradoxes and Problems*. But, for this very reason, there is none further from Dryden's way

[11] Cf. A. P. Rossiter, *Angels with Horns* (London, 1961), 133.

[12] J. Hillis Miller, 'Ariachne's Broken Woof', *The Georgia Review*, 31 (1977), 44–60.

[13] See E. B. Gilman, *The Curious Perspective* (New Haven and London, 1978).

of thinking and of writing. He chose it precisely with the declared intention of remodelling and completing it, even expressing, at times, feelings of impatient distaste for its complex figurality ('that heap of Rubbish').

Nevertheless, as Dryden's remodelling proceeds it reveals an astonishing awareness of the most sophisticated mechanisms of Shakespeare's writing and of its finely measured counterpoint. With great precision he singles out its ambivalent points, if only to smooth them out in the way which seems most compatible with the 'main design' he claims to discover in it.

Something which has generally escaped those who have compared the two plays is wonderfully highlighted by Dryden's systematic efforts to bring a greater uniformity of discourse to Shakespeare's *Troilus and Cressida*. And this is the heightened level of paradox to which Shakespeare brought the story, involving Cressida as much as Troilus by, for the first time, trying to read events also from her point of view, or rather from the point of view of that which she ambiguously represents.

One of the basic paradoxes of the story, on which Shakespeare insists just as much as Dryden tries to play it down, is that though it is meant to symbolize the inconstancy, the volatility, and ultimately the lack of value of the female sex, it arises and develops alongside the story of a woman who is evidently so valuable as to justify a ten-year war for her exclusive possession; even if, on the other hand, this same woman, because she has passed from one man to another, continually risks falling into the abyss of non-value, dragging with her the justification of the conflict of which she is the cause. Perhaps nothing is more significant in this respect than the curious fortune of Gorgias' mock encomium of Helen, at least as Rosalie Colie sums it up:

Originally a mock encomium of the woman who was obviously unworthy of conventional praise since she was the cause of the Trojan war and of the train of disasters following it, Gorgias' oration was so effective that Helen became not a paradoxical but a proper subject for encomium, a source for many set pieces on the most beautiful woman in the world. In this case a paradox became orthodox.[14]

Shakespeare's text is no less effective in outlining the perfect equilibrium between paradox and orthodoxy which underlies the

[14] R. L. Colie, *Paradoxia Epidemica* (Princeton, 1966), 8.

most ancient of all wars, endlessly unbalancing it. In Shakespeare not only is the indispensable *casus belli* called seriously into question, with Helen oscillating ceaselessly between the status of an 'inestimable' jewel and that of 'whore', but consequently the heroes who contest for her can leap, with hardly any intermediate stages, from extremely bellicose attitudes to a sudden lack of all motivation.

Among the Trojans this is the case at times not only with the enamoured Troilus or the cowardly Helenus but even with Hector, the national hero. If, in spite of everything, they all continue to bear arms, it is because they are driven, at best, by a pure spirit of combat, by the need to maintain their honour, and at worst by bloodthirstiness, by a blind instinct for (self)destruction. And indeed, in this respect, the Greek camp presents no more coherent picture. Ajax is a sort of conglomeration of various heroic tendencies which do not succeed in forming a hero. Achilles has actually stopped fighting, either because of an excessive presumptuousness or because he prefers to stay in his tent and laugh at the farce on military and political power which Patroclus, his 'male varlet', stages before him; or again, perhaps because he is secretly in love with an enemy princess: the war which began with one illicit love affair reaches its impasse, paradoxically, with another.

Hector's challenge, designed to break this stalemate ('this long and dull continued truce'), could not have found, in such a context, a more laughable pretext than the honour and worth of one's own lady. Though received enthusiastically even by the decrepit Nestor, it then goes through a rigged lottery only to fail at the crucial point because of the sudden discovery of a distant kinship between the two opponents, which, furthermore, goes back to the woman (Hesione) whose abduction had set the Trojan War in motion. Is it surprising that the warrior whom Hector finally manages to kill between this interrupted duel and his own death at the hands of Achilles' Myrmidons reveals, inside the splendid suit of armour, nothing but a 'most putrified core'? Achilles himself rejoins the fighting, suddenly forgetful of Polyxena's advice, not because he is jealous of Ajax (as Ulysses had predicted), nor out of a renewed awareness of his own role, but only out of a grim desire to avenge the death of his young male lover.

Shakespeare did not invent the paradoxical element in these

situations. Indeed, it was always latent in the post-Homeric materials on which we may presume that he drew. But what caused it to emerge was his way of rewriting them, of juxtaposing them ironically one with another, revealing hidden correspondences and antinomies. This is shown by the fact that Dryden merely had to play down this subtle subtexture (which includes silences and omissions) to draw from the same plot, using large fragments of the same written material, a highly orthodox picture of the Trojan War and not just 'stuff . . . to make paradoxes'.

There is no room here for a step-by-step reconstruction of this stripping away of the paradoxical. But by way of example let us look at two changes, one an expansion, the other a diminution, which critics have scarcely touched upon, perhaps because Dryden in the 'Preface' hardly dwells on them: the enlargement of the role of Andromache and the complete disappearance of that of Helen.

Andromache must surely be seen above all in relation to the heroic stature of her husband and the virile, patriarchal values he embodies, and which she faithfully reproduces for him. Dryden adds her first entrance at the end of the Trojans' dispute (much simplified by him) on whether to send Helen back or not, whether the war should be continued or ended. The pretext, apparently trivial, but in fact fraught with consequences, is a message from little Astyanax (never mentioned by Shakespeare) who, true to his lineage, already burns with the desire to fight:

HECTOR. Welcome *Andromache*: your looks are cheerfull;
  You bring some pleasing news.
ANDROMACHE.   Nothing that's serious.
  Your little Son *Astyanax* has employ'd me
  As his Ambassadresse.
HECTOR.   Upon what errand?
ANDROMACHE. No less than that his Grandfather this day
  Would make him Knight: he longs to kill a *Grecian*
  For shou'd he stay to be a man, he thinks
  You'll kill 'em all; and leave no work for him.
PRIAM. Your own blood, *Hector*.
ANDROMACHE. And therefore he designs to send a challenge
  To *Agamemnon*, *Ajax*, or *Achilles*
  To prove they do not well to burn our fields;
  And keep us coop'd like prisner's in a Town;
  To lead this lazy life.[15]

        [15] *Truth*, II. i. 78–91.

The idea itself is not all that ridiculous and, naturally, it pro-duces the desired effect in Hector.[16] This triggers another dispute between, on the one hand, Hector, and, on the other, Priam and Aeneas, both anxious to point out that a man such as he is must not endanger himself in this way.[17] Priam's unselfish silence concern-ing the consequences, not only for Troy and for his sons, but for himself, should Hector perish by some evil chance, almost induces the latter to defer his action. Seeing the crack in his son's deter-mination, Priam begs his daughter-in-law to increase the pres-sure.[18] But if Andromache speaks again it is only to espouse her husband's point of view, and in tones which go beyond the bounds of femininity to such an extent that she seems to speak from within him, inflamed with the same valour which she has returned to him in his son:

ANDROMACHE. I would be worthy to be *Hector's* wife:
  And had I been a Man, as my Soul's one,
  I had aspir'd a nobler name, his friend.
  How I love *Hector* (need I say I love him?)
  I am not but in him:
  But when I see him arming for his Honour,
  His Country and his Gods, that martial fire
  That mounts his courage, kindles ev'n to me:
  And when the *Trojan* Matrons wait him out
  With pray'rs, and meet with blessings his return;
  The pride of Virtue, beats within my breast,
  To wipe away the sweat and dust of war:
  And dress my Heroe, glorious in his wounds.[19]

Recognizing in her a worthy consort—indeed, more than a wife a perfect comrade, a heroic *alter ego*—Hector embraces her, en-raptured:

HECTOR. Come to my Arms, thou manlier Virtue come;
  Thou better Name than wife! would'st thou not blush   [*Embrace*]
  To hug a coward thus?[20]

Priam can scarcely add 'Yet still I fear!', for Andromache, caught up in her new identification with her husband's masculinity, accuses him of effeminacy ('There spoke a woman; pardon, Royal Sir'), thus winning Hector over definitively to the idea of the

[16] Ibid., II. i. 91–3.   [17] Ibid., II. i. 102–6.   [18] Ibid., II. i. 141–2.
[19] Ibid., II. i. 143–55.   [20] Ibid., II. i. 156–8.

challenge. And he himself dictates it there and then to Aeneas (Dryden's slight changes from Shakespeare here are partly due to the fact that there it reaches us as reported speech, when Aeneas relates it later in the Greek camp to Agamemnon's royal ears).

Having introduced such a virile Andromache, it may seem strange that Dryden later relegates her to her more traditional role as the warrior's anxious wife, in the second and last of her appearances, which finds her intent upon dissuading Hector from putting on arms, as she has had premonitions of his imminent death. It is true that the scene, a *locus classicus*, also figures in Shakespeare, but Dryden gives far more importance to Andromache's arguments, transforming the *concertato* into a duet. With Priam gone, Andromache takes on the voice of Cassandra (whose madness Dryden prefers not to represent on stage), and also manages to recount in detail the dream of blood and destruction which her Shakespearian predecessor merely affirms that she has had.

The dream motif allows this scene to follow the same lines as the scene between Caesar and Calpurnia in the Shakespearian tragedy which Dryden, despite his denials,[21] must have had in mind more than any other when rewriting *Troilus and Cressida*. There is one difference, however, which says a lot about Dryden's intention to restore the precise, necessary relationship between signifier and signified called into question not only by *Julius Caesar*, but by Shakespeare's plays in general, especially those of the problematic phase. For, in Shakespeare we have only one dream (Calpurnia's) which gives rise to at least two contrasting interpretations, while in Dryden we witness the straightforward narration of two dreams, which are not only different but diametrically opposed, and each of which, because of this, presents itself as an unequivocal message: if, on the one hand, Hector has dreams of 'Jove' who from his throne 'on *Ida*'s top' invites him to ascend and take his place with Bacchus, Hercules, and the other 'demigods', Andromache, on the other hand, has seen 'fiery Demons' falling headlong on to *Ilium*, which is in flames and put to the sword.

In any case Hector, like Shakespeare's Caesar, at first irritated by his wife's superstitious fears, finally allows himself to be convinced not to fight that day, though he is more at pains than Caesar to point out that he is not held back by fear, but only by loving

---

[21] See above, n. 5.

consideration for the soft, feminine side which Andromache has, for once, displayed. The discrepancy between these two sides of Andromache, between the various attitudes which they are capable of provoking in Hector, is, however, one of those which Dryden's theatrical theory not only tolerates but fully authorizes.

Certainly, the ideal hero would be one who, like 'Pius Aeneas', manages never to contradict himself:

> The last property of manners is, that they be constant and equal, that is maintain'd the same through the whole design. Thus, when Virgil had once given the name of Pius to Aeneas, he was bound to show him such, in all his words and actions through the whole Poem.[22]

But, though Dryden's theatrical reforms may tend towards the world of the epic, with its uninterrupted heroism, the theatre is still the theatre. And we can see that Dryden was aware of the risks (or the impossibility) of creating an excessively monolithic character from certain observations he makes on acting methods: 'Thus then the passions, as they are considered simply and in themselves, suffer violence when they are perpetually maintain'd at the same height'.[23] Nevertheless, the only type of conflict which may legitimately be portrayed within the hero is in fact a pseudo-conflict, taking the form rather of the coexistence of compatible passions, among which, however, one must clearly predominate:

> A character, or that which distinguishes one man from all others, cannot be suppos'd to consist of one particular Virtue, or Vice, or passion only; but 'tis a composition of qualities which are not contrary to one another in the same person: thus the same man may be liberal and valiant, but not liberal and covetous; so in a comical character or humour ... Falstaff is a lyar, a coward, a Glutton and a Buffoon, because all these qualities may agree in the same man; yet it is still to be observed that one virtue, vice, and passion, ought to be shown in every man, as predominant over all the rest as covetousness in Crassus, love of his Country in Brutus; and the same in characters which are feign'd.[24]

And it is a conflict, or rather an agreement of compatible passions, which Andromache, with her opposing states of mind, brings to light in Hector. By sparking off and then rekindling his combative spirit in the face of Priam's and his brother's uncertainties, Andromache, in her first appearance, allows her husband

---

[22] The Grounds of Criticism in Tragedy, in M. E. Novak, G. R. Guffey, and A. Roper, vol. xiii, p. 236.

[23] The Grounds of Criticism, p. 242. [24] Ibid., p. 236.

to assert his heroism unequivocally, though he still harbours profound feelings of filial devotion. In her second appearance, her attempt to obstruct him shows likewise that the courageous Hector, in yielding momentarily, is not wholly impervious to feelings of affection and love for his wife, for her fully understandable feminine weakness. He is a magnanimous hero, then, a perfect fusion of strength and love, of Venus and Mars, even if it is to the latter deity that Hector must ultimately make sacrifice, if he truly wishes to ascend to the right hand of Jove.

What is particularly important is the way in which these two scenes of conflict are written, carefully avoiding anything which might interfere with the clear definition of the passions involved. These, on the other hand, though their radical, unshakeable nature is fully developed, exist only in relation to their ultimate submission to the one passion most becoming the hero. Thus, they are reduced to mere detours, whose symmetrical architecture never lets us lose sight of the points both of departure and arrival: prearranged variations on the main theme of heroism, which is synonymous with the persistent self-awareness of reason.

And in fact Andromache's two effusions do not merely function as a litmus test of Hector's pseudo-conflicts and heroic resolutions. They are part of a broader plan which goes beyond the remodelling in more orthodox terms of a single character, or his more in-depth psychological development. Their purpose, in the final analysis, is to institute a more rigorous causal relationship between events, thus becoming a part of that frenzy of rationalization and simplification of which the symmetrical rearrangement of the scenes is merely the most striking feature. Thus, Andromache's first appearance provides a motivation for Hector's challenge other than that of a woman's honour (which is inadequate, to say the least). Following closely on the debate over Helen, the insertion of Andromache shows that there really exists at least one woman for whom, regardless of Helen, it is worth going into battle. Which is in effect what Andromache tells him at the end of their duet on valour:

> You shall be
> My knight this day, you shall not wear a cause
> So black as *Helen*'s rape upon your breast.
> Let *Paris* fight for *Helen*: guilt for guilt.

But when you fight for Honour and for me,
Then let our equal Gods behold an Act,
They may not blush to Crown.[25]

The basic dichotomy of the Trojan War has hardly been pointed out when it is immediately resolved by Andromache's offer of herself to fill the void which Helen may have left in Hector's breast.

In the second instance, however, if Dryden prolongs Andromache's presence on stage, including in it Hector's passing concession to her unaccustomed fears, his aim, if we look closely, is also a more decorous and less contradictory use of the secret love of Achilles and Polyxena. This was introduced by Shakespeare as if to counterbalance Achilles' unnatural passion for Patroclus, whose death subsequently causes the Greek hero to break the solemn vows imposed on him by the still living Polyxena. Cutting out Achilles' homo-erotic relationship, Dryden makes use of his involvement with Polyxena only to get a reaction from Hector, who, provocatively informed of it by Troilus, finds in it sufficient reason to renounce his freshly made promise to Andromache not to fight for the last time.[26]

Similar reasons seem to have dictated the removal of Helen. Shakespeare drags her into the play with a little difficulty, causing her to be present during the scene in which Pandarus announces to Paris that Troilus will not show up that evening for supper at Priam's royal table, thus giving Paris a pretext to ask mischievously if Troilus is not perhaps engaged in some other business with the fair Cressida. It is necessary that it be known at court where Troilus has spent the night: otherwise how could Aeneas arrive at dawn on Pandarus' doorstep to break the fatal news that Cressida is to be exchanged for Antenor?

But in fact why take such a circuitous route? Why bring in Pandarus and Paris as intermediaries, and, along with the latter, disturb no less than a queen who, no matter how uncertain her virtue, still deserves a setting more befitting her rank than the antechamber of a bedroom? So Dryden omits this scene, and at the end of the debate on Helen makes Hector glean directly from Troilus a hint of the latter's gallant rendezvous. This also allows him to repair the damage which that debate has caused to the very foundation of the war, with a generic maxim on the universal attraction of

[25] *Truth*, ii. i. 166–72.   [26] Ibid., v. i. 135–57.

women: a maxim which Andromache, the anti-Helen, will fulfil
positively, with her extraordinary example as the virile wife:

TROILUS.   I have business;
   But I am glad to leave you thus resolved.
   When such arms strike, ne'er doubt of the success.
AENEAS. May we not guess?
TROILUS.   You may, and be deceived.
                                  [*Exit Troilus*
HECTOR. A woman on my life: ev'n so it happens,
   Religion, state affairs, whate'er's the theme
   It ends in women still.
                   Enter Andromache
PRIAM.   See here's your wife
   To make that maxim good.[27]

Yet, if Dryden eliminated that one scene which Shakespeare had
dedicated to Helen it was not only for reasons of functionalism or
decorum. Somehow he must have seen intuitively that that scene,
precisely because it was a device to solve a technical problem
which could be resolved more directly, highlighted far more effectively than any discussion the function of Shakespeare's Helen as a
pure pretext for war. Helen is an ambiguous anaphora of value, an
image in which one can believe with the most burning heroism, but
which at times appears in all its emptiness, or at most filled with
putrefaction. If Helen disappears from Dryden's *dramatis personae*,
it is above all to lessen the paradoxical element of the Trojan War,
which Shakespeare had underlined through her as never before.
The war in Dryden tends to be taken much more for granted, as a
natural background for the heroes' deeds. All that remains of the
two disputes which in Shakespeare open up the endless contradictions of that scenario (where 'each thing meets in mere oppug-
nancy') are two formal debates, tending to help the action flow
along in a well-oiled progression of scenes *à la* Rapin, rather than
to obstruct it; designed to open and close the problems rapidly
rather than to dissect them and leave them eternally suspended. Of
these two debates, both placed at the beginning of their respective
acts (partly perhaps in deference to the royal personages who take
part in them), the first is purged of Ulysses' disquieting observations on the disintegration of 'degree' and the obscene meta-

---

[27] *Truth*, II. i. 70-7.

theatrical activities of Achilles and Patroclus. And the second is relieved of the methodological toing and froing with which the participants approach and pretend to resolve the complex question of 'value'. They both end far more reassuringly with the reaffirmation of 'heroic constancy' as the ultimate, indisputable value.

As often happens when dealing with Shakespeare's *Troilus and Cressida*, the present analysis, which had as its starting-point an adaptation of the play, has been drawn in the end towards one of its two main thematic threads: the rape of Helen and the resulting Trojan War. We must now look at how Dryden, while both exploiting and discarding it, helps us to understand Shakespeare's equally paradoxical reading of the homologous story which constitutes the other principal thread in the play and gives it its title.

Critics have repeatedly pointed out that the relationship between the two themes is not merely circumstantial, in so far as one reproduces the other, albeit in an inverted form: on the one hand a Trojan (Paris) takes a woman (Helen) from a Greek (Menelaus); on the other, a Greek (Diomedes) seduces a woman (Cressida) to repay a Trojan (Troilus) in the same coin. It is in Shakespeare, however, that the isomorphism between the two triangles stands out with uncommon clarity. In his medieval precursors the history of the Trojan War appears rather as a backdrop, which the narrative digression on the story of Troilus and Cressida, whether long or short, continuous or interrupted, tends to make us forget. But Shakespeare seems particularly interested in resurrecting the ancestral links between the two stories, making them no less tight than the strictly mirrored relationship between plot and sub-plot in the most finely structured English Renaissance plays.

Not only does Shakespeare, at the risk of a certain over-complexity, take great pains to present on stage both Paris and Helen herself, fresh from the pleasures of the bedchamber, he also scatters other significant references throughout the text: both explicit ones (e.g. the insistent comparison between Troilus and Paris, Cressida and Helen, which Pandarus weaves into the play from the opening scenes) and others more ironic and indirect: from the remarks which, according to Pandarus, the almost beardless Troilus addressed to Helen characterizing Paris as a cuckold, taking his cue from a cleft hair on his own chin, to Cressida's no less impudent remarks to Menelaus, when, on arriving in the

Greek camp, she reminds him of his sorry status as an 'odd' man, and of his other half who now forms an 'even' couple with Paris. Similarly, Helen's main preoccupation in her erotic and musical *otia* is that the mysterious thing which Cressida envies her (again according to Pandarus) might be her own Paris. Nor, in this light, is it less significant that although Troilus delivers Cressida personally into the hands of Diomedes, he does so in the presence of his brother Paris and that, of all possible settings for the scene of the betrayal, Shakespeare should choose precisely the 'threshold' of Menelaus' tent.

Needless to say, these parallels and echoes, along with many others which one could cite, disappear in Dryden, with easily imaginable consequences. For, their object is not so much the setting up of an abstract structural symmetry, the suggestion of a latent order in Shakespeare's apparent chaos, but rather that which Dryden—from the elimination of both Helen and Paris to the reduction of Menelaus to little more than a minor figure in Agamemnon's retinue—seems more than anything else bent on expurgating: that is, Shakespeare's constant, subtle invitation to read each set of events through the other. This reading starts not only from what is palpably there, but also from what is not expressed: from the ambivalence that undermines the two interlocking plots of love and war, in spite of their common tendency to assert themselves as parables of constancy (male) and inconstancy (female).

Thus, on the one hand, the responsibility of Shakespeare's Helen for the war which, officially, she has unleashed, could not be more fully shared by the heroes who are fighting it in her name. Are they not the first to admit, in their inconclusive diatribes, that their motives have little or nothing to do with Helen's dubious worth?

It is also true, on the other hand, that, though Shakespeare allows her on to the stage, Helen does not spare so much as an aside to express the slightest sense of regret. She moves and speaks like a high-class cocotte, supremely indifferent to the holocaust for which she continues, for better or worse, to be the pretext. Her concern goes no further than her attempt to keep Paris in her clutches while the other heroes are arming themselves to go into combat—though it is unclear whether she does this because she genuinely identifies with the role of the absolute lover ('this love will undo us all'), or because she is concerned to keep her one true champion alive as long as possible. He it is who, during the debate on her fate, does not see her merely as a spur to honour, a pretext for his own glory, a means for self-apotheosis, but poses the concrete problem of what might happen to her if the Trojans should decide to send her back to her former consort.[28]

However, we may suspect that the overwhelming passion (and its related jealousy) which Helen feels for him is, if not quite the result of a calculation, at least a willing adaptation to the wishes of the man who, after all, 'abducted' her from her legitimate spouse. And this is not so much because of the ease with which, in Pandarus' account, we see her flirting with her youngest brother-in-law, but rather because of the text's extreme reticence on the matter of *her* desire at the moment of the abduction. Up to what point did it coincide from the beginning with that of Paris, or is it merely the inevitable consequence of this? In Troilus' fleeting reference to that fatal event she in fact appears as nothing more than a magnificent prey, an object to substitute for another, an intermediate link in the chain of women who have been exchanged, substituted, *traditae*, whether willingly or reluctantly, and which stretches from Hesione right down to Cressida.

That it is Troilus who speaks in these terms (and on the very eve of the exchange of Cressida for Antenor) helps to underline not only the links but also the contradictions between the two sets of circumstances, when we stop to consider them from both sides, male and female, as Shakespeare continually forces us to do. For, Cressida too, just as much as Helen, is a fatal source of violence. Naturally, in any account of the myth her infidelity brings about a fierce rivalry between the first and second lover. This never manages to culminate in a cathartic duel which would involve the elimination of at least one of the two. Rather, it gives rise to a series of violent but inconclusive clashes: as if to constitute a metaphor in miniature of the larger but equally protracted, collective war which had its origins in Helen. This rivalry was in any case reconnected with the war (even Boccaccio and Chaucer, who are more interested in the 'sentimental' outcome of the story, feel the need to

---

[28] Although, once again, it is difficult to ascertain whether Paris is declaring a chivalrous principle in which he believes (reinforced very probably by Helen's continued urgings behind the scenes) or whether he is merely trying to put forward valid justifications for his own personal pleasure, as Priam sarcastically points out: 'You have the honey still, but these the gall' (II. ii. 145).

stress this link at the end) through the death of Troilus (the second Hector) at the hands (or on the orders) of that other arch-antagonist Achilles (or of his Myrmidons), in one of the many battles in which he subsequently takes part. And Troilus throws himself into this last combat with a fury in which, along with his accustomed valour and patriotism and his desire to avenge the death of Hector, we must presume there is mingled his bitterness towards Diomedes, his grief for the loss of Cressida.

Shakespeare loosens this well-established reconnection between the love and war plots for the simple reason that Troilus remains unexpectedly alive after his usual inconclusive encounters with Diomedes. Or rather, he remains in that state of suspension between life and death which characterizes him from the beginning of the play; the way in which Achilles orders the Myrmidons to kill Hector being the same as that employed (in Caxton and Lydgate) to kill Troilus. So that for those who knew those highly popular versions of the story it cannot have been difficult to foresee his imminent death, though this climax is then denied to him on stage. But the precariousness of his survival is made clear in any case to the attentive listener by his own final speech. This places his vital, warlike impulse in the same ambiguous relationship with Hector's death as with Cressida's lack of amorous response in the first scene, thus revealing once and for all the morbid tendencies running through them. In both cases a paralysing sense of absolute loss is transformed (at the instigation of Aeneas) into a frenzy of activity: and it matters little that in one case it takes the form of athletic fervour, in the other that of dark revenge.

If, then, by virtue of this isomorphism, Shakespeare's Cressida, though removed from the action immediately after the betrayal, is portrayed more than ever—just as much as Helen—as a cause of conflict, the question of her responsibility becomes reversible, perhaps even more than for Helen. Such is the subtlety with which Shakespeare, while reaffirming her condemnation, invites us to re-examine the peculiar circumstances of her infidelity, which turn it too into a consequence of the war and make her an effect, a 'daughter of the game'. For, we must never forget that Cressida comes into being as the figure of a woman who has been violently separated from her man. The very status of widow which she enjoys in certain versions of the myth (e.g. in Chaucer) tends to emphasize this situation. Even before she transfers her love to another she has in fact suffered forced separation from the first man to whom she gave herself, and this on the basis of an irreversible decision, dictated by reasons of state, by the laws of war, of men, of her father, by something in short which excludes her totally. It is true that Shakespeare passes over her first, incidental widowhood, but he does everything he can to highlight the irrevocable character of the second. Consider the *coup de théâtre* of her father's voice recalling her unexpectedly, immediately after she has retired to the bedchamber with Troilus, in a scene which, precisely because of this, we tend to imagine as simultaneous with their long-awaited embrace, or indeed as a nightmare, a bad dream which intervenes to divide them in their post-coital languor, a dark premonition of the news which will surprise them at dawn. This is a scene which Dryden eliminated, in spite of his desire to make Calchas the villain of the piece. His request comes to us in a shortened form through a third party. And certainly this is not solely because of the author's declared intention of reducing as far as possible the alternation between the two main settings of the play. Rather, independently of the negative emphasis placed on Calchas the 'priest' (dictated, as we have seen, by historical circumstances), he must have been concerned deep down to reconcile the affair in question as far as possible with the patriarchal (and monarchical) values which those same historical circumstances threatened to compromise.

This explains how, on the other hand, the motif of the abandonment of Cressida to her cruel fate, as emphasized in Shakespeare, must have seemed unsustainable to Dryden, beginning with the excessive fatalism with which Troilus, forgetting all his bold resolve, accepts without argument the decision to exchange her for Antenor:

AENEAS. We must give up to Diomedes' hand
 The Lady Cressida.
TROILUS.   Is it so concluded?
AENEAS. By Priam and the general state of Troy.
 They are at hand, and ready to effect it.
TROILUS. How my achievements mock me!
 I will go and meet them.[29]

---

[29] *Troilus and Cressida*, IV. ii. 67–72.

But what he says to them we shall never know. Dryden tries to imagine it. Hence, he adds the noble dispute with Hector, which not only offers Troilus the opportunity to display a more obstinate commitment to defend his lady, but also allows his older brother to give him an important lesson on the duties of the good sovereign. He can only call himself such for as long as he is prepared to sacrifice the 'private' for the 'publick': only by virtue of such self-sacrifice can he hope to soar eagle-like above the flock of crows who are his subjects, to become for them an object of devotion. It is in fact in this veneration from below of a superior sacrifice that Dryden's Hector identifies the surest guarantee of social order, of 'degree', the very essence of the divine power of the monarch. Thus, we might say, he adapts *ad usum delphini* his Shakespearian predecessor's sceptical statement on the excessive sacrifice which Helen's cause has ultimately demanded ('Tis mad idolatry | To make the service greater than the god'):

TROILUS. O, she's my life, my being, and my Soul!
HECTOR. Suppose she were, which yet I will not grant,
   You ought to give her up.
TROILUS.   For whom?
HECTOR.   The publick.
TROILUS. And what are they that I shou'd give up her
   To make them happy? Let me tell you Brother,
   The publick, is the Lees of vulgar slaves:
   Slaves, with the mind of slaves so born, so bred:
   Yet such as these united in a herd
   Are call'd the publique: Millions of such Cyphers
   Make up the publique sum: an Eagle's life
   Is worth a world of Crows: are Princes made
   For such as these, who, were one Soul extracted
   From all their beings, cou'd not raise a Man?
HECTOR. And what are we, but for such men as these?
   'Tis adoration, some say, makes a God:
   And who shou'd pay it, where wou'd be their Altars
   Were no inferiour creatures here on earth?
   Ev'n those who serve have their expectances,
   Degrees of happiness, which they must share,
   Or they'll refuse to serve us.[30]

It is certainly a bitter pill to swallow for the young, enamoured prince, who continues for a time to rage wildly, even going so far as

[30] *Truth*, III. ii. 300–19.

to call the wishes of his king and father 'unjust', to call his friend and brother a 'traytor', and to say that Cressida (who in Hector's words is still 'the Daughter of a fugitive | A Traytor to his Coun-try!') is as 'chaste' as Andromache. This juxtaposition in itself ('What! nam'st thou them together!') would be enough to shatter Hector's stoical attitude, had he not previously vowed to have patience with whatever 'gust of passion' might be provoked in his brother by the bad news which he bears. So, on leaving he only threatens an end to their 'friendship', opening up beyond the admittedly noble passion of 'love' the prospect of a more sublime, disembodied value to hold on to. The threat has an immediate effect on Troilus, and the two brothers, after other variations on the theme of friendship, can finally embrace, forming a sort of pre-Canovian sculptural group in which Hector takes on the character-istics not of a friend and brother but of a father, a king, a demigod.

But to make this happy· symbiosis convincing after so many insults and provocations it is necessary to show that in the breast of each of the disputants friendship has truly prevailed over all other inferior passions. Thus, Hector first hastens to reformulate his judgement of Cressida, in terms which, moreover, are more in line with the new reputation which Dryden is forging for her. Then, deeply moved, he goes so far as to call into question again the definitive decision to exchange her. In the end it is Troilus him-self, now fully caught up in the role of the good prince, who wants the exchange to go ahead immediately:

TROILUS. It must not be, my Brother!
  For then your error would be more than mine:
  I'le bring her forth, and you shall bear her hence;
  That you have pitied me is my reward.[31]

If I pause over Dryden's carefully measured heroic insertions it is because by going back from them to Shakespeare's 'incomplete' reading we can appreciate its obstinate tendency to emphasize the problematic aspects of Cressida's story much better than we can through many subsequent critical analyses.

As I have already mentioned, although it was invariably related to the depravity of *all* women, Cressida's infidelity had never ceased to be connected back to the particular violence committed against her. In this respect, Shakespeare's Cressida is extremely

[31] Ibid., III. ii. 431–4.

explicit. And that the 'conventional signs of grief' (a reminiscence of Chaucer) which she displays at the moment when the exchange is announced are not, as Palmer rightly observes, necessarily 'insincere'[32] is shown I think by the fact that later, in a passage omitted by Dryden, she claims the right, in the face of Pandarus' attempts to appease her, to taste fully the pain of the enforced separation:

> The grief is fine, full, perfect, that I taste
> And violenteth in a sense so strong
> As that which causes it: how can I moderate it?[33]

But, apart from this, what matters is the fact that in Shakespeare the yielding up of Cressida is suspended between the compelling motives of an interminable war (in which, however, no one believes blindly any more) and the feeble protests of the man who had declared himself one with her to the point of being unable to commit himself to any other cause. It is because of this that it appears, all the more, if not quite a gratuitous act of cruelty at least a plausible preface to her infidelity, tempting us as never before to reconsider it as a pretext also, and to discover that it has, at least in part, a justificatory function. It is a function which Shakespeare highlights dramatically by making Troilus the one (as in Chaucer) who delivers Cressida into the hands of Diomedes, accompanying this act (which in Chaucer is deliberately silent) with all his counter-productive advice, in one of the most ironic sequences in the play. It is a sequence which Dryden removes, along with all the other awkward details scattered throughout the various phases of the exchange by Shakespeare, culminating in Cressida's arrival in the Greek camp, with the kisses and biting remarks which she exchanges with all the Greek leaders except Ulysses.

After the noble dispute between Hector and Troilus and the separation scene in Pandarus' house, when Dryden's Cressida re-appears later she is already in a tent in the Greek camp, along with her father who (in a short added scene) instructs her on how to ensnare Diomedes. The tent is no longer that of Menelaus, in which Shakespeare imagines that the deserter and his daughter lodge, but, more simply, 'Calchas's tent'. Evidently concerned to absolve Cressida not only partially but completely, and by some

---

[32] K. Palmer, n. to IV. ii. 110–12, Arden edn., p. 235.
[33] *Troilus and Cressida*, IV. iv. 3–5.

other means than by the precedent of her enforced transfer, Dryden skips this completely, thus side-stepping the principal ambiguity which had always been inherent in her traditional condemnation.

To clarify this point further, a comparison with the story of the almost homonymous Griselda[34] (Criseida-Griselda) may be useful. Compared with this the story of Cressida's betrayal presents a certain imbalance which is instructive. Griselda becomes a paradigm of patience, of steadfastness, and of an absolute attachment to her husband, in spite of the terrible tests to which he submits her, because she stays devoted to him though placed in the optimum conditions to stop loving him. Cressida, on the other hand, becomes the unfaithful woman *par excellence*, though she finds herself in far-from-ideal conditions to remain faithful to her Troilus. The paradox is that the woman who becomes the archetype of female inconstancy is the 'protagonist' of a story which offers at least some extenuating circumstances for her infidelity.

This paradox is by no means negligible, in so far as it detracts from the absolute function of Cressida as an archetype, introducing *ab origine* elements of contradiction. It is not necessary to be, in Shakespeare's words, a 'ticklish reader' to sense, beyond the veil of silence which even Chaucer preferred ultimately to draw over the figure of Cressida, a certain unease in the pronouncement of the final condemnation. We may say that Shakespeare heightens this sense of awkwardness, making it the main thread of his re-elaboration, taking his cues from it to parody, to a point of no return, not so much the story itself as the ethics of love which form its background.

Obviously any infidelity on Cressida's part would have been a different matter if Calchas' request had not been agreed to by the Greeks, or if, at least, among the Trojans,[35] Troilus had strenuously opposed it (as indeed in Dryden he tries, for a time, to do)—if, in short, Cressida had, out of the blue, been unfaithful within the walls of Troy, perhaps with a companion or a kinsman of Troilus. But that, of course, would have been another story. Or rather, a

---

[34] It was Boccaccio who invented both names. See V. Branca's nn. to his edn. of the *Decameron* (Milan, 1976), 1556.

[35] The Trojans have everything to gain from it, as Dryden's Hector feels it his duty to point out: 'all our common safety ... depends on freed *Antenors* wisdome' (III. ii. 289–90).

non-story. Cressida would have been plunged automatically into the void, into the unspeakable role of 'whore'.

The more we consider it, the more we wonder about Cressida's infidelity, with all its gaps, incongruities, extenuating circumstances, and indecisions, all duly underlined by Shakespeare just where Dryden tries hardest to remedy them. We continue, in sum, to ask ourselves whether this infidelity, while certainly an opportunity to re-examine the problems of adultery, is not also and above all a means of voicing something (desire on the part of the woman) which was otherwise destined to be silent, to express itself only in 'tortive and errant' ways.

How else can we interpret Cressida's regret, in the scene of the declaration of love, that she has had to wait for Troilus to decide on this step? Had she been able to speak first, she who has had to 'muster' her own feelings of love *at first sight*, she would perhaps have spared herself many 'weary months'. And yet she still hesitates to confess this love, putting forward the reason that it is better to leave men eternally in suspense, lest they should take advantage. But what ties her tongue is also the ill-concealed fear that as a woman she would decline in worth as soon as she dared utter her desire. Is this not indicated by the fact that she now begs Troilus to break his silence, which he has so far maintained perhaps as an astute stratagem? And how should he do this if not by *literally* stopping her mouth with the longed-for kiss which she immediately denies that she wanted to provoke, as though drawn back into the reticence befitting her sex? Her paradoxical request turns up word for word in Dryden, but without the optatives, the suspensions which precede it in Shakespeare, without the anxiety that certain thoughts may show themselves, without any indication of an uncontrollable urge in Cressida, of a desire which *she too* secretly cherishes:

TROILUS Why was my Cressid then so hard to win?
CRESSIDA Hard to seem won. But I was won, my lord.
~~With the first glance that ever—Pardon me:~~
~~If I confess much, you will play the tyrant.~~
~~I love you now, but till now not so much~~
~~But I might muster it. In faith I lie—~~
~~My thoughts were, like unbridled children, grown~~
~~Too headstrong for their mother. See, we fools!~~
Why have I blabb'd? Who shall be true to us?
          unfaithful
When we are so ~~unsecret~~ to ourselves?

~~But, though I lov'd you well, I woo'd you not;~~
~~And yet, good faith, I wished myself a man,~~
~~Or that we women had man's privilege~~
                            O
~~Of speaking first. Sweet,~~ bid me hold my tongue;
For in this rupture ~~I shall surely speak~~
Sure I shall speak what I shou'd soon repent.
~~The thing I shall repent. See, see, your silence,~~
~~Cunning in dumbness, from my weakness draws~~
~~My very soul of counsel!~~ (But) Stop my mouth.
TROILUS A sweet command; and willingly obey'd
            ~~And shall, albeit sweet music issues thence.~~

                                        [*Kisses her*

PANDARUS Pretty, i'faith.
CRESSIDA My lord, I do beseech you pardon me:
'Twas not my purpose thus to beg a kisse.
I am asham'd. O Heavens! What have I done?
For this time I will take my leave, my lord.[36]

What was once the complex set of symptoms of a desire which could no longer be contained is transformed into a predictable game of feminine seduction: the tactics of a maiden who is as demure as she is wily.

Similar considerations come to mind with regard to the modifications occurring at all the other points where Cressida, even implicitly, or indeed by denying it, ventures to speak of her own sexuality. Thus, at the beginning of the *aubade* scene, Dryden not only cuts out her attempt to detain the hurriedly departing Troilus, but also her regret at having yielded too soon, thus diminishing her power of attraction over him.[37] There remains only, slightly modified, Troilus' urgent request that she return to her empty bed and let her senses sleep like children:

Farewell my life! Leave me and back to bed
                            seal
~~To bed, to bed!~~ Sleep ~~kill~~ those pretty eyes
                            tye
And ~~give as soft attachement to~~ thy senses (in a soft band)
            voyd
As infants ~~empty~~ of ~~all~~ thought.[38]

[36] *Troilus and Cressida*, III. ii. 115–38; *Truth*, III. ii. 37–49.
[37] *Truth*, IV. ii. 15–18.
[38] *Troilus and Cressida*, IV. ii. 4–6; *Truth*, III. ii. 193–6.

So, in the end, the *equivocatio* over Cressida's renewed invitation to retire to the bedroom, because someone is knocking insistently at the door, is stripped of any possible ambiguity on her part ('*As if* I meant naughtily'): in Dryden it is only a thought which she reads on the face of Troilus, whose reply to her invitation, 'Indeed, indeed', is far more vigorous than Shakespeare's enigmatic 'Ha, Ha!' The Cressida who emerges from this is not only chaste, but childishly naïve with regard to the act to which, for better or for worse, she has been a party, and which she is made to live indirectly, as an exclusive projection of the male indignation, without any desire to have a greater say in the matter. Dryden's Cressida is a woman who is quite at ease in her conventional female role and who, for example, with regard to her own sexuality, goes no further than to demand a promise of marriage from the man with whom she is about to go to bed for the first time: what was in Shakespeare a parody of the nuptial rite, staged by Pandarus before ushering them inside, becomes the insistent request for a formal vow of betrothal:

> And will you promise that the holy Priest
> Shall make us one forever? . . .
> I'le not consent unless you swear.[39]

The further paradoxical result is that while this Cressida may, in some ways, seem more chaste or more naïve than Shakespeare's, she is also moved by a slightly less disinterested 'passion', though naturally within the limits allowed to a woman by a ritual of love and courtship which Shakespeare's Cressida, by contrast, is always on the point of overstepping, feeling it to be too restrictive.

So, in the end, we may be inclined to see her infidelity as a possible means of revenge for her misunderstood sexuality. We can sense the first murmurings of this desire to vindicate herself in the growing irritation with which she replies, during their brief moments together before the separation, to Troilus' insistent 'Be thou (but) true'—which he places as a necessary pre-condition (for him) to what is at that moment of far more concern to her: that they will see each other again. So much so that when Troilus hastens to point out that this condition is merely an introduction to his promise to see her, Cressida takes him at his word: she will

---

[39] *Truth*, III. ii. 84–5; 89.

be faithful to him in spite (or by virtue?) of the dangers to which he must expose himself in order to see her. And, as if to stress that she will not be content with the tokens, the empty symbolic substitutes (the glove, the sleeve) which he proposes they exchange, she immediately insists again 'When shall I see you?' But Troilus turns the question around, to make his nightly visits a consequence of her fidelity, which can only irritate her further. This short-circuit of priorities underlines marvellously the impossibility of communication between the two of them, between his idealistic posturing and her uncompromising sensuality. Dryden tried to bridge this gap, obviously by sacrificing the latter term:

TROILUS Hear me, my love: be thou but true ~~of heart~~— *like me*

CRESSIDA I, true? How now, what wicked ~~deem~~ is this? *thought*

TROILUS Nay, we must use expostulation kindly,
 For it is parting from us.
 I ~~speak~~ not 'Be thou true' as fearing thee— *spoke*
 ~~For I will throw my glove to Death himself~~
 ~~That there is no maculation in thy heart~~—
 But 'Be thou true' I ~~say~~ to ~~fashion in~~ *said introduce*
 My ~~sequent~~ protestation: be thou true, *following*
 And I will see thee.

CRESSIDA ~~O~~ you shall be expos'd ~~my lord~~ to dangers
 ~~As infinite as imminent! But I'll be true.~~

TROILUS ~~And I'll grow friend with danger: wear this sleeve~~ *I care not*

CRESSIDA ~~And you this glove: when shall I see you?~~

TROILUS ~~I will corrupt the Grecian sentinels~~
 ~~To give you nightly visitation.~~
 But ~~yet~~ be true.

CRESSIDA ~~O heavens~~—'be true' again.[40]

As we can see, not only does Troilus' imperative imply, more generously, a promise to do likewise himself ('be like me'), but he also expresses of his own accord the desire to see her again, rather than wait for her to draw it out of him. Indeed, she never asks this

[40] *Troilus and Cressida*, IV. iv. 56–73; *Truth*, IV. i. 54–64.

of him, clearly putting his safety first when he declares this intention.

Betrayed in her expectations, exposed to the risk of becoming everybody's woman (and in this respect the collective kiss which greets her as she emerges from no man's land is significant), is it then so surprising that Shakespeare's Cressida should be tempted to replace her first (lost) 'husband' with someone whom she at least *desires* (again) 'at the first glance'? It is impossible to say (since she looks on silently) how much she is influenced in this reorientation of her desire by the bickering between Troilus and Diomedes, during which the former expects to establish respect for her as part of a solemn pact between men, reducing her to the level of a sort of point of honour, while the latter insists that he will decide himself whether or not to respect her, and only on the basis of 'her own worth', which, besides, he has immediately been seen to appreciate greatly. There remains, however, the extreme rapidity of this reorientation, especially in relation to the very long courtship which in the medieval versions usually preceded it. Was Shakespeare forced into this acceleration of the time-scale by the obvious restrictions of the medium which he was using, or did he rather exploit these restrictions to point to something in the myth which had never been sufficiently highlighted?

I hope it has been understood that this analysis is not meant to be the umpteenth apologia for 'woeful Cressid 'mongst the merry Greeks'. Taking its cue precisely from the suddenness with which the object of her love changes, it aims rather to show how, apart from Cressida's traditional female flaws, what emerges in Shakespeare is, in a far more general sense, the incorrigible 'femininity' of desire. By this I understand the totality of negative characteristics (fickleness, inconstancy, irrationality, etc.), traditionally the female heritage, but which, above and beyond sexual distinctions, can be said to constitute the other ('weaker') side of desire—desire which is, with its obsessive persistency, the only manifestation of the infinite which we can experience in life, the model for all our dreams of omnipotence, the matrix of our most unrestrained love-hyperboles. Capable as it is of being reborn phoenix-like from its own ashes, it is ever unchanging in its passage from one object to another. But precisely because of these unpredictable fluctuations, ending always in temporary appeasement ('things won are done | Joy's soul lies in the doing'), nothing is more appropriate than desire to symbolize our inadequacy and finiteness, along with that of the means, acts, and objects to which we have recourse to satisfy it ('the will is infinite, and the execution confined'). It is desire that highlights the presence in us of something which guides us and speaks for us, rather than allow itself to be spoken of and guided: of 'an unkind self, that itself will leave | To be another's fool'.

Towards the end of the leave-taking scene, that which Troilus warns Cressida against may indeed be, obliquely, the greater inclination of women to play with fire, to expose themselves to dangerous temptations. In any case he speaks of it as a 'frailty' found in humanity as a whole, which is well depicted in the subtle distinction between the 'presumed' stability of our 'powers', and the unpredictable changes in their 'potency':

> But something may be done that we will not;
> And sometimes we are devils to ourselves,
> When we will tempt the frailty of our powers,
> Presuming on their changeful potency.[41]

And in fact Cressida remains undoubtedly the clearest example in Shakespeare of the instability of our 'absolute' attachment to one object of desire or another. Yet, there is no character in the play who is not in some measure touched by this, and even in Troilus (though he speaks of his desire for her in terms of a magnetic, cosmic, gravitational adhesion) there are exceptions which confirm the rule. It is this uncontrollable slipping of desire which, in Shakespeare, Cressida's traditional infidelity shows us with extraordinary clarity.

In summing up her first, highly dramatic, face-to-face meeting with Diomedes, Cressida does not present us with a *fait accompli.* What she tries to describe is rather the feeling of being torn between her previous lover (to whom, as she leaves him, she still 'looks' back with her mind's eye) and her future lover, who is tempting her other eye, that of her 'heart', which involves, as well as passion, the senses, a physical 'seeing'; and we are left in no doubt, given the 'poor sex' to which she belongs, given the reputation which has hung over her for centuries, in which direction she will 'err':

> Troilus, farewell! One eye yet looks on thee,
> But with my heart the other eye doth see.

[41] *Troilus and Cressida*, IV. iv. 92–5.

Ah, poor our sex! this fault in us I find:
The error of our eye directs our mind.
What error leads must err; O, then conclude,
Minds sway'd by eyes are full of turpitude.[42]

'Cressida's pose is emblematic', comments Palmer.[43] And yet, how much movement there is in this almost gnomic repetition of the archetype, accentuated by the rhyming couplets, which, though it leads to a highly predictable ethical judgement, outlines with disarming clarity the pure dynamism of desire, how it can switch its centre from one object to another, with the complicity of the senses, while reason is powerless to intervene. A further paradox is that Diomedes, who is so 'present' to Cressida's eyes and senses, has just left, while Troilus is right there with her as an unseen witness to her straying thoughts—although later he will do his best to push this scene, which he has physically seen and registered in every syllable, back into the realm of unreality by opposing it with the ideal image of an *other* Cressida, which has remained fixed forever in his mind. It is a chiasmus of two cross-eyed glances (Venus too was cross-eyed) in which the lovers look at each other without seeing each other, constituting that monster of duplicity, the 'byfold authority' of desire, trapped forever between the limited perspective of the senses and the imagined infinity of the mind: 'as infinite as imminent', as Cressida might say.

It was not the first time that the age-old story of Troilus and Cressida had ended up literally on the 'stage'.[44] But Shakespeare, by 'staging' the betrayal scene as a play within the play, succeeded in postponing its meaning indefinitely.

Ultimately, we have proof of this in the form of a confession from Cressida herself, as the three spectators remark:

THERSITES. A proof of strength she could not publish more
    Unless she said, 'My mind is now turned whore'.
ULYSSES. All's done my lord.
TROILUS.   It is.

And that confession must surely, on the one hand, cast an unedifying light on the preceding scene with Diomedes, showing it as

---

[42] *Troilus and Cressida*, v. ii. 106–11.

[43] K. Palmer, n. to v. ii. 106–7, Arden Edn., p. 275.

[44] We ought to note, e.g., the play *Troilus and Cressida*, by Thomas Dekker and Henry Chettle (1599), of which but two pp. of plot outlines and a few stage directions remain.

an example of the delaying techniques used by women to make up for their inferior status, as Cressida has already theorized, both alone and with Troilus. But, as we have just seen, the very terms of that confession tend rather to show her imminent betrayal as the result literally of a 'proof (or trial) of strength'[45] between reason and the senses, in which the latter are fatefully about to prevail. So that, in the very moment it takes place, the whole shilly-shallying with Diomedes can also be seen as an authentic dramatic reflection of an inner struggle in which she tries not to submit to the allurements of her own and of Diomedes' body by clinging to her memory of Troilus. This is in fact what she seems to do as she conjures up the scene of Troilus on his bed, thinking of her and clasping her token to his breast. And yet, could not this be but another shrewd ploy to arouse her new lover to whom she is about to hand over the pledge given by the old? Neither does the caress with which Troilus at one point maintains he sees her stroke his rival's face help us to decide what her intentions really are. Even if we exclude (though there are no stage directions) the idea that the caress is merely a hallucination on the part of Troilus, a part of his tendency to interpret Cressida's most innocent actions 'naughtily', how then should we interpret it from Cressida's point of view? Is it a calculated gesture meant to hold Diomedes, to whom she has already committed herself? Or is it a sign of her irresistible desire to touch him—a result of the ever-decreasing attraction which the memory of Troilus holds for her?

The suspense is such that an audience hypothetically unaware of the traditional plot could even suppose that Cressida is only marking time because she does not know what else to do. A prisoner, the daughter of a traitor, and the object of a Greek prince's desire, she may simply be acting in this manner on the advice of her cunning father, hidden inside the tent.

And in fact Dryden transforms the scene into just such a performance. He needs only to make certain cuts (mostly insignificant ones, apart from the 'caress' which, though ambiguous, unbalanced the figure of Cressida too much), to replace the discussion between Cressida and Diomedes over when they will meet again with a more laconic exchange (D. 'I shall expect your promise', C. 'I'le perform it'), and naturally to replace her final confession with the

---

[45] I do not agree that this means only 'forceful proof' as Palmer suggests (n. to v. ii. 112, p. 275).

aside: 'Thus to deceive deceivers is no fraud'. Dryden does, indeed, precede all this with a short explanatory scene in which Calchas instructs Cressida in her part. But it is difficult to say whether this can be ascribed to the overwhelming need for clarity and completeness or the desire to burden the conscience of the scheming 'priest' with the downfall of his chaste daughter. This offers her anyway a solid alibi so that she at the end can be believed, if not by Troilus and Diomedes, at least by those in the audience who still remember her famous misdeeds. Perhaps Dryden intended all these things at once. In any case, even without the insertion of the scene with Calchas the new meaning would still be apparent. This is what I have tried to demonstrate: that Cressida's 'new' innocence (which was always implicit to a remote degree even in the versions of the myth most hostile to her) is *almost* brought to the surface by Shakespeare's 'byfold' writing, which always seems on the point of declaring it but then falls back on the traditional view of her 'full turpitude'. This paradoxical twisting ('a lion that will fly | With his face backward'[46]) illustrates perfectly how, under the impact of changing values, the myth had reached its limits, those of self-parody, beyond which only a complete inversion of the meaning was possible. Dryden, a perspicacious reader, sensed this possibility and seized on it wholeheartedly—with the result, however, that he lost the supreme duplicity found in Shakespeare.

Shakespeare partially absolves Cressida by weaving her story into a background where there are no longer any absolute certainties, where a 'cause' no longer produces a commensurate 'effect', where the only unifying factor seems to be the self-destructive 'universal Wolf' of individual appetite. In this context, where the precise meaning of words has been lost, each sentence must comment upon itself and place itself in inverted commas. Then even the soundest of proverbs tends to waver and Cressida's infidelity, rather than symbolizing the lechery of all women, becomes just one more example (and not even the most serious at that) of the general instability and moral decline of the times. This is best summed up in Thersites' judgement: 'Lechery, still wars and lechery, nothing else holds fashion'. And Cressida is ultimately sucked back into this background, as it flares up into a furious conflict, over which hangs the imminent fall of Troy. It is as if by her

---

[46] *Troilus and Cressida*, IV. i. 20–1.

infidelity she had become identified with this scenario: even Troilus, strangely, speaks of her no more, as if he had completely forgotten her. It is up to Pandarus, in his epilogue on the vicissitudes of his occupation, to remind the audience of the failed amorous transaction of which she has been the co-protagonist.

But there is more in Shakespeare than this grim absolute moralism, with its implied lament for the old hierarchies, for angelic women and the valorous knights of old and for 'what not stirs'; a clear (and regressive) condemnation of change. If in another way Shakespeare redeems Cressida's infidelity, along with the failings of Troilus and all the other betrayals in the play (including even Achilles' savage treachery), it is because his writing shows up the sheer mechanisms, the irresolvable contradictions, which underlie them. Thus, his play takes them out of the sphere of morality, relating them rather to something which goes beyond reason and responsibility and mocks our vain attempts to sound 'th'uncomprehensive deep'. So, the play is more than just a moralistic lament for the changing times. It becomes a lucid, melancholy metaphor of all that limits and conditions us despite ourselves: of Chance and Time, which eternally threaten the illusory continuity of desire: 'Now good or bad 'tis but the chance [change?] of war [of love?]'?

Paradoxically, Dryden absolves Cressida *completely* by resolving both the historical and meta-historical contradiction which Shakespeare had opened up as far as possible in order to attenuate her guilt or indeed to suspend her condemnation indefinitely. Thus, on the level of the plot, the background on which she and Troilus move is still divided and fragmented: one way or the other there is a war going on, one of the most controversial and ultimately the most heroic. But in Dryden those who are highest in the hierarchy express far fewer doubts about it, and the only one who still sees it as an absurd battle between cuckolds for the sake of a whore is the vitriolic Thersites. It is left to him to point out the prevalence of lust and corruption, and, along with Pandarus, he is given a monopoly of the sexual puns which in Shakespeare can be found in the most diverse social contexts and linguistic registers. As regards the general malaise, its origins and effects are seen exclusively in the loss of respect for and faith in the supremacy of monarchical power and the divine right on which it is based. So, after Cressida's noble sacrifice and the ensuing blood-bath, the whole play can end cathartically, not with Pandarus' bitter epilogue but with Ulysses' radiant address to the re-enthroned Agamemnon:

> Hayl *Agamemnon*! truly Victor now!
> While secret envy, and while open pride,
> Among thy factious Nobles discord threw;
> While publique good was urg'd for private ends,
> And those thought Patriots, who disturb'd it most;
> Then, like the headstrong horses of the Sun,
> That light which shou'd have cheer'd the World consum'd it:
> Now peacefull order has resum'd the reynes,
> Old time looks young, and Nature seems renew'd:
> Then, since from homebred Factions ruine springs,
> Let Subjects learn obedience to their Kings.[47]

But in practical terms this certainty of renewal is something which is seen not only in the progressive and symmetrical restructuring of the 'plot'. It can be seen even more in the changes in the very 'writing': the removal of the 'heap of Rubbish', of the remarkably tangled style which, playing endlessly with language, symbolized the abominable, 'feminine' wandering of a desire which, unlike Dryden's well-defined passions, can never be brought within the 'main design' of reason.

Thus, while Troilus, Hector, and all the other male parts become, whether comically or tragically, for good or ill, clear-cut characters, Cressida, once her ancestral link with Helen has been cut and she has been raised to the same status as the 'new' virile Andromache, is absolved, not only because she did not commit the crime, but because she did not even remotely desire to (although she plays the part very well on the prompting of her father). Indeed, after her initial manifestation of desire for Troilus (the audience must, after all, be shown that she is deeply in love with him) her desire is taken for granted, appeased, projected exclusively on to the men who exchange and manipulate her, who compete for her and desire her. She becomes a symbol of the 'Woman in Love',[48] but in practice ceases to desire, and so sees her age-old function disappearing all at once. So that, though she is innocent, she is condemned to die, to be literally annihilated on stage, dragging with her her two lovers who for centuries had not succeeded

---

[47] *Truth*, v. ii. 316–26.

[48] See D. S. Smith, 'Dryden's Purpose in Adapting Shakespeare's *Troilus and Cressida*', *Ball State University Forum*, 10 (1969), 51.

in eliminating each other. After all, it was impossible for the myth to go any further than Shakespeare's forced rendition except as something competely different: a 'ghost' which looks to the spirit of Homer rather than to Shakespeare. And Homer, ironically, had not even foreseen that myth, which in any case reappears here dressed in the guise of French classicism.

The myth was born as an unresolved love-story, in which the sorrows of love were portrayed predominantly from the point of view of the man taken unawares by the congenital duplicity of women. In Shakespeare it was balanced by the addition of the 'unfaithful' woman's point of view, which leads to a more equitable highlighting of the ambivalence or, we may say, of the inter-sexuality of desire. And the myth is resolved with the abolition of all differences, the raising up of the woman to the highest levels of male constancy, and the suppression of the femininity of desire. The two worn-out archetypes come together as one (the 'stronger' one) in order 'to make that maxim good'. By doing away with the 'betrayal' Dryden had carried out one of the most instructive mis-readings in English literature.

Perhaps this Cressida was meant to be an allegory of heroic con-stancy pushed to its sacrificial limits, addressed to contemporary England: on the one hand, to the Stuart monarchy, threatened with exclusion from the throne, that it should sacrifice the 'private' to the 'public' good, thus reconsecrating itself in the eyes of its sub-jects; and, on the other hand, to the latter (from the 'lees of vulgar slaves' to the likes of Oates, Shaftesbury, and Buckingham), that they should cease their scheming and show obedience. If this was Dryden's intention we may say that he succeeded in it.

And yet, the circle can never quite be squared. There is some-thing which does not quite work in Dryden's use of Shakespeare's 'inconclusiveness' to make a proper tragedy, one which would exemplify his theories on the passions, and which Rymer would have appreciated; something which shows that those theories have little or no relevance to the irreconcilable contradictions under-lying the tragic, here entrusted solely to the physical extermination of the protagonists. This 'poetic justice' seems to come out of the blue, a necessary event, but inexplicable in the light of the extreme rationalism and good sense which guided the rest of the action: it is sparked off solely by a terrible misunderstanding, an isolated upset which has no roots in the preceding well-balanced presentation of the characters. So that this somewhat kitsch revival of medieval values in a classical guise turns out in fact to be a laughable aspiration to tragedy, a false tragedy, a comedy disguised as tragedy, not permeated with it like Shakespeare's Problem Plays.

Trapped in the new plot, Troilus must yield to a jealous rage which does not even remotely recall his Shakespearian predecessor's radical schizophrenia. Not only that, but he also repudiates the lesson which his brother had taught him the previous day on controlling his 'gusts of passion'. And we see Hector, despite all the evidence of his moderation, equanimity, and foresight, running headlong towards his doom, trampling on Andromache's and Cassandra's premonitions. But it would have been too much to rewrite Homer too.

As for Cressida, we have seen how her exclusive preoccupation with the wedding ring (the object which significantly replaces the two Shakespearian 'pledges') reveals in her characteristics of the 'feigned simpleton' of Restoration comedy. Ultimately, she does not so much resemble the desire-torn heroines of Racine and Corneille as those of later melodrama.

13

Eros and Thanatos: Cressida, Troilus, and the Modern Age

PIERO BOITANI

We have followed the adventures of Troilus from antiquity through the Middle Ages to the Renaissance and into the seventeenth century. The almost purely epic and tragic tradition of classical times and of some medieval versions is radically changed by the introduction into the story of Cressida's character and by the love-and-betrayal plot this generates. After Benoît and Guido the tragedy of Troilus becomes a romantic one within the more general frame or pattern of the adultery-triangle drama.[1] A young man falls desperately in love with a woman and conquers her. She is forced by external circumstances to leave the town where they live and to join the enemy. There, she succumbs to the courtship of another man. When he learns of this, the young man is understandably depressed and seeks to die in battle. This does indeed occur when the greatest of the enemy warriors kills him. There seems to be nothing peculiar to this story: there are countless similar ones in novels, operas, films, and perhaps even in real life. But then, the story of Dante's Paolo and Francesca is an even more banal one of adultery and murder, yet we still read it with great excitement and consider it a masterpiece.

Why were the Troilus-Cressida affair and its consequences so gripping in the Middle Ages and Renaissance that eight major authors from France, Italy, England, and Scotland decided to deal with them? There is of course, as Malcolm Andrew has shown, the fascination produced by a tragic love-story which is itself part of the greater tragedy of Troy's fall. There is also, as Derek Brewer maintains, the simple human interest in the normal dramas of human beings. But there are also, I suspect, two further reasons—

[1] For which see Tony Tanner, *Adultery in the Novel* (Baltimore and London, 1979).

one more strictly literal and one based on the essentially moral and philosophical problems raised by the story.

After Benoît Troilus and Cressida become, with the circulation of manuscripts, and the various translations and adaptations of his *Roman*, European characters. This is strengthened by the widespread popularity of Guido's *Historia*. The success of Boccaccio's *Filostrato* is more limited, although a French translation, *Le Roman de Troïlus et de Criseida*, may have already circulated towards the beginning of the fifteenth century.[2] But Boccaccio's greatest impact is not so much geographic—it consists in having inspired Chaucer to write his *Troilus*. From this moment on and until the end of the nineteenth century the Troilus-Cressida story is an exclusively British affair. And the reason for this is that Chaucer's *Troilus* is the first and greatest narrative poem in the English language, a monument which, as the articles by Barry Windeatt and Karl Reichl have shown, overcomes at once all the barriers of literary genre, embraces antiquity and the present, and is seriously concerned with important philosophical issues. After Chaucer, the Troilus and Cressida story becomes an English *myth*—and David Benson has illustrated the ways in which this phenomenon takes place at all levels. No one can avoid facing this literary masterpiece and this myth of the imagination. Thus, to give but one example, we find Surrey writing a kind of *pastourelle*, 'In winters just returne', where a shepherd hears a man complaining about his having been abandoned by his beloved, and then sees him die. Distraught, the shepherd does not know what to do until he has to bury the body:

> And in my mind it came, from thence not farre away,
> Where Chreseids love, king Priams sonne, the worthy Troilus lay.
> By him I made his tomb, in token he was treew,
> And as to him belonged well, I covered it with bleew.[3]

Yet the fact is—and here we enter a less literary sphere—that Chaucer's masterpiece is a problematic poem, in which loose ends

---

[2] The *Roman*, attributed to Beauvau, seneschal of Anjou, was printed by L. Moland and C. d'Héricault in their edn. of *Nouvelles Françoises en prose du XIV siècle* (Paris, 1858). The dating of the *Roman* is not final, but the most probable period of composition is the early fifteenth century. See B. A. Windeatt (ed.), Geoffrey Chaucer, *Troilus and Criseyde* (London and New York, 1984), 18–24, and refs. therein.

[3] Surrey, *Poems*, ed. E. Jones (Oxford, 1964), p. 14, ll. 77–80.

hang about profusely. Chaucer's story offers no simple moral like Boccaccio's 'Giovine donna, e mobile e vogliosa | è ... volubil sempre come foglia al vento'[4]—the first written formulation of a 'law' proclaimed down to Verdi's *Rigoletto*, Joyce's *Finnegans Wake*, and Walton's *Troilus*.[5] *Troilus* suspends judgement on Criseyde, tries even to defend her, turns the invective against unfaithful ladies upside down by attacking men,[6] and ends with a reversal of Boccaccio's moral: 'Beth war of men, and herkneth what I seye!' Like the *Roman*, the *Historia*, and the *Filostrato*, *Troilus* tells us nothing of the final destiny of Criseyde, but, unlike its predecessors, it follows the ghost of Troilus up to the eighth sphere and then suddenly and mysteriously abandons him 'Ther as Mercurye sorted hym to dwelle'.[7]

Why should the guilty party, Criseyde, survive, and the innocent Troilus die? This is but one of the questions that authors after Chaucer could ask. We have seen, in Anna Torti's essay above, how Lydgate and Henryson answered it in widely different ways. With David Benson we have at the same time witnessed the development of the immensely popular paradigm, 'true Troilus and false Cresseid'. It seems to me that a highly critical moment in the story of Troilus is reached towards the end of the sixteenth and the beginning of the seventeenth century. This, of course, is represented by Shakespeare, but not, in the first place, by his *Troilus*. Shakespeare's first known allusion to Troilus' story occurs in the *Merchant of Venice*, a play usually dated between 1596 and 1598. At the beginning of the last act of that comedy, Lorenzo and Jessica start a duet made up of Chaucerian reminiscences, the first of which comes from Lorenzo and, opening the dialogue, sets the tone for the entire scene:

> The moon shines bright. In such a night as this,
> When the sweet wind did gently kiss the trees,
> And they did make no noise, in such a night
> Troilus methinks mounted the Trojan walls,
> And sigh'd his soul toward the Grecian tents
> Where Cressid lay that night.[8]

[4] *Filostrato*, VIII. xxx.
[5] Verdi, *Rigoletto*, III. i; Joyce, *Finnegans Wake* (London, 3rd edn., 1964), 292 ('la *gonna* è mobile'); Walton, *Troilus*, III, final sextet.
[6] *Troilus*, v. 1779–85.   [7] Ibid., v. 1827.
[8] *Merchant of Venice*, v. i. 1–6.

The reference is to Book V of Chaucer's *Troilus*, where the hero is shown as beholding the moon every night and as sighing while he walks on the walls to watch the Greek camp—a supremely lyrical and pathetic episode which takes place before either the reader or Troilus learns of Criseyde's betrayal.[9]

In the context, Shakespeare's allusion to it at this point in the play is highly significant, because all the references in the opening remarks of Lorenzo and Jessica are to moments of intense pathos in tragic love-stories,[10] while the scene itself will have a happy ending. But what is more important for us is that from the use of it he makes here Shakespeare would seem to think of Troilus' story as an eminently romantic one, something one would treat dramatically as a Romeo-and-Juliet type of tragedy.

Things change by the time Shakespeare writes *As You Like It*, generally ascribed to the period between 1598 and 1600. There, Orlando threatens to die when Rosalind declares she will not have him. 'Men', she replies, 'have died from time to time and worms have eaten them, but not for love'.[11] The two instances she uses are Leander and Troilus:

No, faith, die by attorney. The poor world is almost six thousand years old, and in all this time there was not any man died in his own person, videlicet, in a love-cause. Troilus had his brains dashed out with a Grecian club, yet he did what he could to die before, and he is one of the patterns of love.[12]

Troilus is still a model of romantic eros, but Rosalind's version of his story is not only burlesque—it establishes a strong contrast between the ideal lyrical figure recalled in the *Merchant of Venice* and the cruel, over-realistic truth of his death. Something is happening to Shakespeare's view of the Troilus story. In *Much Ado About Nothing* (late 1598) Benedick calls Troilus but 'the first employer of pandars' and one 'of these quondam carpet-mongers'.[13]

Whether or not this new attitude was influenced by the *Troilus and Cressida* on which Dekker and Chettle are known to have been

[9] *Troilus*, v. 647–75.

[10] After Troilus, the *exempla* are Thisbe, Dido, and Medea, almost certainly inspired by Chaucer's *Legend of Good Women*.

[11] *As You Like It*, iv. i. 101–3.

[12] Ibid., iv. i. 89–94.

[13] *Much Ado About Nothing*, v. ii. 30–1.

[14] *Troilus and Cressida*, v. x. 12–14.

working at the time, the final result of Shakespeare's ruminations was his own play on *Troilus and Cressida* (probably 1602). This has been analysed in detail in the essays by Jill Mann, Agostino Lombardo, and Sergio Rufini earlier in this volume. Here, it will therefore be enough to say that Shakespeare's *Troilus* constitutes the new corner-stone and at the same time the definitive stumbling-block of our tradition. In a sense, Shakespeare deals a mortal blow to the story. He destroys the epic element while inserting the love affair much more thoroughly than before into the framework of the Trojan War; he emphasizes the romantic aspect and at once shows himself to be sceptical about it; he splits the personalities of Troilus and Cressida into such contrasting halves of 'truth' and 'appearance' that we can no longer know them fully. Finally, he leaves Troilus' end suspended in mid-air. After Hector's death, his hero may well re-acquire epic status and take upon himself the tragic destiny of Troy and of ancient Troilus ('I do not speak of flight, of fear, of death, | But dare all imminence that gods and men | Address their dangers in'),[14] but the fact is that we are not shown his death. The play virtually ends in silence,

> Hector is dead: there is no more to say

or else in the empty raging of Troilus against Achilles, or finally in Pandarus' babble.[15]

Chaucer's lyrical, meditative, paralysed Troilus could perhaps become a Hamlet figure.[16] After Shakespeare's handling of the story that way is barred, and there are only three solutions left for Troilus' tragedy. One could either make it worse, degrading Cressida to an unprecedented degree, following and surpassing Henryson—and this, as David Benson shows, is what Thomas Heywood already does in his *Iron Age*. One could return to Chaucer, as Sir Francis Kynaston did with his Latin translation of *Troilus and Criseyde*. And, finally, one could try to turn Shakespeare's version into a 'proper' tragedy, following the rules established by French

---

[14] *Troilus and Cressida*, v. x. 12–14.

[15] Ibid., v. x. 22; 23–31; 35–57.

[16] It is indeed interesting to note that in his rendering of Chaucer's *Troilus*, v. 519–686 Wordsworth replaces Chaucer's lines 622–3 ('And al this nas but his malencolie, | That he hadde of hymself swich fantasie') with 'All which he of himself conceited wholly | Out of his weakness and his melancholy', the second line being a quotation from *Hamlet*, II. ii. 638: *Poetical Works*, ed. E. de Selincourt (Oxford, 1966 reprint), iv. 231.

classicism. This, as Sergio Rufini has shown, is Dryden's solution. All other considerations aside, however, Dryden's play ends in a *cul-de-sac* which is the opposite extreme of Shakespeare's. Shakespeare leaves problems so open that one cannot even imagine a satisfactory tragic *dénouement.* Dryden solves all problems and therefore kills the tragedy. Walter Scott, noting the change of attitude towards Cressida that takes place between the Renaissance and the late seventeenth century, criticizes Dryden's 'solution' sharply:

The preceding age, during which the infidelity of Cressida was proverbially current, could have as little endured a catastrophe turning upon the discovery of her innocence, as one which would have exhibited Helen chaste, or Hector a coward. In Dryden's time, the prejudice against this unfortunate female was probably forgotten as her history had become less popular. There appears, however, something too nice and fastidious in the critical rule which exacts that the hero and the heroine of the drama shall be models of virtuous perfection ... It would have been more natural to have brought about the catastrophe on the plan of Shakespeare and Chaucer, than by the forced mistake in which Dryden's lovers are involved, and the stale expedient of Cressida's killing herself, to evince her innocence.[17]

Be that as it may, after Dryden the 'myth' of Troilus and Cressida disappears from the European *imaginaire* for two and a half centuries. Every now and then, it surfaces in England. Wordsworth, for instance, interestingly translates a beautiful passage from Chaucer's version around 1801. And in Book II of *Endymion* (published in 1818), where the poet celebrates earthly or sexual eros as higher than active life, Keats dreamily forgets the tragedy of betrayal and chooses 'the close of Troilus and Cressid sweet' as an example of the 'sovereign power of love'.[18] This is so strong as to obscure, for the first time in the tradition reviewed in the present volume, the great tragic epos of Troy of which the Troilus story has so far been but one episode:

> The woes of Troy, towers smothering o'er their blaze,
> Stiff-holden shields, far-piercing spears, keen blades,
> Struggling, and blood, and shrieks—all dimly fades

[17] *The Works of John Dryden*, ed. Sir Walter Scott, rev. G. Saintsbury (Edinburgh, 1883), vi. 243.

[18] The echoes in the text are from Shakespeare, but from the context one wonders whether Keats had in mind a blend of Chaucer and Shakespeare.

Into some backward corner of the brain;
Yet, in our very souls, we feel amain
The close of Troilus and Cressid sweet.[19]

However significant, these are minor episodes. Between the last
quarter of the seventeenth and the mid twentieth century the story
of Troilus seems to be not so much forgotten as removed from
European consciousness. Why does baroque, classical, and romantic opera not seize upon a theme which would be melodramatic *par
excellence*?[20] Verdi, to give but one example, takes from Shakespeare the subject for *Macbeth*, *Othello*, and *Falstaff*. For a long
time he toys and struggles with the idea of turning *King Lear* into
music. But he never even thinks of a *Troilus*.

This brings me to a first hypothesis. Before Shakespeare translations began flooding Europe the only versions of the story that
could possibly be known on the Continent would be Benoît's and
Boccaccio's, but both the *Roman* and the *Filostrato* were now long
forgotten. Of all the major European composers only Handel,
because of his emigration to England, would have been aware of
Shakespeare, of Dryden, and perhaps of Chaucer. After the
immense impact Shakespeare had on European culture, the only
version of the Troilus story known in the eighteenth and nineteenth centuries would be his (Chaucer and Dryden, not to
mention Henryson, being unknown in all countries but England).
But Shakespeare, as we have seen, has destroyed the Troilus myth
both as a tragic epos such as antiquity was familiar with and as a
romantic love-story such as the Middle Ages were fond of. Shakespeare has in fact turned it into a 'comedy of tragedy', emptying
the plot and leaving it desperately open to a total lack of meaning.
Even two eminent English critics, both enthusiastic admirers of

---

[19] *Endymion*, ii. 8–13.
[20] Between the end of the seventeenth and the end of the nineteenth century
there are several operas devoted to the Briseis episode of the *Iliad*, with no mention of Troilus. In 1696 Agostino Steffani or Pietro Torri produced a *Briseide* in
Hanover; a 'serenata' on 'Briseide' was composed by F. Corradini and produced
in Madrid in 1745; shortly thereafter, in 1768, a 'zarzuela heróica' by Antonio
Rodriguez de Hita, entitled *Briseida*, was staged in Madrid; there followed:
F. Bianchi, *Briseide* (Turin, 1783); F. Robuschi, *Briseide* (Naples, 1791); D. Capue
Scondito, *Briseide* (1810?); E. Chabrier, *Briseis* (Berlin, 1899, from Goethe's *Braut
von Corinth*). Plays have either a pastoral setting (like Jean Mairet's *Chryséide et
Arimand*, 1625, which has nothing to do with our theme), or a neoclassically
'tragic' subject (like Louis Poinsinet de Sivry's *Briséis ou La colère d'Achille*, 1759).

Shakespeare, were at a loss with *Troilus*. Coleridge said that 'there is none of Shakespeare's plays harder to characterize',[21] although he went on to praise individual characterization in the play. Hazlitt, who presents a very interesting comparison between Chaucer and Shakespeare, begins his essay on the latter's *Troilus* in the following manner: 'This is one of the most loose and desultory of our author's plays: it rambles on just as it happens, but it overtakes, together with some indifferent matter, a prodigious number of fine things in its way.'[22]

The only way of dealing with Troilus' story after Shakespeare's conquest of the European theatre would therefore be that of restoring to it its broadly 'comic' and 'romantic' dimension—that is, of going back to Chaucer or to the medieval versions in general. Neo-classicism, however, dislikes blends of different genres and is generally uninterested in medievalism. By the time Romanticism comes on to the stage, Shakespeare has become too exclusively central in the European imagination. Only the Verdi of *Il trovatore* or, much later, of *Falstaff* could have produced a satisfactory mixture of comic, tragic, and romantic. Berlioz, who composed a monumental and magnificent *Les Troyens* (1856–8) and knew Shakespeare's works well, avoided the Troilus and Cressida episode to concentrate on Troy's fall and the Aeneas-Dido story.

This widespread lack of interest in the Troilus theme may be due not only to the problems raised by Shakespeare's play but also to more generous reasons. Antiquity, as we have seen, did not develop the theme of Troilus' love story not only because it was primarily interested in Troilus' 'function'—his death as a sign of Troy's fall—but also because it already had plenty of illustrious mythological plots of love, betrayal, and death. The European eighteenth and nineteenth centuries create their own models of 'adultery', of 'triangles' and the problems they involve. *La Nouvelle Heloïse*, the *Elective Affinities*, *Madame Bovary*, and *Anna Karenina* are paradigmatic enough. Why should anyone be interested in a distant Cressida when he or she has a contemporary, fascinating Emma Bovary to explore?

If, then, Cressida is no longer so appealing, what about Troilus? Troilus may be a 'pattern of love' in medieval and Renaissance

[21] *Coleridge on Shakespeare*, ed. T. Hawkes (Harmondsworth, 1969), 271.

[22] W. Hazlitt, *Characters of Shakespeare's Plays* (London and New York, 1906), 64.

culture, but new, less aristocratic, more disquieting figures take his place later—schematically, Don Juan on the one hand, Werther on the other. In fact, the ideal itself of a perfect 'courtly' lover slowly disappears from the scene. Anyone who follows an itinerary that goes from Tom Jones to Julien Sorel, and even to the aristocratic Andrei Bolkonsky and Pierre Bezuhov of *War and Peace* knows what this means. Furthermore, the figure of Troilus is not capable of the many transformations of archetypal heroes such as Ulysses, Oedipus, and Faust. Troilus can move from death to love and back to death, but, once Hamlet bars his road to further complexity, he cannot acquire the infinite, ever-receding horizon of torment, guilt, and thirst for knowledge that is required of true heroes. Troilus and Cressida simply are human beings destroyed by events outside their control. This may explain why they appeal to the imagination of a century like ours, which has experienced two World Wars and which, moreover, has been continually engaged in the recovery of all sorts of past myths.

There are several versions of the Troilus and Cressida story in the twentieth century to witness this revival. The opera *Troilus et Cressida*, composed by Paul Antonin Vidal and performed in Paris in 1910,[23] had no impact whatsoever. Similarly indifferent are the operas by Winfried Wolf (Vienna, 1951) and Winfried Zillig (Würzburg, 1951), both entitled *Troilus und Cressida* and based on Shakespeare. Troilus' first successful reappearance takes place in Jean Giraudoux's *La guerre de Troie n'aura pas lieu*,[24] a very popular play in which Hector and Ulysses desperately try to stop the war from breaking out, while love between Helen and Paris is over. In spite of this, Troy will not surrender Helen, and Oiax's obscene treatment of Andromache is enough to spur the Trojan populace to kill him and thus start hostilities.

Troilus' part in this plot is minimal, but emblematic. We first see him, a boy of fifteen, confronted by Helen, who has noticed that he follows her everywhere and who for the first time in her life is 'forced to shout in talking to a man' in order to address him. Asked by her what he wants, Troilus replies, 'All'.[25] Helen understands very well the psychology of this adolescent trembling before her

---

[23] Libretto by G. Duval after Shakespeare.

[24] First performed in 1935.

[25] The edn. used here is J. Giraudoux, *La guerre de Troie n'aura pas lieu* (Paris, 1985).

and who with a mixture of effrontery, pride, shyness, and frustra-
tion shows that he intensely desires what every Trojan dreams of—
herself. She provokingly asks Troilus if he would like to embrace
her. He rejects her offer.[26] Immediately afterwards, Paris finds the
two together and at first threatens to kill Troilus if he embraces
Helen. When, however, he himself allows his younger brother to
do it, Troilus, already on the point of rushing towards the lady,
suddenly stops. The Trojan senators approach. Paris invites
Troilus to embrace Helen before them and thus become famous.
Troilus says he prefers to remain unknown and poor. 'Either you
embrace her before them, or I embrace her before you', Paris continues defiantly, but he is interrupted by Helen, who kisses him
and simultaneously declares that her kiss was destined for Troilus.
The scene[27] ends with Helen repeating her former prophecy that
by sunset Troilus will have embraced her. We lose sight of the boy
for the remaining twelve scenes of the play. But at the very end,
when Oiax is killed and Hector tells Andromache that the war will
take place, the Gates of War slowly open to reveal Helen em-
bracing Troilus.

The figure of Troilus, once more an *andropais* as in antiquity,
sums up the entire meaning of the play. His irresistible infatuation
for Helen is Troy's blind rapture before that face which is Venus
and Beauty.[28] If love between Paris and Helen is over (or has never
really existed), it is replaced by this ecstatic-aesthetic frenzy of a
whole town, Troy, and her namesake, Troilus. Erotic delirium
coincides with nationalistic pride and *furor bellicus*—the most passionate advocate of Helen and of the war is the poet Demokos. But
Helen is not merely beauty and love, an ideal image or a symbol.
There is, as she says to Hector,[29] a deep relationship between this
weakest of women and the future. She sees events that are to come
as grey or coloured shadows, and she 'chooses' the coloured ones—
or, and this is the same thing, they simply happen. Helen is 'life as
it takes place', she represents the hypostasis or incarnation of what
people call 'destiny'.

Her encounter with Troilus at the beginning of the second Act
brings together all these motifs. Helen is that woman, Troilus is
that boy. Both are persons, the former a lady who has noticed an
adolescent, the latter a trembling young lad. Both are more than

---

[26] *La guerre de Troie*, I. i.   [27] Ibid., II. ii.
[28] Ibid., I. iv. p. 38.   [29] I. ix, p. 72.

persons. She is Beauty and Venus, he is Troy and Eros. In her encounter with Troilus, Helen proves that the mythic love affair with Paris no longer matters. What matters now is this boy she suddenly 'sees'. Her seeing him, however, is also projected on to the future: 'Nous nous embrasserons, Troïlus. Je t'en réponds', she cries at the end of the second scene. And the embrace between Troilus and Helen, between Troy and beauty, between fate and man, concludes the play. 'La guerre de Troie aura lieu', and a Greek poet, as Cassandra remarks, will now sing it. Giraudoux certainly shows himself to be a subtle manipulator of the traditional sense of an ending.

A Troilus without Cressida, but coupled with Helen, is unique in our tradition, yet in a sense ideally closer to his classical ancestor than all the medieval and Renaissance Troiluses we have studied— because he once more totally identifies with Troy and her fate. Other twentieth-century treatments of the Troilus story keep Cressida as a now established feature of the myth. What they have in common is a sense of the past and of its distance from and closeness to the present, and a continuous struggle with the 'end' of the episode. When, for instance, the popular American novelist Christopher Morley publishes his *The Trojan Horse*,[30] Troy appears as 'earth's most famous town', which 'belongs to everybody, and to all times at once', where 'among medieval walls and classic temples we see perpendicular modern skyscrapers, radio towers, filling stations'.[31] Pandarus is a financier, the *Evening Trojan* and Radio Ilium interview Cressida after the economist Dr Calchas' flight from Troy, Greek and Trojan officers meet in the evening at a seaside road-house, Sarpedoni's Shore Diner, Troilus and the Trojan royal house are served by a black attendant. The conflict itself has become a true World War—the Greeks fight for Europe and for possession of the Hellespont, the Trojans stand for civilized Asia (but Pandarus, like Calchas, has invested all his money in Greek bonds).

Slowly, individual figures emerge from this misty superimposition of different ages and from 'the pale haze of Romance'.[32] Troilus is a young man who writes love poetry, Cressida a 'ripened

---

[30] The edn. used here is the first (Philadelphia, 1937). It is interesting to note that the book was translated into Italian (Milan, 1942) by the great writer Cesare Pavese.

[31] *The Trojan Horse*, pp. 1, 2.   [32] Ibid., p. 4.

woman'. As in Chaucer, he first sees her in the Palladium, but later, romantically, he can hardly even remember her face.[33] Emphasizing, on the one hand, the humorous, broadly 'comic' situations and, on the other, the lyrical, sentimental features, Morley basically follows Chaucer's plot and praises his 'literary tact'.[34] This return to the medieval author in spite of Shakespeare is significant in itself (only one of Shakespeare's scenes has been adapted, a tea-party in the Greek camp where all the warriors crowd around Cressida), but even a Chaucerophile like Morley feels forced to modify two important details. In the first place, hostility between Troilus and Diomedes goes back to a quarrel between them over Cressida during a party at Sarpedoni's. Secondly, the end of the story is changed.

The Wooden Horse is inside Troy, and Greek warriors pour out of it. Before the burning starts Troilus kills Diomedes and is in turn killed by Achilles. Thus, Troilus' death formally coincides with the fall of Troy—individual end and general 'doom', as Morley calls it, are once more the same. But modern sensitivity requires that Troilus' rival in love should also die. Nor is this the real end of the narrative. In the last chapter Morley offers a modernized 'classical' version of the Epilogue in Chaucer's poem. This time, however, Troilus' final destination is specified. We are in the Elysian Fields, and, as in an American college ground, Greek and Trojan heroes play sports together. Troilus and Diomedes race each other to the river and go for a swim. A newcomer, a lady, is being shown around. The boys do not notice her, but she watches them 'curiously', 'puzzled': 'Who were those boys, she asks the guide. There was something familiar about them?'[35] Cressida does not recognize her old lovers. 'Eternity', as Morley says, 'marches on'[36]—serene, unchangingly beautiful, perfect. Its price is the abolition of thought ('the enemy of life') and total oblivion. The dramatic contrast between the death and ascent of pagan Troilus and the Christian Epilogue of Chaucer's poem is thus smoothed out. A rather dull, if pleasant, ataraxic eternity constitutes the new sense of an ending.

Yet, this, too, is only provisional. The next time we encounter Troilus in the twentieth century he appears, as in Shakespeare,[37] 'like a strange soul upon the Stygian banks | Staying for waftage'. In

---

[33] *The Trojan Horse*, p. 44.   [34] Ibid., p. 26.
[35] Ibid., p. 248.   [36] Ch. heading, p. 246.
[37] *Troilus and Cressida*, III. ii. 7–9.

Louis MacNeice's poem, 'The Stygian Banks',[38] the image of a Troilus forever waiting to enter Cressida's chamber and to cross over to the Elysian fields dominates the beginning and end. Paradoxically, the traditionally sterile Troilus is chosen to address the question why people have children. They may, MacNeice answers, wish 'to keep themselves young, by following their children's growth to move backward from experience to innocence, to live England's history over again as it appears in the experience and growth of a child'.[39] Thus, we go back to the fourteenth century, to the Black Death, to Chaucer's England (I) and to his Alison (VI). It is, however, impossible to establish proper continuity through the generations and hence through time in this fashion—child and father are never completely alike, and our roots are not permanent. If Alison walks through a spring garden with her arms full of flowers, that garden is not our home and time cannot be stopped nor wound and rewound. 'Yes, here we stay—for a little | Strange souls in the daylight'. And the figure of Troilus arises once more, incarnating human eagerness, the supreme value. Waiting before Styx, he stands as if facing the ultimate limit, yet this limit is not an end *tout court*, but the end that makes us 'begin | Again and again'. For the first time in our tradition, Troilus finds himself before 'the infinite dark'—the potentiality of life and perpetuation—on the point of becoming the archetypal hero he never was:

> Troilus
> Patrols the Stygian banks, eager to cross,
> But the value is not on the further side of the river,
> The value lies in his eagerness. No communion
> In sex or elsewhere can be reached and kept
> Perfectly for ever. The closed window,
> The river of Styx, the wall of limitation
> Beyond which the word beyond loses its meaning,
> Are the fertilizing paradox, the grille
> That, severing, joins, the end to make us begin
> Again and again, the infinite dark that sanctions
> Our growing flowers in the light, our having children;
> The silence behind our music . . .[40]

---

[38] Pub. in his collection, *Holes in the Sky* (1948).
[39] E. E. Smith, *Louis MacNeice* (New York, 1970), 131.
[40] vii. 10–22. *The Collected Poems of Louis MacNeice*, ed. E. R. Dodds (London, 1966), 266–7.

MacNeice's Troilus is a poetic image, a symbol without dramatic life, frozen in the posture where the epigraph from Shakespeare's play places him as a literary allusion. It is in 1954 that the ancient Trojan hero returns to the stage, and this time he finally occupies that place which Verdi and Berlioz had denied him. William Walton's opera, *Troilus and Cressida* (libretto by Christopher Hassall) was first performed at Covent Garden on 3 December of that year, and soon afterwards in New York, San Francisco, and at La Scala in Milan.[41]

Four elements characterize it—a more rigorous 'classical' setting than before; a deliberate attention to the conventions, both dramatic and musical, of Italian opera; a return to and reinterpretation of Chaucer in the characterization of Cressida; a tightening up of the plot with, once more, a fundamental change of the ending.

The time of the action is placed 'about the twelfth century B.C.', and in his Preface to the libretto Hassall therefore states his intention of abandoning the conception of 'courtly love' and lifting the story out of the Middle Ages and retelling it in the setting of legendary Troy.[42] A typical version of this kind of 'romantic' classicism is Troilus' prayer to Aphrodite (which becomes a hymn of gratitude at the end of Act I, when Pandarus gives Troilus Cressida's crimson scarf). In Hassall's libretto, this replaces the Narrator's and Troilus' Boethian hymns to Love in Chaucer's Book III with an aria where both the general atmosphere and the words echo Greek poetry, but where the music is decidedly 'romantic':

> Child of the wine-dark wave
>   Mantled in beauty,
> Spirit of mortal love,
>   Tall Aphrodite;
> Thou whose warm footprints fill
>   With flowers of Spring,
> Walk our dry desert ways,
>   Thy fruitful pleasures bring.
> Girdled with foam, on the swell
>   In majesty riding,
> Cradled in sea-blown shell
>   Come shoreward gliding . . .

[41] The edn. of the libretto from which I quote is William Walton, *Troilus and Cressida* (London, 1954).

[42] Ibid., p. 4.

Again, when the curtain rises at the very beginning, worshippers, priests, and priestesses stand before the temple of Pallas praying to the goddess, 'Virgin of Troas | whiter than snow | new fallen, | taste our libation'. The caption for the staging prescribes a scenery such as one would expect for Verdi's *Aida*.

Verdi and Puccini are, indeed, the two models for Walton's melodramatic inspiration. His is very much a singer's opera,[43] with beautifully lyrical and romantic arias such as Cressida's 'Slowly it all comes back' in Act I and 'At the haunted end of the day' in Act II. The former in particular constitutes a good example of the way in which Hassall handles the Chaucerian characterization of Cressida. In his Preface he recalls C. S. Lewis's view of Criseyde's 'ruling passion' as 'fear of loneliness, of old age, of death, of love, and of hostility', from which springs her 'pitiable longing . . . for protection'.[44] Accordingly, in the first half of 'Slowly it all comes back' Cressida remembers being a child 'alone with the night around' her. The 'towering, wavering shade' of her father dominated her unconscious life, but the real man deserted her afterwards. In the second part of Cressida's reverie, Calkas is replaced by the image of a strong warrior who never turns away from her. This she now knows to be Troilus, whom she is still afraid of loving. Walton's Cressida has 'something of the "ill-divining soul" of a Cassandra'.[45] In spite of Chaucer's influence, then, the opera's heroine is a new concretion.

The same is true of the plot, which is Chaucerian in its broad outline, but in fact comes close to Shakespeare on the one hand and to Dryden on the other in the second part of the story. Here, scenes are conflated and rendered more compact. The exchange between Antenor and Cressida, for instance, is announced to Pandarus directly by Diomede. Cressida is then discovered by the Greek himself in the alcove immediately after the awakening of the two lovers and their *aubades*.[46] The situation is thus more similar to Shakespeare's than to Chaucer's. However, the first four scenes of Shakespeare's Act IV have been compressed into a single one, simplified and intensified. In the play, the tension mounts

---

[43] The great exception is the long orchestral interlude that marks the climax of the love scene in Act II.

[44] C. S. Lewis, *The Allegory of Love* (Oxford, 1970 reprint), 185.

[45] Preface, p. 3.

[46] *Troilus and Cressida*, II. ii.

slowly. We first see Diomedes, Antenor, Paris, and Aeneas together in the street and learn of the exchange. We are then shown Troilus and Cressida in the dawn scene, which is interrupted by Pandarus' mockery and soon after by Aeneas' announcement. Troilus promises to deliver Cressida. There follows the long farewell between the two lovers, and finally Diomedes appears with Aeneas and the others. A first threatening exchange between the Greek and Troilus ensues. In the opera, all this has become a single melodramatic explosion of tension, which reaches its climax when Diomede draws back the curtains of the alcove.

A much more fundamental alteration of the traditional plot—at first sight along Drydenian lines—affects the end of the story. In obedience to Calkas, Evadne conceals from Cressida, now in the Greek camp, all messages from Troilus. Feeling abandoned by him and at the same time being attracted by Diomede's charms and mindful of her father's warnings, Cressida yields to Diomede and allows him to take her crimson scarf as a token of her favour. Troilus and Pandarus cross the Greek lines during a truce, to ransom Cressida. 'But ah, too late, it comes too late. | I'm beyond all ransom now ... I'm bought and sold', she tells Troilus as they meet for the first time after ten weeks. She is then hailed queen of Calydon and Argos by Diomede's people, and he appears wearing the crimson token on his helmet. Troilus recognizes it. The two confront each other, both claiming the lady. Cressida 'faces her moment of decision, walks over to Troilus, kneels, and clings to him'. As the Chorus sing 'False Cressida! False!', Diomede, Troilus, Pandarus, and Calkas each proclaim their moral. Diomede accuses Troy, 'false of heart, yet fair', and Cressida, a 'flaunted rose' in which 'the fatal canker grows'. Troilus echoes Boccaccio:

> Woman at wanton play
> with discord fills the earth.
> Her kindness comes and goes
> with ev'ry wind that blows.

Pandarus complains that there is no point in trying 'to ease the world's despair': 'beauty suffers dearth | and crumbles into clay'. Calkas blames destiny, which 'rules the earth'. Evadne urging Diomede to kill Troilus, and Cressida once more desperately crying her love for the Trojan complete the sextet in true Verdian fashion. 'On sudden impulse' Diomede throws the crimson favour

to the ground and tramples on it. Troilus attacks, disarms, and
beats the rival to his knees, but is stabbed in the back by Calkas.
Diomede decides that Troilus' body be returned to Priam, that
Calkas go back to Troy in fetters, and that Cressida, whom he calls
a whore, be kept in the Greek camp. Cressida, however, seizes
Troilus' sword and kills herself over his body as Diomede's
soldiers arrive to fetch it.

In Cressida's last words we see Troilus on the Stygian banks
again, but the Death that has received him there is now Cressida's
hope of forgiveness, the vindication of her love, and the celebration
of their union:

> Turn, Troilus, turn, on that cold river's brim
> beyond the sun's far setting.
> Look back from the silent stream
> of sleep and long forgetting.
> Turn and consider me
> and all that was ours;
> you shall no desert see
> but pale unwithering flowers.
> Oh never with scorn, nor with hate, shall Death receive me.
> He will purge all blemish away,
> and you, even you,
> of all men under his sway,
> may yet forgive me.
>
> .   .   .   .
>
> Open the gates.
> We are riding together into Troy.
> And by this sign I am still your Cressida.
>
> *[She stabs herself*

Once more, it is the end of Troilus' story that is changed. As in
most traditional versions, Cressida has been unfaithful to Troilus
(although her yielding to Diomede is partly due to Calkas' and
Evadne's deception). Yet, when faced by the crucial choice she
returns to Troilus and kills herself for him. To save Cressida,
Dryden had invented the 'false betrayal' device and ended up with
a merely external 'truth found too late'. In Walton's opera, Cressida finds this truth inside herself—it is her love for Troilus. 'False
Cressida' becomes deeply true at the very moment the Chorus
proclaims her falseness aloud. Romantically, she is purged of all
blemish—as she herself says she will be by Death—far beyond the

redemption she may have gained through repentance in Henryson. Modern feeling absolves her but a few minutes after Troilus and Diomede have condemned her on the stage. This, yet another step in the evolution that starts with Chaucer, is the final solution of Cressida's problem, but it in no way helps solve the other crux of the story, Troilus' death. The Trojan hero must of course succumb, or we would have the happy ending of comedy or romance. If, however, one eliminates from the plot the traditional agent of his murder, Achilles, one is left with the rather implausible and unsatisfactory solution of a Calkas stabbing Troilus in the back without any substantial motivation.

Thus, we have in a sense come full circle. Eros, the love professed by Cressida, prevails over Thanatos, the death of Troilus. The different morals proclaimed in the final sextet sum up the meanings the story has had since the Middle Ages: woman is fair yet fickle, the beauty of the world decays, 'destiny rules the earth'. By making love have the last word after these proclamations Walton and Hassall have brought an entire 'cultural' cycle to its end. No further development in this direction is possible. It is interesting that this should happen in a romantic opera with decidedly Italian overtones. It is significant that six centuries after the story arrived in England from Italy by means of a melodramatic romance composed by one of the greatest Italian writers and adapted by one of the greatest English poets it should return to Italy as an opera beautifully translated by the greatest Italian poet of the twentieth century. The 'rhythmic version' of *Troilus and Cressida* for the production at La Scala on 12 January 1956 is the work of Eugenio Montale.

We have now reviewed all the major phases in the life of the Troilus story within the cycle that goes from Benoît to Walton. One feature of it keeps changing with each new version—the end. Boccaccio, Chaucer, Henryson, Shakespeare, Dryden, Morley, Hassall deal with the same myth, but invariably modify something in the central knot of love, betrayal, and death. Boccaccio shows the mechanism at work in its barest outline: Criseida is unfaithful, Troilus is killed by Achilles, beware of young women. Chaucer keeps this, but tries to change the moral and adds an epilogue where we are half shown Troilus' destiny after death and asked to turn our love to the Christian God. Morley imitates Chaucer, but introducing two important variations: before dying, Troilus kills his rival Diomedes; after death, all the characters meet again in the peaceful, forgetful Elysian Fields. Henryson saves Troilus, but has Cressida die, punished by the gods. Shakespeare leaves Troilus' death out of his play. In Dryden and Walton, Cressida commits suicide, thus proving her innocence in the former and her love in the latter. But whereas in Dryden Troilus slays Diomedes before being killed by Achilles, in Walton Troilus is treacherously murdered by Calkas.

All these changes prove that after antiquity the end of the story is felt to be unsatisfactory, disturbing, and hence open to debate and reinvention. One reason for this may be that the Middle Ages inherited from classical and late antique tradition a *mythos* which, as we have seen in the first essay of this book, must end with Troilus' death at the hands of Achilles. However, unaware of or deliberately ignoring the motif of Achilles' love for Troilus, the Middle Ages attach to Troilus' death the love-and-betrayal story with Cressida and gradually make it the central point of the story. These two narrative nuclei, however, have nothing in common. Troilus' murder by Achilles is not the logical consequence of his unfortunate affair with Cressida. Hence, one can plausibly keep it only as a chance event within the epic-tragic frame of Troy's fall. This is why Shakespeare does not feel the need to stage Troilus' death. His play is as much about Troy (and the Greeks) as about Troilus and Cressida. Once Hector is gone, Troy will fall, and Troilus' death no longer matters. If, on the other hand, an author chooses to focus on the love-and-betrayal plot, the problem of the end becomes acute, because the logical conclusion of that kind of plot would have to be either the death of one of the two rivals at the hands of the other (and we have this as one feature of the ending in Dryden and Morley, and a move in this direction in Walton), or the murder of Cressida by either Troilus or Diomedes (which is interestingly avoided by all writers), in the classic jealousy-and-revenge tragedy. Alternatively, one could devise the happy ending of comedy or romance—a truly innocent, or sincerely repenting, Cressida. This type of *dénouement* is what Dryden and Walton move towards, only to make tragedy break into it and thus produce a typical melodramatic mixture.

The problem, however, is not merely 'literary'—a question of dramatic consequentiality and choice of genre—it is also the reflection of basic moral and philosophical attitudes. How does one solve the contrast between justice and fate? If Cressida is guilty, why should she survive while innocent Troilus dies a miserable death? Henryson is the only one of our authors to come up with a radical answer. Cressida must be punished with leprosy and death, Troilus lives on. By their changes to the end of the story, all other versions show that this existential problem, central in our culture ever since the Book of Job, is in fact insoluble—or at leat insoluble in this world. Chaucer and Morley know this so well that in their different ways they feel the need to project the end of the story on to the other world, where the laws of human fate, love, and strife do not apply. The others react to the problem by trying to employ the ethical standards of their own age. Henryson condemns Cressida, Dryden makes her a victim of appearances, Walton and Hassall absolve her because of her love. Unique among all, Shakespeare divides right and wrong equally, suspending judgement. Cressida is a strumpet and a victim, she is one and two, and no one:

> This is, and is not, Cressid.

Finally, what these ever-changing ends reveal is the contrast between reality and fiction that both authors and audiences have felt throughout the centuries. In reality, something may or may not happen to a Troilus, a Cressida, and a Diomedes after the betrayal. If we read their story in a newspaper we would be prepared to accept any development. Yet, from fiction we expect verisimilitude to go hand in hand with completeness, plenitude to be accompanied by both surprise and necessity—in short a satisfying 'sense of an ending'. This the Troilus and Cressida story from Benoît to Walton simply does not provide.

The latest version of the myth however does, and in a powerful manner. Christa Wolf's *Kassandra*, a 'novel' published in Germany but a few years ago, has already acquired the status of a classic.[47] Cassandra is standing before the stone lions of Mycenae's gates. As at the opening of Aeschylus's *Oresteia*, Agamemnon is being butchered inside the palace by his wife, Clytemnestra. Waiting for her own death, the daughter of Priam, the prophetess whom no one in Troy would believe, now only a slave in Agamemnon's

---

[47] The German edn. I use is *Kassandra* (Darmstadt and Neuwied, 1986). The book was originally published in 1983. English quotations are taken from *Cassandra*, trans. J. Van Heurck (London, 1984).

booty, reviews her life, going back in memory to the war that has destroyed her city and her family. The story of Troilus and Briseis (as she is called again for the first time since Benoît) occupies but a few scattered paragraphs in this work which blends all the mythic motifs related to Troy into one single 'recherche du temps perdu' slowly and painstakingly performed by Cassandra in her memories, associations, and reflections.

The way in which those in power deliberately build up a war, hiding futile pretexts and real interests behind propaganda, and the progressive degradation that deception and the real horror of war bring about in human beings are the author's central concerns. This is not the place to illustrate at length how forcefully she manages to convey her message, but even a glance at how she treats our theme will suffice. In dealing with it, Christa Wolf fuses both the classical and medieval traditions, but makes *thanatos* the centre of the myth, brutally severing it from *eros* and debasing the latter to an unprecedented degree.

Even before the war begins Troilus and Briseis are in love with each other, indeed they form 'a pair of lovers if there ever was one'.[48] They are the focus of attention of the entire court, for instance, during the banquet given in honour of Menelaus before Paris' abduction of Helen:

No one who looked their way could help smiling. Briseis was Troilus's first love, and no one could doubt him when he said she would also be his last. Briseis, not much older but more mature, seemed scarcely able to credit her good fortune.[49]

Calchas has already deserted and, as tensions rise in Troy, Cassandra finds herself protecting an endangered couple. Briseis is willing to leave the city in order not to put Troilus at risk, but he does not want to let her go. The girl often cries in Cassandra's bedchamber at night.[50] Christa Wolf is not interested in the love-story as such, in Troilus' conquest of Briseis.[51] She offers us the picture of a fervid, happy, satisfied love relationship—of perfect bliss. Troilus and Briseis are *the* couple of Troy, the symbol of eros as harmony.

Politics, the manipulation of popular feelings, destroys this happiness. It is the first sign of the approaching end—there is something rotten in Priam's kingdom. Then, war ineluctably breaks out.

[48] *Cassandra*, p. 57.   [49] Ibid.   [50] Ibid., p. 63.
[51] Pandarus is therefore eliminated.

The Greeks, looking for free access to the Dardanelles, seize the opportunity offered by Paris' abduction of Helen. The Trojans cannot return her to Menelaus because in reality she is in Egypt.[52] The people, however, are deceived into thinking that she lives in Troy and that it would be a supreme insult to the city's honour to give in to the enemy's requests. The Greeks land and on the very first day of fighting Troilus is killed by Achilles. The council discusses the oracle which says that Troy can win the war only if Troilus reaches the age of twenty. As he has just died at seventeen, a posthumous decree is passed declaring Troilus to have been twenty years old. Priam struggles against it:

No (I was told he had said), insult his dead son further with lies? No. Not with his consent. So there was a time when the dead were sacred, at least to us; and I knew that time. The new time respected neither living nor dead.[53]

A chill comes over Cassandra. But her horror is nothing compared to Briseis' grief. She almost loses her mind, and her shrieks at Troilus' burial curdle the Trojans' blood. Briseis speaks to no one, and lets no one speak to her, for a long time. Finally, she agrees to join her renegade father in the Greek camp. Cassandra accompanies her, and the two are welcomed by the lustful stares of the warriors. Before she leaves to return to Troy, as with a burning heart she is about to embrace Briseis, Cassandra sees her leaning 'with an unmoved face' against Diomedes, whom she has just seen for the first time in her life:

The ungainly lout. I pictured my delicate boyish brother Troilus. 'Briseis!' I said softly, 'what are you thinking of?' 'He loves me,' she replied. 'He says he loves me.' I saw him place his hand on her the way men touch slave women. The Greek men all around us laughed their booming male laughs. I was seized by a ghastly fear of the love of the Greeks.[54]

Thus, the modern Cressida is unfaithful to Troilus after his death—her betrayal is more base than ever before, yet more comprehensible in the context of this kind of war, which turns people's hearts to stone. When Cassandra returns to Troy, she finds that Briseis has been declared a political traitor, and that all her former friends are under suspicion. If the Greeks are mere brutes, the Trojans are fast adapting themselves.

[52] As in some classical versions of her story, for instance in Euripides' *Helen.*
[53] *Cassandra*, p. 76.   [54] Ibid., p. 82.

Briseis' destiny, however, is far worse—worse even than in Henryson. Her fate is Achilles, the man who has murdered Troilus, and Achilles is free to do as he likes with her. Then, she is given to Agamemnon to indemnify him for the loss of Chryseis. When Cassandra ventures to ask how Briseis is, the only reply is 'a long mute look'.[55] Agamemnon himself later brings her back to Achilles, 'in what a state!' Finally, we see her through Cassandra's eyes at the end of the war:

I saw Briseis again after the fall of Troy, when we were driven through the camp of the Greeks [*das Lager der Griechen*]. I thought I had seen all the horror a human being can see. I know what I am saying: Briseis' face surpassed it all.[56]

Homer's plot (the Briseis-Chryseis exchange) is brought in, then, and fused with the medieval and Renaissance version to show the fate of Briseis in its crudest light. Like an object, she is handed over by Diomedes to Achilles to Agamemnon and back to Achilles. Her medieval betrayal of Troilus, her Renaissance falseness, even her leprosy, are nothing compared to this. It is significant that the face of Briseis, full of horror, should be the last sight we are shown of the Trojan War—its end.

The end, however, had started at the beginning, on the very first day of fighting, when Troilus was killed. It is an event that Cassandra has tried to blot out of her memory, but 'nothing in the whole war [has] left a keener imprint'.[57] She is herself shortly to be slaughtered, and an overwhelming fear, she says, forces her to think; yet every 'cursed detail' of Troilus' death occupies her mind even now: 'this one dead man would have lasted me the rest of the war'.[58] Troilus' death is stronger than personal doom—it is *the* death of the Trojan War.

Cassandra is standing in the temple of Apollo outside the city, watching the Greeks leave the ships and wade through the shallow water, trying to reach the shores of Troy. The Trojans, led by Hector, cut down the first and second waves, 'human dolls' falling 'to the ground, soundlessly and sufficiently far away'.[59] Then, something quite different begins. A formation of Greeks in close array, their shields surrounding them as if in an armoured car, storm ashore, howling. Those on the outlying edges are quickly

[55] Ibid., p. 110.   [56] Ibid., p. 83.   [57] Ibid., p. 71.   [58] Ibid., p. 72.
[59] Ibid.

killed by the exhausted Trojans, those inside slay many enemies. The core reaches the shore, 'and with them the core's core: the Greek hero Achilles'.[60] 'So that's how it's done', is Cassandra's first, feverish comment, 'All for one'.[61] Achilles cunningly avoids Hector, engaged by other Greeks. He goes for the boy Troilus, who is driven towards him 'by well-trained men the way game is driven toward the hunter'.[62] 'So that's how it's done', Cassandra repeats. Troilus stands his ground and fights by the rules, the way he has been taught. Achilles 'the brute' (*das Vieh*) does not respond to the boy's offer. He raises his sword high above his head, gripping it with both hands, and lets it whistle down on Troilus. 'All rules fell into the dust forever. So that's how it's done', Cassandra concludes for the third time.[63] Troilus falls to the ground, Achilles on top of him, strangling the lying boy. It is the moment of Cassandra's first and definitive realization that the end is approaching. The fate of Troilus and Troy are once more the same:

Etwas ging vor, was über meine, unsere Begriffe war. Wer sehen konnte, sah am ersten Tag: Diesen Krieg verlieren wir.

[Something happened that went beyond my conception, beyond the conception of us all. Those who could see saw it the first day: we would lose this war.][64]

The dreadful scene, however, is not yet over. As a conclusion to this volume on the European tragedy of Troilus, let us read its final sequences in the English translation of Christa Wolf's words, some of the most powerful and hair-raising that have ever been written on the subject:

The worst was still to come, is still to come. Troilus, wearing light armor, had gotten up again, had wrenched himself free from Achilles' hands, began to run—ye gods, how he could run! Aimlessly at first; then—I signaled, shouted—he found the direction, ran toward me, ran to the temple. Saved. We would lose the war but this brother, who at that moment seemed the dearest of them all, was saved. I ran to him, grabbed his arm, drew him into the interior of the temple—his throat was rattling, he was collapsing—in front of the god's statue, where he was safe. The repulsed Achilles wheezed after him; I no longer needed to pay him any

---

[60] *Cassandra*, p. 72.   [61] Ibid., p. 73.
    [62] The prototype is, as I have remarked in the first essay of the present vol., the account of Dares.
    [63] *Cassandra*, p. 73.   [64] Ibid.

notice. What I needed to do was to unfasten my brother's helmet, loosen his cuirass; he was gasping for air. The old priestess Herophile, whom I never saw weep before or since, helped me. My hands flew. He who lives is not lost. Not lost to me, either. I will take care of you, Brother, I will love you, get to know you at last. 'Briseis will be happy,' I said into his ear.

Then Achilles the brute came. The murderer came into the temple, which darkened as he stood at the entrance. What did this man want? What was he after, wearing weapons here in the temple? Hideous moment: already I knew. Then he laughed. Every hair on my head stood on end and sheer terror came into my brother's eyes. I threw myself over him and was shoved aside as if I were not there. In what role was his enemy approaching my brother? As a murderer? As a seducer? Could such a thing be—the voluptuousness of the murderer and the lover in one? Was that allowed to exist among human beings? The fixed gaze of the victim. The capering approach of the pursuer, whom I now saw from behind, a lewd beast. Who took Troilus by the shoulders, stroked him, handled him—the defenseless boy from whom I, wretched woman, had removed the armor! Laughing, laughing all over. Gripped his neck. Moved to the throat. His plump, stubby-fingered, hairy hand on my brother's throat. Pressing, pressing. I hung on the murderer's arm, on which the veins stood out like cords. My brother's eyes were starting out of their sockets. And the gratification in Achilles' face. The naked hideous male gratification. If that exists, everything is possible. It was deathly still. I was shaken off, felt nothing. Now the enemy, the monster, raised his sword in full view of Apollo's statue and severed my brother's head from his torso. Human blood spurted onto the altar as before it had spurted from the carcasses of our sacrificial animals. Troilus, the sacrificial victim. The butcher fled with a horrid and gratified howl. Achilles the brute. I felt nothing for a long time.[65]

The ambush by the fountain has disappeared, replaced by an even more treacherous assault, but the flight and pursuit, the violence and the lust, the sacrilege and the sacrifice are all there. Now, we really have come full circle. After struggling for 800 years with the problem of how to harmonize a romantic and doomed love-story with the hero's predestined death, after the only comparable scene of our tradition—Shakespeare's cruel staging of Hector's murder—in the 1980s European literature goes back to archaic Greece. With the fragments of Greek culture, it once more faces an ever-present reality and its symbol: the stark, naked tragedy of Troilus' slaughter. And with Cassandra we, too, feel nothing for a long time.

[65] Ibid., pp. 73–4.

Index